Oscar Wilde

A Life
In
Letters

Oscar Wilde

A Life
In
Letters

Selected and edited by

MERLIN HOLLAND

CARROLL & GRAF PUBLISHERS
NEW YORK

To the memory of Rupert Hart-Davis, with love and gratitude.

OSCAR WILDE
A Life in Letters

Carroll & Graf Publishers
An Imprint of Avalon Publishing Group, Inc.
245 West 17th Street, 11th Floor
New York, NY 10011

AVALON
publishing group incorporated

Compilation copyright © 2003, 2007 by Merlin Holland

First published in Great Britain in 2003 by
Fourth Estate, a Division of HarperCollinsPublishers, London

First Carroll & Graf edition 2007

Library of Congress Cataloging-in-Publication Data is available.

ISBN-13: 978-0-78671-907-5
ISBN-10: 0-7867-1907-9

9 8 7 6 5 4 3 2 1

Printed in the United States of America
Distributed by Publishers Group West

Contents

Introduction

The enduring fascination of Oscar Wilde more than a century after his death remains a literary phenomenon. His creative output, by comparison with many other nineteenth century writers, was relatively small, yet it was spread over poetry and prose poems, literary and artistic criticism, essays, lectures, short stories and fairy tales, historical melodramas, society comedies and a single novel, *The Picture of Dorian Gray*, for which he has become known across the world. Both his critics and his admirers have been legion, some insisting that he was merely a passing socio-cultural phenomenon and the author of lightweight popular works, and others viewing him as a modern thinker, bridging two centuries, an astute critic and commentator, a writer at odds with the stuffiness of his age, whose 'over-the-topness in knocking the bottom out of things' in Seamus Heaney's words, amused but finally enraged his tight-laced Victorian contemporaries.

Whether he has a deserved place in the canon of great authors or is merely a first-rate funny-man struggling to rise beyond the second division of literary excellence, one thing is certain: he remains one of the most accessible and appealing writers of all time. Paradoxically, though, for all the thousands of studies published on Wilde, there are aspects of his life which are still enigmatic, unexplained even. The duality in his character with its inherent contradictions, intrigues and confuses: the Anglo-Irishman with Nationalist sympathies; the Protestant with life-long Catholic leanings; the married homosexual. And Oscar himself did nothing to help matters by deliberately donning masks to mislead. In 1885 he cautioned the painter James Whistler against revealing too much of himself and his art in his lectures. 'Be warned in time, James, and remain, as I do, incomprehensible; to be great is to be misunderstood,' he remarked, and spent the rest of his life ensuring that he was.

He left no intimate diary, wrote no memoirs and the Boswell who might have given us a memorable life, Robert Ross, felt that the task of rehabilitating his friend posthumously was best done as an astute literary executor; not that we could have relied much on the accuracy of any sort of personal memoir from the man who referred to 'a morbid and unhealthy faculty of truth-telling' as being fatal to the artistic imagination.

But like anyone of a literary disposition, Oscar Wilde occasionally needed to express himself without his public mask, and his letters, particularly those written to intimate friends without thought of publication, are in effect the autobiography that he never wrote and as close as we shall come to the magic of hearing that legendary talker in person. They comment openly on his life and his work from the early years of undergraduate friendships, through the year-long lecture tour in America of a striving and ambitious young 'Professor of Aesthetics' as he styled himself, to the short period of fame and success in the early 1890s followed by his disgrace and imprisonment. Thereafter they include the most poignant and revealing letters of all, those which cover the five long years between his downfall and his early death in exile at 46, during which he suffered the ultimate indignity for one of his generosity – poverty and having to borrow money from friends. Even in adversity, though, his humour does not desert him and he is able to share with his readers that greatest of gifts – the ability to smile at one's own misfortune.

The first major edition of Wilde's letters appeared in 1962, meticulously edited by the late Rupert Hart-Davis. At the time, homosexuality in Britain was still illegal and I was an impressionable young teenager at school, so naturally the question of expurgation was discussed. Many of Wilde's post-prison letters were quite explicit about his sexual inclinations and it led to much agonising in the family about publishing them in their entirety. My father finally took the advice of his old friend Rebecca West who persuaded him that by then suppression was pointless and, with some lingering unease, he agreed to their uncensored publication. As it turned out, his misgivings were totally unfounded and the first publication of so much autobiographical material gave an entirely new impetus to the study of Wilde and a much greater understanding of the complexities of his character. A supplement was published in 1985 and a much revised and enlarged edition, *The Complete Letters of Oscar Wilde*, bringing the total number to 1562, was produced in 2000 to mark the centenary of his death.

All these editions, however, including a *Selected Letters* in 1976, relied heavily on the scholarly apparatus of copious footnotes to put the letters in context and I feel that the time has now come to make my grandfather's correspondence accessible to a broader public with only a minimum of editorial intervention. To this end, I have made a very personal selection of the letters, some 400 in total, which seem to me to reflect the man, warts and all, whom I have come to love and respect as a relative after twenty years of immersing myself in his life and works. By interspersing the letters with the smallest amount of necessary explanation and biography, I hope that readers will be able to listen to Oscar in his own words more or less uninterrupted and I am certain that anyone unfamiliar with Wilde as a correspondent will find it packed with unexpected delights. For one thing, his letters show that the public perception of Wilde as the lightweight author of society comedies, a few memorable poems and some fairy stories must finally make room for Wilde as a hard-working professional writer, deeply interested by the issues of his day and carrying in his intellectual baggage something that we all too frequently overlook, a quite extraordinary classical, literary and philosophical education.

The editorial principles employed in transcribing the letters have been explained at length in *The Complete Letters of Oscar Wilde* (Fourth Estate, 2000) and given the nature of the present edition, it would seem unnecessary here to do more than summarise them briefly.

Wilde's spelling was mostly good, but he often misspelled proper names, even of places like Babbacombe, Berneval and Posillipo where he stayed for several months. These have been corrected along with other such slips throughout. His punctuation, except in his more formal letters, consisted mainly of short dashes, which he used to represent every kind of stop. They make the letters difficult to read, and normal punctuation has been used as the sense seems to demand. A case in point is the letter to Alfred Douglas in March 1893 which has been reproduced exactly as he wrote it, partly to show his emotional anguish and partly to illustrate the problems of transcription. Ellipses which occur in the text are Wilde's own unless enclosed in square brackets.

Each address from which Wilde wrote is given in full the first time it occurs, and thereafter abbreviated to the essential minimum. No distinction has been made between printed and written addresses. In letters where he failed to indicate the place of writing it has been conjectured between square brackets, but in some instances this has not been possible, as for example when he was on tour in America, and the address has been omitted. For convenience the address is always printed on the right, and the date, in standardised form, on the left.

Wilde seldom dated his letters. Postmarks have often helped (though occasionally letters have strayed into wrong envelopes), and other dates have been deduced from internal evidence or cross-reference. All dates editorially supplied are enclosed within square brackets: doubtful ones are preceded by a query. Such editorial decisions, unless self-evident, were explained in the footnotes to *The Complete Letters*.

I considered carefully whether or not to include Wilde's long letter (50,000 words) from prison to Alfred Douglas, *De Profundis*, and reluctantly decided against it. I realise that this may seem inconsistent with the idea of this selection, since of all his letters it is the one in which he lets us see most deeply into his innermost thoughts. However, since its first integral publication in 1962, it has been made widely available and its inclusion here would have made this volume, intended to be reader-friendly both in size as well as in content, unmanageably large. As an account, though, of his relationship with Alfred Douglas and of the *débâcle* with the Marquess of Queensberry, as well as a reflection on his past glories and excesses, his misery in prison and at his aspirations for the future, it is an intimate and powerful document which should be read alongside this selection.

I have benefited over the years of working on Wilde's letters from the generosity and kindness of many scholars, collectors and friends, all acknowledged at length in *The Complete Letters*; for reasons of space it is not possible here to reiterate my thanks in detail, but they know who they are and I hope that they will accept a general expression of my profound gratitude once more. To Rupert Hart-Davis I owe, together with my family, more than mere words can express; I have dedicated this selection to his memory with much love and respect. It was his decision fifty years ago to publish the first edition of Oscar Wilde's letters which helped to put my grandfather back into the position which he lost in 1895 as one of the most charismatic and fascinating figures in English literary history.

Lastly my thanks to Mitzi Angel and Catherine Blyth at Fourth Estate for their old-style professionalism as true publisher's editors, friends and advisers.

MERLIN HOLLAND
St Martin-sous-Montaigu
August, 2003

Chronological Table

of *Vera* with Marie Prescott in the lead; it is not a success

September   Begins lecture tour of UK which lasts off and on for a year

26 November   Becomes engaged to Constance Lloyd while lecturing in Dublin

1884   *29 May*   Married to Constance Lloyd in London
May–June   On honeymoon in Paris and Dieppe

1885   *January*   Moves into 16 Tite Street, Chelsea
May   'The Truth of Masks' published in the *Nineteenth Century*
5 June   Cyril Wilde born

1886   Meets Robert Ross who remains lifelong friend and after his death becomes his literary executor
3 November   Vyvyan Wilde born

1887   *February–March*   'The Canterville Ghost' published in the *Court & Society Review*
May   'The Sphinx without a Secret' published in the *World* and 'Lord Arthur Savile's Crime' in the *Court & Society Review*
June   'The Model Millionaire' published in the *World*
November   Becomes editor of *Woman's World*

1888   *May*   *The Happy Prince and Other Tales* published
December   'The Young King' published in the *Lady's Pictorial*

1889   *January*   'The Decay of Lying' published in the *Nineteenth Century* and 'Pen, Pencil and Poison' in the *Fortnightly Review*
March   'The Birthday of the Infanta' published in *Paris Illustré*
July   Gives up editorship of *Woman's World*. 'The Portrait of Mr W. H.' appears in *Blackwood's Magazine*

1890   *20 June*   'The Picture of Dorian Gray' appears in *Lippincott's Magazine*
July–September   Both parts of 'The Critic as Artist' published these months in the *Nineteenth Century*

1891   *26 January*   First production of *The Duchess of Padua* under the title *Guido Ferranti*. It opens anonymously in New York and runs for only three weeks
February   'The Soul of Man under Socialism' published in the *Fortnightly Review*
April   *The Picture of Dorian Gray* published in book form with additional chapters and a preface
2 May   *Intentions* published (comprising 'The Truth of Masks', 'The Critic as Artist', 'Pen, Pencil & Poison' and 'The Decay of Lying')

?June   Meets Lord Alfred Douglas (Bosie)

July   Lord Arthur Savile's Crime and Other Stories (the other stories being 'The Sphinx without a Secret', 'The Canterville Ghost' and 'The Model Millionaire') published in book form

November   A House of Pomegranates published. It included 'The Young King', 'The Birthday of the Infanta', 'The Fisherman and his Soul' and 'The Star Child', the last two of which had not been published before

November–December   Writes *Salomé* in Paris

1892   *20 February   Lady Windermere's Fan* produced at St James's Theatre

June   A production of *Salomé* with Sarah Bernhardt in the title role is banned by the Lord Chamberlain

July   Takes cure at Homburg

August–September   Writes *A Woman of No Importance* in Norfolk

1893   *22 February   Salomé* published in French

19 April   A Woman of No Importance produced at Haymarket Theatre

October   Writes *An Ideal Husband*

November   Lady Windermere's Fan published

1894   *9 February   Salomé* published in English with Aubrey Beardsley's illustrations

May   In Florence with Douglas

11 June   The Sphinx published

July   'Poems in Prose' published in the *Fortnightly Review*

August–September   Writes *The Importance of Being Earnest* at Worthing

9 October   A Woman of No Importance published

October   At Brighton with Douglas

November   'A Few Maxims for the Instruction of the Over-Educated' published in the *Saturday Review*

December   'Phrases and Philosophies for the Use of the Young' published in the *Chameleon*

1895   *3 January   An Ideal Husband* produced at Haymarket Theatre

January–February   Visits Algiers with Douglas

14 February   The Importance of Being Earnest produced at St James's Theatre

28 February   Finds Queensberry's card at Albemarle Club

1 March   Obtains warrant for Queensberry's arrest

9 March   Queensberry remanded at Bow Street for trial at Old Bailey

12–20 March   Visits Monte Carlo with Douglas

3 April   Queensberry trial opens

5 April   Queensberry acquitted. Wilde arrested at Cadogan Hotel and charged at Bow Street. Bail refused. Imprisoned at Holloway until first trial

24 April   Sheriff's sale of all Wilde's possessions at his home, 16 Tite Street

26 April   First trial opens

1 May   Jury disagree

7 May   Released on bail

20 May   Second trial opens

25 May   Convicted and sentenced to two years' hard labour. Imprisoned at Pentonville

30 May   *The Soul of Man under Socialism* published in book form

4 July   Transferred to Wandsworth

12 November   Declared bankrupt

20 November   Transferred to Reading

1896   *3 February*   Death of his mother, Lady Wilde

11 February   *Salomé* produced in Paris at the Théâtre de l'Oeuvre

1897   *January–March*   Writes *De Profundis*

19 May   Released. Crosses to Dieppe

26 May   Moves from Dieppe to Berneval-sur-Mer

July–October   Writes and revises *The Ballad of Reading Gaol*

?28 August   Meets Douglas in Rouen

15 September   Leaves Dieppe for Paris

20 September   Arrives at Naples with Douglas

1898   *February*   Returns to Paris

13 February   *The Ballad of Reading Gaol* published

End March   Moves to Hôtel d'Alsace, rue des Beaux-Arts, Paris

7 April   Death of Constance Wilde in Genoa after spinal operation

June–July   At Nogent-sur-Marne

August   At Chevennières-sur-Marne

December   Invited by Frank Harris to spend three months on French Riviera at Napoule near Cannes

1899   *February*   *The Importance of Being Earnest* published. Leaves Napoule for Nice

25 February   Leaves Nice to stay as Harold Mellor's guest at Gland, Switzerland

13 March   Willie Wilde, his brother, dies

1 April   Leaves Gland for Santa Margherita on Italian Riviera

May   Returns to Paris. Stays at Hôtel de la Néva, then at Hôtel Marsollier

July   *An Ideal Husband* published

August   Moves back to the Hôtel d'Alsace

1900   *April–May*   Spends two weeks as Mellor's guest travelling in Italy and Sicily

May   Returns to the Hôtel d'Alsace

10 October   Undergoes ear operation in hotel room

30 November   Dies in Hôtel d'Alsace of cerebral meningitis. Buried at Bagneux

1905   *February   De Profundis* first published in heavily expurgated form by Robert Ross

1906   *July*   Wilde's estate discharged from bankruptcy. Creditors paid 20s in the £ and 4 per cent interest from sales of books and licensing of plays

1908   First collected edition of Wilde's works published by Methuen

1909   *20 July*   Wilde's remains are moved from the cemetery at Bagneux to Père Lachaise and reinterred under Jacob Epstein's monument. The manuscript of *De Profundis* is presented by Ross to the British Museum on the condition that it remain closed for fifty years

1945   *20 March*   Death of Lord Alfred Douglas

1949   Suppressed part of *De Profundis* published by Wilde's son, Vyvyan Holland, from Ross's typescript

1954   Unveiling of plaque on Wilde's London home at 16 Tite Street

1956   First publication of the original four-act version of *The Importance of Being Earnest*

1962   Publication of Wilde's *Collected Letters* including first fully correct version of *De Profundis*

1995   Consecration of a window to Oscar Wilde in Poets' Corner, Westminster Abbey

1998   Erection of a publicly funded sculpture *A Conversation with Oscar Wilde* in Adelaide Street, London

The Student

*'It is too delightful altogether this
display of fireworks at the end
of my career. . . . The dons
are 'astonied' beyond
words – the Bad Boy
doing so well in
the end!'*

It is all too easy to think of Oscar Wilde as a fin de siècle phenomenon, something like the firework in his story 'The Remarkable Rocket', rising apparently from nowhere, exploding in a spectacularly self-destructive way and gasping as he went out, 'I knew I should create a great sensation!' In reality, he was brought up in what today would be considered a well-to-do, upper-middle-class, professional family, living in a fashionable area of Dublin, though not by the conventional parents that such a background might have suggested. His father, William Wilde, was a respected medical man specialising in maladies of the eye and ear, whose work on the Irish census of 1851, hailed at the time as a quite exceptional demographic study, is still in use today as source material for the study of the Great Famine. He was also passionately interested in the history and topography of Ireland and wrote two books on the subject, as well as one on Irish folklore, and catalogued in three volumes the antiquities of the Royal Irish Academy.

Oscar's mother, Jane, was no less extraordinary in her way: she had played a leading role in the Young Ireland movement of the 1840s writing inflammatory, anti-English articles in the Nation under her pen name 'Speranza' and narrowly missed imprisonment alongside the editor, Charles Gavan Duffy, for sedition; she published poetry, essays, and translations from French and German; and she hosted a weekly salon to which came Dublin's foremost doctors, lawyers, artists and literary figures, together with distinguished foreign visitors. The influence of these two remarkable parents, committed Hibernophiles both, he intellectually and she more emotionally, was to remain with Oscar Wilde throughout his life. Indeed, from prison he would write remorsefully to Lord Alfred Douglas, 'She and my father had bequeathed me a name they had made noble and honoured not merely in Literature, Art, Archaeology and Science, but in the public history of my own country in its evolution as a nation. I had disgraced that name eternally.'

Jane Elgee and William Wilde were married on 12 November 1851 and their first child, William Charles Kingsbury, was born on 26 September the following year. Jane was soon pregnant again and on 16 October 1854 she gave birth to her second child. He was christened Oscar Fingal O'Flahertie (he would later add the 'Wills' from his father), a veritable mouthful of names by which he was embarrassed at school, proud of at university and dismissive of in later life, saying, 'As one becomes famous, one sheds some of them, just as a balloonist, when rising higher, sheds unnecessary ballast. All but two have already been thrown overboard. Soon I shall discard another and be known simply as "The Wilde" or "The Oscar".' If Willie had been christened with admirable restraint after his own father, Jane's father and Jane's mother's family name, reflecting her new conformity, the new arrival was an excuse to restate her Irishness. Oscar and Fingal were respectively son and father of Oisin, the third-century Celtic warrior-poet and O'fflahertie, as he would occasionally spell it, was in deference to her husband's links with 'the ferocious O'Flaherties of Galway'.

The Wildes soon began to find that their house at 21 Westland Row, which backed on to Trinity College, was not only too small for the expanding family, but also lacked the social cachet which William's growing status as a doctor demanded. Before Oscar was a year old they moved to an ample Georgian house around the corner at 1 Merrion Square and engaged six servants to run it, as well as employing a French maid and a German governess. The latter permitted the children's education to take place at home until Oscar was ten, when he was sent with his brother to board at Portora Royal School, Enniskillen. It was from there that his first surviving letter was written. His mother had contributed a poem 'To Ireland' for the previous (August) issue of the National Review, *a pale and short-lived imitation of the magazine of her former firebrand days, the* Nation, *and the young thirteen-year-old Oscar's taste for clothes and radical politics is beginning to show.*

To Lady Wilde

8 September 1868   *Portora School*

Darling Mama, The hamper came today, I never got such a jolly surprise, many thanks for it, it was more than kind of you to think of it. The grapes and pears are delicious and so cooling, but the blancmange got a little sour, I suppose by the knocking about, but the rest all came safe.

Don't forget please to send me the *National Review*, is it not issued today?

The flannel shirts you sent in the hamper are both Willie's, mine are one quite scarlet and the other lilac but it is too hot to wear them yet, the weather is so hot.

We went down to the horrid regatta on Thursday last. It was very jolly. There was a yacht race.

You never told me anything about the publisher in Glasgow. What does he say and have you written to Aunt Warren on the green note paper?

We played the officers of the 27th Regiment now stationed in Enniskillen, a few days ago and beat them hollow by about seventy runs.

You may imagine my delight this morning when I got Papa's letter saying he had sent a hamper.

Now dear Mamma, I must bid you goodbye as the post goes very soon. Many thanks for letting me paint. With love to Papa, ever your affectionate son   OSCAR WILDE

In 1871 he won an entrance scholarship to Trinity College, Dublin, and went there armed with an exhibition from Portora. During the next three years he had the distinction of being made a Foundation Scholar and won many prizes for classics, including the Berkeley Gold Medal for Greek. He also came strongly under the influence of the Rev. John Pentland Mahaffy (1839–1919). This remarkable man (who later became Provost of the College and was knighted in 1918) was then Professor of Ancient History. His passion for all things Greek, his study of the art of conversation and his social technique all left their mark on his pupil.

In 1874, at the age of nineteen, Wilde crowned his Irish academic successes by winning a Demyship (scholarship) to Magdalen College, Oxford and in October, a week before his twentieth birthday, he took up residence there to read Classics. What Dublin had sowed, flowered intellectually in Oxford. He made the acquaintance of John Ruskin, Slade Professor of Fine Art, and having attended his lectures on Florentine Aesthetics in his first term, was soon persuaded to take part in his new mentor's practical improvements to the countryside, and found himself rising at dawn to help build a country road. The reward was less in the toil than in the pleasure of breakfasting with Ruskin afterwards. The road, however, soon sank back into Hinksey Marsh but their friendship flourished. When Wilde sent him a copy of The Happy Prince *in 1888 (see p. 108) he accompanied it with a note: 'The dearest memories of my Oxford days are my walks and talks with you, and from you I learned nothing but what was good. . . . There is in you something of prophet, of priest, and of poet.'*

Soon after his arrival in Oxford Wilde read Walter Pater's Studies in the History of the Renaissance. *Pater was a young don at Brasenose College whom Wilde did not meet in person until his third year but on whose theories of art and aesthetics he was already starting to base his own flamboyant style. He found himself disturbingly attuned to the book's philosophies, especially those in the 'Conclusion' in which Pater said: 'Not the fruit of experience but experience itself is the end' and continued, 'To burn always with this hard gem-like flame, to maintain this ecstasy, is success in life.' He also declared that enrichment of our given lifespan consisted of 'getting as many pulsations as possible into the given time' and of having 'the desire for beauty, the love of art for its own sake'. Writing from prison two decades later Wilde would refer to it as 'that book which has had such a strange influence over my life'.*

Ruskin and Pater each appealed to a different Wilde: Ruskin to the intellectual, the noble, the high-minded; Pater, more insidiously, to the sensual, the decadent, the mystical. Pater was less uplifting for the soul but dangerously attractive to the senses.

But the excitement of new teachings did not lead Oscar to abandon old friends. He still found time for Mahaffy and, together with a young Dubliner, William Goulding, they travelled through Italy during the summer vacation of 1875. Ruskin had fired him with the desire to experience the Renaissance for himself and his old tutor provided the opportunity. They visited Venice, Padua, Verona, Milan and Florence from where he wrote to his father, reflecting their shared interest in history and archaeology.

To Sir William Wilde

Tuesday [15 June 1875]   *Florence*

Went in the morning to see San Lorenzo, built in the usual Florentine way, cruciform: a long aisle supported by Grecian pillars: a gorgeous dome in the centre and three small aisles leading off it. Behind it are the two Chapels of the Medici. The first, the Burial Chapel, is magnificent; of enormous height, octagonal in shape. Walls built entirely of gorgeous blocks of marble, all inlaid with various devices and of different colours, polished like a looking-glass. Six great sarcophagi of granite and porphyry stand in six niches: on top of each of them a cushion of inlaid mosaic bearing a gold crown. Above the sarcophagi are statues in gilded bronze of the Medici; on the dome, of course, frescoes and gilded carving.

The other chapel is very small, built simply of white marble. Two mausoleums in it to two great Medici; one bearing Michelangelo's statues of Night and Morning and the other those of Evening and Dawn.

Then to the Biblioteca Laurenziana in the cloisters of San Lorenzo, where I was shown wonderfully illuminated missals and unreadable manuscripts and autographs. I remarked the extreme clearness of the initial letters in the Italian missals and bibles, so different from those in the Book of Kells etc., which might stand for anything. The early illuminations are very beautiful in design and sentiment, but the later are mere mechanical *tours de force* of geometrical scroll-work and absurd designs.

Then to the Etruscan Museum, which is in the suppressed monastery of San Onofrio and most interesting. You come first to a big tomb, transplanted from Arezzo; cyclopean stonework, doorway with sloping jambs and oblong lintel, roof slightly conical, walls covered with wonderfully beautiful frescoes, representing first the soul in the shape of a young man naked, led by a beautifully winged angel or genius to the two-horsed chariot which is to convey them to Elysium – and then represents the banquet which awaits him. This same idea of the resurrection of the soul and a state of happiness after death pervades the whole system of Etruscan art. There were also wonderful sarcophagi which I have roughly drawn for you. [*Overleaf*]

On the top the figure of the dead man or woman holding a plate containing the obol for paying the ferryman over Styx. Also extraordinary jars with heads and arms – funeral of course – I have drawn them. The sarcophagi, of which there are over *a hundred and fifty* to be seen, are about two and a half feet long and about three feet high. The sides of the sarcophagi are sculptured with the achievements and adventures of the dead man, mostly in bas-relief which are sometimes coloured. There were some with frescoes instead of sculpture, beautifully done. Of course urns and vases of every possible shape, and all painted exquisitely.

A great collection of coins, from the old *as*, a solid pound weight of metal about as big as a large bun and stamped with a ship on one side and a double-faced Janus on the other, down to tiny little gold coins the same size as gold five-franc pieces. The goldsmiths' work for beauty of design and delicacy of workmanship exceeded anything I have ever seen. As I was kept there for a long time by an awful thunderstorm I copied a few which I send you.

I cannot of course give you the wonderful grace and delicacy of workmanship, only the design. Goblets and bowls of jasper and all sorts of transparent pebbles – enamelled jars in abundance. Swords of the leaf shape, regular torques but somewhat same design, metal hand-mirrors, and household

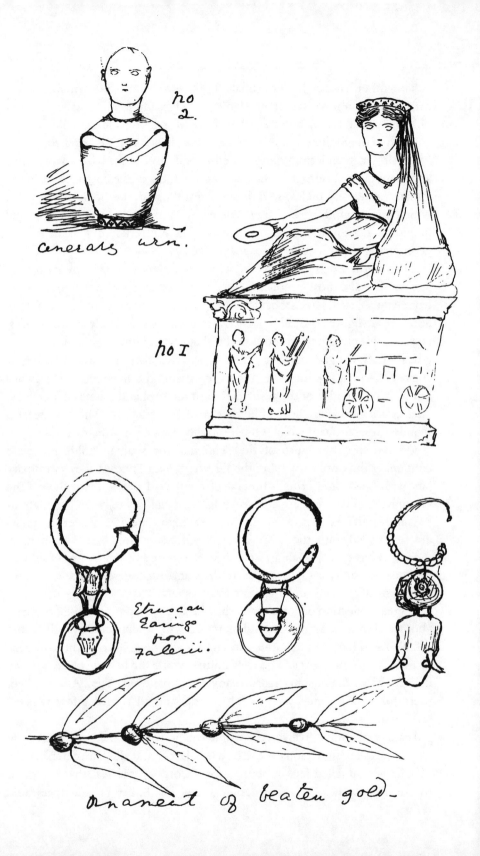

no 2.

cenerary urn.

no I

Etruscan
Earings
from
Falerii.

ornament of beaten gold.

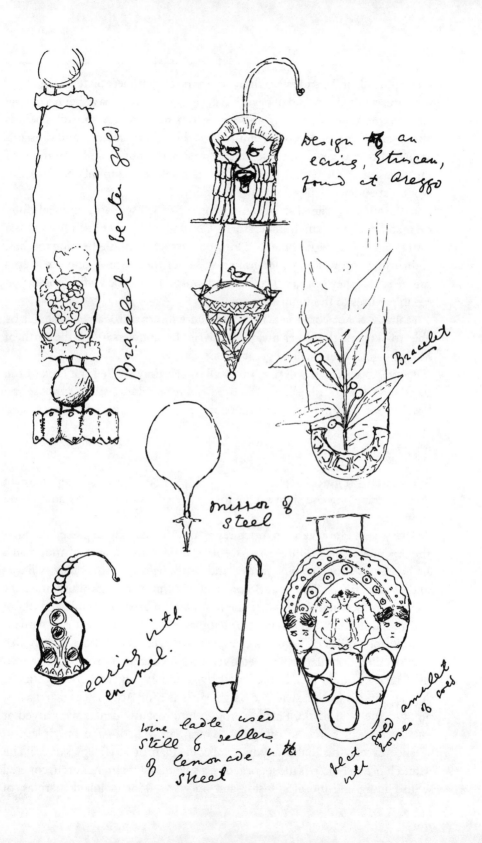

Bracelet - beaten gold

Design for an earing, Etruscan, found at Arezzo

Bracelet

mirror of steel

earing with enamel.

wine ladle used still by sellers of lemonade in the street

flat gold amulet with bosses of coral

utensils of all kinds, and every thing, even the commonest plate or jug, done with greatest delicacy and of beautiful design. They must have been a people among whom artistic feeling and power was most widely spread. There is also a museum of Egyptian antiquities, but their devices and frescoes appeared to me grotesque and uncouth after the purity and sentiment of the Etruscan. You would have been much interested in all the Etruscan work: I spent two delightful hours there.

In the evening I dined at a restaurant on top of San Miniato, air delightfully clear and cool after the thunderstorm. Coming back I met just opposite the Pitti Palace a wonderful funeral; a long procession of monks bearing torches, all in white and wearing a long linen veil over their faces – only their eyes can be seen. They bore two coffins and looked like those awful monks you see in pictures of the Inquisition.

Mahaffy is not come yet. I do hope he will arrive today, as I shan't be able to stay much longer away. Today is the anniversary of the birth of Michelangelo: there will be great fêtes.

Hope Abbotstown will turn out well. It certainly spoiled the look of the place, and that terrible large ditch between us and it will, I suppose, be bridged over. Yours ever truly affectionately   OSCAR O'F. WI. WILDE

To Lady Wilde

Wednesday [23 June 1875]   *Albergo della Francia, Milan*
So busy travelling and sight-seeing for last five days that I have had no time to write.

Diary. Left Florence with much regret on Saturday night; passed through the Apennines, beautiful Alpine scenery; train runs on side of mountains half-way up, above us pine-forests and crags, below us the valley, villages and swollen rivers. Supper at Bologna; about 5.30 in the morning came near Venice. Immediately on leaving the mountains a broad flat tableland (there are no hills in Italy – mountains or flat plains) cultivated like a rich garden. Within four miles of Venice a complete change; a black bog, exactly like Bog of Allen only flatter; crossed over a big *laguna* on a bridge and arrived at Venice 7.30. Seized on immediately by gondoliers and embarked with our luggage, into a *black* hearse-like barge, such as King Arthur was taken away in after the fatal battle. Finally through long narrow canals we arrived at our hotel, which was in the great Piazza San Marco – the only place in Venice except the Rialto anyone walks in. Plan of it. [*Rough sketch.*] The Church of San Marco is most gorgeous; a splendid *Byzantine* church, covered with gilding and mosaics, inside and out. The floor of inlaid marbles, of colour and design indescribable, and through the sinking of the piles undulates in big sweeping waves. Splendid gates of bronze, everything glorious. Next to it the Doge's Palace, which is beyond praise. Inside, giant council chambers; the walls painted with frescoes by Titian of the great battles of the Venetians; the ceiling crossed by gilded beams and rich in gilded carving; rooms fit for the noble-looking grave senators whose pictures are on the walls by Titian or Tintoretto.

Council Room of the celebrated 'Three', black marble and gold. Two dismal passages lead from it across the *Ponte dei Sospiri*. In size and colour and dignity the rooms are beyond description, and the view from the windows across the sea wonderful. Beneath all this greatness are the most dismal dungeons and torture-rooms – most terrible.

Here we spent the morning; afterwards took a gondola and visited some of the islands off Venice; on one an Armenian monastery where Byron used to live. Went to another, the Lido, a favourite place on Sunday, and had oysters and shrimps. Returned home in the flood of a great sunset. Venice as a city just risen from the sea; a long line of crowded churches and palaces; everywhere white or gilded domes and tall campaniles; no opening in the whole city except at the Piazza San Marco. A great pink sunset with a long line of purple thunderclouds behind the city. After dinner went to the theatre and saw a good circus. Luckily a wonderful moon. We landed from our gondola coming from the theatre at the Lion of St Mark. The scene was so romantic that it seemed to be an 'artistic' scene from an opera. We sat on the base of the pillar; on one side of us the Doge's Palace, on the other the King's Palace, behind us the Campanile. The water-steps crowded with black gondolas, and a great flood of light coming right up to us across the water. Every moment a black silent gondola would glide across this great stream of light and be lost in the darkness.

To Lady Wilde

Thursday [24 June 1875]   *Milan*

I believe you left me last looking at the moon from the Piazza San Marco. With difficulty we tore ourselves away to the hotel. Next morning we went up the Grand Canal in a gondola. Great palaces on each side with huge steps leading down to the water, and all round big posts to moor the gondolas to, coloured with the arms of the family. Wonderful colour everywhere – windows hung with striped yellow awnings, domes and churches of white marble, campaniles of red brick, great gondolas filled with fruit and vegetables going to the Rialto where the market is. Stopped to see the picture gallery which, as usual, was in a suppressed monastery. Titian and Tintoretto in great force. Titian's *Assumption* certainly the best picture in Italy. Went to a lot of churches, all however in extravagant 'baroque' style – very rich in worked metal and polished marble and mosaic but as a rule inartistic. In the picture gallery besides the Titians there are two great pictures; one a beautiful Madonna by Bellini, the other a picture of Dives and Lazarus by Bonifazio containing the only *lovely* woman's face I have seen in Italy.

Spent the day in gondolas and markets; in the evening a great band and promenade of all the swells of Venice in the Piazza San Marco. Every woman, nearly, over thirty powdered the front of her hair; most wore veils but I see that bonnets are now made with very high crowns and two wreaths, one under the diadem and one round the crown.

After marriage the Italian women degenerate awfully, but the boys and girls are beautiful. Amongst married women the general types are 'Titiens' and an ugly sallow likeness of 'Trebelli Bettini'.

In the morning breakfasted on board the P & O steamer *Baroda*. I was asked by the doctor, a young Dublin fellow called Fraser. Left for Padua at twelve o'clock. Believe me, Venice in beauty of architecture and colour is beyond description. It is the meeting-place of the Byzantine and Italian art – a city belonging to the *East* as much as to the West.

Arrived at Padua at two o'clock. In the middle of a rich vineyard stands the Baptistery, the great work of Giotto; the walls covered entirely with frescoes by him; one wall the life of Mary, the other the life of Christ; the ceiling blue with gold stars and medallion pictures; the west wall a great picture of Heaven and Hell suggested to him by Dante who, weary of trudging up the steep *stairs*, as he says, of the *Scaligeri* when in exile at Verona, came to stay at Padua with Giotto in a house still to be seen there. Of the beauty and purity of sentiment, the clear transparent colour, bright as the day it was painted, and the harmony of the whole building, I am unable to tell you. He is the first of all painters. We stayed over an hour in the Baptistery filled with wonder and reverence and above all love for the scenes he has painted.

Padua is a quaint town with good colonnades along each street, a university like a barracks, one charming church (Sant' Anastasia) and a lot of bad ones, and the best restaurant in Italy, where we dined.

Arrived at Milan in a shower of rain; went in the evening to the theatre and saw a good ballet.

This morning the Cathedral. Outside most elaborate in pinnacles and statues awfully out of proportion with the rest of the building. Inside most impressive through its huge size and giant pillars supporting the roof; some good old stained glass and a lot of hideous modern windows. These moderns don't see that the use of a window in a church is to show a beautiful massing together and blending of colour; a good old window has the rich pattern of a Turkey carpet. The figures are quite subordinate and only serve to show the sentiment of the designer. The modern fresco style of window has *suâ naturâ* to compete with painting and of course looks monstrous and theatrical.

The Cathedral is an awful failure. Outside the design is monstrous and inartistic. The over-elaborated details stuck high up where no one can see them; everything is vile in it; it is, however, imposing and gigantic as a failure, through its great size and elaborate execution.

From Padua I forgot to tell you we went to Verona at six o'clock, and in the old Roman amphitheatre (as perfect inside as it was in the old Roman times) saw the play of *Hamlet* performed – and certainly indifferently – but you can imagine how romantic it was to sit in the old amphitheatre on a lovely moonlight night. In the morning went to see the tombs of the Scaligeri – good examples of rich florid Gothic work and ironwork; a good market-place filled with the most gigantic umbrellas I ever saw – like young palm trees – under which sat the fruit-sellers. Of our arrival at Milan I have told you.

Yesterday (Thursday) went first to the Ambrosian Library where we saw some great manuscripts and two very good palimpsests, and a bible with Irish glosses of the sixth or seventh century which has been collated by Todd and Whitley Stokes and others; a good collection of pictures besides, particularly a set of drawings and sketches in chalk by Raffaelli – much more interesting I think than his pictures – good Holbeins and Albrecht Dürers.

Then to the picture gallery. Some good Correggios and Peruginos; the gem of the whole collection is a lovely Madonna by Bernardino standing among a lot of trellised roses that Morris and Rossetti would love; another by him we saw in the library with a background of lilies.

Milan is a second Paris. Wonderful arcades and galleries; all the town white stone and gilding. Dined excellently at the Biffi Restaurant and had some good wine of Asti, like good cider or sweet champagne. In the evening went to see a new opera, *Dolores*, by a young maestro called Auteri; a good imitation of Bellini in some parts, some pretty rondos; but its general character was inharmonious shouting. However, the frantic enthusiasm of the people knew no bounds. Every five minutes a terrible furore and yelling of *Bravas* from every part of the house, followed by a frantic rush of all the actors for the composer, who was posted at the side-scenes ready to rush out on the slightest symptom of approval. A weak-looking creature who placed his grimy hand on a shady-looking shirt to show his emotion, fell on the prima donna's neck in ecstasy, and blew kisses to us all. He came out no less than nineteen times, and finally three crowns were brought out, one of which, a green laurel one with green ribbons, was clapped on his head, and as his head was very narrow it rested partly on a very large angular nose and partly on his grimy shirt-collar. Such an absurd scene as the whole

thing was I never saw. The opera except in two places is absolutely devoid of merit. The Princess Margherita was there, very high-bred and pale.

I write this at Arona on the Lago Maggiore, a beautiful spot. Mahaffy and young Goulding I left at Milan and they will go on to Genoa. As I had no money I was obliged to leave them and feel very lonely. We have had a delightful tour.

Tonight at twelve o'clock the *diligence* starts. We go over the Simplon Pass till near Lausanne; eighteen hours *en diligence*. Tomorrow night (Saturday) I get to Lausanne. Yours   OSCAR

It was at Oxford that Wilde started to form his first intense friendships, the most important being with William 'Bouncer' Ward, Reginald 'Kitten' Harding and David 'Dunskie' Hunter-Blair. Wilde admired Ward, also a Classical Scholar, for his intelligence; Harding attracted him by his charm and good looks; and Hunter-Blair's appeal was his devout Catholicism and contacts with the Roman Church in which Wilde was increasingly interested. He also made friends with a young London artist, Frank Miles, whose father was a clergyman and with whom he would share rooms when he came down from Oxford. Between taking his first exams in Honour Moderations (Mods) in June and his viva voce in July, Oscar went to visit his late father's elder brother, who was a clergyman in Lincolnshire. Sir William died in April 1876.

To Reginald Harding

Wednesday [5 July 1876]   *Magdalen College, Oxford*

My dear Kitten, I am very sorry to hear you did not meet the poor Bouncer Boy; see what comes of having rowdy friends fond of practical jokes. I had an awful pencil scrawl from him yesterday, written sitting on the rocks at Lundy. I hope nothing will happen to him.

I had a very pleasant time in Lincolnshire, but the weather was so hot we did nothing but play lawn tennis, as probably Bouncer will tell you when you see him next (I wrote a full account to him). I examined schools in geography and history, *sang* glees, *ate* strawberries and argued fiercely with my poor uncle, who revenged himself on Sunday by preaching on Rome in the morning, and on humility in the evening. Both very 'nasty ones' for me.

I ran up to town yesterday from Lincoln and brought Frank Miles a great basket of roses from the Rectory. I found him sketching the most lovely and dangerous woman in London – Lady Desart. She is very fascinating indeed.

I came down Monday night to read for *viva voce*, but yesterday morning at ten o'clock was woke up by the Clerk of the Schools, and found I was in already. I was rather afraid of being put on in Catullus, but got a delightful exam from a delightful man – not on the books at all but on Aeschylus *versus* Shakespeare, modern poetry and drama and every conceivable subject. I was up for about an hour and was quite sorry when it was over. In Divinity I was ploughed of course.

I am going down to Bingham with Frank Miles and R. Gower on Saturday for a week. They have the most beautiful modern church in England, and the finest lilies. I shall write and tell you about it.

Being utterly penniless I can't go up to town till Friday. It is very slow here – now that Bouncer is gone. But tonight the Mods list comes out so I will have some excitement being *congratulated* – really I don't care a bit (no one ever does now) and quite expect a Second *after* my Logic, though *of course much the cleverest man in.* (Such cheek!)

You will probably see the list on Thursday or Friday; if I get a Second mind you write and condole with me awfully, and if I get a First say it was only what you expected.

See the results of having nothing to do – ten pages of a letter! Yours ever

OSCAR F. O´F. WILLS WILDE

My address will be The Rectory, Bingham, Notts after Saturday. I hope you will write a line and tell me all extra news about Bouncer.

PS no.2. The paper enclosed in Bouncer's letter was *not dirty.*

To William Ward

[Postmark 10 July 1876]   *4 Albert Street, London SW*

My dear Boy, I know you will be glad to hear I have got my First all right. I came up from Lincolnshire to town on Monday and went down that night to Magdalen to read my Catullus, but while lying in bed on Tuesday morning with Swinburne (a copy of) was woke up by the Clerk of the Schools to know why I did not come up. I thought I was not in till Thursday. About one o'clock I *nipped* up and was ploughed immediately in Divinity and then got a delightful *viva voce*, first in the *Odyssey*, where we discussed epic poetry in general, *dogs*, and women. Then in Aeschylus where we talked of Shakespeare, Walt Whitman and the *Poetics*. He had a long discussion about my essay on Poetry in the Aristotle paper and altogether was delightful. Of course I knew I had got a First, so swaggered horribly.

The next day the B.C.s and myself were dining with Nicols in Christ Church and the list came out at seven, as we were walking up the High. I said I would not go up to the Schools, as I knew I had a First etc., and made them all very ill, absolutely. I did not know what I had got till the next morning at twelve o'clock, breakfasting at the Mitre, I read [it] in *The Times*. Altogether I swaggered horribly, but am really pleased with myself. My poor mother is in great delight and I was overwhelmed with telegrams on Thursday from everyone I know. My father would have been so pleased about it. I think God has dealt very hardly with us. It has robbed me of any real pleasure in my First, and I have not sufficient faith in Providence to believe it is all for the best – I know it is not. I feel an awful dread of going home to our old house, with everything filled with memories. I go down today for a week at Bingham with the Mileses. I have been staying here with Julia Tindal who is in great form. Yesterday I heard the Cardinal at the Pro-Cathedral preach a charity sermon. He is more fascinating than ever. I met MacCall and Williamson there who greeted me with much *empressement*. I feel an impostor and traitor to myself on these occasions and must do something decided.

Afterwards I went to the Zoo with Julia and the two Peytons – Tom is nearly all right. Young Stewy dined with us on Saturday. He said he was afraid he must have jarred you by his indecencies and was going to reform. Altogether I found out we were right in thinking that set a little jarred about our carelessness about them. Next term I shall look them up.

I hope you will see the Kitten. I got a very nice letter from him about Mods. Miss Puss has fallen in my estimation if she is fetched with Swan – who to men is irritable, but to women intolerable I think. Write soon to Bingham Rectory, Nottinghamshire. Ever yours   OSCAR O´F. WI. WILDE

To Reginald Harding

[Circa 13 July 1876]   *Bingham Rectory, Notts*
My dear Boy, Thousand thanks for your letter. Half the pleasure of getting a First is to receive such delightful congratulations. I *am* really a little pleased at getting it, though I swaggered horribly and pretended that I did not care a bit. In fact I would not go up to the Schools on Wednesday evening – said it was a bore – and actually did not know certainly till Thursday at twelve o'clock when I read it in *The Times*. The really pleasant part is that my mother is so pleased. I got a heap of telegrams on Thursday from Ireland with congratulations.

I went up to town on Friday and stayed with Julia Tindal; we had a very pleasant time together. Sunday we went to the Zoo with Algy and Tom Peyton. Tom is all right now; he had got paralysis of his face.

I came down here Monday and had no idea it was so lovely. A wonderful garden with such white lilies and rose walks; only that there are no serpents or apples it would be quite Paradise. The church is very fine indeed. Frank and his mother, a very good artist, have painted wonderful windows, and frescoed angels on the walls, and one of his sisters has carved the screen and altar. It is simply beautiful and everything done by themselves.

These horrid red marks are strawberries, which I am eating in basketfuls, during intervals of lawn tennis, at which I am awfully good.

There are four daughters, all very pretty indeed, one of them who is writing at the other side of the table quite lovely. My heart is torn in sunder with admiration for them all, and my health going, so I return to Ireland next week.

We are having a large garden party here today, and tomorrow one at the Duke of Rutland's who is quite close.

I make myself as charming as ever and am much admired. Have had some good arguments with Dean Miles who was a great friend of Newman, Pusey and Manning at Oxford and a very advanced Anglican.

Write me a line soon like a good boy. Ever yours

OSCAR F. O´F. WILLS WILDE

I heard the Cardinal on Sunday preach a charity sermon at the Pro-Cathedral, Kensington. MacCall was there.

To William Ward

Wednesday [26 July 1876]   *1 Merrion Square North, Dublin*

My dear Boy, I confess not to be a worshipper at the Temple of Reason. I think man's reason the most misleading and thwarting guide that the sun looks upon, except perhaps the reason of woman. Faith is, I think, a bright lantern for the feet, though of course an exotic plant in man's mind, and requiring continual cultivation. My mother would probably agree with you. Except for the *people*, for whom she thinks dogma necessary, she rejects all forms of superstition and dogma, particularly any notion of priest and sacrament standing between her and God. She has a very strong faith in that aspect of God we call the Holy Ghost – the divine intelligence of which we on earth partake. Here she is very strong, though of course at times troubled by the discord and jarring of the world, when she takes a dip into pessimism.

Her last pessimist, Schopenhauer, says the whole human race ought on a given day, after a strong remonstrance *firmly but respectfully* urged on God, to walk into the sea and leave the world tenantless, but of course some skulking wretches would hide and be left behind to people the world again I am afraid.

I wonder you don't see the beauty and necessity for the *incarnation* of God into man to help us to grasp at the skirts of the Infinite. The atonement is I admit hard to grasp. But I think since Christ the dead world has woke up from sleep. Since him we have lived. I think the greatest proof of the Incarnation aspect of Christianity is its whole career of noble men and thoughts and not the mere narration of unauthenticated histories.

I think *you* are bound to account (psychologically most especially) for S. Bernard and S. Augustine and S. Philip Neri – and even in our day for Liddon and Newman – as being good philosophers and good Christians. That reminds me of Mallock's *New Republic* in *Belgravia*; it is decidedly clever – Jowett especially. If you have the key to all the actors please send it to me.

I send you this letter and a book together. I wonder which you will open first. It is *Aurora Leigh*, which I think you said you had not read. It is one of those books that, written straight from the heart – and from such a large heart too – never weary one: because they are sincere. We tire of art but not of nature after all our aesthetic training. I look upon it as much the greatest work in our literature.

I rank it with *Hamlet* and *In Memoriam*. So much do I love it that I hated the idea of sending it to you without marking a few passages I felt you would well appreciate – and I found myself marking the whole book. I am really very sorry: it is like being given a bouquet of plucked flowers instead of being allowed to look for them oneself. But I could not resist the temptation, as it *did* instead of writing to you about each passage.

The only fault is that she overstrains her metaphors till they snap, and although one does not like polished emotion, still she is inartistically rugged at times. As she says herself, she shows the mallet hand in carving cherry-stones.

I hope you will have time to read it, for I don't believe your dismal forebodings about Greats.

I wrote to Kitten for your address, and his letter and yours arrived simultaneously. His thoughts and ink rarely last beyond one sheet.

I ride sometimes after six, but don't do much but bathe, and although always feeling slightly immortal when in the sea, feel sometimes slightly heretical when good Roman Catholic boys enter the water with little amulets and crosses round their necks and arms that the good S. Christopher may hold them up.

I am now off to bed after reading a chapter of S. Thomas à Kempis. I think half-an-hour's warping of the inner man daily is greatly conducive to holiness.

Pray remember me to your mother and sisters. Ever yours

OSCAR F. O´F. WILLS WILDE

Post Scriptum

You don't deserve such a long letter, but I must tell you that I met Mr Rigaud (the gentleman who met with that sad accident in early youth) and his brother the General swaggering up Grafton Street here yesterday. I had a long talk with them and the General told me yarns by the dozen about the time he was quartered here 'with the 16th Battalion, sir! Damme, sir! We were the best corps in the Regiment! Service gone to the dogs! Not a well drilled soldier in the country, sir!'

Sir William had built two properties in the west of Ireland, a small fishing lodge in 1853 at Illaunroe, near Leenane, and a comfortable country house at Moytura near Cong. Oscar is known to have spent time there as a boy helping his father record and catalogue Celtic antiquities, and now as a student used both as summer retreats for himself and for entertaining friends.

To Reginald Harding

Wednesday [?16 August 1876]   *Moytura House, Cong, Co. Mayo*
Dear Kitten, Have you fallen into a well, or been mislaid anywhere that you
never write to me? Or has one of your nine lives gone?

Frank Miles and I came down here last week, and have had a very royal
time of it sailing. We are at the top of Lough Corrib, which if you refer to
your geography you will find to be a lake thirty miles long, ten broad and
situated in the most romantic scenery in Ireland. Frank has done some
wonderful sunsets since he came down; he has given me some more of his
drawings. Has your sister got the one he calls 'My Little Lady' – a little girl's
face with a lot of falling hair? If she has not got it I would like to send it to
her in return for her autograph on the celebrated memorial.

Frank has never fired off a gun in his life (and says he doesn't want to)
but as our proper sporting season here does not begin till September I have
not taught him anything. But on Friday we go into Connemara to a charming
little fishing lodge we have in the mountains where I hope to make him
land a salmon and kill a brace of grouse. I expect to have very good sport
indeed this season. Write to me there if your claws have not been clipped.
Illaunroe Lodge, Leenane, Co. Galway.

Best love to Puss. I hope he is reading hard. Ever yours

OSCAR F. O´F. WILLS WILDE

To William Ward

Wednesday [?6 September 1876]   *1 Merrion Square North*
My dear Bouncer, Note paper became such a scarcity in the West that I had
to put off answering your letter till I came home.

I had a delightful time, and capital sport, especially the last week, which
I spent shooting, and got fair bags.

I am afraid I shall not cross to England via Bristol, as I hear the boats are
rather of the 'Ancient Mariner' type! but I may be down in Bristol with
Frank Miles as I want to see S. Raphael's and the pictures at Clevedon.

I would like very much to renew my friendship with your mother and
sisters so shall write to you if I see any hope of going down.

I have given up my pilgrimage to Rome for the present: Ronald Gower
and Frank Miles were coming: (we would have been a great Trinity) but at
the last hour Ronald couldn't get time, so I am staying in Dublin till the
20th, when I go down to Longford, and hope to have good sport.

I have heard from many people of your father's liberality and noble spirit, so I know you will take interest in the report I send you of my father's hospital, which he built when he was only twenty-nine and not a rich man. It is a great memorial of his name, and a movement is being set on foot to enlarge it and make it still greater.

I have got some charming letters lately from a great friend of my mother, Aubrey de Vere – a cultured poet (though sexless) and a convert to Catholicity. I must show you them; he is greatly interested in me and is going to get one of my poems into the *Month*. I have two this month out: one in the *Dublin University Magazine*, one in the *Irish Monthly*. Both are brief and Tennysonian.

I hope you are doing good work, but I suppose at home you are hardly allowed 'to contemplate the abstract' (whatever that means) undisturbed.

I am bothered with business and many things and find the world an ἀναρχία [chaos] at present and a Tarpeian Rock for honest men.

I hope you will write when you have time. Ever yours

OSCAR F. O´F. WILLS WILDE

I like signing my name as if it was to some document of great importance as 'Send two bags of gold by bearer' or 'Let the Duke be slain tomorrow and the Duchess await me at the hostelry'.

I send you one of Aubrey de Vere's letters. I know you will be amused at them. Return it when you have committed it to memory.

In the Michaelmas term of 1876 both Ward and Hunter-Blair took their finals and went down. Wilde moved into Ward's rooms overlooking the River Cherwell and continued to agonise over whether or not to become a Catholic. For the time being his mystical leanings had to be satisfied with the quasi-religious rituals and fancy dress of freemasonry. The following spring, though, he again went on a Classical tour with Mahaffy, this time to Greece, and came back via Rome where he met Ward and Hunter-Blair who had arranged a private audience with the Pope.

To William Ward

[Week ending 3 March 1877]   [*Oxford*]

I have got rather keen on Masonry lately and believe in it awfully – in fact would be awfully sorry to have to give it up in case I secede from the Protestant Heresy. I now breakfast with Father Parkinson, go to St Aloysius, talk sentimental religion to Dunlop and altogether am caught in the fowler's snare, in the wiles of the Scarlet Woman – I may go over in the vac. I have dreams of a visit to Newman, of the holy sacrament in a new Church, and of a quiet and peace afterwards in my soul. I need not say, though, that I shift with every breath of thought and am weaker and more self-deceiving than ever.

If I *could hope* that the Church would wake in me some earnestness and purity I would go over *as a luxury*, if for no better reasons. But I can hardly hope it would, and to go over to Rome would be to sacrifice and give up my two great gods 'Money and Ambition'.

Still I get so wretched and low and troubled that in some desperate mood I will seek the shelter of a Church which simply enthrals me by its fascination.

I hope that now in the Sacred City you are wakened up from the Egyptian darkness that has blinded you. *Do* be touched by it, *feel* the awful fascination of the Church, its extreme beauty and sentiment, and let every part of your nature have play and room.

We have had our Sports and are now in the midst of Torpids and tomorrow the pigeons are shot. To escape I go up to town to see the Old Masters *with the Kitten!* who is very anxious to come. Dear little Puss is up, and looks wretched, but as pleasant and bright as ever. He is rather keen on going to Rome for Easter with me, but I don't know if I can afford it, as I have been elected for the St Stephen's [Club] and have to pay £42. I did not want to be elected for a year or so but David Plunket ran me in in three weeks some way rather to my annoyance.

I would give worlds to be in Rome with you and Dunskie. I know I would enjoy it awfully but I don't know if I can manage it. You would be a safeguard against Dunskie's attacks.

I am in for the 'Ireland' on Monday. God! how I have wasted my life up here! I look back on weeks and months of extravagance, trivial talk, utter vacancy of employment, *with feelings so bitter that I have lost faith in myself.* I am too ridiculously easily led astray. So I have idled and won't get it and will be wretched in consequence. I feel that if I had read I would have done well up here but I have not.

I enjoy your rooms awfully. The inner room is filled with china, pictures, a portfolio and a piano – and a grey carpet with stained floor. The whole get-up is much admired and a little made fun of on Sunday evenings. They are more delightful than I ever expected – the sunshine, the cawing rooks and waving tree-branches and the breeze at the window are too charming.

I do nothing but write sonnets and scribble poetry – some of which I send you – though to send anything of mine to Rome is an awful impertinence, but you always took an interest in my attempts to ride Pegasus.

My greatest chum, except of course the Kitten, is Gussy who is charming though not educated well: however he is *'psychological'* and we have long chats and walks. The rest of Tom's set are capital good fellows but awful children. They talk nonsense and smut. I am quite as fond of the dear Kitten as ever but he has not enough power of character to be more than a pleasant affectionate boy. He never exerts my intellect or brain *in any way*. Between his mind and mine there is no *intellectual friction to rouse me up to talk or think*, as I used when with you – especially on those dear rides through the greenwood. I ride a good deal now and the last day rode an awful brute which by a skilful buckjump threw me on my head on Shotover. I escaped however unhurt and got home all safe.

The Dean comes sometimes and we talk theology, but I usually ride by myself, and have got such new trousers – quite the dog! I have written a very foolish letter; it reads very rambling and absurd, but it is so delightful writing to you that I just put down whatever comes into my head.

Your letters are charming and the one from Sicily came with a scent of olive-gardens, blue skies and orange trees, that was like reading Theocritus in this grey climate. Goodbye. Ever, dear boy, your affectionate friend

OSCAR WILDE

I have a vacant page.

I won't write to you theology, but I only say that for you to feel the fascination of Rome would to me be the greatest of pleasures: I think it would *settle me*.

And really to go to Rome with the bugbear of formal logic on one's mind is quite as bad as to have the 'Protestant jumps'.

But I know you are keenly alive to beauty, and do try and see in the Church not man's hand only but also a little of God's.

To the Rev. H. R. Bramley

2 April 1877   *Hotel St George, Corfu*

My dear Mr Bramley, My old tutor Mr Mahaffy, Fellow of Trinity College Dublin, met me on my way to Rome and insisted on my going with him to Mykenae and Athens. The chance of seeing such great places – and in such good company – was too great for me and I find myself now in Corfu. I am afraid I will not be able to be back at the beginning of term. I hope you will not mind if I miss ten days at the beginning: seeing Greece is really a great education for anyone and will I think benefit me greatly, and Mr Mahaffy is such a clever man that it is quite as good as going to lectures to be in his society.

We came first to Genoa, which is a beautiful marble city of palaces over the sea, and then to Ravenna which is extremely interesting on account of the old Christian churches in it of enormous age and the magnificent mosaics of the *fourth century*. These mosaics were very remarkable as they contained two figures of the Madonna enthroned and receiving adoration; they completely upset the ordinary Protestant idea that the worship of the Virgin did not come in till late in the history of the Church.

I read the book you kindly lent me with much interest; the Roman Catholics certainly do seem to confuse together Catholic doctrines which we may all hold and the supremacy of the Pope which we need not hold.

I hope your health has been good this Easter. We expect to be in Athens by the 17th and I will post back to Oxford immediately. Yours very truly

OSCAR WILDE

The Easter term at Oxford started on 4 April and Wilde must have arrived back at least three weeks late. The Rev. Bramley (Dean of Arts at Magdalen, and responsible for internal college discipline) and the other Fellows decided that Wilde's cavalier behaviour was intolerable, fined him half his annual scholarship and rusticated him for the rest of the academic year. As he later remarked to his friend Charles Ricketts, 'I was sent down from Oxford for being the first undergraduate to visit Olympia.' Turning adversity to advantage, he immediately had himself invited to the opening of the new Grosvenor Gallery, and networked his way around artistic and literary London.

To W. E. Gladstone

[14 May 1877]   1 *Merrion Square North*
Sir, Your noble and impassioned protests, both written and spoken, against the massacres of the Christians in Bulgaria have so roused my heart that I venture to send you a sonnet which I have written on the subject.

I am little more than a boy, and have no literary interest in London, but perhaps if you saw any good stuff in the lines I send you, some editor (of the *Nineteenth Century* perhaps or the *Spectator*) might publish them: and I feel sure that you can appreciate the very great longing that one has when young to have words of one's own published for men to read. I remain, in deepest admiration, your obedient servant   OSCAR WILDE

To Reginald Harding

Tuesday [15 May 1877]   1 *Merrion Square North*
My dear Boy, Thanks for your letter: I had made out the facts by a careful study of the statutes going up to town, but it was comforting all the same to have it confirmed by such an authority as the Schools Clerk.

I had a delightful time in town with Frank Miles and a lot of friends and came home on Friday. My mother was of course awfully astonished to hear my news and very much disgusted with the wretched stupidity of our college dons, while Mahaffy is *raging*! I never saw him so indignantly angry; he looks on it almost as an insult to himself.

The weather is charming, Florrie more lovely than ever, and I am going to give two lectures on Greece to the Alexandra College girls here, so I am rapidly forgetting the Boeotian ἀναισθησία [insensibility] of Allen and the wretched time-serving of that old woman in petticoats, the Dean.

As I expected, all my friends here refuse to believe my story, and my brother who is down at Moytura at present writes me a letter marked 'Private' to ask 'what it *really* is all about and *why* have I been rusticated', treating my explanations as mere child's play.

I hope you will write and tell me all about the College, who is desecrating my rooms and what is the latest scandal.

When Dunskie comes tell him to write to me and remember me to Dick and Gussy and little Dunlop and everyone you like or I like. Ever yours

OSCAR

I am going down I hope for my May fishing soon, but I am overwhelmed with business of all kinds.

Get *Aurora Leigh* by Mrs Browning and read it carefully.

To Lord Houghton

[Circa 17 May 1877]   *1 Merrion Square North*

Dear Lord Houghton, Knowing your love and admiration for John Keats I venture to send you a sonnet which I wrote lately at Rome on him: and should be very glad to know if you see any beauty or stuff in it.

Someway standing by his grave I felt that he *too* was a Martyr, and worthy to lie in the City of Martyrs. I thought of him as a Priest of Beauty slain before his time, a lovely Sebastian killed by the arrows of a lying and unjust tongue.

Hence – my sonnet. But I really have other views in writing to you than merely to gain your criticism of a boyish poem.

I don't know if you have visited Keats's grave since a marble tablet in his memory was put up on the wall close to the tomb. There are some fairly good lines of poetry on it, but what is really objectionable in it is the bas-relief of Keats's head – or rather a *medallion profile*, which is *extremely ugly*, exaggerates his facial angle so as almost to give him a hatchet-face and instead of the finely cut nostril, and Greek sensuous delicate lips that he had, gives him thick almost negro lips and nose.

Keats we know was lovely as Hyakinthos, or Apollo, to look at, and this medallion is a very terrible lie and misrepresentation. I wish it could be removed and a tinted bust of Keats put in its place, like the beautiful coloured bust of the Rajah of Koolapoor at Florence. Keats's delicate features and rich colour could not be conveyed I think in plain white marble.

In any case I do not think this very ugly thing ought to be allowed to remain: I am sure a photograph of it could easily be got, and you would see how horrid it is.

Your influence and great name could achieve anything and everything in the matter, and I think a really beautiful memorial might be erected to him. Surely if everyone who loves to read Keats gave even half-a-crown, a great sum of money could be got for it.

I know you always are engaged in *Politics and Poetry*, but I feel sure that with your name at the head of the list, a great deal of money would be got: in any case the ugly libel of Keats could be taken down.

I should be very glad to hear a line from you about it, and feel sure that you will pardon my writing to you on the subject. For you are fitted above all others to do anything for Keats's memory.

I hope we will see you again in Ireland: I have very pleasant memories of some delightful evenings passed in your society. Believe me yours truly

OSCAR WILDE

Oscar turned the spare time on his hands to good account. Apart from writing to Lord Houghton about Keats (which gained him a valuable letter of introduction when he went to America four years later) he penned his first piece of art criticism on the Grosvenor Gallery and had it published by the Dublin University Magazine. *If the pleasure he took in this was somewhat soured by the death that summer of his 'cousin', Henry Wilson (actually one of Sir William's three illegitimate children), it was later increased by the notice which Walter Pater took of the copy of the review which Wilde had calculatingly sent him.*

To Keningale Cook

[May–June 1877]   1 *Merrion Square North*
I return proof. What I meant by two proofs was one with your marginal corrections for my guide, the other plain, but of course both from the same type. Naturally, one of the great sorrows of youthful artists is that they always 'expurgate' bits of their articles, the very bits that they think best. However, I am glad to get the article published in your July number before the Gallery closes. Please have all my corrections attended to. Some of them

are merely 'style' corrections, which, for an Oxford man, must be always attended to. As regards the additions, they are absolutely necessary, and as I intend to take up the critic's life, I would not wish the article published without them. I would sooner pay for the proof and publish elsewhere.

(1) I and Lord Ronald Gower and Mr Ruskin, and all artists of my acquaintance, hold that Alma-Tadema's drawing of men and women is disgraceful. I could not let an article signed with my name state he was a powerful drawer.

(2) I always say I and not 'we'. We belongs to the days of anonymous articles, not to signed articles like mine. To say 'we have seen at Argos' either implies that I am a Royal Personage, or that the whole staff of the *DUM* visited Argos. And I always say clearly what I know to be true, such as that the revival of culture is due to Mr Ruskin, or that Mr Richmond has not read Aeschylus's *Choephoroe*. To say 'perhaps' spoils the remark.

(3) I have been obliged to explain what I mean by imaginative colour, and what Mr Pater means by it. We mean thought expressed by colour such as the sleep of Merlin being implied and expressed in the colour. I do not mean odd, unnatural colouring. I mean 'thought in colour'.

(4) I think Mr Legros's landscape very smudgy and the worst French style. I cannot say it is bold or original – and I wish my full remarks on Mr Whistler to be put in (as per margin). I know he will take them in good part, and besides they are really clever and amusing. I am sorry you left out my quotation from Pater at the end. However, I shall be glad to get a second proof before you go to press with my corrections. I am afraid you would find my account of our ride through Greece too enthusiastic and too full of metaphor for the *DUM*.

When I receive the second proof I am going to have small notes of the article appearing in *DUM* by me sent to the Oxford booksellers. I know it would have a good sale there and also here if properly advertised, but for the past year the articles have been so terribly dull in the *DUM* that people require to be told beforehand what they are to get for 2/6.

I hope we will come to terms about this article – and others. Believe me I am most anxious to continue my father's connection with the *DUM* which, I am sure, under your brilliant guidance will regain its lost laurels. Yours truly   OSCAR WILDE

To Reginald Harding

[Circa 16 June 1877]   1 *Merrion Square North*
My dear Kitten, Many thanks for your delightful letter. I am glad you are in the midst of beautiful scenery and *Aurora Leigh*.

I am very much down in spirits and depressed. A cousin of ours to whom we were all very much attached has just died – quite suddenly from some chill caught riding. I dined with him on Saturday and he was dead on Wednesday. My brother and I were always supposed to be his heirs but his will was an unpleasant surprise, like most wills. He leaves my father's hospital about £8000, my brother £2000, and me £100 on condition of my being a Protestant!

He was, poor fellow, bigotedly intolerant of the Catholics and seeing me 'on the brink' struck me out of his will. It is a terrible disappointment to me; you see I suffer a good deal from my Romish leanings, in pocket and mind.

My father had given him a share in my fishing lodge in Connemara, which of course ought to have reverted to me on his death; well, even this I lose 'if I become a Roman Catholic for five years' which is very infamous.

Fancy a man going before 'God and the Eternal Silences' with his wretched Protestant prejudices and bigotry clinging still to him.

However, I won't bore you with myself any more. The world seems too much out of joint for me to set it right.

I send you a little notice of Keats's grave I have just written which may interest you. I visited it with Bouncer and Dunskie.

If you would care to see my views on the Grosvenor Gallery send for the enclosed, and write soon to me. Ever yours   OSCAR WILDE
I heard from little Bouncer from Constantinople lately: he said he was coming home. Love to Puss.

To William Ward

[Postmark 19 July 1877]   1 *Merrion Square North*
Dear old Boy, I hear you are back: did you get my telegram at the Lord Warden? Do write and tell me about the Turks. I like their attitude towards life very much, though it seems strange that the descendants of the wild Arabs should be the Sybarites of our day.

I sent you two mags, to Frenchay: one with a memoir of Keats, the other religious.

Do you remember our delightful visit to Keats's grave, and Dunskie's disgust. Poor Dunskie: I know he looks on me as a renegade; still I have suffered very much for my Roman fever in mind and *pocket* and happiness.

I am going down to Connemara for a month or more next week to try and read. I have not opened a book yet, I have been so bothered with business and other matters. I shall be quite alone. Will you come? I will give you fishing and scenery – and bring your books – *and some notebooks for me.* I am in despair about 'Greats'.

It is roughing it, you know, but you will have

(1) bed

(2) table and chair

(3) knife and fork

(4) fishing

(5) scenery – sunsets – bathing – heather – mountains – lakes

(6) whisky and salmon to eat. Write and say when you can come, and also send me please *immediately* the name and address of Miss Fletcher whom I rode with at Rome, and of her stepfather. I have never sent her some articles of Pater's I promised her.

I want you to read my article on the Grosvenor Gallery in the *Dublin University Magazine* of July – my first art-essay.

I have had such delightful letters from many of the painters, and from Pater *such sympathetic praise.* I must send you his letter: or rather do so, but return it in *registered letter* by next post: don't forget. Ever yours   OSCAR

After all I can't trust my letter from Pater to the mercies of the postman, but I send you a copy:

> Dear Mr Wilde, Accept my best thanks for the magazine and your letter. Your excellent article on the Grosvenor Gallery I read with very great pleasure: it makes me much wish to make your acquaintance, and I hope you will give me an early call on your return to Oxford.
>
> I should much like to talk over some of the points with you, though on the whole I think your criticisms very just, and they are certainly very pleasantly expressed. The article shows that you possess some beautiful, and, for your age, quite exceptionally cultivated tastes: and a considerable knowledge too of many beautiful things. I hope you will write a great deal in time to come. Very truly yours   WALTER PATER

You won't think me snobbish for sending you this? After all, it *is* something to be honestly proud of.   O. F. W.

To William Ward

[August 1877]   *Illaunroe Lodge, Lough Fee, Connemara*
My dear Bouncer, So very glad to hear from you at last: I was afraid that you were still seedy.

I need not say how disappointed I was that you could not come and see this part of the world. I have two fellows staying with me, Dick Trench and Jack Barrow, who took a lodge near here for July and came to stay with me about three weeks ago. They are both capital fellows, indeed Dick Trench is I think my oldest friend, but I don't do any reading someway and pass my evenings in 'Pool, Ecarté and Potheen Punch'. I wish you had come; one requires sympathy to read.

I am however in the midst of two articles, one on Greece, the other on Art, which keep me thinking if not writing. But of Greats work I have done nothing. After all there are more profitable studies, I suppose, than the Greats course: still I would like a good Class awfully and want you to lend me your notes on Philosophy: I know your style, and really it would be a *very great advantage* for me to have them – Ethics, Politics (*Republic*) and general Philosophy. Can you do this for me? If you could send them to me in Dublin? Or at least to Oxford next term? And also *give me advice* – a thing I can't stand from my elders because it's like preaching, but I think I would like some from you 'who have passed through the fire'.

The weather is fair but not good for fishing. I have only got one salmon but our 'bag' yesterday of 'twelve white trout and twenty brown' was not bad. I have also had capital hare-shooting, but mountain-climbing is not my *forte*.

I heard, by the same post which brought me your letter, from Miss Fletcher, who is still in the Tyrol. She sends her best wishes to you of course, and writes as cleverly as she talks: I am much attracted by her in every way.

Please give my very best wishes to your sister on her approaching marriage. I remember Mr St John's *window* very well, and will hope to have the pleasure of knowing him some day. He must be a very cultured artist. Will the wedding be soon? *What* form you *will* be in! Ever yours

OSCAR WILDE

I am going to Longford on Friday to shoot. Write to me Clonfin House, Granard, Co. Longford.

Few letters survive from his last year at Oxford, if indeed many were written, since Oscar was, as he put it, 'reading hard for a Fourth in Greats'. In the end his Finals papers were judged overall to be the best of his year and he had achieved the coveted distinction

of a 'Double First' in Mods and Greats. And if that was not enough, he was also awarded the Newdigate poetry prize. He left Oxford in a blaze of academic glory.

To William Ward

[Circa 24 July 1878]   *Magdalen College*
My dear old Boy, You are the best of fellows to telegraph your congratulations: there were none I valued more. It is too delightful altogether this display of fireworks at the end of my career. I cannot understand my First except for the essays which I was fairly good in. I got a very complimentary *viva voce*.

The dons are 'astonied' beyond words – the Bad Boy doing so well in the end! They made me stay up for the Gaudy and said nice things about me. I am on the best terms with everyone including *Allen!* who I think is remorseful of his treatment of me.

Then I rowed to Pangbourne with Frank Miles in a birchbark canoe! and shot rapids and did wonders everywhere – it was delightful.

I cannot, I am afraid, yacht with you. I am so troubled about my law suit, which I have won but find my own costs heavy, though I was allowed them. I have to be in Ireland.

Dear old boy, I wish I could see you again. Ever yours   OSCAR

To the Rev. Matthew Russell SJ

[?September 1878]   *Illaunroe Lodge, Connemara*
Dear Father Russell, Thanks for the magazine. With regard to the Newdigate, if you look in the *Oxford Calendar* you will find the whole account of it. The subject is given out at the June Encaenia and is the same for all. There is besides the κῦδος a prize of twenty guineas. It was originally limited to fifty lines, and the subject used to be necessarily taken from some *classical* subject, either Greek or Latin, and generally a work of art. The metre is heroic couplets, but as you have seen perhaps from my poem, of late years laxity is allowed from the horrid Popeian jingle of regular heroics, and *now* the subject may be taken from any country or time and there is no limit to the length. I rather think it is very much older than 1841. There is a picture of the Founder hanging in the dining hall of University College, Oxford, which as well as I remember is very old. Besides I have an idea that Ruskin and Dean Stanley got it. You might by looking at the *Oxford Calendar* get all information and make your article the *locus classicus* for the History of the Newdigate Prize.

There was a strange coincidence about my getting it. On the 31st of March 1877 (long before the subject was given out) I entered Ravenna on my way to Greece, and on 31st March 1878 I had to hand my poem in. It is quite the blue ribbon of the Varsity and my college presented me with a marble bust of the 'young Augustus' which had been bequeathed by an old Fellow of Magdalen, Dr Daubeny, to the first undergraduate who should get the Newdigate.

I am resting here in the mountains – great peace and quiet everywhere – and hope to send you a sonnet as the result. Believe me, very truly yours

OSCAR WILDE

Because Dublin held little in the way of a future for the newly self-styled 'Professor of Aesthetics', he bade farewell to his home town and the woman he once described as 'an exquisitely pretty girl . . . with the most perfectly beautiful face I ever saw and not a sixpence of money'. To his chagrin Florrie Balcombe had accepted a proposal of marriage from Bram Stoker, who had just been appointed Henry Irving's manager at the Lyceum Theatre and would later become known as the author of Dracula.

To Florence Balcombe

Monday night [?30 September 1878]   *1 Merrion Square North*
Dear Florrie, As I shall be going back to England, probably for good, in a few days, I should like to bring with me the little gold cross I gave you one Christmas morning long ago.

I need hardly say that I would not ask it from you if it was anything you valued, but worthless though the trinket be, to me it serves as a memory of two sweet years – the sweetest of all the years of my youth – and I should like to have it always with me. If you would care to give it to me yourself I could meet you any time on Wednesday, or you might hand it to Phil, whom I am going to meet that afternoon.

Though you have not thought it worth while to let me know of your marriage, still I cannot leave Ireland without sending you my wishes that you may be happy; whatever happens I at least cannot be indifferent to your welfare: the currents of our lives flowed too long beside one another for that.

We stand apart now, but the little cross will serve to remind me of the bygone days, and though we shall never meet again, after I leave Ireland, still I shall always remember you at prayer. Adieu and God bless you.

OSCAR

To Florence Balcombe

Thursday [?3 October 1878]   *1 Merrion Square North*

Dear Florence, As you expressed a wish to see me I thought that *your mother's house* would be the only suitable place, and that we should part where we first met. As for my calling at Harcourt Street, you know, my dear Florence, that such a thing is quite out of the question: it would have been unfair to you, and me, and to the man you are going to marry, had we met anywhere else but under your mother's roof, and with your mother's sanction. I am sure that you will see this yourself on reflection; as a man of honour I could not have met you except with the full sanction of your parents and in their house.

As regards the cross, there is nothing 'exceptional' in the trinket except the fact of my name being on it, which of course would have prevented you from wearing it ever, and I am not foolish enough to imagine that you care now for any memento of me. It would have been impossible for you to keep it.

I am sorry that you should appear to think, from your postscript, that I desired any clandestine '*meeting*': after all, I find you know me very little.

Goodbye, and believe me yours very truly   OSCAR WILDE

Charming London

*'We live in an age of inordinate
personal ambition and I am
determined that the world
shall understand me.'*

After Wilde's academic triumphs in the summer of 1878, Magdalen renewed his Demyship for a further (fifth) year. He was obliged to keep an extra Oxford term in order to pass the Divinity exam, which he had failed two years earlier, and found lodgings for that period at 71 High Street. On 22 November he satisfied the examiners in the Rudiments of Religion and on 28 November took his degree as Bachelor of Arts. It is not known how much of 1879 he spent in Oxford, but like other graduates of the time he seems to have been unable to make the final break with his Alma Mater for a while and made periodic visits to see undergraduate friends still in residence. From the first letter below it is clear that he was already looking for accommodation in London by the end of 1878, and planning to develop his aesthetic tastes and to charm Society with his conversation. However, in his application for a reader's ticket to the British Museum in February he is unsure whether to give his Oxford college or London address, and George Macmillan's reply to his letter of 22 March is addressed to Wilde at Oxford. By the time he came to review the opening of the 1879 Grosvenor Gallery exhibition in May, his feet seem to have been firmly planted in the metropolis. At first he appears to have been reluctant to put aside his classical background. He joined the newly founded Hellenic Society, becoming a member of the Council, suggested translations from the Greek to Macmillan (with whom he had travelled to Greece in 1877), applied for an archaeological studentship at Athens and even considered becoming an Inspector of Schools.

To George Macmillan

22 March 1879   *St Stephen's Club, Westminster, London*
Dear Macmillan, I was very glad to get your note and to see that the Society is really to be set on foot: I have every confidence in its success.

Nothing would please me more than to engage in literary work for your House. I have looked forward to this opportunity for some time.

Herodotos I should like to translate very much indeed – selections from that is – and I feel sure that the wonderful picturesqueness of his writings, as well as the pathos and tenderness of some of his stories, would command a great many readers. It is a work I should enjoy doing and should engage to have it done by September 1st next.

I do not know how many Greek plays you intend publishing, but I have been working at Euripides a good deal lately and should of all things wish to edit either the *Mad Hercules* or the *Phoenissae*: plays with which I am well acquainted. I think I see what style of editing is required completely.

I shall be glad to hear from you soon, as well as to see you at Salisbury Street any time you are not busy. Believe me very truly yours

OSCAR WILDE

Once in London, Oscar set up house with his friend Frank Miles in Salisbury Street just off the Strand, moving in the summer of 1880 to 1 Tite Street, Chelsea, which Wilde quickly renamed 'Keats House'. Frank was well connected through his work as an artist and introduced Oscar to Lillie Langtry, 'Professional Beauty' and mistress of the Prince of Wales, who in turn opened the door to London Society. He consolidated a friendship with the Cambridge don, Oscar Browning, and flattered the most prominent actresses of the day with sonnets, among them Sarah Bernhardt and Ellen Terry. That summer of 1879 Bernhardt was making the first of many visits to London with the Comédie Française and Wilde was said to have met her off the Channel ferry with an armful of lilies.

To Oscar Browning

[3 June 1879]   *St Stephen's Club*
My dear Browning, Your bible and prayer book only exists in a bookseller's Utopia! There is no such thing: I ransacked all Paternoster Row on this wretched rainy day and found nothing that would suit you. I told however the Bible Society to send you down a small paragraph Bible 10/- plainly rather uglily bound. The only thing I could find.

I am afraid you will have to take refuge in an Edition de Luxe of *Keble's Christian Year* if you want something nice. I am so sorry my search is so unsuccessful.

I wish so much you could have been with me last night. Sarah Bernhardt's Phèdre was the most splendid creation I ever witnessed. The scene only lasted 10 minutes yet she worked the audience to a strained pitch of excitement such as I never saw. It seems so foolish to call French Tragedy stilted: the scene last night was not a bit 'ἐκ δϱυός καὶ πέτϱης' [out of oak and stone] but the most impassioned human nature.

About Tuesday 17th I fear I must be in Oxford. I could not say definitely if I could come with you or not; it's so far off and life is so intricate. I had a charming time at Cambridge for which accept my best thanks. Truly yours

OSCAR WILDE

Please remember me to your charming friend Stokes whom I like so much.

To Ellen Terry

[Early July 1879]   *13 Salisbury Street, London*
Dear Miss Ellen Terry, Will you accept from me a poem which I have written to you in your character of Henrietta Maria as a small proof of my great and loyal admiration for your splendid artistic powers, and the noble tenderness and pathos of your acting.

No actress has ever affected me as you have. What I have said to you in my sonnet to you expresses quite inadequately the great effect your acting has had on me.

You will have many more triumphs but I do not think you will ever have a more sincere and impassioned admirer than I am.

I look forward to your winning new laurels in new parts, and remain most sincerely yours   OSCAR WILDE

To Reginald Harding

[28 November 1879]   *St Stephen's Club*
Dear Reggie, I was only in Cambridge for the night with Oscar Browning (I wish he was *not* called Oscar) and left the next morning for the Hicks-Beachs' in Hampshire, to kill time and pheasants and the *ennui* of not having set the world quite on fire as yet.

I will come some day and stay with you, though your letters are rather what boys call 'Philippic'.

I am going to night with *Ruskin* to see Irving as Shylock, and afterwards to the *Millais* Ball. How odd it is. Dear Reg, ever yours   OSCAR
Remember me to Tom Peyton.

Important though Society contacts were, Wilde was also anxious to be seen in literary and artistic circles. The Forbes-Robertsons (Norman, Ian, Johnston, Eric and Frankie) were predominantly an acting family with whom he remained friendly for many years, Frankie being especially kind to him after his imprisonment (see p. 346). Margaret Hunt was a successful popular novelist married to the landscape painter Alfred Hunt. Wilde toyed briefly with the idea of marrying her daughter Violet.

To Norman Forbes-Robertson

[?Circa 16 March 1880]   *St Stephen's Club*

My dear Norman, I suppose you are engaged for Saturday and that there is no chance of our going to the Boat Race together? If you have any time do come and see me soon.

I don't know if I bored you the other night with my life and its troubles. There seems something so sympathetic and gentle about your nature, and you have been so charming whenever I have seen you, that I felt somehow that although I knew you only a short time, yet that still I could talk to you about things, which I only talk of to people whom I like – to those whom I count my friends.

If you will let me count *you* as one of my friends, it would give a new pleasure to my life.

I hope so much to see you again. Till I do, ever yours   OSCAR WILDE

To Mrs Alfred Hunt

25 August [1880]   *1 Tite Street, Chelsea, London*

Dear Mrs Hunt, It was so good of you to take the trouble of sending me such a long account of your little village. I have been hoping to go every week, but have had so many engagements that it has been out of my power; which, believe me, is no small disappointment. I should like so much to be with you all.

And now I am trying to settle a new house, where Mr Miles and I are going to live. The address is *horrid* but the house very pretty. It is much nearer you than my old house, so I hope we shall often, if you let me, have 'dishes of tea' at one another's houses.

I have broken a promise shamefully to Miss Violet about a poem I promised to send her. My only excuse is that nowadays the selection of colours and furniture has quite taken the place of the cases of conscience of the middle ages, and usually involves quite as much remorse. However I send her one I have just published. I hope she will see some beauty in it, and that your wonderful husband's wonderful radicalism will be appeased by my first attempt at political prophecy, which occurs in the last verse. If she will send me a little line to say what she thinks of it, it will give me such pleasure.

I hope she has been writing herself. After all, the Muses are as often to be met with in our English fields as they ever were by Castaly, or Helicon, though I have always in my heart thought that the simultaneous appearance of *nine (unmarried)* sisters at a time must have been a little embarrassing.

Please remember me *most* kindly to your husband, and all yours, and believe me very truly yours OSCAR WILDE

Wilde by this time had spent the best part of a year and a half in London making himself seen and talked about, regularly caricatured by du Maurier in Punch. *He now needed to show that he was capable of more than a few sonnets to actresses and accordingly wrote and published privately his first play,* Vera; or, the Nihilists, *a drama set in mid-nineteenth-century Russia. He sent copies to leading theatrical figures, among them two Americans, Clara Morris and Hermann Vezin (who later gave him voice coaching before his lecture tour of America), but received no offer to produce it.*

To Clara Morris

[Circa September 1880] *Keats House, Tite Street*
Dear Madam, Permit me to send you a copy of a new and original drama I have written: the character of the heroine is drawn in all those varying moods and notes of passion which you can so well touch. Your great fame, which has long ago passed over here, and a suggestion of my friend Mr Dion Boucicault have emboldened me, being a very young writer, to send you my first play; and if you do not think it suitable for dramatic representation in America, at any rate accept it as a homage to your genius.

On account of its avowedly republican sentiments I have not been able to get permission to have it brought out here, but with you there is more freedom, and though democracy is the note through which the play is expressed, yet the tragedy is an entirely human one. Believe me, Madam, your obedient servant OSCAR WILDE
In case you approve of the play I shall be so happy to correspond on the subject.

To Norman Forbes-Robertson

[Circa 1 October 1880] *Keats House, Tite Street*
My dear Norman, I am so glad you have not forgotten about the play and send you a copy with great pleasure. I hope you are getting stronger as your dear mother was rather anxious about you. I have not yet finished furnishing

my rooms, and have spent all my money over it already, so if no manager gives me gold for the *Nihilists* I don't know what I shall do; but then I couldn't really have anything but Chippendale and satinwood – I shouldn't have been able to write.

Modjeska has asked me to adapt some play for her – we have not yet settled what – probably *Luisa Miller*. I am looking forward to her first night for which Barrett has just sent me stalls. I envy you so much being with dear Nellie, the kindest-hearted, sweetest, loveliest of women. As for me I am lonely, *désolé* and wretched. I feel burned out – so do come back soon and let me see a great deal of you and believe me, your affectionate friend

OSCAR WILDE

To Hermann Vezin

[4 October 1880]   *Tite Street*

My dear Vezin, I send you a copy of my drama which you were kind enough to hear me read some months ago; any suggestions about situations or dialogue I should be so glad to get from such an experienced artist as yourself: I have just found out what a difficult craft playwriting is.

Will you let me tell you what immense pleasure your *Iago* gave me. It seems to me the most perfect example I have ever seen of that right realism which is founded on consummate art, and sustained by consummate genius: the man Iago walked and talked before us. Two points particularly delighted me – the enormous *character* you gave to otherwise trivial *details*: a rare and splendid art, to make all common things *symbolic* of the leading idea, as Albert [*sic*] Dürer loved to do in his drawings. The other is your delivery of asides, notably in Act II: I never knew how they ought to be given before – but perhaps you are saying in an aside now '*Ohé jam satis!*' [well, that's enough], so believe me your friend and admirer   OSCAR WILDE

To Lawrence Alma-Tadema

[Late 1880–early 1881]   *Keats House, Tite Street*

Dear Mr Tadema, There is a good deal of difficulty in obtaining a *really* correct idea of Greek writing at the time of Sappho: Sappho is so early, 610 BC, that we have no inscriptions at all contemporary, and the earliest Aeolic coin is about 550. Taking this as my starting point and following out the Aeolic shapes of the letters, which are quite different from the Attic, I have drawn out the enclosed list, which is as accurate probably as one can get it.

The early shapes are curious and I imagine are conditioned by the material on which they wrote – paper or parchment – as opposed to the later forms when *stone* inscriptions became usual: and the lines consequently more rigid and straight, and, it seems to me, less beautiful.

I have written *Mnasidika* instead of *Mnasidion* as in your letter; all the MSS read Mnasidika in the line from Sappho, and besides Mnasidion is a man's name. Gyrinnos is the Aeolic form for Gyrinna.

I remember your talking about Catullus the other night – one of the most beautiful of his poems is taken from a still extant song of Sappho's beginning,

(only a blot!)

I don't know if you would care to strike that literary note and scrawl it on your marble?

I hope that whenever you want any kind of information about Greek things, in which I might help you that you will let me know.

It is always a pleasure for me to work at any Greek subject, and a double pleasure to do so for anyone whose work mirrors so exquisitely and rightly, as yours does, that beautiful old Greek world. Believe me sincerely yours

OSCAR WILDE

To Ellen Terry

[3 January 1881]   *Tite Street, Chelsea*

My dear Nellie, I write to wish you *every success* tonight. *You* could not do anything that would not be a mirror of the highest artistic beauty, and I am so glad to hear you have an opportunity of showing us that passionate power which *I know you have*. You will have a great success – perhaps one of your greatest.

I send you some flowers – two crowns. Will you accept one of them, whichever you think will suit you best. The other – don't think me treacherous, Nellie – but the other please give to Florrie *from yourself*. I should like to think that she was wearing something of mine the first night she comes on the stage, that anything of mine should touch her. Of course if you think – but you won't think she will suspect? How could she? She thinks I never loved her, thinks I forget. My God how could I!

Dear Nellie, if you can do this – in any case accept these flowers from your devoted admirer, your affectionate friend   OSCAR WILDE

To Mrs Alfred Hunt

[17 February 1881]   *Keats House, Tite Street*

Dear Mrs Hunt, Thank you so much for your kind invitations but I am in the 'lion's den' on both days. Sunday I dine to meet Mr Lowell, a poet, statesman, and an American in one! A sort of three-headed Cerberus of civilisation who barks when he is baited and is often mistaken for a lion, at a distance.

And on Wednesday the 2nd I have a long-standing engagement to dine with Sir Charles Dilke, a lion who has clipped his radical claws and only roars through the medium of a quarterly review now – a harmless way of roaring. So I cannot come to you, which *makes me very sad*.

I ought, like Sir Boyle Roche's bird, to be able to be in two places at once, but in that case I should always be at Tor Villas. I hope to see you all soon again. Very truly yours   OSCAR WILDE

In 1881 Wilde published his second book, a volume of poems, this time with a publisher. There were 750 copies printed which he cannily divided into three equal 'editions' between June and September in the hope that it would attract more attention. Despite a complimentary review from Oscar Browning and an encouraging letter from Arnold the notices were generally unfavourable – Punch's reviewer describing it as 'Swinburne and water'. The library of the Oxford Union even went so far as to request a copy and then reject it as being too derivative. It also ended the friendship with Miles, whose clergyman father read dangerous sensuality into the volume and urged his son to have nothing more to do with the author.

To David Bogue

[May 1881]   *Keats House, Tite Street*

Dear Sir, I am anxious to publish a volume of poems immediately, and should like to enter into a treaty with your house about it. I can forward you the manuscript on hearing that you will begin negotiations.

Possibly my name requires no introduction. Yours truly   OSCAR WILDE

To Oscar Browning

[June 1881]   *Keats House, Tite Street*

My dear Browning, If you get the opportunity, and would care for it, I wish you would review my first volume of poems just about to appear: books so often fall into stupid and illiterate hands that I am anxious to be really *criticised*: ignorant praise or ignorant blame is so insulting. Truly yours

OSCAR WILDE

To Robert Browning

[June 1881]   *Keats House, Tite Street*

Dear Mr Browning, Will you accept from me the first copy of my poems – the only tribute I can offer you in return for the delight and the wonder which the strength and splendour of your work has given me from my boyhood.

Believe me, in all affectionate admiration, very truly yours OSCAR WILDE

To Matthew Arnold

[June–July 1881]   *Keats House, Tite Street*

Dear Mr Arnold, Will you accept from me my first volume of poems . . . of the constant source of joy and wonder that your beautiful work was to all of us at Oxford . . . for I have only now, too late perhaps, found out how all art requires solitude as its companion, only now indeed know the splendid difficulty of this great art in which you are a master illustrious and supreme. Still, such as it is, let me offer it to you, and believe me in all affectionate admiration, truly yours   OSCAR WILDE

To Violet Hunt

[Postmark 22 July 1881]   *Keats House, Tite Street*

Dear Miss Violet Hunt, I thank you very much for your kind letter, and am infinitely delighted that you have thought my poems beautiful. In an age like this when Slander, and Ridicule, and Envy walk quite unashamed among us, and when any attempt to produce serious beautiful work is greeted with a very tornado of lies and evil-speaking, it is a wonderful joy, a wonderful spur for ambition and work, to receive any such encouragement and appreciation as your letter brought me, and I thank you for it again and again.

The poem I like best is 'The Burden of Itys' and next to that 'The Garden of Eros'. They are the most lyrical, and I would sooner have any power or quality of 'song' writing than be the greatest sonnet writer since Petrarch.

I go to the Thames this afternoon with Mr Burne-Jones but will hope to see you when I return.

You have made me very happy. Believe me ever sincerely yours

OSCAR WILDE

When both her sons moved to London in 1879, Lady Wilde came to join them and was living in somewhat reduced circumstances, her London tea parties being a pale imitation of her famous Saturday conversazioni in Dublin. Although not yet able to help her financially, Oscar seemed to realise that his mother's mantle had fallen on his shoulders and attempted to puff her to the editor of the Nineteenth Century.

To James Knowles

[October 1881]   *Keats House, Tite Street*

Dear Mr Knowles, I send you a – rather soiled – copy of my mother's pamphlet on the reflux wave of *practical* republicanism which the return of the Irish emigrants has brought on Ireland. It was written three years ago nearly, and is extremely interesting as a political prophecy. You probably know my mother's name as the 'Speranza' of the *Nation* newspaper in 1848. I don't think that age has dimmed the fire and enthusiasm of that pen which set the young Irelanders in a blaze.

I should like so much to have the privilege of introducing you to my mother – all brilliant people should cross each other's cycles, like some of the nicest planets. In any case I am glad to be able to send you the article. It is part of the thought of the nineteenth century, and will I hope interest you. Believe me, truly yours   OSCAR WILDE

To the Hon. George Curzon

[November 1881]   *9 Charles Street, Grosvenor Square, London*

My dear Curzon, You are a brick! and I thank you very much for your chivalrous defence of me in the Union. So much of what is best in England passes through Oxford that I should have been sorry to think that discourtesy so gross and narrow-mindedness so evil could have been suffered to exist without some voice of scorn being raised against them.

Our sweet city with its dreaming towers must not be given entirely over to the Philistines. They have Gath and Ekron and Ashdod and many other cities of dirt and dread and despair, and we must not yield them the quiet cloister of Magdalen to brawl in, or the windows of Merton to peer from.

I hope you will come and see me in town. I have left my house at Chelsea but will be always delighted to see you, for, in spite of the story of Aristides, I have not got tired yet of hearing Rennell Rodd call you perfect.

I send you a bill of my first attack on Tyranny. I wish you could get it posted in the 'High', but perhaps I bother you? Very truly yours

OSCAR WILDE

Discovering America

*'Great success here; nothing
like it since Dickens, they
tell me. I am torn in bits
by Society. Immense
receptions, wonderful
dinners, crowds wait
for my carriage. I
wave a gloved
hand and an
ivory cane
and they
cheer.'*

The great break for which Wilde had been waiting came in about October 1881. Earlier that year, in April, Richard D'Oyly Carte had produced Gilbert and Sullivan's Patience at the Opera Comique, London. The opera satirised the contemporary 'aesthetic' movement, and the character of Bunthorne, the Fleshly Poet, though perhaps intended for Rossetti, was generally taken as a caricature of Wilde. Patience opened in New York on 22 September and Colonel W. F. Morse, Carte's American representative, thought that a tour by Wilde himself, lecturing on aesthetics, might provide useful publicity, since the American public had not experienced the butt of the satire first-hand. After some last-minute negotiations in London it was agreed that he would receive one-third of the net receipts from the tour once expenses had been deducted. He was accordingly booked to give a series of lectures, sailed on the Arizona on 24 December 1881 and landed at New York on 2 January 1882, where he was reported to have said to the examining customs official (though there is sadly no hard evidence for the anecdote), 'I have nothing to declare but my genius.'

His first lecture, at the Chickering Hall, New York on 9 January, was on 'The English Renaissance' but it was too lengthy and theoretical for many in his audience and the press was critical of his lacklustre delivery. He immediately set about shortening it and within a month it had become 'The Decorative Arts' with a much wider popular appeal. He added a second lecture to his repertoire, 'The House Beautiful', for cities in which he had more than one engagement. He also prepared a lecture on 'Irish Poets and Poetry of the Nineteenth Century', which he gave in April in San Francisco, accepting with good grace the introductory label of 'Speranza's Boy', bestowed on him by the expatriate Irish, whose memories of Jane's role in the famine years were still warm.

To Norman Forbes-Robertson

[15 January 1882]   *New York*

My dear Norman, I have been to call on Ian and his wife. She is so pretty and sweet and simple, like a little fair-haired Madonna, with a baby who already shows a great dramatic power and behaved during my visit (I stayed about an hour, breaking fifty-four engagements) like Macbeth, Hamlet, King John, and all the remarkable characters in Shakespeare. They seem very happy, and she is very loving to Ian, and unaffected.

I go to Philadelphia tomorrow. Great success here; nothing like it since Dickens, they tell me. I am torn in bits by Society. Immense receptions, wonderful dinners, crowds wait for my carriage. I wave a gloved hand and an ivory cane and they cheer. Girls very lovely, men simple and intellectual. Rooms are hung with white lilies for me everywhere. I have 'Boy' at intervals, also two secretaries, one to write my autograph and answer the hundreds of letters that come begging for it. Another, whose hair is brown, to send locks of his own hair to the young ladies who write asking for mine; he is rapidly becoming bald. Also a black servant, who is my slave – in a free country one cannot live without a slave – rather like a Christy minstrel, except that he knows no riddles. Also a carriage and a black tiger who is like a little monkey. I give sittings to artists, and generally behave as I always have behaved – '*dreadfully*'. Love to your mother and Forby and all of them. Ever your affectionate friend.   OSCAR

Initially Wilde's tour was not without its incidents. Another lecturer, Archibald Forbes, a war correspondent whose tour was also managed by D'Oyly Carte, crossed swords with Wilde in a train while they were both travelling to lecture in Baltimore. Forbes's disparaging remarks about aestheticism apparently needled Wilde who responded by staying on the train and going straight on to Washington. The dispute became public in the newspapers and threatened to jeopardise Wilde's entire tour.

To Archibald Forbes

[20 January 1882]   *Arlington Hotel, Washington*

Dear Mr Forbes, I felt quite sure that your remarks on me had been misrepresented. I must however say that your remarks about me *in your lecture* may be regarded as giving *some* natural ground for the report. I feel bound to say quite frankly to you that I do not consider them to be either in good taste or appropriate to your subject.

I have something to say to the American people, something that I know will be the beginning of a great movement here, and all foolish ridicule does a great deal of harm to the cause of art and refinement and civilisation here.

I do not think that your lecture will lose in brilliancy or interest by expunging the passage, which is, as you say yourself, poor fooling enough.

You have to speak of the life of action, I of the life of art. Our subjects are quite distinct and should be kept so. Believe me, yours truly

OSCAR WILDE

To Richard D'Oyly Carte

[?24 or 25 January 1882]   *Washington*

My dear Carte, Another such fiasco as the Baltimore business and I think I would stop lecturing. The little wretched clerk or office boy you sent to me in Col. Morse's place is a fool and an idiot. Do let us be quite frank with one another. I must have, according to our agreement, Morse or some responsible experienced man always with me. This is for your advantage as well as for mine. I will not go about with a young office boy, who has not even the civility to come and see what I want. He was here for five minutes yesterday, went away promising to return at eleven o'clock a.m. and I have not seen him since. I had nine reporters, seven or eight telegrams, eighteen letters to answer, and this young scoundrel amusing himself about the town. I must never be left again, and please do not expose me to the really brutal attacks of the papers. The whole tide of feeling is turned by Morse's stupidity.

I know you have been ill, and that it has not been your doing but we must be very careful for the future. Very sincerely yours   OSCAR WILDE

To Archibald Forbes

[Circa 29 January 1882]   *Boston*

Dear Mr Forbes, I cannot tell you how surprised and grieved I am to think that there should have been anything in my first letter to you which seemed to you discourteous or wrong.

Believe me, I had intended to answer you in the same frank spirit in which you had written to me. Any such expressions however unintentional I most willingly retract.

As regards my motive for coming to America, I should be very disappointed if when I left for Europe I had not influenced in *however* slight a way the growing spirit of art in this country, very disappointed if I had not out of the many who listen to me made one person love beautiful things a little more, and very disappointed if in return for the dreadfully hard work of lecturing – hard to me who am inexperienced – I did not earn enough money to give myself an autumn at Venice, a winter at Rome, and a spring at Athens; but all these things are perhaps dreams.

Letter-writing seems to lead to grave misunderstandings. I wish I could have seen you personally: standing face to face, and man to man, I might have said what I wished to say more clearly and more simply. I remain yours truly   O. WILDE

Forbes was not alone in his mockery of what he saw as Wilde's namby-pamby aesthetics. The students at Harvard and Rochester, where he went in early February, attempted to disrupt his lectures and newspaper columnists questioned his sincerity of purpose, hinting that his motives were purely financial. The poet Joaquin Miller and the anti-slavery campaigner Julia Ward Howe both came to his defence in print, and Wilde consoled himself with recounting his American adventures to friends back home, among them the solicitor George Lewis and his wife.

To George Lewis

[9 February 1882]   *Prospect House, Niagara Falls, Canada Side*
My dear Mr Lewis, Things are going on very well, and you were very kind about answering my telegrams. Carte blundered in leaving me without a manager, and Forbes through the most foolish and mad jealousy tried to lure me into a newspaper correspondence. His attack on me, entirely unprovoked, was one of the most filthy and scurrilous things I ever read – so much so that Boucicault and Hurlbert of the *World* both entreated me to publish it, as it would have brought people over to my side, but I thought it wiser to avoid the garbage of a dirty-water-throwing in public. It was merely on Forbes's part that the whole thing began, I really declining always to enter into any disquisition. I will show you his letter – it was infamous. He has been a dreadful failure this year and thought he would lure me on to a public quarrel.

I am hard at work, and I think making money, but the expenses seem very heavy. I hope to go back with £1000: if I do it will be delightful.

Your friend Whitelaw Reid, to whom I brought two letters of introduction, has not been very civil – in fact has not helped me in any way at all. I am sorry I brought him any letters, and the *New York Herald* is most bitter. I wonder could you do anything for it? Pray remember me to Mrs Lewis, and with many thanks, yours most affectionately   OSCAR WILDE

To the Hon. George Curzon

[15 February 1882]   *US*

My dear George Curzon, Yes! You are on the black list, and, if my secretary does his work properly, every mail shall hurl at your young philosophic head the rage of the American eagle because I do not think trousers beautiful, the excitement of a sane strong people over the colour of my necktie, the fear of the eagle that I have come to cut his barbaric claws with the scissors of culture, the impotent rage of the ink-stained, the noble and glorious homage of the respectable – you shall know it all: it may serve you for marginal notes περὶ δημοκρατίας [about democracy].

Well, it's really wonderful, my audiences are enormous. In Chicago I lectured last Monday to 2500 people! This is of course nothing to anyone who has spoken at the Union, but to me it was delightful – a great sympathetic electric people, who cheered and applauded and gave me a sense of serene power that even being abused by the *Saturday Review* never gave me.

I lecture four times a week, and the people are delightful and lionise one to a curious extent, but they follow me, and start schools of design when I visit their town. At Philadelphia the school is called after me and they really are beginning to love and know beautiful art and its meaning.

As for myself, I feel like Tancred or Lothair. I travel in such state, for in a free country one cannot live without slaves, and I have slaves – black, yellow and white. But you must write again. Your letter had a flavour of Attic salt. Yours (from Boeotia)   OSCAR WILDE

Renell Rodd, a friend of Wilde's from Oxford days, had published a book of poems in 1881 entitled Songs of the South. *Wilde, anxious as much to promote his own ideas as Rodd's poetry, arranged for the volume to be produced in Philadephia by Stoddart, with an aesthetic* envoi *or preface of his own and an effusive dedication to himself: 'To Oscar Wilde, "heart's brother", these few songs and many songs to come'. The book duly appeared in October as* Rose Leaf and Apple Leaf, *but Rodd was disturbed and upset by Wilde's parading of their friendship, and a volume of poetry proved its undoing, as it had with Frank Miles the year before.*

To J. M. Stoddart

[?19 February 1882]   *Cincinnati*

Dear Mr Stoddart, I send you the volume of poems and the preface. The preface you will see is most important, signifying my new departure from Mr Ruskin and the Pre-Raphaelites, and marks an era in the aesthetic movement. Please send proofs to *New York*: they will forward them to me as I race from town to town. I also wish to ask Mr Davis a favour. I should like to be able to send Mr Rodd some money: if Mr Davis will advance £25 on the whole half-profits that fall to Mr Rodd and myself it would be to this young poet a great encouragement, and would give him good hope of success. If Mr Davis would do this he would be encouraging a young fellow of, as you know, great poetical promise: by sending me the whole draft I could forward it to Rennell Rodd – his £25. As for your paper it is charming. I would undertake to be your art-correspondent for London and Paris – two articles a month – and in the summer letters from Italy on art.

You will think this over. Ever yours   OSCAR WILDE

Post Scriptum

Yes: *The Daisy* will be the title, *and Other Poems*. You can print the little poem on the daisy first. As regards the binding, have it a bound book – not in loose sheets like Tiffany's monstrosity. Send me your ideas of a cover. Lathrop could do a delightful thing for you.

Look at dedication.

To J. M. Stoddart

[Postmark 24 February 1882]   *Cincinnati*

Dear Mr Stoddart, This is the type I like. I have not received proofs yet: please let me have them soon or I will be in California, with an Indian to disturb me at every comma and a grizzly at every semi-colon.

OSCAR WILDE

To Colonel W. F. Morse

[?26 February 1882]   *St Louis, Missouri*

Dear Colonel Morse, Will you kindly go to a good costumier (theatrical) for me and get them to make (you will not mention my name) two coats, to wear at matinées and perhaps in evening. They should be beautiful; tight velvet doublet, with large flowered sleeves and little ruffs of cambric coming up from under collar. I send you design and measurements. They should be

ready at *Chicago* on Saturday for matinée there – at any rate the black one.
Any good costumier would know what I want – sort of Francis I dress: only

knee-breeches instead of long hose. Also get me two pair of grey silk
stockings to suit grey mouse-coloured velvet. The sleeves are to be flowered
– if not velvet then plush – stamped with large pattern. They will excite a
great sensation. I leave the matter to you. They were dreadfully disappointed
at Cincinnati at my not wearing knee-breeches. Truly yours OSCAR WILDE

To Mrs George Lewis

Tuesday, 28 February [1882]   *Grand Pacific Hotel, Chicago*
Dear Mrs Lewis, I send you a line to say that since Chicago I have had two
great successes: Cincinnati where I have been invited to lecture a second
time – this time to the workmen, on the handicraftsman – and St Louis.
Tomorrow I start to lecture eleven consecutive nights at eleven different
cities, and return here on Saturday week for a second lecture. I go to Canada
then, and also return to New England to lecture. Of course I have much to
bear – I have always had that – but still as regards my practical influence I
have succeeded beyond my wildest hope. In every city they start schools of
decorative art after my visit, and set on foot public museums, getting my
advice about the choice of objects and the nature of the building. And the
artists treat me like a young god. But of this I suppose little reaches England.
My play will probably come out, but this is not settled, and I will be back
about May I hope.

Pray remember me most affectionately to Mr Lewis, and believe me very
truly yours   OSCAR WILDE

To Walt Whitman

[Postmark 1 March 1882]   *Chicago*
My dear dear Walt, Swinburne has just written to me to say as follows:

'I am sincerely interested and gratified by your account of Walt Whitman
and the assurance of his kindly and friendly feeling towards me: and I
thank you, no less sincerely, for your kindness in sending me word of it.
As sincerely can I say, what I shall be freshly obliged to you if you will
[– should occasion arise –] assure him of in my name, that I have by no

manner of means [either 'forgotten him' or] relaxed my admiration of his noblest work – such parts, above all, of his writings, as treat of the noblest subjects, material and spiritual, with which poetry can deal. I have always thought it, and I believe it will hereafter be generally thought, his highest and surely most enviable distinction that he never speaks so well as when he speaks of great matters – liberty, for instance, and death. This of course does not imply that I do – rather it implies that I do not – agree with all his theories or admire all his work in anything like equal measure – a form of admiration which I should by no means desire for myself and am as little prepared to bestow on another: considering it a form of scarcely indirect insult.'

There! You see how you remain in our hearts, and how simply and grandly Swinburne speaks of you, knowing you to be simple and grand yourself.

Will you in return send me for Swinburne a copy of your *Essay on Poetry* – the pamphlet – with your name and his on it: it would please him so much.

Before I leave America I must see you again. There is no one in this wide great world of America whom I love and honour so much.

With warm affection, and honourable admiration   OSCAR WILDE

To Mrs George Lewis

[Early March 1882]   *Griggsville, Illinois*
Dear Mrs Lewis, I am sorry to say that an art-movement has begun at Griggsville, for I feel it will not last long and that Colvin will be lecturing about it. At present the style here is Griggsville rococo, and there are also traces of 'archaic Griggsville', but in a few days the Griggsville Renaissance will blossom: it will have an exquisite bloom for a week, and then (Colvin's fourth lecture) become 'debased Griggsville', and the Griggsville Decadence. I seem to hear the Slade Professor, or dear Newton, on it. As for myself I promise you never, never to lecture in England, *not even* at dinner.

The Giottos of Griggsville are waiting in a deputation below, so I must stop. With kind remembrances to Mr Lewis, and remembrances to Katie, yours sincerely   OSCAR WILDE

Wilde's revolutionary drama Vera *had been scheduled for production in London shortly before he left, but partly for political reasons – the American President and the Russian Czar had been assassinated in 1881 – and partly through lack of funds, it was cancelled. Once across the Atlantic, though, he felt its republican sentiments would have greater appeal in America where it was eventually produced to savage criticism in August 1883.*

To Richard D'Oyly Carte

16 March 1882   *Metropolitan Hotel, St Paul, Minnesota*

Dear Mr Carte, I have received your letter about the play. I agree to place it entirely in your hands for production on the terms of my receiving half-profits, and a guarantee of £200 paid down to me on occasion of its production, said £200 to be deducted from my share of subsequent profits if any. This I think you will acknowledge is fair. Of course for my absolute work, the play, I must have absolute certainty of some small kind.

As regards the cast: I am sure you see yourself how well the part will suit Clara Morris: I am however quite aware how *difficile* she is, and what practical dangers may attend the perilling of it on her. If you, exercising right and careful judgment, find it impossible to depend on her – then, while the present excitement lasts, let us go to Rose Coghlan, and Wallack's Theatre – they have a good company – and if Miss Morris cannot be really retained I am willing to leave it in your hands for Rose Coghlan. In case of producing it here, I will rely on you to secure a copyright for England also by some simultaneous performance. This however you can manage naturally without any advice of mine.

Please let me know your acceptance of my terms, and your decision of the cast by wire, as soon as possible. Yours very truly   OSCAR WILDE

Prologue follows soon: have been so tired – too tired to write.

By the middle of March, Wilde had completed the New England leg of his tour and was deep into the Mid-West on his way to California. Sidney Colvin was the Slade Professor of Fine Arts at Cambridge and Robert Kerr a teetotal Scottish judge sitting in the City of London. The reason for Wilde's apparent dislike of them both can only be conjectured.

To Mrs George Lewis

[Circa 20 March 1882]   *Sioux City*

Dear Mrs Lewis, I am sure you will be interested to hear that I have met Indians. They are really in appearance very like Colvin, when he is wearing his professorial robes: the likeness is quite curious, and revived pleasant literary reminiscences. Their conversation was most interesting as long as it was unintelligible, but when interpreted to me reminded me strangely and vividly of the conversation of Mr Commissioner Kerr.

I don't know where I am: somewhere in the middle of coyotes and cañons: one is a 'ravine' and the other a 'fox', I don't know which, but I think they change about. I have met miners: they are big-booted, red-shirted, yellow-bearded and delightful ruffians. One of them asked me if I was not 'running an art-mill', and on my pointing to my numerous retinue, said he 'guessed I hadn't need to wash my own pans', and his 'pardner' remarked that 'I hadn't need to sell clams neither, I could toot my own horn'. I secretly believe they read up Bret Harte privately; they were certainly almost as real as his miners, and quite as pleasant. With my usual passion for personality I entertained them, and had a delightful time, though on my making some mention of early Florentine art they unanimously declared they could neither 'trump or follow it'.

Weary of being asked by gloomy reporters 'which was the most beautiful colour' and what is the meaning of the word 'aesthetic', on my last Chicago interview I turned the conversation on three of my heroes, Whistler, Labouchere, and Irving, and on the adored and adorable Lily. I send you them all.

I hope you are all well. Pray remember me to your husband, and to the Grange when you visit there next.

Colvin in a blanket has just passed the window: he is decked out with feathers, and wants me to buy bead slippers; it is really most odd, and undoubtedly Colvin, I could hardly be mistaken.

Give my love to Katie please!!! and believe me, most sincerely and truly yours   OSCAR WILDE

In a lecture at Louisville, Kentucky on 21 February, Wilde had quoted Keats's 'Sonnet on Blue'. By sheer coincidence, the poet's niece was sitting in the audience. She so enjoyed Wilde's lecture that she invited him home to see her uncle's papers and three weeks later sent him the manuscript of the sonnet itself.

To Emma Speed

21 March 1882   [*Omaha, Nebraska*]

What you have given me is more golden than gold, more precious than any treasure this great country could yield me, though the land be a network of railways, and each city a harbour for the galleys of the world.

It is a sonnet I have loved always, and indeed who but the supreme and perfect artist could have got from a mere colour a motive so full of marvel: and now I am half enamoured of the paper that touched his hand, and the ink that did his bidding, grown fond of the sweet comeliness of his charactery, for since my boyhood I have loved none better than your marvellous kinsman, that godlike boy, the real Adonis of our age, who knew the silver-footed messages of the moon, and the secret of the morning, who heard in Hyperion's vale the large utterance of the early gods, and from the beechen plot the light-winged Dryad, who saw Madeline at the painted window, and Lamia in the house at Corinth, and Endymion ankle-deep in lilies of the vale, who drubbed the butcher's boy for being a bully, and drank confusion to Newton for having analysed the rainbow. In my heaven he walks eternally with Shakespeare and the Greeks, and it may be that some day he will lift

> his hymenaeal curls from out his amber gleaming wine, With ambrosial lips will kiss my forehead, clasp the hand of noble love in mine.

Again I thank you for this dear memory of the man I love, and thank you also for the sweet and gracious words in which you give it to me: it were strange in truth if one in whose veins flows the same blood as quickened into song that young priest of beauty, were not with me in this great renaissance of art which Keats indeed would have so much loved, and of which he, above all others, is the seed.

Let me send you my sonnet on Keats's grave, which you quote with such courteous compliment in your note, and if you would let it lie near his own papers it may keep some green of youth caught from those withered leaves in whose faded lines eternal summer dwells.

I hope that some day I may visit you again at St Louis, and see the little Milton and the other treasures once more: strange, you call your house 'dingy and old', ah, dear Madam, fancy has long ago made it a palace for me, and I see it transfigured through the golden mists of joy. With deep respect, believe me, most truly yours   OSCAR WILDE

To Norman Forbes-Robertson

27 March 1882   *San Francisco*
My dear Norman, Here from the uttermost end of the great world I send you love and greeting, and thanks for your letters which delight me very much. But, dear boy, your hair will lose its gold and your cheek its roses if you insist on being such a chivalrous defender of this much abused young man. It is so brave and good of you! Of course I will win: I have not the slightest intention of failing for a moment, and my tour here is triumphal. I was four days in the train: at first grey, gaunt desolate plains, as colourless as waste land by the sea, with now and then scampering herds of bright red antelopes, and heavy shambling buffaloes, rather like Joe Knight in manner and appearance, and screaming vultures like gnats high up in the air, then up the Sierra Nevadas, the snow-capped mountains shining like shields of

polished silver in that vault of blue flame we call the sky, and deep cañons full of pine trees, and so for four days, and at last from the chill winter of the mountains down into eternal summer here, groves of orange trees in fruit and flower, green fields, and purple hills, a very Italy, without its art.

There were 4000 people waiting at the 'depot' to see me, open carriage, four horses, an audience at my lecture of the most cultivated people in 'Frisco, charming folk. I lecture again here tonight, also twice next week; as you see I am really appreciated – by the cultured classes. The railway have offered me a special train and private car to go down the coast to Los Angeles, a sort of Naples here, and I am fêted and entertained to my heart's content. I lecture here in California for three weeks, then to Kansas; after that I am not decided.

These wretched lying telegrams in the *Daily News* are sent by Archibald Forbes, who has been a fiasco in his lecturing this season and is jealous of me. He is a coward and a fool. No telegram can kill or mar a man with anything in him. The women here are beautiful. Tonight I am escorted by the Mayor of the city through the Chinese quarter, to their theatre and joss houses and rooms, which will be most interesting. They have 'houses' and 'persons'.

Pray remember me to all at home, also to that splendid fellow Millais and his stately and beautiful wife.

Love to Johnston. Ever yours   OSCAR WILDE
(My new signature – specially for California)

To Mrs Bernard Beere

[17 April 1882]   *Kansas City, Missouri*
My dear Bernie, I have lectured to the Mormons. The Opera House at Salt Lake is an enormous affair about the size of Covent Garden, and holds with ease fourteen families. They sit like this and are very, very ugly.The

President, a nice old man, sat with five wives in the stage box. I visited him in the afternoon and saw a charming daughter of his.

I have also lectured at Leadville, the great mining city in the Rocky Mountains. We took a whole day to get up to it on a narrow-gauge railway 14,000 feet in height. My audience was entirely miners; their make-up excellent, red shirts and blond beards, the whole of the first three rows being filled with McKee Rankins of every colour and dimension. I spoke to them of the early Florentines, and they slept as though no crime had ever stained the ravines of their mountain home. I described to them the pictures of Botticelli, and the name, which seemed to them like a new drink, roused them from their dreams, but when I told them in my boyish eloquence of the 'secret of Botticelli' the strong men wept like children. Their sympathy touched me and I approached modern art and had almost won them over to a real reverence for what is beautiful when unluckily I described one of Jimmy Whistler's 'nocturnes in blue and gold'. Then they leaped to their feet and in their grand simple way swore that such things should not be. Some of the younger ones pulled their revolvers out and left hurriedly to see if Jimmy was 'prowling about the saloons' or 'wrastling a hash' at any eating shop. Had he been there I fear he would have been killed, their feeling was so bitter. Their enthusiasm satisfied me and I ended my lecture there. Then I found the Governor of the State waiting in a bullock *wagon* to bring me down the great silver-mine of the world, the Matchless. So off we drove, the miners carrying torches before us till we came to the shaft and were shot down in buckets (I of course true to my principle being graceful even in a bucket) and down in the great gallery of the mine, the walls and ceilings glittering with metal ore, was spread a banquet for us.

The amazement of the miners when they saw that art and appetite could go hand in hand knew no bounds; when I lit a long cigar they cheered till the silver fell in dust from the roof on our plates; and when I quaffed a cocktail without flinching, they unanimously pronounced me in their grand simple way 'a bully boy with no glass eye' – artless and spontaneous praise which touched me more than the pompous panegyrics of literary critics ever did or could. Then I had to open a new vein, or lode, which with a silver drill I brilliantly performed, amidst unanimous applause. The silver drill was presented to me and the lode named 'The Oscar'. I had hoped that in their simple grand way they would have offered me shares in 'The Oscar', but in their artless untutored fashion they did not. Only the silver drill remains as a memory of my night at Leadville.

I have had a delightful time all through California and Colorado and am now returning home, twice as affected as ever, my dear Bernie. Please remember me to dear Dot, to Reggie and all our mutual friends including Monty Morris, who won't write to me or even criticise me. Goodbye. Your sincere friend   OSCAR WILDE

Your letter was charming. Write to New York, 1267 Broadway.

Helena, aged eighteen, was the young sister of the painter Walter Sickert. Wilde had known the family for some time and had presented her with her first volume

of poetry, Matthew Arnold's poems, three years before. There is an uncanny presaging of Wilde's own fate in his visit to the prison; on the other side of the bars fourteen years later he too would read Dante to console himself.

To Helena Sickert

25 April 1882   *Fremont, Nebraska*

My dear Miss Nellie, Since I wrote to you I have been to wonderful places, to Colorado which is like the Tyrol a little, and has great cañons of red sandstone, and pine trees, and the tops of the mountains all snowcovered, and up a narrow-gauge railway did I rush to the top of a mountain 15,000 feet high, to the great mining city of the west called Leadville, and lectured the miners on the old workers in metal – Cellini and others. All I told them about Cellini and how he cast his Perseus interested them very much, and they were a most courteous audience; typical too – large blond-bearded, yellow-haired men in red shirts, with the beautiful clear complexions of people who work in silver-mines.

After my lecture I went down a silver-mine, about a mile outside the little settlement, the miners carrying torches before me as it was night. After being dressed in miner's dress I was hurled in a bucket down into the heart of the earth, long galleries of silver-ore, the miners all at work, looking so picturesque in the dim light as they swung the hammers and cleft the stone, beautiful motives for etching everywhere, and for Walter's impressionist sketches. I stayed all night there nearly, the men being most interesting to talk to, and was brought off down the mountain by a special train at 4.30 in the morning.

From there I went to Kansas where I lectured a week. At St Joseph the great desperado of Kansas, Jesse James, had just been killed by one of his followers, and the whole town was mourning over him and buying relics of his house. His door-knocker and dust-bin went for fabulous prices, two speculators absolutely came to pistol-shots as to who was to have his hearth-brush, the unsuccessful one being, however, consoled by being allowed to purchase the water-butt for the income of an English bishop, while his sole work of art, a chromo-lithograph of the most dreadful kind, of course was sold at a price which in Europe only a Mantegna or an undoubted Titian can command!

Last night I lectured at Lincoln, Nebraska, and in the morning gave an address to the undergraduates of the State University there: charming audience – young men and women all together in the same college, attending lectures and the like, and many young admirers and followers among them.

They drove me out to see the great prison afterwards! Poor sad types of humanity in hideous striped dresses making bricks in the sun, and all mean-looking, which consoled me, for I should hate to see a criminal with a noble face. Little whitewashed cells, so tragically tidy, but with books in them. In one I found a translation of Dante, and a Shelley. Strange and beautiful it seemed to me that the sorrow of a single Florentine in exile should, hundreds of years afterwards, lighten the sorrow of some common prisoner in a modern gaol, and one murderer with melancholy eyes – to be hung they told me in three weeks – spending that interval in reading novels, a bad preparation for facing either God or Nothing. So every day I see something curious and new, and now think of going to Japan and wish Walter would come or could come with me.

Pray give my love to everybody at home, and believe me your affectionate friend   OSCAR WILDE

Perhaps the most important aspect of Wilde's American tour was that he found a voice of his own. After his synthetic utterances in the first month with their often verbatim borrowings from Ruskin, Morris and Pater, and their lukewarm reception by the press, Wilde soon realised that what interested the New World were his views on art education and what they should be doing about their own arts and crafts. The lectures changed accordingly with Wilde even becoming involved in the practical application of his theories. This enthusiasm was to reflect itself in much of his writing until the end of the decade. Leland had spent ten years in England and on his return to Philadelphia in 1881 founded the Industrial Art School.

To Charles Godfrey Leland

[Circa 15 May 1882]   [Montreal]
My dear Mr Leland, Your letter was very very welcome to me, and indeed I do think that as regards that part of my lecture in which I spoke of the necessity of art as the factor of a child's education, and how all knowledge comes in doing something not in thinking about it, and how a lad who learns any simple art learns honesty, and truth-telling, and simplicity, in the most practical school of simple morals in the world, the school of art, learns too to love nature more when he sees how no flower by the wayside is too lowly, no little blade of grass too common but some great designer has seen it and loved it and made noble use of it in decoration, learns too to be kind to animals and all living things, that most difficult of all lessons to teach a child (for I feel that when he sees how lovely the little leaping squirrel is on the beaten brass, or the bird arrested in marble flight on the carven stone,

he will never be cruel to them again), learns too to wonder and worship at God's works more, the carving round a Gothic cathedral with all its marvels of the animal and vegetable world always seeming to me a *Te Deum* in God's honour, quite as beautiful and far more lasting than that chanted *Te Deum* of the choir which dies in music at evensong – well, I felt my audience was with me there both in Philadelphia and in New York. When I showed them the brass work and the pretty bowl of wood with its bright arabesque at New York they applauded to the echo, and I have received so many letters about it and so many congratulations that your school will be known and honoured everywhere, and you yourself recognised and honoured as one of the great pioneers and leaders of the art of the future. If you come across the *Tribune* of last Friday you will see an account of my lecture, though badly reported.

For your kind words of confidence accept my thanks. I feel that I am gaining ground and better understood every day. Yes: I shall win, for the great principles are on our side, the gods are with us! Best regards to Mrs Leland. Very truly yours   OSCAR WILDE

To Julia Ward Howe

6 July [1882]   *Augusta, Georgia*
My dear Mrs Howe, My present plan is to arrive in New York from Richmond on Wednesday evening, and to leave that night for Newport, being with you Thursday morning and staying, if you will have me, till Saturday. I have an enormous trunk and a valet, but they need not trouble you. I can send them to the hotel. With what incumbrances one travels! It is not in the right harmony of things that I should have a hat-box, a secretary, a dressing-case, a trunk, a portmanteau, and a valet always following me. I daily expect a thunderbolt, but the gods are asleep, though perhaps I had better not talk about them or they will hear me and wake. But what would Thoreau have said to my hat-box! Or Emerson to the size of my trunk, which is Cyclopean! But I can't travel without Balzac and Gautier, and they take up so much room: and as long as I can enjoy talking nonsense to flowers and children I am not afraid of the depraved luxury of a hat-box.

I write to you from the beautiful, passionate, ruined South, the land of magnolias and music, of roses and romance: picturesque too in her failure to keep pace with your keen northern pushing intellect; living chiefly on credit, and on the memory of some crushing defeats. And I have been to Texas, right to the heart of it, and stayed with Jeff Davis at his plantation (how fascinating all failures are!) and seen Savannah, and the Georgia forests, and bathed in the Gulf of Mexico, and engaged in Voodoo rites with the Negroes, and am dreadfully tired and longing for an idle day which we will have at Newport.

Pray remember me to Miss Howe, and believe me very truly yours

OSCAR WILDE

Would you send a line to me at 1267 Broadway to say if it is all right.

The lecture tour, which was only planned to last until April, was extended to the middle of May when Col. Morse offered him a further two months in the Southern States and Canada. Wilde accepted and by the middle of July was glad of a two-week break (not three as it turned out) in Rhode Island and New York. The visit to Japan never took place because Morse arranged a further tour of New England in August, and Canada again in October. Wilde had met Donoghue when in Chicago and his championing of the young sculptor publicly in America made Donoghue's career.

To Charles Eliot Norton

[Circa 15 July 1882]   *Ocean House, Newport [Rhode Island]*

Dear Mr Norton, I send you the young Greek: a photograph of him: I hope you will admire him. I think it is very strong and right, the statue: and the slight asceticism of it is to me very delightful. The young sculptor's name is John Donoghue: pure Celt is he: and his address is Reaper Block, Chicago: any word of interest from you would be very cheering to him. I feel sure he could do any one of your young athletes, and what an era in art that would be to have the sculptor back in the palaestra, and of much service too to those who separate athletics from culture, and forget the right ideal of the beautiful and healthy mind in a beautiful and healthy body. I can see no better way of getting rid of the mediaeval discord between soul and body than by sculpture. Phidias is the best answer to Thomas à Kempis, but I wish you could see the statue itself, and not the sun's libel on it.

When I had the privilege of dining with you you spoke to me, if I remember right, of Professor Morse, the Japanese traveller. As I am going to Japan myself it would be of great service to me to get any instructions or letters from him which would enable me to see their method of studying art, their schools of design and the like. I hardly like to ask you to do this for me, knowing how busy your days are, but I am so anxious to see the artistic side of Japanese life that I have ventured to trespass on your courtesy. I have just returned from the South and have a three-weeks holiday now before Japan, and so find it not unpleasant to be in this little island where idleness ranks among the virtues. I suppose you are still among your beautiful trees. How rich you are to have a Rossetti and a chestnut tree. If I happen to be in Boston pray allow me to call on you, and believe me yours truly   OSCAR WILDE

Wilde used the little free time that he had to work on the scenario of a new play, The Duchess of Padua, a blank verse tragedy set in mediaeval Italy. Despite what he always said later about never having written a play for a particular actress, he appears to have approached his leading actress in early September in order to persuade the director Steele Mackaye and the producer Lawrence Barrett to take it on. Hamilton Griffin, Anderson's stepfather and manager, finally agreed terms with Wilde in late November, $1000 down and $4000 on acceptance of the play to be delivered by 31 March 1883.

To Mary Anderson

[September 1882]   *1267 Broadway, New York*
Dear Miss Anderson, I am very anxious to learn what decision you have come to as regards the production of my play. It is in our power to procure all the conditions of success by the beauty of costume, the dignity of scenery, the perfection of detail and dramatic order, without which, in England at any rate, you could not get your right position as an artist.

I will merely remind you of the complete fiasco made by Edwin Booth this summer in London merely through the inartistic style of the stage management, and the mediocre company. If you desire, as I feel that you at any rate do, to create an era in the history of American dramatic art, and to take your assured rank among the great artists of our time, here is the opportunity: and remember we live in an age when without art there is really no true success, *financial* or otherwise.

That I can create for you a part which will give your genius every scope, your passion every outlet, and your beauty every power, I am well assured. The bare, meagre outline I have given you is but a faint shadow of what Bianca Duchess of Padua will be.

Mr Lawrence Barrett has made me a very large offer for the play, but I feel that it is for you to create the part and I have told him that the acceptance of the play rests at present with you.

Mr Steele Mackaye has written to me estimating the cost of production at 10,000 dollars: you will appear in a more gorgeous frame than any woman of our day. This price I do not consider at all excessive, as, for your production of it in London, the properties, dresses, etc. will of course be available.

I will hope to hear from you soon on the matter. Mr Barrett is a good manager and actor, but for my Duchess I need you.

However there it lies. Think seriously and long about it. Perhaps for both of us it may mean the climacteric of our lives.　　　OSCAR WILDE

To Steele Mackaye

[Postmark 11 October 1882]　　　　　　　　　　　　*Halifax, Nova Scotia*

My dear Steele, Mary Anderson has written to me, accepting you as director and supreme autocrat (I think that over the 'supers' you should have the power of life and death: we will have no serious dramatic art until we hang a super), offering to take Booth's Theatre for October, and to get a good young actor for the hero, and indeed she seems most willing to do everything requisite for our success. She is simple and nice, and the Griffin must have his claws clipped.

I will see of course that in our contract you shall be named as the man under whose direction the play shall walk the stage. I will be back in a fortnight; and we will settle matters about *The Duchess* and about *Vera*. Any and all of your suggestions will be most valuable. I am glad you like it and if we can get Miss Mather it will be a great thing.

Pray go over the play carefully, and note on the blank interleaf your changes, so that over the walnuts and the wine at some little Brunswick dinner we may settle everything.

I long to get back to real literary work, for though my audiences are really most appreciative I cannot write while flying from one railway to another and from the cast-iron stove of one hotel to its twin horror in the next.

I will be at the Vendome Hotel, Boston, on Sunday next. Send me a line there to say how things are going with you.

Remember me to Frank Pierrson, and believe me, very truly yours

OSCAR WILDE

The Conformist Rebel

*'I write because it gives me the
greatest possible artistic
pleasure to write. If my
work pleases the few,
I am gratified. If it
does not, it causes
me no pain.'*

Wilde sailed home from New York on the Bothnia *on 27 December 1882 and arrived in Liverpool on 6 January. During his year in America he had delivered nearly 150 lectures and earned himself around $6000. After two or three weeks in London he used what was left of his American earnings to spend three months in Paris. He stayed at the Hôtel Voltaire on the Left Bank, had his hair curled in imitation of a bust of Nero in the Louvre and dressed in the height of fashion. 'We are now concerned with the Oscar of the second period,' he said, 'who has nothing whatever in common with the gentleman who wore long hair and carried a sunflower down Piccadilly.' Some years later he would further modify his account of this stunt by saying that he never carried a flower down Piccadilly: 'To have done it was nothing, but to make people think one had done it – that was a triumph.'*

It was in Paris that he met and befriended a young English journalist, Robert Sherard, a great-grandson of Wordsworth. Sherard was later to become his first and most voluminous biographer, though in his muddle-headed way and spaniel-like devotion he entirely overlooked his friend's homosexuality before his arrest and misunderstood it thereafter. It was through Sherard that Wilde met many of the foremost literary Frenchmen of the time: Verlaine and Victor Hugo, Mallarmé, Zola, Alphonse Daudet and Edmond de Goncourt, as well as the painters Degas and Jacques-Emile Blanche. Impressing Paris was considerably more difficult than London or New York, which had looked upon his eccentricities and showmanship with amused tolerance; Zola and de Goncourt were especially critical, the latter writing rather unflatteringly of Wilde in his diary as 'cet individu au sexe douteux, au langage de cabotin, aux récits blagueurs'.

The Duchess of Padua *was duly sent off to Mary Anderson, who within a month had turned it down, which was as much of a blow to his finances as it was to his ego. However it must have been some consolation that he had almost finalised the arrangements for* Vera *to be produced with Marie Prescott in the title role in August.*

To Mary Anderson

23 March 1883   *Paris*

My dear Miss Anderson, The play was duly forwarded some days ago: I hope it arrived safe: I have no hesitation in saying that it is the masterpiece of all my literary work, the *chef-d'oeuvre* of my youth.

As regards the characters, the Duke is a type of the Renaissance noble: I felt that to have made him merely a common and vulgar villain would have been 'banal': he is a cynic, and a philosopher: he has no heart, and his vileness comes from his intellect: it is a very strong acting part as you see, and must be given to an experienced actor. To write a comedy one requires comedy merely, but to write a tragedy, tragedy is not sufficient: the strain of emotion on the audience must be lightened: they will not weep if you have not made them laugh: so I proceeded in the following fashion.

At the beginning of the play I desired merely to place the audience in full possession of the facts, of the foundation of the play: comedy would have been disturbing, so with the exception of Ascanio's few prose speeches there is none: the action begins with the entrance of the Duke, whose comedy is bitter but comedy still, and the culmination of the act is the entrance of the Duchess: I have ended the act with the words

'The Duchess of Padua'

which strike the keynote of the play, and make a very novel and striking effect.

The comedy of Act II is the Duke's comedy, which is bitter, the citizens', which is grotesque, and the Duchess's comedy which is the comedy of Viola, and Rosalind; the comedy in which joy smiles through a mask of beauty.

Act III. Here there is no need of comedy: the act is short, quick, terrible: what we want is to impress the audience clearly with the two great speculations and problems of the play, the relations of Sin and Love: they must see that both Guido and the Duchess have rights on their side: Guido is cruel, and the Duchess has done wrong: but they represent great principles of Life and Love. The Duchess's

Sure it is the guilty
Who being very wretched need love most:

Guido's

There is no love where there is any sin:

and the great speech of the Duchess that follows give to the audience exactly what one wants to produce: *intense emotion with a background of intellectual speculation*. Which is right? That is what they will ask.

The comedy of Act IV is elaborate, and necessary to relieve the audience: you must not think it too long: believe me it is vitally necessary to make our audience merry after the horror in the corridor. I have selected, as you see, the style of comedy which never fails to raise laughter: the unconscious comedy of stupidity, missing the meaning of words, yet in all its solemn ignorance stumbling now and then on a real bit of truth.

Act V. The comedy of the soldiers: this relieves the audience from the strain of the trial: and is a bit of realism not I think put before into a dungeon scene.

Well, there is my comedy: and I hope that you have laughed over it as you read it: for myself, I am devoted to the 'second citizen' who seems to me an unconscious humorist of the highest order: he should get a great deal of fun out of his part. [. . .]

Will you present my compliments to Mr and Mrs Griffin: and believe me that writing this play for you has been a task of pleasure, and a labour of love. I remain, dear Miss Anderson, most truly yours   OSCAR WILDE

To Marie Prescott

[?March–April 1883]   [?Paris]

My dear Miss Prescott, I have received the American papers and thank you for sending them. I think we must remember that no amount of advertising will make a bad play succeed, if it is not a good play well acted. I mean that one might patrol the streets of New York with a procession of vermilion caravans twice a day for six months to announce that *Vera* was a great play, but if on the first night of its production the play was not a strong play, well acted, well mounted, all the advertisements in the world would avail nothing. My name signed to a play will excite some interests in London and America. Your name as the heroine carries great weight with it. What we want to do is to have *all* the real conditions of success in our hands. Success is a science; if you have the conditions, you get the result. Art is the mathematical result of the emotional desire for beauty. If it is not thought out, it is nothing.

As regards dialogue, you can produce tragic effects by introducing comedy. A laugh in an audience does not destroy terror, but, by relieving it, aids it. Never be afraid that by raising a laugh you destroy tragedy. On the contrary, you intensify it. The canons of each art depend on what they appeal to. Painting appeals to the eye, and is founded on the science of optics. Music appeals to the ear and is founded on the science of acoustics. The drama appeals to human nature, and must have as its ultimate basis the science of psychology and physiology. Now, one of the facts of physiology is the desire of any very intensified emotion to be relieved by some emotion that is its opposite. Nature's example of dramatic effect is the laughter of hysteria or the tears of joy. So I cannot cut out my comedy lines. Besides, the essence of good dialogue is interruption. All good dialogue should give the effect of its being made by the reaction of the personages on one another. It should never seem to be ready made by the author, and interruptions have not only their artistic effect but their physical value. They give the actors time to breathe and get new breath power. I remain, dear Miss Prescott, your sincere friend   OSCAR WILDE

To Jacques-Emile Blanche

5 April [1883]   *Hôtel Voltaire*
Cher Monsieur Blanche, Je vous remercie beaucoup pour ces trois charmants souvenirs de votre art. Quant à la petite fille qui lit mes poèmes, je l'adore déjà, mais hélas! elle ne veut pas lever ses yeux de mon livre, même pour un instant. Traître, vous l'avez fait préférer le poète à l'amant, et les vers aux baisers!

Cependant c'est intéressant de trouver une femme comme ça, car elle n'existe pas. A Dimanche prochain, votre bien devoué   OSCAR WILDE

To Edmond de Goncourt

[?April 1883]   *Hôtel Voltaire, Paris*
Monsieur, Daignez recevoir mes poèmes, témoignage de mon admiration infinie pour l'auteur de *La Faustin*.

Je serai bien content de penser qu'il y aura une place, peut-être, pour mes premières fleurs de poésies, près de vos Watteau, et de vos Boucher, et de ce trésor de laque, d'ivoire, et de bronze, que dans votre *Maison d'un Artiste* vous avez pour toujours immortalisé.

Acceptez, Monsieur, l'assurance de mes compliments les plus distingués.
                                                          OSCAR WILDE

Back in London about the beginning of May, Wilde's American resources were fast dwindling, and since his somewhat tenuous new asset was his reputation as a lecturer, he decided to make the most of it. Apart from bringing him money and

experience, his transatlantic year had given him a lifelong supply of gentle jibes at the Americans and to his existing lectures, 'The Decorative Arts' and 'The House Beautiful' he now added 'Personal Impressions of America' which he first gave in London on 11 July.

To R. H. Sherard

[Postmark 17 May 1883]   *8 Mount Street, Grosvenor Square, London*
Dear Robert, Your letter was as loveable as yourself, and this is my first moment after channel-crossings, train-catchings, and my natural rage at the charges for extra luggage from Paris, for sitting down to tell you what pleasure it gave me, and what memories of moonlit meanderings, and sunset strolls, the mere sight of your handwriting brought.

As for the dedication of your poems, I accept it: how could I refuse a gift so musical in its beauty, and fashioned by one whom I love so much as I love you?

To me the mirror of perfect friendship can never be dulled by any treachery, however mean, or disloyalty, however base. Individuals come and go like shadows but the ideal remains untarnished always: the ideal of lives linked together not by affection merely, or the pleasantness of companionship, but by the capacity of being stirred by the same noble things in art and song. For we might bow before the same marble goddess, and with hymns not dissimilar fill the reeds of her flutes: the gold of the night-time, and the silver of the dawn, should pass into perfection for us: and from each string that is touched by the fingers of the player, from each bird that is rapturous in brake or covert, from each hill-flower that blossoms on the hill, we might draw into our hearts the same sense of beauty, and in the House of Beauty meet and join hands.

That is what I think true friendship should be, like that men could make their lives: but friendship is a fire where what is not flawless shrinks into grey ashes, and where what is imperfect is not purified but consumed. There may be much about which we may differ, you and I, more perhaps than we fancy, but in our desire for beauty in all things we are one, and one in our search for that little city of gold where the flute-player never wearies, and the spring never fades, and the oracle is not silent, that little city which is the house of art, and where, with all the music of the spheres, and the laughter of the gods, Art waits for her worshippers. For we at least have not gone out into the desert to seek a reed shaken by the wind, or a dweller in kings' houses, but to a land of sweet waters, and to the well of life; for the nightingale has sung to both of us, and the moon been glad of us, and not

77

to Pallas, or to Hera, have we given the prize, but to her who from the marble of the quarry and the stone of the mine can give us pillared Parthenon and glyptic gem, to her who is the spirit of Beauty, and who has come forth from her hollow hill into the chill evening of this old world, and walks among us visible.

That is, I think, what we are seeking, and that you should seek it with me, you who are yourself so dear to me, gives me faith in our futures, confidence in our love.   OSCAR

To Euphemia Millais

[Circa 3 June 1883]   *9 Charles Street, Grosvenor Square*
Dear Mrs Millais, Here are the Lily's views on American women. Very sweetly expressed, I think they are, and a lesson in courtesy to a nation which has been discourteous to her. I hope they will interest you. They are really very clever, but then all beautiful women are more or less verbally inspired. Believe me most truly yours   OSCAR WILDE

'Violet Fane' was the pseudonym of the poet and novelist Mary Singleton, whose acquaintance Wilde had probably made through Lillie Langtry in 1880. She later became one of his favourite contributors when he edited the Woman's World *magazine. The Love Sonnets of Proteus by Wilfrid Blunt had been published anonymously in 1881.*

To Violet Fane

[?July 1883]   *9 Charles Street*
Of course I am coming! How could one refuse an invitation from one who is a poem and a poet in one, an exquisite combination of perfection and personality, which are the keynotes of modern art.

It was horrid of me not to answer before, but a nice letter is like a sunbeam and should not be treated as an epistle needing a reply. Besides your invitations are commands.

I look forward to meeting Proteus very much: his sonnets are the cameos of the decadence. Very sincerely yours   OSCAR WILDE

To the Hon. George Curzon

16 July 1883   9 *Charles Street*
My dear George Curzon, I have been so busy – too busy to answer any nice
letters – but I hope to see you soon. When are you at home? I will come
round one morning and smoke a cigarette with you. You must tell me about
the East. I hope you have brought back strange carpets and stranger gods.
Very truly yours   OSCAR WILDE

To Wilfrid Scawen Blunt

[Circa 25 July 1883]   9 *Charles Street, Grosvenor Square*
Dear Mr Blunt, I am quite suddenly telegraphed for to go to America as
they do not like beginning the rehearsals of my play without my being there
and I find myself obliged to deprive myself of the pleasure of a day of steeds
and sonnets with you, as I have to go to Liverpool early on Monday
morning. I will not cease to regret the chance that has prevented my coming
to you, and I beg you to offer to Lady Anne my most sincere apologies.

   If when I return in September you are still in the country perhaps you
will allow me to come and spend an afternoon with you. Believe me truly
yours   OSCAR WILDE

*Vera opened in New York on 21 August. It played to small houses, was slated by
the critics and taken off after only a week. The* New York Herald *described it as
'long-drawn dramatic rot' and Wilde did not risk the stage again for eight years.
He stayed on in America for a month, and on his return to England realised that
lecturing was his only immediate source of income. According to his American
manager Col. Morse, who was now in London, he arranged 150 lectures for Wilde
for the 1883–4 season, as many as he had given in the States but without the frenetic
pace and the long-distance travelling. Wilde also expanded his repertoire to include
'The Value of Art in Modern Life' and 'Dress'. His schedule in November took him
to Dublin where he renewed a close friendship with Constance Lloyd who was there
visiting relations. Constance, whom he had first met in 1881, was the daughter of
an eminent London QC who had died when she was sixteen. She had been attracted
to Oscar from the moment they met and the feeling was mutual. This time it went
further; within four days of meeting again they were engaged.*

Constance Lloyd to Otho Holland Lloyd

26 November 1883   *1 Ely Place, Dublin*

My dearest Otho, Prepare yourself for an astounding piece of news! I am engaged to Oscar Wilde and perfectly and insanely happy. I am sure you will be glad because you like him, and I want you now to do what has hitherto been my part for you, and make it all right. Grandpapa will, I know, be nice, as he is always so pleased to see Oscar. The only one I am afraid of is Aunt Emily. Oscar will write to Grandpapa and to Mama when he arrives at Shrewsbury today, and probably to you at the same time, and he will call next Sunday (he is going up to town on purpose) so you must be at home and be nice to him. I shall probably be there myself, but I shall let you know in a day or two about that. I want to go because otherwise I shall not see him until Christmas. [. . .] Now that he is gone, I am so dreadfully nervous over my family; they are so cold and practical. Everyone in this house is quite charmed, especially Mama Mary who considers me very lucky. Mind you write to me soon, dear old boy, and congratulate me. I am longing to know how you will all take it. I won't stand opposition, so I hope they won't try it. Ever your loving sister   CONSTANCE M. LLOYD

To Lillie Langtry

[Circa 22 January 1884]   *Royal Victoria Hotel, Sheffield*

My dear Lil, I am really delighted at your immense success; the most brilliant telegrams have appeared in the papers here on your performance in *Peril*. You have done what no other artist of our day has done, invaded America a second time and carried off new victories. But then, you are made for victory. It has always flashed in your eyes, and rung in your voice.

And so, I write half to tell you how glad I am at your triumphs – you, 'Venus Victrix of our age'! – and the other half to tell you that I am going to be married to a beautiful young girl called Constance Lloyd, a grave, slight, violet-eyed little Artemis, with great coils of heavy brown hair which make her flower-like head droop like a flower, and wonderful ivory hands which draw music from the piano so sweet that the birds stop singing to listen to her. We are to be married in April. I hope so much that you will be over then. I am so anxious for you to know and to like her.

I am hard at work lecturing and getting quite rich, tho' it is horrid being so much away from her, but we telegraph to each other twice a day, and I rush back suddenly from the uttermost parts of the earth to see her for an hour, and do all the foolish things which wise lovers do.

Will you write and wish me happiness, and believe me, ever your devoted and affectionate friend   OSCAR WILDE

Waldo Story was an American sculptor whose family lived in Italy whom Wilde most probably met through James Whistler.

To Waldo Story

[Postmark 22 January 1884]   *Royal Victoria Hotel, Sheffield*
Yes! my dear Waldino, yes! Amazing of course – that was necessary.

Naturally I did not write – the winds carry tidings over the Apennines better than the 2½d post: of course it accounts for the splendid sunsets about which science was so puzzled. Hurrah! *You* had no sunsets when you were engaged – only moonlights. Well, we are to be married in April, as you were, and then go to Paris, and perhaps to Rome – what do you think? Will Rome be nice in May? I mean, will you and Mrs Waldo be there, and the Pope, and the Peruginos? If so we will arrive.

Her name is Constance and she is quite young, very grave, and mystical, with wonderful eyes, and dark brown coils of hair: quite perfect except that she does not think Jimmy the only painter that ever really existed: she would like to bring Titian or somebody in by the back door. However, she knows I am the greatest poet, so in literature she is all right: and I have explained to her that you are the greatest sculptor: art instruction can not go further.

We are of course desperately in love. I have been obliged to be away nearly all the time since our engagement, civilising the provinces by my remarkable lectures, but we telegraph to each other twice a day, and the telegraph clerks have become quite romantic in consequence. I hand in my messages, however, very sternly, and try to look as if 'love' was a cryptogram for 'buy Grand Trunks' and 'darling' a cypher for 'sell out at par'. I am sure it succeeds.

Dear Waldo, I am perfectly happy, and I hope that you and Mrs Waldo will be very fond of my wife. I have spoken to her so much about you both that she knows you quite well already, and of course I can not imagine anyone seeing her and not loving her.

Please give my love to Uncle Sam and the young robust transcendentalist from Boston, Mass. whose novels we all delight in. And remember me most kindly to your wife, and tell her how much I look forward to introducing Constance to her. *Addio*   OSCAR

Oscar and Constance were married on 29 May 1884 and spent their honeymoon in Dieppe and Paris. They took a lease on a house at 16 Tite Street in Chelsea and

commissioned the architect and theatre designer E. W. Godwin to make internal changes and decorate it. In the meantime they moved back into Oscar's old lodgings in Charles Street until the work was finished in January of the following year.

To the Editor of the *Pall Mall Gazette*

[Circa 13 October 1884]   [*London*]

The 'Girl Graduate' must of course have precedence, not merely for her sex but for her sanity: her letter is extremely sensible. She makes two points: that high heels are a necessity for any lady who wishes to keep her dress clean from the Stygian mud of our streets, and that without a tight corset 'the ordinary number of petticoats and etceteras' cannot be properly or conveniently held up. Now it is quite true that as long as the lower garments are suspended from the hips, a corset is an absolute necessity; the mistake lies in not suspending all apparel from the shoulders. In the latter case a corset becomes useless, the body is left free and unconfined for respiration and motion, there is more health, and consequently more beauty. Indeed all the most ungainly and uncomfortable articles of dress that fashion has ever in her folly prescribed, not the tight corset merely, but the farthingale, the vertugadin, the hoop, the crinoline, and that modern monstrosity the so-called 'dress-improver' also, all of them have owed their origin to the same error, the error of not seeing that it is from the shoulders, and from the shoulders only, that all garments should be hung.

And as regards high heels, I quite admit that some additional height to the shoe or boot is necessary if long gowns are to be worn in the street; but what I object to is that the height should be given to the heel only, and not to the sole of the foot also. The modern high-heeled boot is, in fact, merely the clog of the time of Henry VI, with the front prop left out, and its inevitable effect is to throw the body forward, to shorten the steps, and consequently to produce that want of grace which always follows want of freedom.

Why should clogs be despised? Much art has been expended on clogs. They have been made of lovely woods, and delicately inlaid with ivory, and with mother-of-pearl. A clog might be a dream of beauty, and, if not too high or too heavy, most comfortable also. But if there be any who do not like clogs, let them try some adaptation of the trouser of the Turkish lady, which is loose round the limb, and tight at the ankle.

The 'Girl Graduate', with a pathos to which I am not insensible, entreats me not to apotheosise 'that awful, befringed, beflounced, and bekilted divided skirt'. Well, I will acknowledge that the fringes, the flounces, and the kilting do certainly defeat the whole object of the dress, which is that of ease and liberty; but I regard these things as mere wicked superfluities, tragic proofs that the divided skirt is ashamed of its own division. The principle of the dress is good, and, though it is not by any means perfection, it is a step towards it.

Here I leave the 'Girl Graduate', with much regret, for Mr Wentworth Huyshe. Mr Huyshe makes the old criticism that Greek dress is unsuited to our climate, and the, to me, somewhat new assertion, that the men's dress of a hundred years ago was preferable to that of the second part of the seventeenth century, which I consider to have been the exquisite period of English costume.

Now, as regards the first of these two statements, I will say, to begin with, that the warmth of apparel does not depend really on the number of garments worn, but on the material of which they are made. One of the chief faults of modern dress is that it is composed of far too many articles of clothing, most of which are of the wrong substance; but over a substratum of pure wool, such as is supplied by Dr Jaeger under the modern German system, some modification of Greek costume is perfectly applicable to our climate, our country, and our century. This important fact has already been pointed out by Mr E. W. Godwin in his excellent, though too brief, handbook on Dress, contributed to the Health Exhibition. I call it an important fact because it makes almost any form of lovely costume perfectly practicable in our cold climate. Mr Godwin, it is true, points out that the English ladies of the thirteenth century abandoned after some time the flowing garments of the early Renaissance in favour of a tighter mode, such as northern Europe seems to demand. This I quite admit, and its significance; but what I contend, and what I am sure Mr Godwin would agree with me in, is that the principles, the laws of Greek dress may be perfectly realised, even in a moderately tight gown with sleeves: I mean the principle of suspending all apparel from the shoulders, and of relying for beauty of effect, not on the stiff ready-made ornaments of the modern milliner – the bows where there should be no bows, and the flounces where there should be no flounces – but on the exquisite play of light and line that one gets from rich and rippling folds. I am not proposing any antiquarian revival of an ancient costume, but trying merely to point out the right laws of dress, laws which are dictated by art and not by archaeology, by science and not by fashion; and just as the best work of art in our days is that which combines classic grace with absolute reality, so from a continuation of the Greek principles of beauty with the German principles of health will come, I feel certain, the costume of the future.

And now to the question of men's dress, or rather to Mr Huyshe's claim of the superiority, in point of costume, of the last quarter of the eighteenth century over the second quarter of the seventeenth. The broad-brimmed hat of 1640 kept the rain of winter and the glare of summer from the face; the same cannot be said of the hat of one hundred years ago, which, with its comparatively narrow brim and high crown, was the precursor of the modern 'chimney-pot': a wide turned-down collar is a healthier thing than a strangling stock, and a short cloak much more comfortable than a sleeved overcoat, even though the latter may have had 'three capes': a cloak is easier to put on and off, lies lightly on the shoulder in summer, and, wrapped round one in winter, keeps one perfectly warm. A doublet, again, is simpler than a coat and waistcoat; instead of two garments we have one; by not being open, also, it protects the chest better.

Short loose trousers are in every way to be preferred to the tight knee-breeches which often impede the proper circulation of the blood; and, finally, the soft leather boots, which could be worn above or below the knee, are more supple, and give consequently more freedom, than the stiff Hessian which Mr Huyshe so praises. I say nothing about the question of grace and picturesqueness, for I suppose that no one, not even Mr Huyshe, would prefer a macaroni to a cavalier, a Lawrence to a Vandyke, or the third George to the first Charles; but for ease, warmth and comfort this seventeenth-century dress is infinitely superior to anything that came after it, and I do not think it is excelled by any preceding form of costume. I sincerely trust that we may soon see in England some national revival of it.

To Philip Griffiths

[Postmark 2 December 1884]   *9 Charles Street, Grosvenor Square*
My dear Philip, I have sent a photo of myself for you to the care of Mr MacKay which I hope you will like and in return for it you are to send me one of yourself which I shall keep as a memory of a charming meeting and golden hours passed together. You have a nature made to love all beautiful things and I hope we shall see each other soon. Your friend   OSCAR WILDE

Little is known about Griffiths but this letter is significant in that it marks the start of Wilde's correspondence with young men over the next few years, among them Harry Marillier, Douglas Ainslie, Herbert Horne and Richard Le Gallienne. They were all about ten years his junior and he was clearly attracted by their flattery and adulation, as well as by their looks. Despite the intensity of his letters, though, there is nothing to suggest that his relationship with them was other than platonic.

To Constance Wilde

Tuesday [Postmark 16 December 1884]   *The Balmoral, Edinburgh*
Dear and Beloved, Here am I, and you at the Antipodes. O execrable facts, that keep our lips from kissing, though our souls are one.

What can I tell you by letter? Alas! nothing that I would tell you. The messages of the gods to each other travel not by pen and ink and indeed your bodily presence here would not make you more real: for I feel your fingers in my hair, and your cheek brushing mine. The air is full of the music of your voice, my soul and body seem no longer mine, but mingled in some exquisite ecstasy with yours. I feel incomplete without you. Ever and ever yours   OSCAR
Here I stay till Sunday.

Apart from two perfunctory notes shortly before and during his trials, this is the only letter of Oscar's to his wife which is known to have survived. The rest were probably destroyed by her family after her death. It is unlikely that Constance destroyed them, as in her own correspondence after the trials she still writes of him with affection, if with regular exasperation.

To J. S. Blackie

[Circa 16 December 1884]   *The Balmoral, Edinburgh*
My dear Professor, I am in Edinboro' for three days, and the man who comes to Scotland without scenting the heather on the mountain, or talking to you among your books, misses what is best in the land. So as I can see no glory of purple on the hillside, may I come and see you, when you have, if you ever have, an idle hour?

My excuse must be that all Celts gravitate towards each other. Believe me, in any case, your sincere admirer   OSCAR WILDE

John Blackie had been Professor of Greek at Edinburgh until 1882. He was much loved, famous for his eccentricities and said to teach his pupils everything except Greek. He visited the Wildes when he was in Dublin in 1874. He died, coincidentally, on the day that Wilde had the Marquess of Queensberry arrested, 2 March 1895.

To E. W. Godwin

[19 December 1884]   *The Balmoral, Edinburgh*

My dear Godwin, I cannot understand Sharpe's account, enclosed. What is (1) extra painting? What is (2) 14 gas brackets? What is deal shelf overmantel and case in dining-room etc.? Sharpe has been paid first £40 for the overmantel in bedroom and drawing-room, and the sideboard – which by the bye I thought very dear – then £120 for his contract, but this new £100 takes me by surprise. I thought the £120 was for everything. Surely Green fixed the gas stoves? I may be wrong, but would you look over it again?

I hope you have been able to choose the stuffs. I don't think the oriental blue and red hanging is big enough for two curtains on landing at drawing-room. Would you choose something for that place, and see my wife about them? I do hope to see things nearly ready when I come home – the coverings for settees especially.

I wish you were in Edinboro' with me: it is quite lovely – bits of it. The house must be a success: do just add the bloom of colour to it in curtains and cushions. Ever yours   OSCAR

Wilde had been billed as one of the speakers at a meeting in Leicester of the Funeral and Mourning Reform Association which had been inaugurated the year before.

To the Rev. J. Page Hopps

14 January 1885   *[London]*

Dear Mr Hopps, I am very sorry to say that I am confined to the house with a severe cold, caught by lecturing in a Lincolnshire snowstorm, and am not allowed by my doctor to travel. It is with much regret that I find myself unable to join in the meeting tomorrow, as I sympathise most strongly with the object in question. The present style of burying and sorrowing for the dead seems to me to make grief grotesque, and to turn mourning to a mockery. Any reform you can bring about in these customs would be of value quite inestimable. The present ostentation and extravagance of burial rites seems to me to harmonise but ill with the real feeling of those at the doors of whose house the Angel of Death has knocked. The ceremony by which we part from those whom we have loved should not merely be noble in its meaning, but simple in its sincerity. The funeral of Ophelia does not seem to me 'a maimed rite' when one thinks of the flowers strewn on her grave. I regret exceedingly that I cannot hear the actual suggestions on the matter which will be made at your meeting. I have always been of opinion that the coffin should be privately conveyed at night-time to the churchyard chapel, and that there the mourners should next day meet. By these means the public procession through the streets would be avoided; and the publicity of funerals is surely the real cause of their expense. As regards dress, I consider that white and violet should be recognised as mourning, and not black merely, particularly in the case of children. The habit of bringing flowers to the grave is now almost universal, and is a custom beautiful in its symbolism; but I cannot help thinking that the elaborate and expensive designs made by the florist are often far less lovely than a few flowers held loose in the hand. There are many other points on which I should have liked to listen, and one point on which I had hoped to have the privilege of speaking. I mean the expression of sorrow in art. The urns, pyramids and sham sarcophagi – ugly legacies from the eighteenth century to us – are meaningless as long as we do not burn or embalm our dead. If we are to have funeral memorials at all, far better models are to be found in the beautiful crosses of Ireland, such as the cross at Monasterboice, or in the delicate bas-reliefs on Greek tombs. Above all, such art, if we are to have it, should concern itself more with the living than the dead – should be rather a noble symbol for the guiding of life than an idle panegyric on those who are gone. If a man needs an elaborate tombstone in order to remain in the memory of his country, it is clear that his living at all was an act of absolute superfluity. Keats's grave is a hillock of green grass with a plain headstone, and is to me the holiest place in Rome. There is in Westminster Abbey a periwigged admiral in a nightgown hurried off to heaven by two howling cherubs, which is one of the best examples I know of ostentatious obscurity.

Pray offer to the committee of the society my sincere regrets at my inability to be present, and my sincere wishes for the success of your movement. Believe me, sincerely yours OSCAR WILDE

Wilde's relationship with Whistler, which had started when he came to London in 1879, was always a stormy one; Whistler generally accusing Wilde of plagiarism and appropriating his views on art. It passed through good-natured banter while Wilde was in America but started to become acrimonious after Wilde reviewed Whistler's 'Ten O'Clock' lecture on 20 February. Whistler's hostility finally brought it to an end in 1890, though Wilde managed to have the last word by publishing 'The Critic as Artist' six months after their last public exchange (see pp. 121–2).

To James McNeill Whistler

[Circa 23 February 1885]
Dear Butterfly, By the aid of a biographical dictionary I discovered that there were once two painters, called Benjamin West and Paul Delaroche, who recklessly took to lecturing on Art.

As of their works nothing at all remains, I conclude that they explained themselves away. Be warned in time, James; and remain, as I do, incomprehensible: to be great is to be misunderstood. *Tout à vous*   OSCAR
Private
Jimmy! You must *stamp* your letters – they are dear at two pence – and also do send them in proper time. 2.30 on Monday! *Ciel!*

To T. H. S. Escott

[?Late February 1885]   *16 Tite Street, Chelsea*
Dear Mr Escott, There is an ominous silence from 'Jimmy' over the way: if he sends any letter to the *World* I wish you would not publish it till I can write my answer. There is no delight unless both guns go off together. Truly yours   OSCAR WILDE

To Helena Sickert

[Circa 1 March 1885]   *16 Tite Street*
Dear Miss Nellie, Is it in accordance with the right principles of political economy to sell a poet's love letters? Your sincere friend   OSCAR WILDE

William Benson, elder brother of Frank Benson, the actor, was an architect and designer in metalwork. Since decorating his own 'House Beautiful' in Tite Street, Wilde's views on house decoration had developed considerably from the rather theoretical lectures he was giving three years before in America.

To W. A. S. Benson

[16 May 1885]   *16 Tite Street*
My dear Benson, I don't at all agree with you about the decorative value of Morris's wallpapers. They seem to me often deficient in real beauty of colour: this may be due as you say to his workmen, but Art admits of no excuses of that kind. Then as regards the design, he is far more successful with those designs which are meant for textures which hang in folds, than

for those which have to be seen flat on a stretched material: a fact which may be due to the origin of many of his patterns, but which is a fact still.

Setting aside however a point on which we were sure for obvious reasons to disagree, I am surprised to find we are at such variance on the question of the value of pure colour on the walls of a room. No one I think would paint a room in distemper entirely: for the ceiling and the upper part of the wall distemper is excellent, for the lower part (as for the woodwork) one uses oil paint which has the great advantage of being cleanable, if there is such a word.

Nor are the colours one gets in distemper and oils necessarily spoiled by the introduction of silk embroideries or oil pictures. These things depend entirely on the scheme of colour one selects for the room, and on one's own knowledge of colour harmonies. I have for instance a dining-room done in different shades of white, with white curtains embroidered in yellow silk: the effect is absolutely delightful, and the room is beautiful.

I have seen far more rooms spoiled by wallpapers than by anything else: when everything is covered with a design the room is restless and the eye disturbed. A good picture is always improved by being hung on a coloured surface that suits it, or by being placed in surroundings which are harmonious to it, but the delicacy of line in an etching for instance is often spoiled by the necessarily broad, if not coarse, pattern on a block-printed wallpaper.

My eye requires in a room a resting-place of pure colour, and I prefer to keep design for more delicate materials than papers, for embroidery for instance. Paper in itself is not a lovely material, and the only papers which I ever use now are the Japanese gold ones: they are exceedingly decorative, and no English paper can compete with them, either for beauty or for practical wear. With these and with colour in oil and distemper a lovely house can be made.

Some day if you do us the pleasure of calling I will show you a little room with blue ceiling and frieze (distemper), yellow (oil) walls, and white woodwork and fittings, which is joyous and exquisite, the only piece of design being the Morris blue-and-white curtains, and a white-and-yellow silk coverlet. I hope, and in my lectures always try and bring it about, that people will study the value of pure colour more than they do. The ugly ceilings of modern houses are often due to the excessive use of wallpapers, and I do not think Morris himself sets the exaggerated value on wallpapers which you do.

Anybody with a real artistic sense must see the value and repose of pure colour, and even taking the matter in a practical light, wallpapers collect dirt and dust to a great extent and cannot be cleaned. They are economical and often pretty and charming but they are not the final word of Art in decoration by any means. I hope they will be used much less frequently than they are, and that Morris will devote his time, as I think he is doing, to textile fabrics, their dyes and their designs, and not so much to a form of wall decoration which has its value of course, but whose value has been overestimated, and whose use is often misunderstood.

I saw Frank at Oxford: there was a charming performance, and lovely costumes: he seemed very pleased at it and so was I. Believe me, very truly yours   OSCAR WILDE

How can you see socialism in *The Earthly Paradise*? If it is there it is an accident not a quality – there is a great difference.

The first of Wilde's children, Cyril, was born on 5 June. Nellie, who was married to Constance's brother Otho, gave birth later in the month. After Wilde was released from prison Otho stayed in touch with him and was the least judgemental of Constance's relations.

To Nellie Lloyd

[Postmark 5 June 1885]   [*16 Tite Street*]

My dear Little Nellie, You will be delighted to hear that Constance got through her confinement all right, suffering hardly any pain. The child – an amazing boy! – was born when she was under chloroform, and on coming to she absolutely declined to believe it was born at all! And was only convinced of the fact by the nurse producing a stalward [sic] boy, *who already knows me quite well.* She is very happy and peaceful but cannot see anyone for some days. The doctor has posted a bulletin in the hall to that effect.

You must have a little girl and we will make up a match at once. I will let you and Otho, the important uncle and aunt of our son and heir, know how she gets on. I hope you will get through your own confinement as easily as Constance – I am sure you will. It really is very little after all – you must not be nervous. I have sent Otho a telegram and send you a letter (my first!). I know you will be delighted – both of you. Ever affectionately yours

OSCAR

To Edward Heron-Allen

[Postmark 12 June 1885]   *[16 Tite Street]*

My dear E. H. A., Thank you for your letter. Will you cast the child's horoscope for us? It was born at a quarter to eleven last Friday morning. My wife is very anxious to know its fate, and has begged me to ask you to search the stars. Ever yours   OSCAR WILDE

Heron-Allen was a writer, polymath and eccentric with interests as varied as violin-making, zoology, Persian literature, asparagus culture and cheiromancy (palm-reading), and he may well have suggested to Wilde the idea for 'Lord Arthur Savile's Crime'. He did indeed cast Cyril's horoscope and delivered it to the Wildes later in the year, noting in his diary, 'It grieved them very much.' Cyril was killed in action in 1915.

To Norman Forbes-Robertson

[Early June 1885]   *[16 Tite Street]*

Dear Norman, Thanks for your congratulations. Yes, come tomorrow. The baby is wonderful: it has a bridge to its nose! which the nurse says is a proof of genius! It also has a superb voice, which it freely exercises: its style is essentially Wagnerian.

Constance is doing capitally and is in excellent spirits.

I was delighted to get your telegram. You must get married *at once*! Ever yours   OSCAR

To the Hon. George Curzon

20 July 1885   16 *Tite Street*

Dear Curzon, I want to be one of Her Majesty's Inspectors of Schools! This is ambition – however, I want it, and want it very much, and I hope you will help me. Edward Stanhope has the giving away and, as a contemporary of mine at Oxford, you could give me great help by writing him a letter to say (if you think it) that I am a man of some brains. I won't trouble you with the reasons which make me ask for this post – but I want it and could do the work, I fancy, well.

If you could give me and get me any help you can I will be so much obliged to you, and I know how the party think of you – you brilliant young Coningsby!

I hope to get this and to get it with your approval and your good word. I don't know Stanhope personally and am afraid he may take the popular idea of me as a real idler. Would you tell him it is not so? In any case, ever yours   OSCAR WILDE

To an Unidentified Correspondent

[?1885]   16 *Tite Street*

I have been laid up with a severe attack of asthma, and have been unable to answer your letter before this. I return you your manuscript, as you desire, and would advise you to prune it down a little and send it to either *Time* or *Longman's*. It is better than many magazine articles, though, if you will allow me to say so, it is rather belligerent in tone.

As regards your prospects in literature, believe me that it is impossible to live by literature. By journalism a man may make an income, but rarely by pure literary work.

I would strongly advise you to try and make some profession, such as that of a tutor, the basis and mainstay of your life, and to keep literature for your finest, rarest moments. The best work in literature is always done by those who do not depend upon it for their daily bread, and the highest form of literature, poetry, brings no wealth to the singer. For producing your best work also you will require some leisure and freedom from sordid care.

It is always a difficult thing to give advice, but as you are younger than I am, I venture to do so. Make some sacrifice for your art, and you will be repaid; but ask of Art to sacrifice herself for you, and a bitter disappointment may come to you. I hope it will not, but there is always a terrible chance.

With your education you should have no difficulty in getting some post which should enable you to live without anxiety, and to keep for literature your most felicitous moods. To attain this end, you should be ready to give up some of your natural pride; but loving literature as you do, I cannot think that you would not do so.

Finally, remember that London is full of young men working for literary success, and that you must carve your way to fame. Laurels don't come for the asking. Yours   OSCAR WILDE

To Herbert Warren

[Circa 18 October 1885]   *Athenaeum Club*

My dear Warren, Will you accept my warm congratulations on the high and well-deserved honour that has been given to you. With you as President, Magdalen should hold in intellectual matters as high a position as Balliol does – I am delighted at the prospect.

I often think with some regret of my Oxford days and wish I had not left Parnassus for Piccadilly – all the more now that my College has gained so fine a President. Believe me, truly yours   OSCAR WILDE

Harry Marillier had lodged at 13 Salisbury Street at the same time as Wilde and Miles had been living there in 1879–80. He was now a classical scholar at Cambridge.

To H. C. Marillier

[Postmark 5 November 1885]   *Albemarle Club, 25 Albemarle Street*

Of course I remember the blue-coat boy, and am charmed to find he has not forgotten me.

Your letter gave me great pleasure and if possible I will come down to see the *Eumenides* – which I suppose will look like Hamlet surrounded by the witches of *Macbeth* – but you have not told me the date of the production yet, so I cannot say if I will be really free.

I have a very vivid remembrance of the bright enthusiastic boy who used to bring me my coffee in Salisbury Street, and am delighted to find he is devoted to the muses, but I suppose you don't flirt with all nine ladies at once? Which of them do you really love? Whether or not I can come and see you, you must certainly come and see me when you are in town, and we will talk of the poets and drink Keats's health. I wonder are you all Wordsworthians still at Cambridge, or do you love Keats, and Poe, and Baudelaire? I hope so.

Write and tell me what things in art you and your friends love best. I do not mean what pictures, but what moods and modulations of art affect you most.

Is it five years ago really? Then I might almost sign myself an old friend, but the word old is full of terror.   OSCAR WILDE

To H. C. Marillier

[Postmark 14 November 1885]   16 *Tite Street*

My dear Harry, The army is a noble profession. I would sooner see you in a cocked hat than see you a curate, or a solicitor. A man of brains can always be fine, and I think you are right to go in for the examination, though I wonder you dislike the idea of being a schoolmaster. With your quick sympathies, your delicate intuition, and your enthusiasm, you could teach wonderfully. You have the power of making others love you, which is the first essential of a teacher. For my own part I think the life of a teacher the loveliest in the world. But wherever you are, whatever your profession, you will make a mark and carve a destiny. I felt that when I met you, I know it now that we have written to each other.

I wonder are you all as cold in Cambridge as we are. I love the languor of hot noons, and hate our chill winter – so pitiless, so precise – giving one form where one wants colour, definiteness where one needs mystery, and making poor humanity red-nosed and blue-nosed and horrid. I think I had better not come down to Cambridge. You should be reading and I would idle you. You should dream of parallelograms not of poetry, and only talk of x and y. What do you say? Life is long and we will see each other often. In the meantime we can write. Also, send me a photograph of yourself.

Sayle of New College has sent me his poems. Do you know him? There is one very lovely sonnet. Affectionately yours   OSCAR

To H. C. Marillier

[Postmark 12 December 1885]   *Central Station Hotel, Glasgow*

Dear Harry, I am away in the region of horrible snow and horrible note paper! Lecturing and wandering – a vagabond with a mission! But your letter has reached me, like a strain of music wind-blown from a far land. You too have the love of things impossible – ἔρως τῶν ἀδυνάτων – *l'amour de l'impossible* (how do men name it?). Some day you will find, even as I have found, that there is no such thing as a romantic experience; there are romantic memories, and there is the desire of romance – that is all. Our most fiery moments of ecstasy are merely shadows of what somewhere else we have felt, or of what we long some day to feel. So at least it seems to me. And, strangely enough, what comes of all this is a curious mixture of ardour and of indifference. I myself would sacrifice everything for a new experience, and I know there is no such thing as a new experience at all. I think I would more readily die for what I do not believe in than for what I hold to be true. I would go to the stake for a sensation and be a sceptic to the last! Only one thing remains infinitely fascinating to me, the mystery of moods. To be master of these moods is exquisite, to be mastered by them more exquisite still. Sometimes I think that the artistic life is a long and lovely suicide, and am not sorry that it is so.

And much of this I fancy you yourself have felt: much also remains for you to feel. There is an unknown land full of strange flowers and subtle perfumes, a land of which it is joy of all joys to dream, a land where all things are perfect and poisonous. I have been reading Walter Scott for the last week: you too should read him, for there is nothing of all this in him.

Write to me at Tite Street, and let me know where you will be. Ever yours   O. W.

The Pall Mall Gazette *had been running a series on 'The Best Hundred Books' by 'The Best Hundred Judges'. Wilde, increasingly confident in his ability to challenge the established order, turned the series on its head.*

To the Editor of the *Pall Mall Gazette*

[Early February 1886]   [*London*]
Books, I fancy, may be conveniently divided into three classes:

1. Books to read, such as Cicero's *Letters*, Suetonius, Vasari's *Lives of the Painters*, the *Autobiography of Benvenuto Cellini*, Sir John Mandeville, Marco Polo, St Simon's *Memoirs*, Mommsen, and (till we get a better one) Grote's *History of Greece*.

2. Books to re-read, such as Plato and Keats: in the sphere of poetry, the masters not the minstrels; in the sphere of philosophy, the seers not the savants.

3. Books not to read at all, such as Thomson's *Seasons*, Rogers's *Italy*, Paley's *Evidences*, all the Fathers except St Augustine, all John Stuart Mill except the *Essay on Liberty*, all Voltaire's plays without any exception, Butler's *Analogy*, Grant's *Aristotle*, Hume's *England*, Lewes's *History of Philosophy*, all argumentative books and all books that try to prove anything.

The third class is by far the most important. To tell people what to read is, as a rule, either useless or harmful; for the appreciation of literature is a question of temperament not of teaching; to Parnassus there is no primer and nothing that one can learn is ever worth learning. But to tell people what not to read is a very different matter, and I venture to recommend it as a mission to the University Extension Scheme.

Indeed, it is one that is eminently needed in this age of ours, an age that reads so much that it has no time to admire, and writes so much that it has no time to think. Whoever will select out of the chaos of our modern curricula 'The Worst Hundred Books', and publish a list of them, will confer on the rising generation a real and lasting benefit.

After expressing these views I suppose I should not offer any suggestions at all with regard to 'The Best Hundred Books', but I hope that you will allow me the pleasure of being inconsistent, as I am anxious to put in a claim for a book that has been strangely omitted by most of the excellent judges who have contributed to your columns. I mean the *Greek Anthology*. The beautiful poems contained in this collection seem to me to hold the same position with regard to Greek dramatic literature as do the delicate little figurines of Tanagra to the Pheidian marbles, and to be quite as necessary for the complete understanding of the Greek spirit.

I am also amazed to find that Edgar Allan Poe has been passed over. Surely this marvellous lord of rhythmic expression deserves a place? If, in order to make room for him, it be necessary to elbow out someone else, I should elbow out Southey, and I think that Baudelaire might be most advantageously substituted for Keble. No doubt, both in *The Curse of Kehama* and in *The Christian Year* there are poetic qualities of a certain kind, but absolute catholicity of taste is not without its dangers. It is only an auctioneer who should admire all schools of art.

To Violet Fane

[13 February 1886]   *16 Tite Street*
Dear Mrs Singleton, On Tuesday with pleasure. Who would not be charmed to visit '*la Sappho de nos jours*'?

But how to write anything these grey days? I hate our sunless, loveless winter, and in Tite Street there are no terracotta Caesars! However, some little swallow-flight of song may come to me as I am running down to Oxford. If so you shall have it.

The Oxford theatre opens tomorrow and I am going to see our 'young barbarians all at play'. Young Oxonians are very delightful, so Greek, and graceful, and uneducated. They have profiles but no philosophy. Very sincerely yours   OSCAR WILDE

By early 1886 with a household to support, Constance pregnant again (his second son Vyvyan was born in November) and the lecture circuit less lucrative than in the previous two years, Wilde's thoughts turned to some form of permanent employment. The Beaumont Trust was responsible for 'The People's Palace' which opened in the East End of London the following year. It was designed 'as an institution, in which, whether in Science, Art or Literature, any student may be able to follow up his education to the highest point by means of Technical and Trades Schools, Reading Rooms and Libraries'. He was not offered the post.

To the Secretary of the Beaumont Trust

22 February 1886 16 Tite Street

Sir, I beg to offer myself as a candidate for the Secretaryship to the Beaumont Trust Fund, an office which I understand will shortly be vacant.

During my university career I obtained two First Classes, the Newdigate Prize, and other honours, and since taking my degree, in 1878, I have devoted myself partly to literature and partly to the spreading of art-knowledge and art-appreciation among the people.

I have had the opportunity in America of studying the various forms of technical education, from the Cooper Institute in New York to Mr Leland's Art-School for Children in Philadelphia, and have constantly lectured on the subject in this country before Art-Schools, Mechanics' Institutes and Literary Societies.

Should the trustees of the Beaumont Scheme consider me worthy to hold the post of Secretary, I would be able to devote all my time to the fulfilment of the necessary duties and the furtherance of the proposed movement, as I have no formal profession but that of literature and art-culture.

This People's Palace will be to me the realisation of much that I have long hoped for, and to be in any way officially connected with it would be esteemed by me a high and noble honour. I remain, sir, your obedient servant, OSCAR WILDE

To Douglas Ainslie

[?May–June 1886] *Albemarle Club*

Dear Douglas, I have lost your note. What is your address, and what day have you asked me for? I am really 'impossible' about letters: they vanish from my room. I don't think Constance will be able to come, but I will certainly manage some day. I hope you and Osborne are reading hard. He is quite charming, with his low musical voice, and his graceful incapacity for a career. He is a little like the moon.

You were very sweet to come and see us; we must have many evenings together and drink yellow wine from green glasses in Keats's honour. Ever yours OSCAR

Horne, architect and art historian, had founded a quarterly magazine entitled the Century Guild Hobby Horse in January. Wilde published an article on the manuscript of Keats's 'Sonnet on Blue' (see p. 60) in the third number and their friendship seems to have started that summer. Both men shared a fascination for the eighteenth-century poet and forger Thomas Chatterton, and Wilde lectured on him in November at Birkbeck College. Despite their efforts, nothing was done to commemorate Chatterton until the middle of the last century when Pyle Street School was pulled down and its façade, together with a memorial plaque, incorporated into the schoolmaster's house where Chatterton had been born.

To Herbert P. Horne

[Postmark 16 August 1886]   16 Tite Street

My dear Horne, Thank you for the copy of your letter. I am afraid it reads as if we wanted to entirely renovate the school, and the more I think of that little grey building the more I feel we should proceed cautiously, and not do anything in a hurry.

We must not have William Morris down on us to begin with, and we must not alter the tone of the room.

Perhaps after all, cleaning, repairing, and a tablet would be enough. I wish you were in town to talk it over. But do not send circulars out till after the magazine appears, nor commit us to anything definite.

I am sure you regret that the muniment room is not as the 'marvellous boy' saw it; there may be others who would have the same view about the school.

Of course we will do something, and put up a tablet, but more than this we should seriously think about. And above all things let us not rashly commit ourselves: there is lots of time before us.

Write to me soon, and believe me, truly yours   OSCAR WILDE

To Herbert P. Horne

[7 December 1886]   16 Tite Street

My dear Horne, Of course we will have the tablet. I thought we had fully settled that at Bristol. The little classical façade of the school-house is just the place for it, and it will add historic interest to the building without marring its antiquarian value or eighteenth-century look. I remember your telling me in the train that one of your friends had promised to design one, and I was talking the other day about it to an ardent Chattertonian.

Do you think we should have a bas-relief of T. C.? It seems to me that there is really no picture of the poet extant. What do you say to a simple inscription

To the Memory

of

Thomas Chatterton

One of England's greatest poets and sometime pupil at this school.

I prefer the inscription, though a symbolic design might accompany it.

I was very nearly coming to fetch you the night of the fog to come and hear my lecture on Chatterton at the Birkbeck, but did not like to take you out on such a dreadful night. To my amazement I found 800 people there! And they seemed really interested in the marvellous boy.

You must come in for a cigarette some night soon. Sincerely yours

OSCAR WILDE

To J. S. Little

[29 April 1887]   *16 Tite Street*

Dear Mr Little, It will give me great pleasure to become a Fellow of the Society of Authors, and I hope we will have some more meetings. I hope also that for the future no one who is not a man of letters will be invited on the platform. Brett's speech was a gross impertinence at Gosse's lecture, and we should keep clear of the journeymen painters who usurp the name of artist.

Why not have a *soirée*? The artists have their *fêtes*, let us have ours, and try to get the thinkers and the men of style, not merely the scribblers and second-rate journalists. I enclose you a cheque for £1. 1. I think you could work up the Society into something very good. You have the qualifications and the opportunity. Truly yours   OSCAR WILDE

Vian was the editor of the Court & Society Review *in which Wilde had published his first work of fiction, 'The Canterville Ghost', in February–March. His article on 'The Child Philosopher' appeared in April. One of the other definitions which Wilde particularly liked was 'Plagiarist: a writer of plays' and which he said 'is the most brilliant thing which has been said on modern literature for a long time'. It is from about now that Wilde's most creative years begin with almost all his literary work, other than articles and reviews, being published between 1887 and 1895.*

To Alsagar Vian

[Postmark 13 April 1887]   16 *Tite Street*

My dear Vian, Shall I do for you an article called 'The Child Philosopher'? It will be on Mark Twain's amazing and amusing record of the answers of American children at a Board School.

Some of them such as *Republican* – 'a sinner mentioned in the Bible', or *Democrat* – 'a vessel usually filled with beer', are excellent.

Come and dine at *Pagani's* in Portland Street on Friday – 7.30. No dress, just ourselves and a flask of Italian wine. Afterwards we will smoke cigarettes and talk over the Journalistic article. Could we go to your rooms, I am so far off, and clubs are difficult to talk in. This however is for you entirely to settle. Also send me your address again like a good fellow. I have lost it.

I think your number is excellent, but as usual had to go to St James's Street to get a copy. Even Grosvenor Place does not get the *C & S* till Thursday night! This is all wrong, isn't it. Truly yours   OSCAR WILDE

Reid was the general manager of Cassell's which had started to publish the Lady's World *in November 1886. It had not been particularly successful and Wilde's carefully crafted reviews at the time, mainly for the* Pall Mall Gazette, *had undoubtedly brought him to Reid's attention as the man to revive the ailing magazine. He edited it for two years from November 1887 to October 1889 under its new title the* Woman's World.

To Wemyss Reid

[April 1887]   16 *Tite Street*

Dear Mr Wemyss Reid, I have read very carefully the numbers of the *Lady's World* you kindly sent me, and would be very happy to join with you in the work of editing and to some extent reconstructing it. It seems to me that at present it is too feminine, and not sufficiently womanly. No one appreciates more fully than I do the value and importance of Dress, in its relation to good taste and good health: indeed the subject is one that I have constantly lectured on before Institutes and Societies of various kinds, but it seems to me that the field of the *mundus muliebris*, the field of mere millinery and trimmings, is to some extent already occupied by such papers as the *Queen* and the *Lady's Pictorial*, and that we should take a wider range, as well as a high standpoint, and deal not merely with what women wear, but with what they think, and what they feel. The *Lady's World* should be made the recognised organ for the expression of women's opinions on all subjects of literature, art, and modern life, and yet it should be a magazine that men could read with pleasure, and consider it a privilege to contribute to. We should get if possible the Princess Louise and the Princess Christian to contribute to it: an article from the latter on needlework for instance in connection with the Art School of which she is President would be very interesting. Carmen Sylva and Madame Adam should be got to write: Mrs Julia Ward Howe of Boston should be invited to contribute, as well as some of the other cultured women of America, while our list should include such women as Lady Archibald Campbell, a charming writer, Lady Ardilaun, who might give us some of her Irish experiences, Mrs Jeune, Miss Harrison, Miss Mary Robinson, Miss Olive Schreiner, the author of *South African Farm*; Lady Greville, whose life of Montrose is a very clever monograph, Miss Dorothy Tennant, Lady Verney, Lady Dilke, Lady Dufferin, Lady Constance Howard, Matthew Arnold's daughter, Lady Brassey, Lady Bective, Lady Rosebery, Lady Dorothy Nevill, who could write on the Walpoles, Mrs Singleton (Violet Fane), Lady Diana Huddleston, Lady Catherine Gaskell, Lady Paget, Miss Rosa Mulholland, Hon. Emily Lawless, Lady Harberton, Mrs Charles McLaren, Lady Pollock, Mrs Fawcett, Miss Pater (sister of the author of *Marius*) and others too numerous to name in a letter.

We should try to get such articles as Mrs Brookfield's on Thackeray's Letters, Miss Stoker's on the Letters of Sheridan, both of which appear this month in two magazines, and though many of our charming women have not had much literary experience they could write for us accounts of great collections of family pictures and the like. Lady Betty Lytton might give us an account of Knebworth (illustrated), or Lady Salisbury a description of Hatfield House: these last have of course written and published, but I don't see why many who have not done so should not make an essay. All women are flattered at being asked to write. Mrs Proctor also would be invaluable if she would give us some of her recollections, and an article by Lady Galway if we could get it would be delightful. But we should not rely exclusively on women, even for signed articles: artists have sex but art has none, and now and then an article by some man of letters would be of service.

Literary criticism I think might be done in the form of paragraphs: that is to say, not from the standpoint of the scholar or the pedant, but from the standpoint of what is pleasant to read: if a book is dull let us say nothing about it, if it is bright let us review it.

From time to time also we must have news from Girton and Newnham Colleges at Cambridge, and from the Oxford colleges for women, and invite articles from the members: Mrs Humphry Ward and Mrs Sidgwick should not be forgotten, and the wife of the young President of Magdalen, Oxford, might write on her own college, or, say, on the attitude of Universities towards women from the earliest times down to the present – a subject never fully treated of.

It seems to me also that just at present there is too much money spent on illustrations, particularly on illustrations of dress. They are also extremely unequal; many are charming, such as that on page 224 of the current number, but many look like advertisements and give an air to the magazine that one wants to avoid, the air of directly puffing some firm or *modiste*. A new cover also would be an improvement: the present one is not satisfactory.

With the new cover we should start our new names, and try and give the magazine a *cachet* at once: let dress have the end of the magazine; literature, art, travel and social studies the beginning. Music in a magazine is somewhat dull, no one wants it; a children's column would be much more popular. A popular serial story is absolutely necessary for the start. It need not be by a woman, and should be exciting but not tragic.

These are the outlines which for the moment suggest themselves to me, and in conclusion let me say that I will be very happy indeed to give any assistance I can in reconstructing the *Lady's World*, and making it the first woman's paper in England. To work for Messrs Cassell is a privilege which I fully recognise, to work with you a pleasure and a privilege that I look forward to. Believe me, dear Mr Reid, truly yours   OSCAR WILDE

To Wemyss Reid

[Late May 1887]   16 *Tite Street*
Dear Mr Wemyss Reid, The agreement seems to me to be right in every particular except that the preliminary salary should begin from May 1st, not June 1st. It is absolutely necessary to start at once, and I have already devoted a great deal of time to devising the scheme, and having interviews with people of position and importance.

Yesterday for instance I spent the whole afternoon with Mrs Jeune, who was very delighted with the idea of our project, and I drew up with her our list of names. Tonight I am sending her a letter to put before the Princess Christian, who will I think aid us. Tomorrow I start for Oxford to arrange about the Lady Margaret's article, and to meet some women of ability. We must have the Universities on our side. On Monday I have a meeting at Mrs Jeune's, about which she will write to you. I hope that Lady Salisbury will be there and I shall deliver a brief address.

I have already engaged Lady Greville and some others, and will go to Cambridge before the end of the month. All this and innumerable letters take up time and money, and to defer operations till June would be a mistake. I am resolved to throw myself into this thing, and have already had to give up work for several papers. I feel you will recognise this, and see that the salary should begin when the work begins. June, as you know, will be for the aristocracy a very busy month, so I want to complete our arrangements now. To start well is half the race. I also wish to go to Paris to see Madame Adam about a letter every two months. I find personal interviews necessary. And though I do not expect to make much till the magazine is started, I feel sure Messrs Cassell would not wish me to be at a loss however small. I am to see Lady Dilke soon, and though I do not propose to have her *till next year*, I feel we *should* have her. I hope to call on you soon and have another talk: I think I am sure of Lady Tweeddale, Lady Malmesbury, and Maud Stanley. With the exception of the date I accept the agreement, and the date I leave to you.

I grow very enthusiastic over our scheme, and *with your assistance* will make it a success. Truly yours   OSCAR WILDE

To Helena Sickert

[27 May 1887]   *16 Tite Street*
Dear Miss Nellie, I am going to become an Editor (for my sins or my virtues?) and want you to write me an article. The magazine will try to be representative of the thought and culture of the women of this century, and I am very anxious that those who have had university training, like yourself, should have an organ through which they can express their views on life and things.

As for the subject – a review of the change of Political Economy during the last few years? Or on the value of Political Economy in education? But choose *your own aspect* of the question. About eight pages of printed matter in length, the honorarium a guinea a page, which is the same as the *Nineteenth Century* pays, and more than most of the magazines. I hope you will do this for me, but let me know what subject you like best to write on.

My wife is at home the first and third Thursdays in each month. Do come next Thursday with your mother, and talk over the matter. Believe me, very sincerely yours   OSCAR WILDE
The magazine will be published by *Cassell's*. It is of course a secret just at present.

To an Unidentified Correspondent

[?September 1887]   *16 Tite Street*

Dear Madam, I am very much gratified at your kind permission to add your name to my list of contributors. The poem is full of power and pathos, and I will let you have a proof of it before publication.

How tragic the stories of the Irish Famine are! My father worked all through it, and afterwards wrote the Blue Book on it for the Government. He used to tell me marvellous tales about it. I am very glad you have taken one of the incidents in it as a motive for a poem. Very faithfully yours

OSCAR WILDE

Despite living in London and integrating himself into English Society, Wilde retained a strong sense of his Irish background and was a keen though passive supporter of the Nationalist cause. The poem never appeared in the magazine, possibly because of the increasingly sensitive issue of Irish Home Rule.

To Wemyss Reid

[5 September 1887]   *16 Tite Street*

Dear Mr Wemyss Reid, I am very anxious that you should make a final appeal to the Directors to alter the name of the magazine I am to edit for them from the *Lady's World* to the *Woman's World*. The present name of the magazine has a certain taint of vulgarity about it, that will always militate against the success of the new issue, and is also extremely misleading. It is quite applicable to the magazine in its present state; it will not be applicable to a magazine that aims at being the organ of women of intellect, culture, and position.

This is not merely my view, but is undoubtedly the view of those whom we want to contribute. In writing to the various women whose names stand now on the contributors' list I carefully avoided mentioning the name of the magazine, but in certain cases I have been obliged to tell it, and on every occasion of this kind the name has met with the strongest opposition.

Miss Thackeray has spoken to me more than once on the subject, and has told me very candidly that she does not care about having her name connected with a magazine that has so vulgar a title, and that had I not been the editor she would have definitely refused. Lady Verney first consented to write an article, but on hearing the name of the magazine withdrew her promise; 'I have not the courage', she writes, 'to contribute to a magazine with such a title,' so I have been obliged to remove her name from the list. Miss Fletcher, the author of the serial, has spoken and written to me on the subject in the strongest terms. Some days ago I received the enclosed post-card from Lady Margaret Majendie, which I beg you will read to the Directors: Lady Lindsay writes to the same effect: the same view has been expressed by Miss Agnes Giberne, Miss Edmonds, Mrs Frederika MacDonald, and Miss Orne, and I feel quite sure that the retention of the present name will be a serious bar to our success. It would also be impossible to ask any prominent man of letters to contribute to the magazine under its present title, and I see quite clearly that it will not be possible to rely entirely on women for our contributions.

From the commercial point of view I see that the slight change demanded by the contributors will be of no small advantage in emphasising the new departure: I may mention that the *Girls' Own Magazine* by altering its name to *Atalanta* has succeeded in gaining a staff of writers of a very distinguished order, including men like Ruskin, Walter Besant, Andrew Lang, Rider Haggard, Anstey and others, and I have no doubt that it will be a great success. For our magazine there is a definite opening and a definite mission, but without an alteration in the title it will not be able to avail itself of its opportunity. Its name should definitely separate itself from such papers as the *Lady* and the *Lady's Pictorial*. I remain, yours truly   OSCAR WILDE

To Anne Richardson

[?September 1887]   *16 Tite Street*
Dear Miss Richardson, I think an article on *The Family of Augustus* would be most interesting, an account of the home life of the imperial ménage, taking in Augustus himself, Livia, Julia, the mother of Marcellus, etc. The artificial efforts of Augustus to recreate the old Roman type of household, and the terrible tragedy of the shame and exile of Julia, are full of suggestion. It was too late in the world's history for the basis of morals to be found in legislation and state sanction – Augustus hardly realised that, but the Stoics had done so for centuries: a few remarks on the Stoic men and women would be valuable in this connection, as few people – amongst the magazine public – realise what an era was *individualism* in morals. We are now returning to the old conception of socialism, of the state – progress being really, in my opinion, a *pendulum* affair. The poets and artists in their relation to the court of Augustus should be noticed and something said about the influence of the personality of Cleopatra – but all lightly touched as the French, who are so good on the Roman Empire, have done. Any busts in the museum will be copied that you select. The article should not be more than 3000 or 3500 words. I do not require it this year. Very faithfully yours   OSCAR WILDE

To Mrs Bernard Beere

[?Late October 1887]   *Beaufort Club, 32 Dover Street*
My dear Bernie, I am sure you will be very sorry to hear that I have been in great trouble. Our youngest boy has been so ill that we thought he could never recover, and I was so unhappy over it that all my duties and letters escaped me, otherwise I would have been delighted to have had the chance of seeing you.

I am afraid as it is ten years since I lived in Dublin that all my friends have vanished – all that is who would have appreciated you, and whom you would have liked, but I have no doubt that by this time you are the idol of Hibernia, and all the College boys are in love with you. If they are not, at least, they must have lost their old admiration for wit and beauty.

I hope you drive about on outside cars: there are several Dion Boucicaults on the stand opposite the Shelbourne who are delightful creatures.

How nice of the Earthquake to wait till you had left. *Après vous* – *le tremblement de terre!* Poor Edmund! I hope he had not to run about *en déshabille*.

When do you come back? Why should the cottage be left lonely? Your last dinner was a marvel, one of the pleasantest I was ever at. We have no *lionne* now but Ouida. With best wishes, believe me, ever yours   OSCAR

To Violet Fane

[Circa 12 November 1887]   *16 Tite Street*
Dear 'Violet Fane', I am charmed to think I may have the chance of publishing some of your dainty, witty, fascinating prose, and if you abandon 'the harmless necessary cauliflower' for a diet of roast snipe and burgundy I feel sure that you will not regret it. However, even vegetarianism, in your hands, would make a capital article – its connection with philosophy is very curious – dating from the earliest Greek days, and taken by the Greeks from the East – and so is its connection with modern socialism, atheism, nihilism, anarchy, and other political creeds. It is strange that the most violent republicans I know are all vegetarians: Brussels sprouts seem to make people bloodthirsty, and those who live on lentils and artichokes are always calling for the gore of the aristocracy, and for the severed heads of kings. Your vegetarianism has given you a wise apathy – so at least you told me once – but in the political sphere a diet of green herbs seems dangerous. Pray send me your poem on the Mer-baby, and I will try and get Dorothy Tennant's illustration. It will be a dainty page of the magazine, and shall have the best place. Very truly yours   OSCAR WILDE

Granger was a pupil of E. W. Godwin and had overseen some of the building work on Wilde's Tite Street house. He was now a lecturer (later Professor) in Classics and Philosophy at Nottingham University and had sent Wilde his book The Psychological Basis of Fine Art.

To Frank Granger

[Postmark 17 November 1887]   *16 Tite Street*
Dear Mr Granger, Many thanks for your interesting book, which I am reading with great pleasure. There are some few points in which I cannot help differing from you, but your style is quite admirable, and your ideas most suggestive. If people would study art from the psychological and physiological point of view, as you do, there would be far less prejudice in aesthetic matters, and far more understanding. After all, preferences in art are very valueless, what is needed is to understand the conditions of each art, and to be, as Goethe said, ready for the reception of impressions.

I am delighted to see dear Godwin's name on the dedication page. In the November number of the *Woman's World* you will find a most appreciative notice of him by Lady Archibald Campbell. Believe me, truly yours

OSCAR WILDE

The book which Little had sent Wilde was his novel Whose Wife Shall She Be?. *Gil Blas, in Le Sage's picaresque novel of the same name, is entrusted with the delicate task of criticising his master, the Archbishop's homilies should the need arise, only to find himself dismissed the first time he dares to do so.*

To J. S. Little

[15 January 1888]   *16 Tite Street*
My dear Little, Thank you very much for your charming book, which I have read with great pleasure. You ask me to give you a criticism of it, but Gil Blas is plucking my sleeve and reminding me of the Archbishop. However, here is my opinion.

The book is a little too crowded: the motive is hardly clear enough: if Gwendoline is the heroine we should hear more of her: if she is not, the last chapters emphasise her too much. Captain Breutnall is not a success: his death is merely the premature disappearance of a shell-jacket: I decline to mourn with Gwendoline over someone who is not properly introduced.

Upon the other hand Ralph, Grace, and Mrs Landford are all admirable: they are your real characters: Gwendoline seems to me unnecessary. Your

descriptions are excellent, whether of scenery or of women, and I wish that I could write a novel, but I can't! Give my love to Grace, who is very adorable, and believe me, truly yours OSCAR WILDE
(A rash letter)

The Happy Prince and Other Tales was published in May by David Nutt. It was illustrated by Walter Crane and Jacomb Hood. Despite what Wilde wrote to Gladstone, elsewhere he described the volume as 'meant partly for children, and partly for those who have kept the childlike faculties of wonder and joy', and also 'written, not for children, but for childlike people from eighteen to eighty'.

To John Ruskin

[June 1888] *16 Tite Street*
Dear Mr Ruskin, I send you my little book, *The Happy Prince and Other Tales*, and need hardly say how gratified I will be if you find in it any charm or beauty.

It was a great pleasure to me to meet you again: the dearest memories of my Oxford days are my walks and talks with you, and from you I learned nothing but what was good. How else could it be? There is in you something of prophet, of priest, and of poet, and to you the gods gave eloquence such as they have given to none other, so that your message might come to us with the fire of passion, and the marvel of music, making the deaf to hear, and the blind to see. I wish I had something better to give you, but, such as it is, take it with my love. OSCAR WILDE

To Florence Balcombe Stoker

[June 1888] *[London]*
Dear Florrie, Will you give me the pleasure of accepting a copy of my book of fairy tales? I hope you will like them, simple though they are; and I think you will enjoy Crane's pretty pictures, and Jacomb Hood's designs. With kind regards to Bram OSCAR

To W. E. Gladstone

[June 1888] *16 Tite Street*
Dear Mr Gladstone, Will you do me the honour of accepting a copy of a little book I have just brought out, called *The Happy Prince*? It is only a collection of short stories, and is really meant for children, but I should like to have the pleasure of presenting it, such as it is, to one whom I, and all

who have Celtic blood in their veins, must ever honour and revere, and to whom my country is so deeply indebted. Believe me, dear Mr Gladstone, most faithfully and sincerely yours   OSCAR WILDE

To Alfred Nutt

[Circa 13 June 1888]   *16 Tite Street*
Dear Mr Nutt, I will try and arrange with Miss Terry: it certainly would be charming to hear her read 'The Happy Prince'.

I find I have forgotten the *Century Guild Hobby Horse*. Will you kindly send them a copy for review – at 28 Southampton Street, Strand, WC. The *Irish Times* I suppose has got its copy? Also, would it not be well to have a card for the booksellers to hang up in their shops? It may show Crane's frontispiece as well as the title etc. of the book. And is it not time for a few advertisements? *Punch* and the *World* are capital papers to advertise in – once. Mr Pater has written me a wonderful letter about my prose, so I am in high spirits. Yours faithfully   OSCAR WILDE

To Richard Le Gallienne

[?15 June 1888]   *16 Tite Street*
This is in case you have not got my letter – come and dine at 7 o'c. Don't dress. I am so sorry you are leaving on Saturday.

Since I have met you I have been re-reading your poems, seeing you, hearing you through them. How the finely woven veil of form reveals in all the arts! I can recognise a whole life in the choice of an adjective. All your romance, your fine and ardent love of beauty, your delicacy and refinement of mood, I recognise them all in your work. I have no doubt you will, in every form of literature, do delightful work, and your prose should be very good for you have distinction. Your sincere friend

OSCAR WILDE

To Lady Monckton

[?June–July 1888]   *16 Tite Street*
Dear Lady Monckton, I hope your son is better and that he won't go on reckless yachting tours again.

With regard to the article, if you did not care to write about acting as an art, you might still write on acting as a profession – on the advisability of training actors: on the advantages of learning by *experience* in the provinces, as opposed to the French method of teaching the *principles* in a *conservatoire*: or on modern plays? melodrama, farcical comedy, high comedy, drama, poetical tragedy, which is the best suited for our stage: why the French write, as a rule, better plays than the English.

Any subject of this kind treated by you in an article of four or five pages would be most attractive. When you get your holiday think it over – it would only take you a few days to write.

We look forward to seeing you on the 13th. Truly yours   OSCAR WILDE

To Thomas Hutchinson

[13 July 1888]   *16 Tite Street*

My dear Sir, I must thank you for your very charming and graceful letter, but I am afraid that I don't think as much of the young Student as you do. He seems to me a rather shallow young man, and almost as bad as the girl he thinks he loves. The nightingale is the true lover, if there is one. She, at least, is Romance, and the Student and the girl are, like most of us, unworthy of Romance. So, at least, it seems to me, but I like to fancy that there may be many meanings in the tale, for in writing it, and the others, I did not start with an idea and clothe it in form, but began with a form and strove to make it beautiful enough to have many secrets, and many answers. Truly yours   OSCAR WILDE

Smithers, a Sheffield solicitor with a sideline in printing erotica, was to figure largely in Wilde's post-prison years as the only publisher who would still touch his books. He collaborated with Sir Richard Burton, translator of the unexpurgated Arabian Nights, *during Burton's last years and published much of Aubrey Beardsley's work. Wilde later gave him the manuscript of* The Happy Prince.

To Leonard Smithers

[Postmark 13 July 1888]   *16 Tite Street*

My dear Sir, I must very sincerely thank you for your charming letter, and am glad to think that 'The Happy Prince' has found so sympathetic an admirer, so gracious a lover. The story is an attempt to treat a tragic modern problem in a form that aims at delicacy and imaginative treatment: it is a reaction against the purely imitative character of modern art – and now that literature has taken to blowing loud trumpets I cannot but be pleased that some ear has cared to listen to the low music of a little reed. So I thank you again, and remain, faithfully yours   OSCAR WILDE

'The Young King' was due to be published in the Christmas number of the Lady's
Pictorial *with illustrations by Partridge. In 1892 Partridge caricatured Wilde
good-naturedly in* Punch *over smoking during his curtain-call at the première of*
Lady Windermere's Fan *and over his threat to emigrate to France when* Salomé
was banned from the English stage.

To Bernard Partridge

[Postmark 12 October 1888]   16 *Tite Street*
My dear Partridge, I was away at Clumber and unable to come and see you
while you were at work on my story, but Gibbons yesterday showed me
some of the drawings and I cannot help writing to you to tell you how
charmed I am by them. You have seen the Young King just as I hoped you
would see him, and made him by delicate line and graceful design the most
winsome and fascinating lad possible. I thank you very much for your
beautiful and poetic work, and I can only hope that I may again have you
to illustrate some story of mine. Crane, whom I admire very much, is always
haunted by a touch of formal mannerism: you have perfect freedom and
grace in all you do. Believe me, very sincerely yours   OSCAR WILDE

*Ross, a young man of seventeen from a well-connected Canadian background, was
about to go up to King's College, Cambridge. He had stayed with the Wildes for
two months the previous year when, it is said, he became Wilde's first homosexual
lover. Their friendship was more constant and less tempestuous than Wilde's with
Alfred Douglas and flourished after Wilde's release from prison. After Wilde's death
Ross became his literary executor.*

To Robert Ross

[Circa 13 October 1888]   16 *Tite Street*
My dear Bobbie, I congratulate you. University life will suit you admirably,
though I shall miss you in town. Enclosed is the praise of the Philistines. Are
you in College or in lodgings? I hope in College; it is much nicer. Do you know
Oscar Browning? You will find him everything that is kind and pleasant.

I have been speaking at Stratford about Shakespeare, but in spite of
that enjoyed my visit immensely. My reception was semi-royal, and the
volunteers played God Save the Queen in my honour. Ever yours

OSCAR WILDE

William Henley was a poet as well as being the editor of the Scots Observer *and
Wilde's review of* A Book of Verses *appeared in the December issue of the*

Woman's World. *His friendship with Wilde was short-lived and ended after the* Scots Observer's *vicious attack on* Dorian Gray *in 1890. Wilde never did join the Savile Club despite being put up for membership.*

To W. E. Henley

[Circa 16 October 1888]   16 *Tite Street*

My dear Henley, It will give me great pleasure to lunch with you at the Savile on Saturday, though I am afraid that I shall be like a poor lion who has rashly intruded into a den of fierce Daniels. As for proposing me for the Savile, that is of course one of your merry jests.

I am still reading your volume, preparatory to a review which I hope will be ready by the year 1900. I have decided that a great deal of it is poetry, and that, of the rest, part is poesy, and part . . . [*Wilde's ellipsis*]

The weather here is rather cloudy this morning, but I hope it will clear up, though I am told that dampness is good for agriculture. Pray remember me to Mrs Henley, and believe me, ever yours   OSCAR WILDE

In October Jane Wilde, now sixty-seven, moved from Mayfair to Oakley Street not far from where her son was living. Her income from property in Ireland was small and sporadic and she made little from her regular contributions to the Pall Mall Gazette *and the* Queen, *but Oscar discreetly paid her bills when he could afford to. He helped canvass support for a grant of £100 from the Royal Literary Fund which she received the following month, and applied on her behalf for a Civil List Pension based on his father's work for the Irish Censuses. It was approved in May 1890 and she was paid £70 a year until she died.*

To Theodore Watts

[?October 1888]   16 *Tite Street*

My dear Watts, Thank you for your kind letter, and tell Swinburne how gratified my mother is at his prompt and generous response to her request. I hope to be able to get my mother on the Civil List, but it takes a long time and there are many applicants, though few I think with my mother's claims.

Wednesday is our day. You will always be most welcome if you come. I want to talk to you about a lot of things from the moon down to Henley, my last pet lunatic and hers. Ever yours   OSCAR WILDE

To W. E. Henley

[November–December 1888]   *16 Tite Street*

My dear Henley, I am charmed you like my article. I tried to express as nicely as I could my feelings about the Marsyas of the early part of your book, and the Apollo of the latter, to me the lovelier portion. I hope you have read what I say about poor Sharp. I think I have been fair all round – as fair as an Irishman with a temperament ever wants to be. I am dining with Willie Richmond at Hammersmith on Saturday, but if I can come in late will try to do so. I have sent Dunn a wicked little symphony in yellow, suggested by seeing an omnibus (yellow omnibus) crawl across Blackfriars Bridge one foggy day about a week ago. He expresses himself 'quite charmed' but says, not unwisely, that he is uncertain about publishing poetry! So I have produced my effect. Ever yours   OSCAR

Marsyas was a mortal who challenged Apollo to a musical competition, lost and was flayed alive for his pains. Wilde refers often to this myth in his work, and especially after prison in his letters, casting himself in the tragic and hubristic role of the loser.

To W. E. Henley

[?December 1888]   *16 Tite Street*

Quite right, my dear 'Marsyas et Apollo'; to learn how to write English prose I have studied the prose of France. I am charmed that you recognise it: that shows I have succeeded. I am also charmed that no one else does: that shows I have succeeded also.

Yes! Flaubert is my master, and when I get on with my translation of the *Tentation* I shall be Flaubert II, *Roi par grâce de Dieu*, and I hope something else beyond.

Where do you think I am not so good? I want very much to know. Of course it is, to me, a new genre. Ever yours   OSCAR

Despite Wilde's glowing review of his book, Henley took a puritan dislike to Wilde, doubtless tinged with envy at Wilde's apparently effortless success. Apart from his attack on Dorian Gray he also described The Portrait of Mr W. H. *as immoral and condemned* The Ballad of Reading Gaol *in 1898 as unrealistic rubbish.*

To W. E. Henley

[?December 1888]   16 *Tite Street*

My dear Henley, Your distinction is admirable. Flaubert did not write French prose, but the prose of a great artist who happened to be French. As for your critics, when a book has so much of life and so much of beauty as yours has, it must inevitably appeal differently to different temperaments.

Beauty of form produces not one effect alone, but many effects. Surely you do not think that criticism is like the answer to a sum? The richer the work of art the more diverse are the true interpretations. There is not one answer only, but many answers. I pity that book on which critics are agreed. It must be a very obvious and shallow production. Congratulate yourself on the diversity of *contemporary* tongues. The worst of posterity is that it has but one voice. *A vous*   OSCAR

To Robert Ross

[?Late December 1888]   16 *Tite Street*

My dear Bobbie, The kitten is quite lovely. It does not *look* white, indeed it looks a sort of tortoise-shell colour, or a grey barred with velvety dark browns, but as you *said* it was white I have given orders that it is always to be spoken of as the 'white kitten'. The children are enchanted with it, and sit, one on each side of its basket, worshipping. It seems pensive. Perhaps it is thinking of some dim rose-garden in Persia, and wondering why it is kept in this chill England.

I hope you are enjoying yourself at Cambridge. Whatever people may say against Cambridge it is certainly the best preparatory school for Oxford that I know. After this insult I had better stop. Ever yours   OSCAR WILDE

A chance meeting laid the ground for a new phase in Wilde's literary development – the controversial essay in the form of a Platonic dialogue. The first to be published in the January issue of the Nineteenth Century *was 'The Decay of Lying' arguing for a return to imagination in literature rather than the current vogue for realism. In it he refers to Mrs Humphry Ward's best-selling three-volume novel* Robert Elsmere *as 'a masterpiece of the genre ennuyeux', a judgement with which today few would disagree. The essay became, in a sense, his literary manifesto, the practical application of which, a year later, found its voice in* The Picture of Dorian Gray.

To an Unknown Correspondent

[?1888–9]   16 *Tite Street*

My dear Sir, I was very sorry that I had not the opportunity of talking to you at the McLarens – English people are stupid about introductions and it was not till after you had left that I realised who you were.

As for an article – well, I am horribly, or delightfully indolent, and really write very little – but dialogues always fascinate me. Would you like a dialogue of about 10,000 words? I think it would be about the relations of Art to Ethics – I have something to say about the subject. If so what price would you offer me? I never resist large temptations. If you have a day to spare in London, pray let me have the pleasure of calling on you. Truly yours   OSCAR WILDE

William Courtney was a Fellow of New College, Oxford, an author and a journalist. His Life of John Stuart Mill *had just appeared. He joined the* Daily Telegraph *in 1890 and became its literary editor and dramatic critic. When Wilde's* De Profundis *appeared posthumously in 1905, he wrote to Robert Ross describing it as 'a wonderful book'.*

To W. L. Courtney

[?January 1889]   16 *Tite Street*

My dear Courtney, Thank you very much for your admirable little book on Mill, which I have read with great pleasure. It seems to me to be excellently done, and its conciseness and directness are excellent examples for others to follow. The whole account of Mrs Taylor (who I suppose is the representative of the Seductive Method in thought) interests me very much. As for Mill as a thinker – a man who knew nothing of Plato and Darwin gives me very little. His reputation is curious to me. I gain nothing, I have gained nothing from him – an arid, dry man with moods of sentiment – a type that is poor, and, I fancy, common. But Darwinism has of course shattered many reputations besides his, and I hope that individual liberty has had its day, for a time. His later religious views show an astounding silliness and sentimentality. But your book is admirable. Many thanks for it. Ever yours   OSCAR WILDE

To Mrs George Lewis

[January 1889]   16 Tite Street
My dear Mrs Lewis, Thank you so much for your charming and welcome letter. I am delighted you like the article: underneath the fanciful form it hides some truths, or perhaps some great half-truths, about art, which I think require to be put forward, and of which some are, I think, quite new, and none the worse for that. I have blown my trumpet against the gates of dullness, and I hope some shaft has hit *Robert Elsmere* between the joints of his nineteenth edition. It was delightful work writing the article, and it is equally delightful to know that Lady Betty enjoyed it. Ever yours

OSCAR WILDE

To an Income-Tax Inspector

[?April 1889]   Woman's World, *La Belle Sauvage, Ludgate Hill*
Sir, It was arranged last year that I should send in my income-tax return from Chelsea where I reside, as I am resigning my position here and will not be with Messrs Cassell after August. I think it would be better to continue that arrangement. I wish your notices were not so agitating and did not hold out such dreadful threats. A penalty of fifty pounds sounds like a relic of mediæval torture. Your obedient servant   OSCAR WILDE

Wilde's story on Mr W. H. for which he received £25, was published in the July issue of Blackwood's Magazine. *He later expanded it, hoping for publication in book form, but the critics' reception of* Dorian Gray *in the meantime frightened off potential publishers, who felt that even the literary treatment of same-sex love was too dangerous a subject to handle (see p. 180). The full version was only published in 1921.*

To William Blackwood

[April 1889]   16 Tite Street
Dear Sir, I remember reading some interesting articles on Shakespeare's Sonnets in *Blackwood*, and would be very pleased if you would care to publish a story on the subject of the Sonnets which I have written. It is called 'The Portrait of Mr W. H.' and contains an entirely new view on the subject of the identity of the young man to whom the sonnets are addressed. I will ask you to return me the manuscript in case you decide not to publish it. Truly yours   OSCAR WILDE

Robert Cunninghame Graham was the most picturesque Scot of his time. A traveller, poet, horseman, socialist and sometime politician, he was involved in the Trafalgar Square Riot of November 1887, beaten by the police and imprisoned for six weeks. A few days after this letter, his wife lectured to the Bloomsbury Socialists insisting on the complete political emancipation of women. Wilde's own somewhat idealistic essay 'The Soul of Man under Socialism' was published in 1891.

To Mrs R. B. Cunninghame Graham

[Circa 30 June 1889]   16 *Tite Street*

Dear Mrs Cunninghame Graham, I wish so much I could come and hear you on Tuesday, but I am dining out. I think your subject most interesting, but what is to become of an indolent hedonist like myself if Socialism and the Church join forces against me? I want to stand apart, and look on, being neither for God nor for his enemies. This, I hope, will be allowed.

Seriously speaking, however, what I want to see is a reconciliation of Socialism with Science. Ritchie, in his *Darwinism and Politics*, has tried to do this, but his book, which I suppose you have seen, is very slight and amateurish.

Give my love to your delightful and dangerous husband. Ever yours

OSCAR WILDE

To Robert Ross

[July 1889]   16 *Tite Street*

Dear Bobbie, Your telegram (of course it was *yours*) has just arrived. So many thanks for it: it was really sweet of you to send it, for indeed the story is half yours, and but for you would not have been written. Are you well again? Terror for Cyril kept me away, but now I may come, may I not?

Write to me a letter. Now that Willie Hughes has been revealed to the world, we must have another secret. Ever yours, dear Bobbie   O. W.

To W. E. Henley

[July 1889]   16 *Tite Street*

My dear Henley, To be exiled to Scotland to edit a Tory paper in the wilderness is bad enough, but not to see the wonder and beauty of my discovery of the real Mr W. H. is absolutely dreadful. I sympathise deeply with you, and can only beg you to return to London where you will be able to appreciate a real work of art.

The Philistines in their vilest forms have seized on you. I am so disappointed.

Still, when you return you will be welcome; all is not lost. Ever yours

OSCAR

Lawrence Barrett, the American actor-manager, was in Europe and had reopened negotiations with Wilde about The Duchess of Padua. *It was eventually produced for three weeks in New York in January 1891, but to little critical enthusiasm.*

To Robert Ross

[Late July 1889]   *Kreuznach*

Dear Bobbie, I am actually in Germany! I had an invitation to come here to see somebody about a play, and I thought it would be a superb opportunity for forgetting the language. So I arrived on Saturday after a day's journey from Cologne by steamer.

The Rhine is of course tedious, the vineyards are formal and dull, and as far as I can judge the inhabitants of Germany are American.

I return this week, via Wiesbaden and Ostend. Somebody I used to like is at Ostend, and I have promised to stay a day.

I am charmed with what you say about the little Princess – the Infanta: in style (in *mere* style as honest Besant would say) it is my best story. The *Guardian* on Mr W. H. you must send to me at Tite Street. Write to me there: I shall be home on Saturday. And oh! Bobbie, let us have an evening together. What ages since we had a talk! Yours, with much love   OSCAR

The publication of 'Mr W. H.' prompted Charles Ricketts to 'produce' the portrait itself and send it to Wilde. He lived with Charles Shannon in The Vale, Chelsea from where they published a magazine, the Dial. *Ricketts and Shannon together were responsible for the design and decoration of most of Wilde's books from this time on.*

To Charles Ricketts

[?Autumn 1889]   *16 Tite Street*

My dear Ricketts, It is not a forgery at all; it is an authentic Clouet of the highest *artistic* value. It is absurd of you and Shannon to try and take me in! As if I did not know the master's touch, or was no judge of frames!

Seriously, my dear fellow, it is quite wonderful, and your giving it to me is an act so charming that, in despair of showing you any return, I at once call upon the gods to shower gold and roses on the Vale, or on that part of the Vale where the De Morgans do not live. I am really most grateful (no! that is a horrid word: I am never grateful) I am flattered and fascinated, and I hope we shall always be friends and see each other often.

I must come round and enjoy the company of the Dialists – *par nobile* as they are. Sincerely yours   OSCAR WILDE

In August Stoddart had come to London in search of stories to publish in Lippincott's Magazine. *As a result Wilde offered him first 'The Fisherman and his Soul', which Stoddart rejected, and then* The Picture of Dorian Gray.

To J. M. Stoddart

30 September [1889]   16 *Tite Street*
Dear Mr Stoddart, I have just returned from France, and find your letter of 18th waiting for me.

You ask me to try and send you my story 'early in October'; surely you mean 'early in November'? If you could be content with 30,000 words I might be able to post the manuscript to you the first week in November, but October is of course out of the question. If this date, and 30,000 words will do, telegraph to me on receipt of this. If not, it will be sufficient to write. I was very pleased to see you again, and I hope you will often come to London. Believe me truly yours   OSCAR WILDE

To Henrietta Barnett

[?November 1889]   16 *Tite Street*
Dear Mrs Barnett, I am afraid I have nothing just at present suitable for a lecture, and I have been ill for a long time with malaria, caught during a rash visit to Provence at vintage time – it comes and goes, but I can never be certain of myself. Some day I will give Toynbee Hall a lecture on Irish Art if I can get someone to help me with a magic lantern – I think that pictures are really necessary to give a proper idea of what one is talking of – but I have never yet had pictures in any lecture.

I hope to have the pleasure of seeing you tomorrow and remain truly yours   OSCAR WILDE

To Mrs Bernard Beere

[?December 1889]   *Lyric Club, Piccadilly East*

My dear Bernie, I am so sorry to hear you are tired and worn out. Remember that Sarah never really *acts* more than twice a week, if so often. You must be careful, and yet I know your intense artistic conscientiousness, and your dislike of merely sauntering through a part. I long to see you. Last Sunday I was with the Abbot of Abbots Hill. If possible, I will come tomorrow.

Do take care of yourself, and believe me, ever affectionately yours

OSCAR

To J. M. Stoddart

[Date of receipt 17 December 1889]   *16 Tite Street*

Dear Mr Stoddart, Thanks for your letter. I am glad to say that I am much better now: it was an attack of malaria, that enervating and wretched malady.

I have invented a new story, which is better than 'The Fisherman and his Soul', and I am quite ready to set to work at once on it. It will be ready by the end of March. But I would ask you to let me have half the honorarium in advance – £100 – as I have a great many offers of work, and having been idle for four months require some money. I hope you will let me have this as soon as possible.

Believe me with kind regards ever yours   OSCAR WILDE

The Woman's World *and Wilde parted company in October 1889. It must have been an amicable arrangement, as Reid asked Wilde to contribute to his new magazine, the* Speaker. *Wilde wrote on the Chinese philosopher Chuang Tzu for the February issue and on Pater's latest book,* Appreciations, *in March.*

To Wemyss Reid

[18 December 1889]   *16 Tite Street*

My dear Wemyss Reid, Thanks for your letter: I am of course a little disappointed at not being either your Dramatic or your Art Critic. I had hoped indeed to have had both offices. I will try what I can to do in the way of a Causerie, but I know I write best on a definite subject and have not much discursive journalistic faculty. The other article I will let you have by the 28th.

Your dinner was really delightful, and I enjoyed myself immensely. With best wishes for the *Speaker*, believe me truly yours   OSCAR WILDE

James Whistler to the Editor of *Truth*

[Early January 1890]   *Chelsea*

Most valiant Truth, Among your ruthless exposures of the shams of today, nothing, I confess, have I enjoyed with keener relish than your late tilt at that arch-impostor and pest of the period – the all-pervading plagiarist!

I learn, by the way, that in America he may, under the 'Law of '84', as it is called, be criminally prosecuted, incarcerated, and made to pick oakum, as he has hitherto picked brains – and pockets!

How was it that, in your list of culprits, you omitted that fattest of offenders – our own Oscar?

His methods are brought again freshly to my mind, by the indefatigable and tardy Romeike, who sends me newspaper cuttings of 'Mr Herbert Vivian's Reminiscences', in which, among other entertaining anecdotes, is told at length the story of Oscar simulating the becoming pride of author, upon a certain evening, in the club of the Academy students, and arrogating to himself the responsibility of the lecture, with which, at his earnest prayer, I had in good fellowship crammed him, that he might not add deplorable failure to foolish appearance, in his anomalous position as art expounder, before his clear-headed audience.

He went forth, on that occasion, as my St John – but, forgetting that humility should be his chief characteristic, and unable to withstand the unaccustomed respect with which his utterances were received, he not only trifled with my shoe, but bolted with the latchet!

Mr Vivian, in his book, tells us, further on, that lately, in an article in the *Nineteenth Century* on 'The Decay of Lying', Mr Wilde has deliberately and incautiously incorporated, 'without a word of comment', a portion of the well-remembered letter in which, after admitting his rare appreciation and amazing memory, I acknowledge that 'Oscar has the courage of the opinions – of others!'

My recognition of this, his latest proof of open admiration, I send him in the following little note, which I fancy you may think *à propos* to publish, as an example to your readers, in similar circumstances, of noble generosity in sweet reproof, tempered, as it should be, to the lamb in his condition:

'Oscar, you have been down the area again, I see!

I had forgotten you, and so allowed your hair to grow over the sore place. And now, while I looked the other way, you have stolen *your own scalp*! and potted it in more of your pudding.

Labby has pointed out that, for the detected plagiarist, there is still one way to self-respect (besides hanging himself, of course), and that is for him boldly to declare, *"Je prends mon bien là où je le trouve."*

You, Oscar, can go further, and with fresh effrontery, that will bring you the envy of all criminal confrères, unblushingly boast, *"Moi, je prends son bien là où je le trouve!"'*

To the Editor of *Truth*

[Early January 1890]   16 *Tite Street*
Sir, I can hardly imagine that the public are in the very smallest degree interested in the shrill shrieks of 'Plagiarism' that proceed from time to time out of the lips of silly vanity or incompetent mediocrity.

However, as Mr James Whistler has had the impertinence to attack me with both venom and vulgarity in your columns, I hope you will allow me to state that the assertions contained in his letter are as deliberately untrue as they are deliberately offensive.

The definition of a disciple as one who has the courage of the opinions of his master is really too old even for Mr Whistler to be allowed to claim it, and as for borrowing Mr Whistler's ideas about art, the only thoroughly original ideas I have ever heard him express have had reference to his own superiority over painters greater than himself.

It is a trouble for any gentleman to have to notice the lucubrations of so ill-bred and ignorant a person as Mr Whistler, but your publication of his insolent letter left me no option in the matter. I remain, sir, faithfully yours

OSCAR WILDE

To Charles Whitmore

[?Late January 1890]   16 *Tite Street*
Dear Mr Whitmore, I write to you as our Chelsea member to ask you to help with your influence and recommendation my old friend Dr Fisher of Oakley Street, who is applying for the post of Divisional Surgeon to the Police vacant by poor Daniell's death.

Dr Fisher, like Dr Daniell, was a pupil of my Father's, and we have known him and respected him for many years. He is hard working, energetic, and full of sound sense – just the man for the post. Since my marriage he has been my family doctor, and though you converted him to Unionism at the last election, we have not changed him! So I am not helping my party in this matter. Believe me, truly yours   OSCAR WILDE

To Beatrice Allhusen

[?Early 1890]   16 *Tite Street*

Dear Mrs Allhusen, It is most kind of you to ask me to Bournemouth. I am so busy at present I cannot get away, but if I can manage it a little later I will certainly ask you to take me in for a couple of nights. Bournemouth is delightful, and we would have long talks, on the things of Life and Art. I have just finished my first long story, and am tired out. I am afraid it is rather like my own life – all conversation and no action. I can't describe action: my people sit in chairs and chatter. I wonder what you will think of it. I will send you a copy. You are quite right to assail me about letters being unanswered. My only excuse is that I am incorrigible. With many thanks, believe me yours   OSCAR WILDE

As before with Whistler, Wilde very seldom allowed himself to express anger in his correspondence and only when he felt personally insulted. Vivian was a young journalist on the Sun *with whom Wilde had conversed socially at some length in mid-1889 and to whom he had recounted in light-hearted fashion how Cyril was refusing to say his prayers. Vivian included this story and a personal letter of Wilde's in a series of memoirs which were serialised in the* Sun *without Wilde's permission. In them he accused Wilde of plagiarism and also referred to him as the 'fairy godfather' of the work.*

To Herbert Vivian

[Postmark 17 May 1890]   16 *Tite Street*

Dear Mr Vivian, I am so sorry that you do not appreciate the courtesy of the form I used in addressing you on Wednesday night. I was not asking you to do me a favour: I was asserting my right to prevent my name being in any way associated with a book that, from the extracts I have read of it, I must admit I consider extremely vulgar and offensive. No one has the right to make one godfather to a dirty baby against one's will, or to put forward as a result of a suggestion of one's own a book with which no gentleman would wish to have his name associated. You may say that you refuse to recognise this right: that is possible: but by doing so you make a very wilful surrender of that position you hold as a gentleman, a position for which your birth and culture give you the fullest qualifications. Believe me, it would be an ungentlemanly thing to do, and I should be sorry to think that any Cambridge man could be wilfully guilty of such conduct, conduct which combines the inaccuracy of the eavesdropper with the method of the blackmailer. Meeting you socially, I, in a moment which I greatly regret, happened to tell you a story about my little boy. Without asking my permission you publish this in a vulgar newspaper and in a vulgar, inaccurate and offensive form, to the great pain of my wife, who naturally does not wish to see her children paraded for the amusement of the uncouth. As a gentleman you had no right to do that, any more than you had to publish a letter of mine without my permission. You wrote of me personally with gross and impertinent familiarity. You may not be conscious of this, but you did so. It was an error of taste on your part. When you are older you will recognise it. As you cannot or will not understand the courtesy of a form of address, pray understand that you have no right to make use of my name in connection with your book, or to report any private conversation I may have had with you, or to publish any letter of mine without my permission, and I must insist that you do not do so. Truly yours   OSCAR WILDE

The Picture of Dorian Gray appeared in Lippincott's Magazine for July. The storm of critical protest was remarkable – as were the sales. A single bookstall in the Strand sold eighty copies of the magazine in a single day when they normally sold three copies a month, and W. H. Smith withdrew it from circulation describing the story as 'a filthy one'.

To the Editor of the *St James's Gazette*

25 June 1890   *16 Tite Street*

Sir, I have read your criticism of my story, *The Picture of Dorian Gray*, and I need hardly say that I do not propose to discuss its merits or demerits, its personalities or its lack of personality. England is a free country, and ordinary English criticism is perfectly free and easy. Besides, I must admit that, either from temperament or from taste, or from both, I am quite incapable of understanding how any work of art can be criticised from a moral standpoint. The sphere of art and the sphere of ethics are absolutely distinct and separate; and it is to the confusion between the two that we owe the appearance of Mrs Grundy, that amusing old lady who represents the only original form of humour that the middle classes of this country have been able to produce. What I do object to most strongly is that you should have placarded the town with posters on which was printed in large letters: MR OSCAR WILDE'S LATEST ADVERTISEMENT; A BAD CASE.

Whether the expression 'A Bad Case' refers to my book or to the present position of the Government, I cannot tell. What was silly and unnecessary was the use of the term 'advertisement'.

I think I may say without vanity – though I do not wish to appear to run vanity down – that of all men in England I am the one who requires least advertisement. I am tired to death of being advertised. I feel no thrill when I see my name in a paper. The chronicler does not interest me any more. I wrote this book entirely for my own pleasure, and it gave me very great pleasure to write it. Whether it becomes popular or not is a matter of absolute indifference to me. I am afraid, sir, that the real advertisement is your cleverly written article. The English public, as a mass, takes no interest in a work of art until it is told that the work in question is immoral, and your réclame will, I have no doubt, largely increase the sale of the magazine; in which sale, I may mention with some regret, I have no pecuniary interest.

I remain, sir, your obedient servant   OSCAR WILDE

To the Editor of the *St James's Gazette*

26 June 1890   *16 Tite Street*

In your issue of today you state that my brief letter published in your columns is the 'best reply' I can make to your article upon *Dorian Gray*. This is not so. I do not propose to fully discuss the matter here, but I feel bound to say that your article contains the most unjustifiable attack that has been made upon any man of letters for many years. The writer of it, who is quite incapable of concealing his personal malice, and so in some measure destroys the effect he wishes to produce, seems not to have the slightest idea of the temper in which a work of art should be approached. To say that such a book as mine should be 'chucked into the fire' is silly. That is what one does with newspapers.

Of the value of pseudo-ethical criticism in dealing with artistic work I have spoken already. But as your writer has ventured into the perilous grounds of literary criticism I ask you to allow me, in fairness not merely to myself but to all men to whom literature is a fine art, to say a few words about his critical method.

He begins by assailing me with much ridiculous virulence because the chief personages in my story are 'puppies'. They *are* puppies. Does he think that literature went to the dogs when Thackeray wrote about puppydom? I think that puppies are extremely interesting from an artistic as well as from a psychological point of view. They seem to me to be certainly far more interesting than prigs; and I am of opinion that Lord Henry Wotton is an excellent corrective of the tedious ideal shadowed forth in the semi-theological novels of our age.

He then makes vague and fearful insinuations about my grammar and my erudition. Now, as regards grammar, I hold that, in prose at any rate, correctness should always be subordinate to artistic effect and musical cadence; and any peculiarities of syntax that may occur in *Dorian Gray* are deliberately intended, and are introduced to show the value of the artistic theory in question. Your writer gives no instance of any such peculiarity. This I regret, because I do not think that any such instances occur.

As regards erudition, it is always difficult, even for the most modest of us, to remember that other people do not know quite as much as one does oneself. I myself frankly admit I cannot imagine how a casual reference to Suetonius and Petronius Arbiter can be construed into evidence of a desire to impress an unoffending and ill-educated public by an assumption of superior knowledge. I should fancy that the most ordinary of scholars is perfectly well acquainted with the *Lives of the Caesars* and with the *Satyricon*. The *Lives of the Caesars*, at any rate, forms part of the curriculum at Oxford for those who take the Honour School of *Literæ Humaniores*; and as for the *Satyricon*, it is popular even among passmen, though I suppose they are obliged to read it in translations.

The writer of the article then suggests that I, in common with that great and noble artist Count Tolstoi, take pleasure in a subject because it is dangerous. About such a suggestion there is this to be said. Romantic art deals with the exception and with the individual. Good people, belonging as they do to the normal, and so, commonplace, type, are artistically uninteresting. Bad people are, from the point of view of art, fascinating studies. They represent colour, variety and strangeness. Good people exasperate one's reason; bad people stir one's imagination. Your critic, if I must give him so honourable a title, states that the people in my story have no counterpart in life; that they are, to use his vigorous if somewhat vulgar phrase, 'mere catchpenny revelations of the non-existent'. Quite so. If they existed they would not be worth writing about. The function of the artist is to invent, not to chronicle. There are no such people. If there were I would not write about them. Life by its realism is always spoiling the subject-matter of art. The supreme pleasure in literature is to realise the non-existent.

And finally, let me say this. You have reproduced, in a journalistic form, the comedy of *Much Ado about Nothing*, and have, of course, spoilt it in your reproduction. The poor public, hearing, from an authority so high as your own, that this is a wicked book that should be coerced and suppressed by a Tory Government, will, no doubt, rush to it and read it. But, alas! they will find that it is a story with a moral. And the moral is this: All excess, as well as all renunciation, brings its own punishment. The painter, Basil Hallward, worshipping physical beauty far too much, as most painters do, dies by the hand of one in whose soul he has created a monstrous and absurd vanity. Dorian Gray, having led a life of mere sensation and pleasure, tries to kill conscience, and at that moment kills himself. Lord Henry Wotton seeks to be merely the spectator of life. He finds that those who reject the battle are more deeply wounded than those who take part in it. Yes; there is a terrible moral in *Dorian Gray* – a moral which the prurient will not be able to find in it, but which will be revealed to all whose minds are healthy. Is this an artistic error? I fear it is. It is the only error in the book.

To the Editor of the *Scots Observer*

9 July 1890   *16 Tite Street, Chelsea*
Sir, You have published a review of my story, *The Picture of Dorian Gray*. As this review is grossly unjust to me as an artist, I ask you to allow me to exercise in your columns my right of reply.

Your reviewer, sir, while admitting that the story in question is 'plainly the work of a man of letters', the work of one who has 'brains, and art, and style', yet suggests, and apparently in all seriousness, that I have written it in order that it should be read by the most depraved members of the criminal and illiterate classes. Now, sir, I do not suppose that the criminal and illiterate classes ever read anything except newspapers. They are certainly not likely to be able to understand anything of mine. So let them pass, and on the broad question of why a man of letters writes at all let me say this. The pleasure that one has in creating a work of art is a purely personal pleasure, and it is for the sake of this pleasure that one creates. The artist works with his eye on the object. Nothing else interests him. What people are likely to say does not even occur to him. He is fascinated by what he has in hand. He is indifferent to others. I write because it gives me the greatest possible artistic pleasure to write. If my work pleases the few, I am gratified. If it does not, it causes me no pain. As for the mob, I have no desire to be a popular novelist. It is far too easy.

Your critic then, sir, commits the absolutely unpardonable crime of trying to confuse the artist with his subject-matter. For this, sir, there is no excuse at all. Of one who is the greatest figure in the world's literature since Greek days Keats remarked that he had as much pleasure in conceiving the evil as he had in conceiving the good. Let your reviewer, sir, consider the bearings of Keats's fine criticism, for it is under these conditions that every artist works. One stands remote from one's subject-matter. One creates it, and one contemplates it. The further away the subject-matter is, the more freely can the artist work. Your reviewer suggests that I do not make it sufficiently clear whether I prefer virtue to wickedness or wickedness to virtue. An artist, sir, has no ethical sympathies at all. Virtue and wickedness are to him simply what the colours on his palette are to the painter. They are no more, and they are no less. He sees that by their means a certain artistic effect can be produced, and he produces it. Iago may be morally horrible and Imogen stainlessly pure, Shakespeare, as Keats said, had as much delight in creating the one as he had in creating the other.

It was necessary, sir, for the dramatic development of this story to surround Dorian Gray with an atmosphere of moral corruption. Otherwise the story would have had no meaning and the plot no issue. To keep this atmosphere vague and indeterminate and wonderful was the aim of the artist who wrote the story. I claim, sir, that he has succeeded. Each man sees his own sin in Dorian Gray. What Dorian Gray's sins are no one knows. He who finds them has brought them.

In conclusion, sir, let me say how really deeply I regret that you should have permitted such a notice as the one I feel constrained to write on to have appeared in your paper. That the editor of the *St James's Gazette* should have employed Caliban as his art-critic was possibly natural. The editor of the *Scots Observer* should not have allowed Thersites to make mows in his review. It is unworthy of so distinguished a man of letters. I am, etc.

OSCAR WILDE

To the Editor of the *Scots Observer*

[23 July 1890]   16 *Tite Street*
Sir, In a letter dealing with the relations of art to morals recently published in your columns – a letter which I may say seems to me in many respects admirable, especially in its insistence on the right of the artist to select his own subject-matter – Mr Charles Whibley suggests that it must be peculiarly painful for me to find that the ethical import of *Dorian Gray* has been so strongly recognised by the foremost Christian papers of England and America that I have been greeted by more than one of them as a moral reformer!

Allow me, sir, to reassure, on this point, not merely Mr Charles Whibley himself but also your no doubt anxious readers. I have no hesitation in saying that I regard such criticisms as a very gratifying tribute to my story. For if a work of art is rich, and vital, and complete, those who have artistic instincts will see its beauty, and those to whom ethics appeal more strongly than aesthetics will see its moral lesson. It will fill the cowardly with terror, and the unclean will see in it their own shame. It will be to each man what he is himself. It is the spectator, and not life, that art really mirrors.

And so, in the case of *Dorian Gray*, the purely literary critic, as in the *Speaker* and elsewhere, regards it as a 'serious and fascinating work of art': the critic who deals with art in its relation to conduct, as the *Christian Leader* and the *Christian World*, regards it as an ethical parable. *Light*, which I am told is the organ of the English mystics, regards it as 'a work of high spiritual import'. The *St James's Gazette*, which is seeking apparently to be the organ of the prurient, sees or pretends to see in it all kinds of dreadful things, and hints at Treasury prosecutions; and your Mr Charles Whibley genially says that he discovers in it 'lots of morality'. It is quite true that he goes on to say that he detects no art in it. But I do not think that it is fair to expect a critic to be able to see a work of art from every point of view. Even Gautier had his limitations just as much as Diderot had, and in modern England Goethes are rare. I can only assure Mr Charles Whibley that no moral apotheosis to which he has added the most modest contribution could possibly be a source of unhappiness to an artist.

I remain, sir, your obedient servant OSCAR WILDE

To Norman Forbes-Robertson

[?September 1890] *16 Tite Street*

Dear Norman, I have carefully considered the whole question, and am afraid that I could not afford to let my work be quite speculative. If you want a play from me I would require £100 down on the scenario being drawn out and approved of, and £100 on the completion of the manuscript. Then royalties of course to follow. If you can give these terms, well and good. If not, I fear I could not give up paying work for speculative. I am always in need of money, and have to work for certainties. If I were rich I would of course gladly do it for you, but, as it is, it would not be fair to others who are in a large measure dependent on me.

Speaking quite generally, I think that as a manager you will find it good economic policy to pay a good price for good plays: the play is always 'the thing'. Everything else is nothing. Ever yours OSCAR

Against the Grain

*'To the world I seem, by intention
on my part, a dilettante merely
– it is not wise to show one's
heart to the world. . . . In
so vulgar an age as this
we all need masks.'*

The year 1891 changed Wilde's life and set in motion the train of events which would lead to his downfall four years later. For a start he more or less abandoned his work as a critic: the last of his pronouncements on art and aesthetics had been his dialogue-essay 'The Critic as Artist' in the summer of 1890 and he now confined himself to responding to criticisms of his own work in the newspapers. His essay 'The Soul of Man under Socialism' appeared in February. In April the expanded version of The Picture of Dorian Gray was issued as a book with a short and defiant preface in the form of twenty-five aphorisms, designed to goad his critics further but later used in court as indicative of his dubious moral stance in literature. In November he published A House of Pomegranates, a collection of stories including 'The Fisherman and his Soul' in which the concept of beauty had become associated with temptation, danger and death. An element of what to him was Greek, dark and tragic had begun to intrude itself into his writing. It was a tormented period in Wilde's life. Still married, he had become aware of both his homosexuality and the need, at that stage at least, to conceal it. Then, almost as if to compensate, he started work on his Society plays which, with their characters' double lives and sparkling dialogue, gave expression to his own ambivalence. He spent longer periods away from his family, often in Paris, and although a neglectful husband, he was still, in his way, a loving father.

It was probably in the summer of 1891 that Nature, as Oscar would always have it, imitated Art, and into his life stepped his own nemesis, his own Dorian Gray, in the form of Lord Alfred 'Bosie' Douglas, third son of the Marquess of Queensberry. Douglas was a twenty-one-year-old undergraduate at Oxford, and a talented poet. They met occasionally as acquaintances during the next year, until Douglas came to Wilde for help over an indiscreet letter with which he was being blackmailed. Soon after they must have become lovers (though Douglas would later say that their physical relationship lasted only a short time) and from then until Wilde's arrest three years later they were in each other's company as much as possible. But 'Bosie' was no innocent when he met Oscar; he was already at home in the homosexual *underworld and it was partly through him that Oscar met the rent boys who would later testify at his trial. Whether Bosie was more Oscar's evil genius or his literary muse we shall never know, but it is significant that the four great plays and Salomé, on which much of his reputation still rests, were written during their affair.*

George Alexander had commissioned Wilde to write a play the year before and, now that he had just taken over the St James's Theatre, was pressing Wilde to deliver. Inspiration came that summer and Lady Windermere's Fan *was ready in October.*

To George Alexander

[2 February 1891]   16 *Tite Street*

My dear Aleck, I am not satisfied with myself or my work. I can't get a grip of the play yet: I can't get my people real. The fact is I worked at it when I was not in the mood for work, and must first forget it, and then go back quite fresh to it. I am very sorry, but artistic work can't be done unless one is in the mood; certainly my work can't. Sometimes I spend months over a thing, and don't do any good; at other times I write a thing in a fortnight.

You will be interested to hear that *The Duchess of Padua* was produced in New York last Wednesday, under the title of *Guido Ferranti*, by Lawrence Barrett. The name of the author was kept a dead secret, and indeed not revealed till yesterday when at Barrett's request I acknowledged the authorship by cable. Barrett wires to me that it was a huge success, and that he is going to run it for his season. He seems to be in great delight over it.

With regard to the cheque for £50 you gave me, shall I return you the money, and end the agreement, or keep it and when the play is written let you have the rights and refusal of it? That will be just as you wish.

I am delighted to hear you had a brilliant opening at the St James's. Ever yours   OSCAR WILDE

To Henry Irving

[Circa 3 February 1891]   16 *Tite Street*

My dear Irving, On Wednesday last a poetic tragedy of mine called *Guido Ferranti* was produced in New York by Lawrence Barrett, the name of the author being concealed. It achieved, Barrett cabled to me, an immense success, which, of course, pleased me very much, as it was entirely on its own merits. On Sunday, at Barrett's request, I acknowledged authorship by cabling my thanks to the public for their reception of my play.

Now, of course, you are the one artist in England who can produce poetic blank-verse drama, and as I have pointed out in this month's *Fortnightly* you have created in the theatre-going public both taste and temperament, so that there is an audience for a poet inside a theatre, though there is no or but a small audience for a poet outside a theatre. The public as a class don't read poetry, but you have made them listen to it.

You have my play already under its first title *The Duchess of Padua*. Why not produce it? I should be quite content to have it produced for one performance, to be put regularly in the bills if you and the public take pleasure in it. I need not say what a delight it would be to me to have my work produced by you. You know that you have no warmer and sincerer admirer than myself, and your theatre has always been to me the one link between our stage and our literature.

If you wish I will send you a copy of the play, and Barrett will send the acting version I have no doubt, if I ask him. Or you may like to make your own. In the copy I have there is no cutting, and the play is long – too long – but in his version it plays three hours.

In any case, believe me, always yours   OSCAR WILDE

Grant Allen's 'The Celt in English Art' appeared alongside Wilde's 'The Soul of Man under Socialism' in the February issue of the Fortnightly Review. *Allen had written at the same time praising Wilde's essay, 'Will you allow me to thank you most heartily for your noble and beautiful essay in this month's* Fortnightly? *I would have written every line of it myself – if only I had known how.'*

To Grant Allen

[Circa 7 February 1891]   *16 Tite Street*
Dear Mr Grant Allen, I beg you will allow me to express to you my real delight in your article in the *Fortnightly*, with its superb assertion of that Celtic spirit in Art that Arnold divined, but did not demonstrate, at any rate in the sense of scientific demonstration, such as yours is.

I was dining at the House of Commons on Thursday, and proposed to some Scotch and Welsh members, who had read your article with pride and pleasure, that as to break bread and drink wine together is, as Christ saw, the simplest and most natural symbol of comradeship, *all* of us who are Celts, Welsh, Scotch, and Irish, should inaugurate a Celtic Dinner, and assert ourselves, and show these tedious Angles or Teutons what a race we are, and how proud we are to belong to that race. You are, of course, a Celt. You must be. What do you think of the idea? It is the outcome of your article, so I want you to join in getting our gorgeous banquet up. Think over it. In any case, we all owe you a debt.

My mother is fascinated and delighted by your article, and begs me to tell you so. Truly yours   OSCAR WILDE

To Cyril Wilde

Tuesday, 3 March [1891]   *Hôtel de l'Athénée, 15 rue Scribe, Paris*
My dearest Cyril, I send you a letter to tell you I am much better. I go every day and drive in a beautiful forest called the Bois de Boulogne, and in the evening I dine with my friend, and sit out afterwards at little tables and see the carriages drive by. Tonight I go to visit a great poet, who has given me a wonderful book about a Raven. I will bring you and Vyvyan back some chocolates when I return.

I hope you are taking great care of dear Mamma. Give her my love and kisses, and also love and kisses to Vyvyan and yourself. Your loving Papa
          OSCAR WILDE

To J. S. Little

[21 March 1891]   *16 Tite Street*
My dear Little, I have been ill, and away in Paris to recruit, or I would have answered your charming letter before. Let me thank you now for it. I am very glad you liked the article. The attempt made by the journalists to dictate to the artist and to limit his subject matter is of course quite monstrous, and everyone who cares at all for Art must strongly protest against it.

My novel appears in volume form next month, and I am curious to see whether these wretched journalists will assail it so ignorantly and pruriently as they did before. My preface should teach them to mend their wicked ways. Believe me, sincerely yours   OSCAR WILDE

Morris had almost certainly sent Wilde The Roots of the Mountains, *his fantasy novel, bound in chintz. In 1893 Wilde gave Morris permission to reprint his mother's translation of Wilhelm Meinhold's* Sidonia the Sorceress *at the Kelmscott Press.*

To William Morris

[?March–April 1891]   *16 Tite Street*

Dear Mr Morris, The book has arrived! And I must write you a line to tell you how gratified I am at your sending it. How proud indeed so beautiful a gift makes me. I weep over the cover which is not nearly lovely enough, not nearly rich enough in material, for such prose as you write. But the book itself, if it is to have suitable raiment, would need damask sewn with pearls and starred with gold. I have always felt that your work comes from the sheer delight of making beautiful things: that no alien motive ever interests you: that in its singleness of aim, as well as in its perfection of result, it is pure art, everything that you do. But I know you hate the blowing of trumpets. I have loved your work since boyhood: I shall always love it. That, with my thanks, is all I have to say. Sincerely yours

OSCAR WILDE

To Arthur Conan Doyle

[?April 1891]

Between me and life there is a mist of words always. I throw probability out of the window for the sake of a phrase, and the chance of an epigram makes me desert truth. Still I do aim at making a work of art, and I am really delighted that you think my treatment subtle and artistically good. The newspapers seem to me to be written by the prurient for the Philistine. I cannot understand how they can treat *Dorian Gray* as immoral. My difficulty was to keep the inherent moral subordinate to the artistic and dramatic effect, and it still seems to me that the moral is too obvious. OSCAR WILDE

To R. Clegg

[?April 1891]   *16 Tite Street*

My dear Sir, Art is useless because its aim is simply to create a mood. It is not meant to instruct, or to influence action in any way. It is superbly sterile, and the note of its pleasure is sterility. If the contemplation of a work of art is followed by activity of any kind, the work is either of a very second-rate order, or the spectator has failed to realise the complete artistic impression.

A work of art is useless as a flower is useless. A flower blossoms for its own joy. We gain a moment of joy by looking at it. That is all that is to be said about our relations to flowers. Of course man may sell the flower, and so make it useful to him, but this has nothing to do with the flower. It is not part of its essence. It is accidental. It is a misuse. All this I fear is very obscure. But the subject is a long one. Truly yours   OSCAR WILDE

To W. L. Courtney

[Circa 19 May 1891]   16 *Tite Street*
My dear Courtney, I think I detected your pleasant friendly touch in the review of my essays that appeared in the *Daily Telegraph*. In any case I write to ask you whether my novel of *Dorian Gray* could not be noticed also in the paper. The reason I ask it is this: when it first appeared it was very grossly and foolishly assailed as an immoral book, and I am anxious to have it treated purely from the art-standpoint: from the standpoint of style, plot, construction, psychology, and the like. From this standpoint much, no doubt, may be urged against it. Every true critic has his own temperament by whose laws he abides, and I may candidly admit that I admire my own work far too much to ask other people to praise it. But one does want, especially in England, to have one's work treated from the proper point of view. Could you do this for me? Of course I know your reviews are quite brief. That doesn't matter. Very sincerely yours   OSCAR WILDE

To George Alexander

[?Summer 1891]   16 *Tite Street*
My dear Alick, Of course I am in your debt £50 and I am very much disappointed I have not been able to write the play, but I want you not to ask me to pay you at present, as I am in a great mess about money, and really will not have any till September, when *The Duchess of Padua* goes on tour in America. Do let me wait till then, and believe me to be, with great regret for not having done the play, sincerely yours   OSCAR WILDE

Elkin Mathews and John Lane had become partners in a publishing business in 1887. This first book of Wilde's which they 'published' the following year and which he termed the 'Author's Edition', was in fact the leftover sheets from his 1882 Poems with a new title-page and cover by Ricketts. They issued all Wilde's books until his arrest, when they were quick enough to dissociate themselves from him.

To Elkin Mathews

[?Mid-October 1891]   [?*London*]
Dear Mr Elkin Mathews, It will give me great pleasure to have my book announced in your list, but I don't see how advertisement could rank among the first charges on the book. It is quite an indefinite thing. Do you call the leaflet of your publication an advertisement, for instance? Or do you confine the term to the paid advertisements in newspapers? It would be easy to spend £30 or £40 in advertising, and the book would not stand it. I am of opinion that advertising is entirely for the publisher, and that the author should under no circumstances be called upon to contribute even indirectly towards it. If you choose to set a limit of £5 for advertising to be charged against the book, I will agree to that, so as to avoid any further trouble. But that should be the limit. I am truly yours   OSCAR WILDE

Wilde spent nearly two months in Paris from October to December, mainly to finish writing Salomé *in French but also to see about a possible translation and staging of* Lady Windermere's Fan. *He made new friends, among them two young authors, André Gide, who professed to be captivated by him, and Pierre Louÿs who corrected some errors in the French play and to whom he dedicated it. It was 'The Fisherman and his Soul' that Wilde dedicated to Alice of Monaco.*

To HSH the Princess of Monaco

[?28 October 1891]   *Hôtel Normandie, rue de l'Echelle, Paris*
Dear Princess, I am in Paris, but *you* are away! I am so disappointed. However, I hope to remain for about a month, so perhaps you will be back before then.

I have finished my play, and have arranged for its production in London. But I want to have it produced first in Paris. It would be delightful. When you come back we must talk about it; I want your advice.

In a few weeks my volume of Faery Tales comes out, and I have taken the liberty of dedicating the best to you. Pray accept this slight homage, and believe me, dear Princess, sincerely yours   OSCAR WILDE

To HSH the Princess of Monaco

[?Late November 1891]   *29 boulevard des Capucines, Paris*
My dear Princess, It was a great pleasure seeing you in Paris, though I was so sorry you were ill. I must come south in February, and have charming days, if you will allow me, with you. By that time, of course I shall have become a French author!

Coquelin has recommended me to have my play translated by Delair, who has done *La Mégère* for the Française. I have had an interview with him, and he is fascinated by the plot, but I don't know if he understands *society*-English sufficiently well, I mean the English of the salon and the boudoir, the English one talks. I am sending him the manuscript tomorrow.

Madame Straus was *quite* charming to me. What delightful friends you have. But of Le Roux I have seen nothing, which I regret. *Votre ami dévoué et sincère*   OSCAR WILDE

To Pierre Louÿs

28 November 1891   *29 boulevard des Capucines*
Cher Monsieur Louÿs, J'accepte avec le plus vif plaisir la gracieuse et charmante invitation que vous et M. Gide ont eu la bonté de m'adresser. Vous m'indiquerez, n'est-ce-pas, l'endroit et l'heure.

Je garde un souvenir délicieux de notre petit déjeuner de l'autre jour, et de l'accueil sympathique que vous m'avez fait.

J'espère que les jeunes poètes de France m'aimeront un jour, comme moi à ce moment je les aime.

La poésie française a toujours été parmi mes maîtresses les plus adorées, et je serai très content de croire que parmi les poètes de France je trouverai de véritables amis.

Veuillez présenter à M. Gide l'assurance de mes sentiments les plus distingués. Veuillez, cher Monsieur Louÿs, l'agréer   OSCAR WILDE

Robert, Earl of Lytton, was the British Ambassador and had died on 24 November. He published much verse under the pseudonym Owen Meredith. Wilde dedicated Lady Windermere's Fan *to him when it was published in 1893.*

To Lady Dorothy Nevill

[Circa 30 November 1891]   *29 boulevard des Capucines*

My dear Lady Dorothy, I would have answered your charming letter before, but the death of poor dear Lytton has quite upset me. We had become during the last year very great friends, and I had seen him only a few days before he died, lying in Pauline Borghese's lovely room at the Embassy, and full of charm and grace and tenderness.

His funeral, in spite of the hideous Protestant service, was most impressive; the purple-covered bier with its one laurel wreath being a solemn note of colour and sadness in the midst of the gorgeous uniforms of the Ambassadors.

He was a man of real artistic temperament. I had grown to be very fond of him, and he was most kind always to me.

By all means send your book: I will get Zola's name. Poor Maupassant is dying, I fear. Believe me, dear Lady Dorothy, sincerely yours OSCAR WILDE

To an Unidentified Correspondent

[November–December 1891]   *29 boulevard des Capucines*

Dear Sir, I regret extremely that I am unable to accept the very courteous and flattering invitation extended to me by your Society. Were I in London it would give me great pleasure to attend your meeting, and to say a few words on the tendencies of modern Art, but I am at present in Paris, studying the curious and fascinating development of Art in France, which, I am glad to say, is in the direction of a richer Romanticism, with subtleties of new colour and strange music and extended subject matter. An artist gains his best, his truest inspiration, from the material he uses, and the transformation of the French language, in the hands of the leaders of the new schools, is one of the most interesting and attractive things to watch and wonder at.

I have read the journal of your society with interest and beg you to convey my thanks to your committee for it, as for the desire they have expressed to have my presence at your meeting. I remain, Sir, faithfully yours   OSCAR WILDE

To the Editor of the *Speaker*

[Early December 1891]   *[29] boulevard des Capucines*
Sir, I have just, at a price that for any other English sixpenny paper I would
have considered exorbitant, purchased a copy of the *Speaker* at one of the
charming kiosks that decorate Paris; institutions, by the way, that I think
we should at once introduce into London. The kiosk is a delightful object,
and, when illuminated at night from within, as lovely as a fantastic Chinese
lantern, especially when the transparent advertisements are from the clever
pencil of M. Chéret. In London we have merely the ill-clad newsvendors,
whose voice, in spite of the admirable efforts of the Royal College of Music
to make England a really musical nation, is always out of tune, and whose
rags, badly designed and badly worn, merely emphasise a painful note of
uncomely misery, without conveying that impression of picturesqueness
which is the only thing that makes the spectacle of the poverty of others at
all bearable.

It is not, however, about the establishment of kiosks in London that I
wish to write to you, though I am of opinion that it is a thing that the
County Council should at once take in hand. The object of my letter is to
correct a statement made in a paragraph of your interesting paper.

The writer of the paragraph in question states that the decorative designs
that make lovely my book *A House of Pomegranates*, are by the hand of Mr
Shannon, while the delicate dreams that separate and herald each story are
by Mr Ricketts. The contrary is the case. Mr Shannon is the drawer of
dreams, and Mr Ricketts is the subtle and fantastic decorator. Indeed, it is
to Mr Ricketts that the entire decorative design of the book is due, from the
selection of the type and the placing of the ornamentation, to the completely
beautiful cover that encloses the whole. The writer of the paragraph goes
on to state that he does not 'like the cover'. This is, no doubt, to be regretted,
though it is not a matter of much importance, as there are only two people
in the world whom it is absolutely necessary that the cover should please.
One is Mr Ricketts, who designed it, the other is myself, whose book it
binds. We both admire it immensely! The reason, however, that your critic
gives for his failure to gain from the cover any impression of beauty seems
to me to show a lack of artistic instinct on his part, which I beg you will
allow me to try to correct.

He complains that a portion of the design on the left-hand side of the
cover reminds him of an Indian club with a house-painter's brush on top of
it, while a portion of the design on the right-hand side suggests to him the
idea of 'a chimney-pot hat with a sponge in it'. Now, I do not for a moment

dispute that these are the real impressions your critic received. It is the spectator, and the mind of the spectator, as I pointed out in the preface to *The Picture of Dorian Gray*, that art really mirrors. What I want to indicate is this: the artistic beauty of the cover of my book resides in the delicate tracing, arabesques, and massing of many coral-red lines on a ground of white ivory, the colour-effect culminating in certain high gilt notes, and being made still more pleasurable by the overlapping band of moss-green cloth that holds the book together.

What the gilt notes suggest, what imitative parallel may be found to them in that chaos that is termed Nature, is a matter of no importance. They may suggest, as they do sometimes to me, peacocks and pomegranates and splashing fountains of gold water, or, as they do to your critic, sponges and Indian clubs and chimney-pot hats. Such suggestions and evocations have nothing whatsoever to do with the aesthetic quality and value of the design. A thing in Nature becomes much lovelier if it reminds us of a thing in Art, but a thing in Art gains no real beauty through reminding us of a thing in Nature. The primary aesthetic impression of a work of art borrows nothing from recognition or resemblance. These belong to a later and less perfect stage of apprehension. Properly speaking, they are not part of a real aesthetic impression at all, and the constant preoccupation with subject-matter that characterises nearly all our English art-criticism is what makes our art-criticism, especially as regards literature, so sterile, so profitless, so much beside the mark, and of such curiously little account.

I remain, sir, your obedient servant,   OSCAR WILDE

To Pierre Louÿs

[December 1891]   *[Paris]*
Mon cher ami, Voilà le drame de *Salomé*. Ce n'est pas encore fini ou même corrigé, mais ça donne l'idée de la *construction*, du motif et du mouvement dramatique. Ici et là, il y a des lacunes, mais l'idée du drame est claire.

Je suis encore très enrhumé et je me porte assez mal. Mais je serai tout à fait bien lundi et je vous attendrai à une heure chez Mignon pour déjeuner, vous et M. Fort.

Je vous remercie beaucoup, mon cher ami, pour l'intérêt que vous daignez prendre à mon drame. A toi   OSCAR

Although Wilde had been writing to various correspondents at the beginning of the year that his play 'was an immense success', it only ran in New York for three weeks. Gale and Barrett in the leading roles planned to take it on tour in America

but Barrett died in March. Gale had in fact been touring it rather half-heartedly from the end of August. It was never produced in England in Wilde's lifetime.

To Minna K. Gale

[Postmark 20 December 1891]   *16 Tite Street*

Dear Miss Gale, I have to thank you for the very beautiful impersonation of *The Duchess of Padua* that you are presenting, and also for a charming and fascinating photograph of yourself that you have been kind enough to send me, and for which I should have before thanked you, but I have been suffering from overwork and unable to write.

I wish I could limit my letter to expression of thanks and appreciation, but I am obliged to write to you on business also, which is as painful to me as I have no doubt it is to you.

The business matter is this: I gave you the American rights of my play because you had been the original impersonator of the Duchess, and I felt that to give the rights away from you to any other actress would be a wrong to you, and imply some doubt of your powers, of which I had no doubt, and might do you harm at the outset of your career as an actress directing your own company.

Accordingly I let you have the play on absurdly low terms, understanding also from your letter and from what my friend Mr Anderson, acting for you, told me, that my play was to be the prominent feature and basis of your tour, as Mr Barrett had purposed to make it of his. Mr Anderson told me he understood you intended playing matinées of Juliet and Beatrice, but that my play was to occupy the evening bill for most, if not all, the nights of the week.

Instead of that I find that my play is played about once a fortnight, usually on the *last* night of your engagement in an important place, as recently at Harlem, so that on a tour of three months, I have received royalties for eight performances!

This is of course extremely unjust to me. Had I understood that such was to be the position accorded to my play I would not, of course, have given it to you on the very low terms I did, or indeed given it to you at all. My play, having been a great success in New York, should have been your opening production at Harlem, and should have been played during the week if the houses warranted it. To play it only once, and on your last night, was to assign it a position it of course does not deserve, and to rob it of its proper artistic importance.

I understood you were to emphasise my play, to go on tour with it as the new romantic tragedy, to assert it in each town. I find it treated as if it was an old-fashioned, outworn piece, to be played twice a month, and I feel deeply wounded by the treatment it has received.

It is also a severe monetary loss to me. I fixed the royalties ridiculously low so as not to hamper you at the outset in any way, understanding you were starting on tour with an important, beautiful, artistic production of my play. It has not been so. My play has been put on the shelf, and played on a few Saturday evenings when I suppose you have had an exhausting morning performance. You must realise that as an artist I have not received the treatment I expected, and was led to believe I would get. A grave injustice has been done to me and my work.

And now, what is to be done? The present state of things cannot go on. Will you let me have my play back? Or will you buy my play out and out? If you like I will sell you the *English* and American rights, provided of course that you produce the play in London within three years. Or will you buy the American rights alone? To be forwarded a few dollars at the end of each month for my play is of course absurd and annoying.

For you personally as an actress of genius and power and beauty I have the greatest admiration. My friends tell me you realise perfectly the image put forth in the poetry and passion of my play, but had I known that my play was to be treated in the way it has been, I would of course, in justice to myself, have put it in other hands. Pray think over my letter, and let me hear from you soon. Sincerely yours   OSCAR WILDE

Barlas, a Scottish poet and socialist like Cunninghame Graham, took part in the 1887 'Bloody Sunday' riot in Trafalgar Square. He, too, was arrested after a severe beating from the police which affected his mind. He had fired off a revolver outside Parliament in December shouting, 'I am an anarchist. What I have done is to show my contempt for the House of Commons.' When he was bound over to keep the peace, Wilde guaranteed half his surety of £200.

To John Barlas

[Postmark 19 January 1892]   16 *Tite Street*
My dear friend and poet, Thanks, a thousand thanks, for your charming letter. Whatever I did was merely what you would have done for me or for any friend of yours whom you admired and appreciated. We poets and dreamers are all brothers.

I am so glad you are feeling better. I now know nerves myself, what they are, and what rest can do for them. We will have many days of song and joy together when the spring comes, and life shall be made lovely for us, and we will pipe on reeds. I must come and see you soon. Your affectionate friend OSCAR

Lady Windermere's Fan, Wilde's first critically acclaimed play, was produced at the St James's Theatre on 20 February. Alexander was infuriated by what he saw as the author's inexperienced interference at rehearsals. At the first night curtain call Wilde appeared on stage, cigarette in hand, and addressed the audience: 'Ladies and Gentlemen: I have enjoyed this evening immensely. The actors have given us a charming rendering of a delightful play, and your appreciation has been most intelligent. I congratulate you on the great success of your performance, which persuades me that you think almost as highly of the play as I do myself.'

To George Alexander

[Mid-February 1892]   16 Tite Street

Dear Aleck, I heard by chance in the theatre today – after you had left the stage – that you intended using the first scene a second time – in the last act. I think you should have told me this, as after a long consultation on the subject more than four weeks ago you agreed to have what is directed in the book of the play, namely Lady Windermere's boudoir, a scene which I consider very essential from a dramatic point of view.

My object, however, in writing is not to reproach you in any way – reproaches being useless things – but to point this out. If through pressure of time, or for reasons of economy, you are unable to give the play its full scenic mounting, the scene that has to be repeated should be *the second, not the first*. Lady Windermere *may* be in her drawing-room in the fourth act. *She should not be in her husband's library.* This is a very important point.

Now, from the point of view of stage-management, the advantages of using Scene II are these:

In Act 2 the scene is night. The ballroom is open, and so is the terrace. In Act 4, the scene being day, the ballroom is closed, the window shut, and the furniture can be differently arranged. Rooms are cleared out of some of their contents for a reception. These contents are restored the next day. That is to say, the repetition of the library would have to be an exact replica: the repetition of the drawing-room would not have this disadvantage.

And the disadvantage is a great one, because the scene – a vital one in the play – between the Duchess and Lady Windermere takes place on the sofa on the right of the stage. Now Mrs Erlynne should not have her scene in the same place. It impoverishes the effect. I want you to arrange Mrs

Erlynne on a sofa more in the centre of the stage and towards the left side. In my own rough draft of the stage-setting of this act, made when I was writing the piece, I placed Mrs Erlynne on a high-backed Louis Seize sofa so:

She would then be, what she should be, in full view of the audience. She should not be at the side. The situation is too important. The sofa is of course not parallel with the footlights. It is placed like this and Mrs Erlynne

sits on the upper side naturally. Will you kindly think very seriously over this. The use of the second act, instead of the first, enables us to give Mrs Erlynne a very much better position on the stage. There are only three people in the last act (setting aside the servants) till the arrival of Lord Augustus, and the play should not go on in a corner. Mrs Erlynne should hold the centre of the stage, and be its central figure.

This also is to be remembered. Windermere, being in his own house, can pace up and down – does, in fact, do so; Mrs Erlynne, of course, cannot do anything of the kind. She rises from the sofa, as marked in the play, and sits down, but with the possibility of Lady Windermere entering at any moment, for her to walk about, or cross, or the like, would be melodramatic, but not dramatic or artistic.

All this, of such importance to the play, I should have liked to have talked over with you personally, but, in spite of my earnest request to you conveyed in my letter of some days ago, you have not given me what I wanted, and what my position, as the creator of the play, entitles me to, and that is a formal quiet interview with you at the end of each day's rehearsal. In the interests of the play, that should be done. It saves a great trouble. It would in the present instance have saved me writing this long letter, the points of which could have been more easily put forward in conversation, when I would also have had the advantage of hearing your own views on the many points.

One last point. When Windermere says, on Mrs Erlynne's exit, 'Allow me', he goes to the door. His wife on Mrs Erlynne's exit goes towards him, and I want you both to get to the *back of the stage*. Lord Augustus enters below you, takes you by the arm to the front of stage. Lady Windermere watches from the back, till her anxiety becomes unbearable, and then comes down. It is essential that Lady Windermere should not hear one word of Lord Augustus's account of Mrs Erlynne's explanation.

Pray give your serious attention to all these points, and believe me very sincerely yours   OSCAR WILDE

To George Alexander

[Mid-February 1892]   *Hotel Albemarle, Piccadilly*
Dear Alexander, I am too unwell to attend rehearsal this morning. If there is one this evening I will come. Perhaps Mr Shone will kindly let me know. In any case I hope that there will be no repetition of the painful scene of last night. I have always treated you with personal courtesy, and I expect to be treated with equal courtesy in return.

And now, about the play. Will you kindly consider these points. Details in life are of no importance, but in art details are vital.

In the comedy scenes people should speak out more, be more assertive. Every *word* of a comedy dialogue should reach the ears of the audience. This applies specially to the Duchess, who should be larger in assertion. The chatter that drowned her speech in *Act 2* about Mrs Erlynne and the Savile girls might be *before* her entrance, and the guests pass chattering on to the terrace, leaving two on the sofa at back, and two on the seat at entrance.

Hopper had better have either his own hair or a quiet wig. His face last night was far too white, and his appearance far too ridiculous. Personally I think his own hair, and his face made up younger than it is naturally.

Last night, whether by inadvertence or direction I don't know, the Duchess left out some essential words in her first speech to Hopper. It should run, '. . . kangaroos flying about. <u>Agatha has found Australia on the map. What a curious shape it is</u>! However, it's a very young country, isn't it?'

The words she left out are those I have underlined. They give the point to the remark about the young country. To omit them is to leave out the point of the climax, and in point of time nothing is saved by their omission. The words take less than ten seconds to speak.

I think also that C. Graham should not take his aunt into the ballroom – young dandies dislike their aged relatives – at least rarely pay them attention. Lady J. should have a debutante in tow, and Mrs Erlynne might give the speech about Dumby to Graham, and then turn to you.

With regard to yourself, when Cecil Graham bores you with his chatter you broke off last night by saying 'How amusing!', or some word like that. I think it would be better to say 'Excuse me for a moment', as I suggested. Lord W. is terribly agitated about Mrs Erlynne's coming, and the dandy's chatter bores him, does not please him. He has no taste for it.

Also, on going on to the terrace with Mrs Erlynne, last night you said 'Come on to the terrace'. Now Lord W. is not anxious to keep Mrs Erlynne in his house. She forces him to do what she wants. Let her say, 'Let us go on to the terrace.' He, cold and somewhat disdainful, though that is too strong a word, has to do her will.

Will you kindly think over these two points.

Also, would you remind Lady Plymdale to say 'That woman!' not 'That *dreadful* woman'. We must not make Mrs E. look like a cocotte. She is an adventuress, not a cocotte.

I hope everything is going right. It seemed to me that only the details wanted finishing. Your truly   OSCAR WILDE

Act 3. Lord A's coat is too horsy: also he should take it off. He wants to make a night of it.

I write from bed which accounts for pencil.

To George Alexander

[Mid-February 1892]   *Hotel Albemarle*

Dear Alexander, I am still in bed by my doctor's orders or would have come down to rehearsal, but will be there tonight for certain. With regard to the speech of Mrs Erlynne at the end of Act II, you must remember that until Wednesday night Mrs Erlynne rushed off the stage leaving Lord Augustus in a state of bewilderment. Such are the stage directions in the play. When the alteration in the business was made I don't know, but I should have been informed at once. It came on me with the shock of a surprise. I don't in any degree object to it. It is a different effect, that is all. It does not alter the psychological lines of the play . . . To reproach me on Wednesday for not having written a speech for a situation on which I was not consulted and of which I was quite unaware was, of course, a wrong thing to do. With regard to the new speech written yesterday, personally I think it adequate. I want Mrs Erlynne's whole scene with Lord Augustus to be a 'tornado' scene, and the thing to go as quickly as possible. However, I will think over the speech, and talk it over with Miss Terry. Had I been informed of the change I would of course have had more time and when, through illness caused by the worry and anxiety I have gone through at the theatre, I was unable to attend the rehearsals on Monday and Tuesday, I should have been informed by letter.

With regard to your other suggestion about the disclosure of the secret of the play in the second act, had I intended to let out the secret, which is the element of suspense and curiosity, a quality so essentially dramatic, I would have written the play on entirely different lines. I would have made Mrs Erlynne a vulgar horrid woman and struck out the incident of the fan. The audience must not know till the last act that the woman Lady Windermere proposed to strike with her fan was her own mother. The note would be too harsh, too horrible. When they learn it, it is after Lady Windermere has left her husband's house to seek the protection of another man, and their interest is concentrated on Mrs Erlynne, to whom dramatically speaking belongs the last act. Also it would destroy the dramatic wonder excited by the incident of Mrs Erlynne taking the letter and opening it and sacrificing herself in the third act. If they knew Mrs Erlynne was the mother, there would be no surprise in her sacrifice – it would be expected. But in my play the sacrifice is dramatic and unexpected. The cry with which Mrs Erlynne flies into the other room on hearing Lord Augustus's voice, the wild pathetic cry of self-preservation, 'Then it is I who am lost!' would be repulsive coming from the lips of one known to be the mother by the audience. It seems natural and is very dramatic coming from one who seems to be an adventuress, and who while anxious to save Lady Windermere thinks of her own safety when a crisis comes. Also it would destroy the last act: and the chief merit of my last act is to me the fact that it does not contain, as most plays do, the explanation of what the audience knows already, but that it is the sudden explanation of what the audience desires to know, followed immediately by the revelation of a character as yet untouched by literature.

The question you touch on about the audience misinterpreting the relations of Lord Windermere and Mrs Erlynne depends entirely on the acting. In the first act Windermere must convince the audience of his absolute sincerity in what he says to his wife. The lines show this. He does not say to his wife 'there is nothing in this woman's past life that is against her'; he says openly, 'Mrs Erlynne years ago sinned. She now wants to get back. Help her to get back.' The suggestions his wife makes he doesn't treat trivially and say, 'Oh, there is nothing in it. We're merely friends, that is all.' He rejects them with horror at the suggestion.

At the ball his manner to her is cold, courteous but somewhat hard – not the manner of a lover. When they think they are alone Windermere uses no word of tenderness or love. He shows that the woman has a hold on him, but one he loathes and almost writhes under.

What is this hold? That is the play.

I have entered at great length into this matter because every suggestion you have made to me I have always carefully and intellectually considered. Otherwise it would have been sufficient to have said, what I am sure you yourself will on reflection recognise, and that is that a work of art wrought out on definite lines, and elaborated from one definite artistic standpoint, cannot be suddenly altered. It would make every line meaningless, and rob each situation of its value. An equally good play could be written in which the audience would know beforehand who Mrs Erlynne really was, but it would require completely different dialogue, and completely different situations. I have built my house on a certain foundation, and this foundation cannot be altered. I can say no more.

With regards to matters personal between us, I trust that tonight will be quite harmonious and peaceful. After the play is produced and before I leave for the South of France where I am obliged to go for my health, it might be wise for us to have at any rate one meeting for the purpose of explanation. Truly yours   OSCAR WILDE

To the Editor of the *St James's Gazette*

26 February 1892

Sir, Allow me to correct a statement put forward in your issue of this evening, to the effect that I have made a certain alteration in my play in consequence of the criticism of some journalists who write very recklessly and very foolishly in the papers about dramatic art. This statement is entirely untrue, and grossly ridiculous.

The facts are as follows. On last Saturday night, after the play was over, and the author, cigarette in hand, had delivered a delightful and immortal speech, I had the pleasure of entertaining at supper a small number of personal friends: and, as none of them was older than myself, I naturally listened to their artistic views with attention and pleasure. The opinions of the old on matters of Art are, of course, of no value whatsoever. The artistic instincts of the young are invariably fascinating; and I am bound to state that all my friends, without exception, were of opinion that the psychological interest of the second act would be greatly increased by the disclosure of the actual relationship existing between Lady Windermere and Mrs Erlynne – an opinion, I may add, that had previously been strongly held and urged by Mr Alexander. As to those of us who do not look on a play as a mere question of pantomime and clowning, psychological interest is everything, I determined consequently to make a change in the precise moment of revelation. This determination, however, was entered into long before I had the opportunity of studying the culture, courtesy, and critical faculty displayed in such papers as the *Referee, Reynolds*, and the *Sunday Sun*.

When criticism becomes in England a real art, as it should be, and when none but those of artistic instinct and artistic cultivation is allowed to write about works of art, artists will no doubt read criticisms with a certain amount of intellectual interest. As things are at present, the criticisms of ordinary newspapers are of no interest whatsoever, except in so far as they display in its crudest form the extraordinary Boeotianism of a country that has produced some Athenians, and in which other Athenians have come to dwell.

I am, sir, your obedient servant   OSCAR WILDE

To an Unidentified Editor

[?February 1892]   *16 Tite Street*

Sir, John is an admirable name. It was the name of the most charming of all the Disciples, the one who did not write the Fourth Gospel. It was the name of the most perfect of all the English poets of this century, as it was of the greatest English poets of all the centuries. Popes and Princes, wicked or wonderful, have been called John. John has been the name of several eminent journalists and criminals. But John is not amongst the many delightful names given to me at my baptism. So kindly let me correct the statement made by your reckless dramatic critic in his last and unavailing attack on my play. The attempt he makes to falsify one of the most important facts in the History of Art must be checked at once. I remain sir your obedient servant   OSCAR WILDE

To Robert Ross

[?May–June 1892]   *Royal Palace Hotel, Kensington*

My dearest Bobbie, Bosie has insisted on stopping here for sandwiches. He is quite like a narcissus – so white and gold. I will come either Wednesday or Thursday night to your rooms. Send me a line. Bosie is so tired: he lies like a hyacinth on the sofa, and I worship him.

You dear boy. Ever yours   OSCAR

Wilde's signed, large-paper edition of his Poems *had just appeared. Grant Richards was working for the* Review of Reviews *under W. T. Stead, whose campaign against organised vice had helped the passing of the Criminal Law Amendment Act of 1885 under which Wilde was later arrested. The* Review of Reviews *was surprisingly generous about Wilde on his conviction and Stead wrote to Robert Ross in 1905, 'I am glad to remember . . . that he always knew that I, at least, never joined the herd of his assailants.'*

To Grant Richards

[June 1892]   *16 Tite Street*

Dear Sir, The new edition of my poems is limited to 200 copies, and these are meant not for reviewers, but merely for lovers of poetry, a small and quite unimportant sect of perfect people, so I fear I cannot bid my book wander towards Mowbray House. Its raiment, gold smeared on tired purple, might attract attention in the Strand, and that would annoy it, books being delicate and most sensitive things, and, if they are books worth reading, having a strong dislike of the public.

So you see I must perforce refuse your request. Yours truly

OSCAR WILDE

Kernahan was closely involved in the book publication of Dorian Gray. *His story, 'The Garden of God', was subtitled 'A Story for Children from Eight to Eighty' after Wilde's own description of* The Happy Prince.

To Coulson Kernahan

[Postmark 20 June 1892]   *16 Tite Street*

My dear Kernahan, I should have thanked you long ago for sending me your charming fairy tale, but the season with its red roses of pleasure has absorbed me quite, and I have almost forgotten how to write a letter. However I know you will forgive me, and I must tell you how graceful and artistic I think your story is; full of delicate imagination, and a symbolism suggestive of many meanings, not narrowed down to one moral, but many-sided as, I think, symbolism should be. But your strength lies not in such fanciful, winsome work. You must deal directly with Life – modern terrible Life – wrestle with it, and force it to yield you its secret. You have the power and the pen. You know what passion is, what passions are; you can give them their red raiment, and make them move before us. You can fashion puppets with bodies of flesh, and souls of turmoil: and so, you must sit down, and do a great thing. It is all in you. Your sincere friend

OSCAR WILDE

Arthur Fish had been Wilde's assistant editor on the Woman's World. *They kept in touch for some years after Wilde resigned from the magazine.* Salomé *had been*

in rehearsal when the Lord Chamberlain banned its production, as a result of which Wilde told the Pall Mall Budget *that he was seriously considering emigrating to France, whose censorship laws were less severe.*

To Arthur Fish

[Postmark 11 July 1892]   *51 Kaiser-Friedrichs Promenade, Bad Homburg*
My dear Arthur, I was charmed to get your letter, but so sorry to hear your wife had been ill. As regards the idea of my becoming a French citizen, I have not yet decided. I am very much hurt not merely at the action of the Licensor of Plays, but at the pleasure expressed by the entire Press of England at the suppression of my work. However, the Press only represents the worst side of English life – there are a few, like yourself, who love art and have sympathy with the artist. I confess I should be sorry to separate from them. When I return I hope to see you, and am always your affectionate friend   OSCAR WILDE

Rothenstein, a young artist of nineteen and living in Paris, had met Wilde there the previous autumn. Their friendship survived Wilde's disgrace and Rothenstein visited him after prison both in Berneval and Paris. The burlesque of Lady Windermere's Fan, *to which Wilde objected, was a musical travesty,* The Poet and the Puppets, *by the actor Charles Brookfield, staged in May that year. Brookfield, who afterwards had a small part in* An Ideal Husband, *was jealous of Wilde's reputation and is said to have helped Queensberry's lawyers to collect evidence for the defence in Wilde's libel action against the Marquess in 1895.*

To William Rothenstein

[Mid-July 1892]   *51 Kaiser-Friedrichs Promenade*
My dear Will, The *Gaulois*, the *Echo de Paris*, and the *Pall Mall* have all had interviews. I hardly know what new thing there is to say. The licensor of plays is nominally the Lord Chamberlain, but really a commonplace official – in the present case a Mr Pigott, who panders to the vulgarity and hypocrisy of the English people, by licensing every low farce and vulgar melodrama. He even allows the stage to be used for the purpose of the caricaturing of the personalities of artists, and at the same moment when he prohibited *Salomé*, he licensed a burlesque of *Lady Windermere's Fan* in which an actor dressed up like me and imitated my voice and manner!!!

The curious thing is this: all the arts are free in England, except the actor's art; it is held by the Censor that the stage degrades and that actors desecrate fine subjects, so the Censor prohibits not the publication of *Salomé* but its production. Yet not one single actor has protested against this insult to the stage – not even Irving, who is always prating about the Art of the Actor. This shows how few actors are artists. All the *dramatic* critics, except Archer of the *World*, agree with the Censor that there should be a censorship over actors and acting! This shows how bad our stage must be, and also shows how Philistine the English journalists are.

I am very ill, dear Will, and can't write any more. Ever yours

OSCAR WILDE

To John Lane

[July 1892]   *Homburg*

Dear Mr Lane, I return you the agreement signed and witnessed. I have made some alterations in it. The maker of a poem is a 'poet', not an 'author': author is misleading.

Also the selection of reviews to which the book is sent must be a matter of arrangement between you and your partner and me. A book of this kind – very rare and curious – must not be thrown into the gutter of English journalism. No book of mine, for instance, ever goes to the *National Observer*. I wrote to Henley to tell him so, two years ago. He is too coarse, too offensive, too personal, to be sent any work of mine. I hope that the book will be subscribed for before publication, and that as few as possible will be sent for review. Where in a magazine of art, either French or English, we know that an important appreciation will be written, we can send a copy, but ordinary English newspapers are not merely valueless, but would do harm, just as they are trying in every way to harm *Salomé*, though they have not read it. The *St James's Gazette*, again, I would not have a copy sent to. They are most scurrilous.

With regard to the copies given to other than reviewers, I will have six myself. You and Mr Mathews will of course have a copy each, besides a copy to be kept in your place of business, and Mr Ricketts will have a copy.

I did not contemplate assigning to you the copyright of so important a poem for so small an honorarium as ten per cent, but will do so, it being clearly understood that no new edition is to be brought out without my sanction: I mean no such thing as a popular or cheap edition is to be brought out: nor are you to be able to assign the right of publishing the poem to any other firm. You will see that this is a quite reasonable demand on my part.

I hope *The Sphinx* will be a great success. Will you have a type-written copy made for me, so that I can correct the text before Ricketts writes it out: it would be a saving of time and money. Truly yours   OSCAR WILDE

Archer, dramatic critic of the World, *had written to the* Pall Mall Gazette *supporting Wilde's attack on the banning of* Salomé.

To William Archer

[Postmark 22 July 1892]   *Homburg*
Dear Archer, I am here taking the waters, and have not a copy of *Salomé* with me, or would gladly lend it to you, though the refusal of the Licensor to allow the performance of my tragedy was based entirely on his silly vulgar rule about no Biblical *subject* being treated. I don't fancy he ever *read* the play, and if he did, I can hardly fancy even poor Pigott objecting to an artist *treating* his subject in any way he likes. To object to that would be to object to Art entirely – a fine position for a man to adopt, but a little too fine for Pigott, I should imagine.

I want to tell you how gratified I was by your letter in the *PMG*, not merely for its very courteous and generous recognition of my work, but for its strong protest against the contemptible official tyranny that exists in England in reference to the drama. The joy of the ordinary dramatic critic that such tyranny should exist is to me perfectly astounding. I should have thought there would be little pleasure in criticising an art where the artist was not free. The whole affair is a great triumph for the Philistine, but only a momentary one. We must abolish the censure. I think we can do it. When I come back I must see you. Ever yours   OSCAR WILDE

Some time in the summer, probably for the last half of August and September, Wilde rented a house near Cromer in Norfolk. At the beginning Constance and the children were with him, but then went to stay at Babbacombe Cliff, near Torquay, the home of her distant cousin Lady Mount-Temple. Bosie Douglas spent ten days in Cromer with Oscar, and when he fell ill Constance wrote from Babbacombe to ask whether she should come back and help. At this stage she seems to have been quite unaware of the true nature of the relationship between the two men. It was at Cromer that Wilde started work on A Woman of No Importance *and finished it later at Babbacombe. Tree produced it at the Haymarket Theatre in April the following year.*

To Herbert Beerbohm Tree

13 October 1892   *Central Station Hotel [Glasgow]*

My dear Tree, I hereby agree to assign you the rights in my play entitled *A Woman of No Importance* for performance in Great Britain and Ireland, on condition that you produce it at the Haymarket Theatre after *Hypatia* (reserving to yourself the right to interpose revival) and pay me the following fees: when the gross receipts for six performances are under £600 you shall pay me nothing, when the gross weekly receipts are over £600 and under £800 you shall pay me 6%, when the gross weekly receipts are over £800 and under £1000 you shall pay me 7½%, and when the gross weekly receipts are over £1000 you shall pay me 10% of such gross receipts, it being understood that the sums stated are in each case for six performances and that £100 shall be added to such sums for seven or eight or more performances.

In the provinces of Great Britain and Ireland, the said play shall be our joint property, but if you elect to play it yourself in the provinces you shall pay me 5% of the gross receipts.   OSCAR WILDE

To Lady Mount-Temple

[October–November 1892]   *16 Tite Street*

Dear Lady Mount-Temple, I need hardly say how grateful Constance and I are to you for your kindness in promising to let us your lovely house at Babbacombe, where Constance has passed such beautiful days. I hope you will not mind my writing to you on business matters. If you would allow us to have it for three months for £100, we would both feel very grateful to you, and I need not say we will take the greatest care possible of your lovely home, and remember always who its *châtelaine* is, and how gracious is her courtesy in permitting us to sojourn for a season in her own house.

If you would let us carry out the scheme we propose, we would have the great joy of being still more in your debt for many kindnesses and gracious acts, Believe me, truly yours   OSCAR WILDE

To Lady Mount-Temple

[?November 1892]   *Royal Bath Hotel, Bournemouth*
Dear and gracious Lady, With the children of the gods one dare not argue,
and so I submit to your decision without a murmur save one of thanks and
gratitude, and your lovely house will be treasured and watched over by us,
and the spirit of the *châtelaine* will preside over all things.

The week after next we would like to go down, and I look forward
immensely to being at Babbacombe, as I want to write two plays, one in
blank verse, and I know the peace and beauty of your home will set me in
tune, so that I can hear things that the ear cannot hear, and see invisible
things. I need not tell you how delighted Constance is at the prospect of
being at a place she so much loves, and where so much love has been given
her. Believe me gratefully and truly yours   OSCAR WILDE

*It was about this time that Wilde met Maurice Schwabe and Alfred Taylor who
were to introduce him to the rent boys on whose evidence he was eventually
convicted. On his November visit to Paris to arrange for the publication of* Salomé,
*Wilde was persuaded by Schwabe, whose departure had been delayed, to take Fred
Atkins, a young blackmailer, over to France until Schwabe could join them. Atkins
later testified against Wilde in court.*

To Lord Alfred Douglas

[?November 1892]
Dearest Bosie, I am so glad you are better. I trust you like the little card-case.
Oxford is quite impossible in winter. I go to Paris next week – for ten days
or so. Are you really going to the Scilly Isles?

I should awfully like to go away with you somewhere where it is hot and
coloured.

I am terribly busy in town. Tree running up to see me on all occasions,
also strange and troubling personalities walking in painted pageants.

Of the poem I will write tomorrow. Ever yours   OSCAR
Love to Encombe.

To Robert Ross

[Circa 18 December 1892]   *Babbacombe Cliff, Torquay*

My dearest Bobbie, Thank you so much for the *New Review*. Gosse's mention of me is most charming and courteous. Pray tell him from me what pleasure it gave me to receive so graceful a recognition from so accomplished a man of letters. As a rule, journalists and literary people write so horribly, and with such gross familiarity, and virulent abuse, that I am rather touched by any mention of me that is graceful and civil.

How are you? Are there beautiful people in London? Here there are none; everyone is so unfinished. When are you coming down? I am lazy and languid, doing no work. I need stirring up. With best love. Ever yours

OSCAR

To Lord Alfred Douglas

[?January 1893]   *Babbacombe Cliff*

My Own Boy, Your sonnet is quite lovely, and it is a marvel that those red rose-leaf lips of yours should have been made no less for music and song than for madness of kissing. Your slim gilt soul walks between passion and poetry. I know Hyacinthus, whom Apollo loved so madly, was you in Greek days.

Why are you alone in town, and when do you go to Salisbury? Do go there and cool your hands in the grey twilight of Gothic things, and come here whenever you like. It is a lovely place – it only lacks you; but go to Salisbury first. Always, with undying love, yours   OSCAR

To John Lane

[Early February 1893]   *Babbacombe Cliff*

Dear Mr Lane, Your letter has not yet arrived, but I have received your telegram, which I will now regard as a formal record of our agreement. You see now, I feel sure, how right I was in continually pressing you for a written agreement, and I cannot understand why you would not do so. I spoke to you on the subject at your own place; you promised to forward the agreement next day; this was in November last; I spoke to you twice about it at the Hogarth Club, you made the same promise. I wrote to you endless letters – a task most wearisome to me – on this plain business matter. I received promises, excuses, apologies, but no agreement. This has been going on for three months, and the fact of your name being on the title-page was an act of pure courtesy and compliment on my part: you asked me to allow it as a favour to you; just as my increasing the numbers printed from 250 to 600 was done to oblige you. I make no profit from the transaction, nor do I derive any benefit. As you are interested in literature and curious works of art I was ready to oblige you. The least return you might have made would have been to have spared me the annoyance of writing endless business letters. I can only tell you that when I did not hear from you in Paris last week I very nearly struck your name off the title-page of the book, and diminished the edition. As you had advertised it, however, I felt this would have been somewhat harsh and unkind to you.

I will now look on the incident as over, and accept the regrets expressed in your telegram. I hope that we may publish some other book of mine, but it must clearly be understood that the business matters are to be attended to by your firm properly and promptly: my sphere is that of art, and of art merely.

With regard to the edition on Dutch paper, I am only putting twenty-five on the market. Of these I have reserved ten for you. Yours very truly

OSCAR WILDE

In the advertisements at the end of Mr Symonds's book, I observe you state of *Salomé*, 'This is the play the Lord Chamberlain refused to license etc.' Please do not do this again. The interest and value of *Salomé* is not that it was suppressed by a foolish official, but that it was written by an artist. It is the tragic beauty of the work that makes it valuable and of interest, not a gross act of ignorance and impertinence on the part of the censor.

Also pray remember that it was agreed that no copy of *Salomé* is to be sent either to the *National Observer* or to Mr O'Connor's *Sunday Sun*.

To Lady Mount-Temple

[8–11 February 1893]   *Babbacombe Cliff*

Dear Lady Mount-Temple, As I suppose Constance has told you, I have returned to your lovely house in order to be with the children while she is away, and if you still allow me I will gladly and gratefully accept your kind invitation to stay on for a couple of weeks more – till March 1st if it will not inconvenience you, as I find the peace and beauty here so good for troubled nerves, and so suggestive for new work.

Indeed, Babbacombe Cliff has become a kind of college or school, for Cyril studies French in the nursery, and I write my new play in Wonderland, and in the drawing-room Lord Alfred Douglas – one of Lady Queensberry's sons – studies Plato with his tutor for his degree at Oxford in June. He and his tutor are staying with me for a few days, so I am not lonely in the evenings.

Constance seems very happy in Florence. No doubt you hear from her.

I venture to enclose the formal tribute due to the Lady of The Manor, and with many thanks for your kindness remain most sincerely yours

OSCAR WILDE

To Florence Balcombe Stoker

[Postmark 22 February 1893]   *Babbacombe Cliff*

My dear Florence, Will you accept a copy of *Salomé* – my strange venture in a tongue that is not my own, but that I love as one loves an instrument of music on which one has not played before. You will get it, I hope, tomorrow, and I hope you will like it. With kind regards to Bram, believe me, always your sincere friend   OSCAR WILDE

To Richard Le Gallienne

[22 or 23 February 1893]   *Babbacombe Cliff*

My dear Richard, I have just read the *Star*, and write to tell you how pleased I am that you, with your fluid artistic temperament, should have glided into the secret of the soul of my poem, swiftly, surely, just as years ago you glided into my heart.

There are of course things I regret, for yourself. Journalism is a terrible cave where the divine become tainted – for a moment only. Why should the young prophet, rising from the well of darkness, be like a 'jack in the box'? Why is it that you describe the chill, sceptical, rationalistic Herodias as an 'unimaginative worldly creature'? She is far more than that: she is reason in its tragic raiment, reason with its tragic end – and, oh! Richard, why say I am amusing, when Herod hears that in his *royaume* there is one who can make the dead come to life, and (filled with terror at so hideous a prospect) says in his insolence and his fear 'That I do not allow. It would be terrible if the dead came back.'

But nothing matters much. You have got into the secret chamber of the house in which *Salomé* was fashioned, and I rejoice to think that to you has my secret been revealed, for you are the lover of beauty, and by her much – perhaps over-much – loved and worshipped. Ever yours   OSCAR

To Bernard Shaw

[Postmark 23 February 1893] *Babbacombe Cliff*

My dear Shaw, You have written well and wisely and with sound wit on the ridiculous institution of a stage-censorship: your little book on Ibsenism and Ibsen is such a delight to me that I constantly take it up, and always find it stimulating and refreshing: England is the land of intellectual fogs but you have done much to clear the air: we are both Celtic, and I like to think that we are friends: for these and many other reasons Salomé presents herself to you in purple raiment.

Pray accept her with my best wishes, and believe me, very truly yours

OSCAR WILDE

To Frances Forbes-Robertson

[Circa 23 February 1893] *Babbacombe Cliff*

My dear Frankie, I fear I shall not be in town on the fourth, as I am here with my two boys who are devoted to the sea. Constance is in Rome with her aunt, and we don't like the children to be quite alone.

This is a lovely house, belonging to Lady Mount-Temple whom Norman knows, and has Rossetti drawings, and a Burne-Jones window, and many lovely things.

But today the sea is rough, and there are no dryads in the glen, and the wind cries like a thing whose heart is broken, so I am consoling myself by reading *Salomé*, that terrible coloured little tragedy I once in some strange mood wrote. A copy in Tyrian purple and tired silver is on its way to you. Pray accept it from me as a token of our old friendship, and believe me, always yours OSCAR WILDE

Bosie, still nominally at Oxford, was falling badly behind with his work and was to have been privately tutored at his mother's house in Salisbury by Dodgson, a young classical scholar. Shortly after Dodgson's arrival, Bosie announced that they were going to stay with Oscar in Babbacombe. Dodgson stayed for about two weeks, fascinated and bemused by the domestic arrangements, before returning to London and his job at the British Museum.

To Campbell Dodgson

[Postmark 23 February 1893]   *Babbacombe Cliff*

My dear Dodgson, We are charmed you like the paper-knife and hope it really brings a pleasant memory to you. For myself, I can only assure you how much I enjoyed your visit. I look forward to seeing you in town – either guarding marvellous Rembrandt etchings, or simply existing beautifully, which is even better – and we must talk of purple things and drink of purple wine.

I am still conducting the establishment on the old lines and really think I have succeeded in combining the advantages of a public school with those of a private lunatic asylum, which, as you know, was my aim. Bosie is very gilt-haired and I have bound *Salomé* in purple to suit him. That tragic daughter of passion appeared on Thursday last, and is now dancing for the head of the English public. Should you come across her, tell me how you like her. I want you to like her.

All the boys of the school send their best love, and kindest wishes. Sincerely yours   OSCAR WILDE

Headmaster Babbacombe School

Babbacombe School
Headmaster – Mr Oscar Wilde
Second Master – Mr Campbell Dodgson
Boys – Lord Alfred Douglas

Rules.

Tea for masters and boys at 9.30 a.m.

Breakfast at 10.30.

Work. 11.30–12.30.

At 12.30 Sherry and biscuits for headmaster and boys (the second master objects to this).

12.40–1.30. Work.

1.30. Lunch.

2.30–4.30. Compulsory hide-and-seek for headmaster.

5. Tea for headmaster and second master, brandy and sodas (not to exceed seven) for boys.

6–7. Work.

7.30. Dinner, with compulsory champagne.

8.30–12. Ecarté, limited to five-guinea points.

12–1.30. Compulsory reading in bed. Any boy found disobeying this rule will be immediately woken up.

At the conclusion of the term the headmaster will be presented with a silver inkstand, the second master with a pencil-case, as a token of esteem, by the boys.

To Pierre Louÿs

[Postmark 27 February 1893]   *[Torquay]*

My dear Pierre, Is the enclosed really all that you have to say to me in return for my choosing you out of all my friends to whom to dedicate *Salomé*? I cannot tell you how hurt I am.

Those to whom I merely gave copies have written me charming letters coloured with delicate appreciation of my work. You alone – you whose name I have written in gold on purple – you say nothing, and I don't understand what your telegram means; some trivial jest I suppose; a drop of froth without wine. How you disappoint me! Had you wired '*Je vous remercie*' it would have been enough.

It is new to me to think that friendship is more brittle than love is.

OSCAR WILDE

To the Editor of *The Times*

[Circa 1 March 1893]

Sir, My attention has been drawn to a review of *Salomé* which was published in your columns last week. The opinions of English critics on a French work of mine have, of course, little, if any, interest for me. I write simply to ask you to allow me to correct a misstatement that appears in the review in question.

The fact that the greatest tragic actress of any stage now living saw in my play such beauty that she was anxious to produce it, to take herself the part of the heroine, to lend the entire poem the glamour of her personality, and to my prose the music of her flute-like voice – this was naturally, and always will be, a source of pride and pleasure to me, and I look forward with delight to seeing Mme Bernhardt present my play in Paris, that vivid centre of art, where religious dramas are often performed. But my play was in no sense of the words written for this great actress. I have never written a play for any actor or actress, nor shall I ever do so. Such work is for the artisan in literature, not for the artist.

I remain, sir, your obedient servant   OSCAR WILDE

To Lord Alfred Douglas

[Early March 1893]   *Savoy Hotel, London*

Dearest of all Boys – Your letter was delightful – red and yellow wine to me
– but I am sad and out of sorts – Bosie – you must not make scenes with
me – they kill me – they wreck the loveliness of life – I cannot see *you*, so
Greek and gracious, distorted by passion; I cannot listen to *your* curved lips
saying hideous things to me – don't do it – you break my heart – I'd sooner
be rented all day, than have you bitter, unjust, and horrid – horrid –

I must see you soon – you are the divine thing I want – the thing of grace
and genius – but I don't know how to do it – Shall I come to Salisbury –?
There are many difficulties – my bill here is £49 for a week! I have also got
a new sitting-room over the Thames – but you, why are you not here, my
dear, my wonderful boy –? I fear I must leave; no money, no credit, and a
heart of lead – Ever your own   OSCAR

To J. P. Mahaffy

[?April 1893]   *Haymarket Theatre*

My dear Mahaffy, I am so pleased you like the play, and thank you for your
charming letter, all the more flattering to me as it comes not merely from
a man of high and distinguished culture, but from one to whom I owe so
much personally, from my first and my best teacher, from the scholar who
showed me how to love Greek things.

Let me sign myself, in affection and admiration, your old pupil and your
old friend   OSCAR WILDE

Opus 1, Wilde seems to have regarded as his own Lady Windermere's Fan; *Opus
2, Shaw's* Widowers' Houses *which had been first produced in 1892; and Opus
3,* A Woman of No Importance *which had opened three weeks before.*

To Bernard Shaw

[Postmark 9 May 1893]   *16 Tite Street*

My dear Shaw, I must thank you very sincerely for Op.2 of the great Celtic
School. I have read it twice with the keenest interest. I like your superb
confidence in the dramatic value of the mere facts of life. I admire the
horrible flesh and blood of your creatures, and your preface is a masterpiece – a real masterpiece of trenchant writing and caustic wit and
dramatic instinct. I look forward to your Op.4. As for Op.5, I am lazy, but

am rather itching to be at it. When are you coming to the Haymarket?
Sincerely yours   OSCAR WILDE

Douglas returned to Oxford for the Trinity term, but had not done enough work to sit his Finals and left without a degree. He spent some of the summer months at the cottage which Wilde had taken near Henley translating Salomé *into English, while Oscar tried to work on his next play,* An Ideal Husband. *The quotation is from Act III of* A Woman of No Importance.

To Lady Randolph Churchill

[?June 1893]   *The Cottage, Goring-on-Thames*
Dear Lady Randolph, 'The only difference between the saint and the sinner is that every saint has a past, and every sinner has a future!' That, of course, is the quotation. How dull men are! They should listen to brilliant women, and look at beautiful ones, and when, as in the present case, a woman is both beautiful and brilliant, they might have the ordinary common sense to admit that she is verbally inspired.

   I trust your bet will be promptly paid, as I want to begin writing my new comedy, and have no pen! Believe me, yours sincerely   OSCAR WILDE

To William Wilde

[?Circa 10 July 1893]   *The Cottage, Goring-on-Thames*
My dear Willie, This Saturday is, I fear, impossible, as people are staying here, and things are tedious. You and Dan should have come down for the regatta, even in the evening; there were fireworks of surpassing beauty.

   I am greatly distressed to hear you and the fascinating Dan are smoking American cigarettes. You really must not do anything so horrid. Charming people should smoke gold-tipped cigarettes or die, so I enclose you a small piece of paper, for which reckless bankers may give you gold, as I don't want you to die. With best love, ever yours   OSCAR

Ada Leverson, the Sphinx as Wilde always called her, had published a brief skit on Dorian Gray *in* Punch. *She was one of Wilde's closest women friends. She and her husband Ernest were generous and supportive to Wilde throughout his trials and later they were among the first to greet him on his release from prison.*

To Ada Leverson

[?Circa 15 July 1893]   *Albemarle Club, 13 Albemarle Street*
Your sketch is brilliant, as your work always is. And Dorian Gray looks quite charming. It is quite tragic for me to think how completely he has been understood on all sides!

Why don't you collect your wonderful, witty, delightful sketches – so slight, so suggestive, so full of *esprit* and intellectual sympathy?

You are one of those who, in art, are always, by intuition, behind the scenes, so you see how natural art is.   OSCAR WILDE

By early autumn Bosie's and Oscar's relationship had become severely strained. The translation of Salomé, *which had been more to keep Bosie occupied than because of Oscar's confidence in his French, was a disaster, Oscar later referring to it as full of 'schoolboy faults'. From October 1893 until March 1894 Wilde rented rooms in St James's Place in an attempt to finish his play without the distraction of day-to-day family life and an increasingly demanding Douglas. Lady Queensberry followed Wilde's advice and sent Bosie to Egypt from December until the end of March.*

To Lady Queensberry

[8 November 1893]   *16 Tite Street*
Dear Lady Queensberry, You have on more than one occasion consulted me about Bosie. Let me write to you now about him.

Bosie seems to me to be in a very bad state of health. He is sleepless, nervous, and rather hysterical. He seems to me quite altered.

He is doing nothing in town. He translated my French play last August. Since then he has really done nothing intellectual. He seems to me to have lost, for the moment only I trust, his interest even in literature. He does absolutely nothing, and is quite astray in life, and may, unless you or Drumlanrig do something, come to grief of some kind. His life seems to me aimless, unhappy and absurd.

All this is a great grief and disappointment to me, but he is very young, and terribly young in temperament. Why not try and make arrangements of some kind for him to go abroad for four or five months, to the Cromers in Egypt if that could be managed, where he would have new surroundings, proper friends, and a different atmosphere? I think that if he stays in London he will not come to any good, and may spoil his young life irretrievably, quite irretrievably. Of course it will cost money no doubt, but here is the life of one of your sons – a life that should be brilliant and distinguished and charming – going quite astray, being quite ruined.

I like to think myself his greatest friend – he, at any rate, makes me think so – so I write to you quite frankly to ask you to send him abroad to better surroundings. It would save him, I feel sure. At present his life seems to be tragic and pathetic in its foolish aimlessness.

You will not, I know, let him know *anything about my letter*. I can rely on you, I feel sure. Sincerely yours   OSCAR WILDE

To Lord Alfred Douglas

[Circa 20 December 1893]   *10 & 11 St James's Place, London SW*
My dearest Boy, Thanks for your letter. I am overwhelmed by the wings of vulture creditors, and out of sorts, but I am happy in the knowledge that we are friends again, and that our love has passed through the shadow and the night of estrangement and sorrow and come out rose-crowned as of old. Let us always be infinitely dear to each other, as indeed we have been always.

I hear Bobbie is in town, lame and bearded! Isn't it awful? I have not seen him yet. Lesly Thomson has appeared; he is extremely anxious to devote his entire life to me. Tree has written a long apologetic letter. His reasons are so reasonable that I cannot understand them: a cheque is the only argument I recognise. Hare returns to town early next week. I am going to make an effort to induce him to see that my new play is a masterpiece, but I have grave doubts. This is all the news. How horrid news is. I think of you daily, and am always devotedly yours   OSCAR

To Aubrey Beardsley

[?December 1893]   *10 & 11 St James's Place*
My dear Aubrey, I am charmed to find you are in town. Will you join Bobbie and me at dinner tonight at *Kettner's* (Church St, Soho) at 7.30. We are not going to dress. Ever yours   OSCAR

To John Lane

[Circa December 1893]   *10 & 11 St James's Place*
Dear Mr Lane, The cover of *Salomé* is quite dreadful. Don't spoil a lovely book. Have simply a folded vellum wrapper with the design in scarlet – much cheaper, and much better. The texture of the present cover is coarse

and common: it is quite impossible and spoils the real beauty of the interior. Use up this horrid Irish stuff for stories, etc.: don't inflict it on a work of art like *Salomé*. It really will do you a great deal of harm. Everyone will say that it is coarse and inappropriate. I loathe it. So does Beardsley. Truly yours

OSCAR WILDE

Leo Maxse was a diehard Tory journalist and editor of the National Review.

To Leo Maxse

[Circa 1894]   *16 Tite Street*

Dear Sir, I never write 'slashing' articles: slash does not seem to me to be a quality of good prose. Still less would I feel inclined to write an article attacking all that is known by the term '*Fin-de-Siècle*'.

All that is known by that term I particularly admire and love. It is the fine flower of our civilisation: the only thing that keeps the world from the commonplace, the coarse, the barbarous.

But perhaps your letter was intended for someone else. It seems to me to be addressed to a journalist, not to an artist. However, I merely judge by internal evidence. Faithfully yours   OSCAR WILDE

The paranormal held a constant fascination for Wilde, and not just as a subject of literary study; he had his palm read on several occasions, with disturbing results. This letter was written in reply to the Thirteen Club whose aim was to defy popular superstition and who arranged dinners of thirteen courses with thirteen guests at thirteen tables, after which they smashed mirrors.

To William Harnett Blanch

[January 1894]

Dear Mr Blanch, I have to thank the members of your club for their kind invitation, for which convey to them, I beg you, my sincere thanks. But I love superstitions. They are the colour element of thought and imagination. They are the opponents of common sense. Common sense is the enemy of romance.

The aim of your society seems to be dreadful. Leave us some unreality. Don't make us too offensively sane.

I love dining out; but with a society with so wicked an object as yours I cannot dine. I regret it. I am sure you will all be charming; but I could not come, though thirteen is a lucky number.   OSCAR WILDE

To Lewis Waller

[Circa 6 January 1894]   *16 Tite Street*

My dear Waller, What would you give me for a Triple Bill? I would require a certain sum of money down, and a certain sum on completion; the money down to be returned if you don't like the plays. Royalties on a triple bill which would be played at most two nights a week would not be anything important. I would sell you the plays right out – for Great Britain.

I have finished three acts of the play for Hare, and will do the fourth in the next fortnight, so I could not begin to write till the end of the month, but I could have them ready by the middle of March. Make me an offer, if you care to, and be sure that it is a temptation, for I never resist temptation. Truly yours   OSCAR WILDE

The idea of a triple bill came to nothing, but Waller did produce An Ideal Husband *in January 1895 after John Hare had turned it down.*

To Ralph Payne

[Postmark 12 February 1894]   *16 Tite Street*

Dear Mr Payne, The book that poisoned, or made perfect, Dorian Gray does not exist; it is a fancy of mine merely.

I am so glad you like that strange coloured book of mine: it contains much of me in it. Basil Hallward is what I think I am: Lord Henry what the world thinks me: Dorian what I would like to be – in other ages, perhaps.

Will you come and see me?

I am writing a play, and go to St James's Place, number 10, where I have rooms, every day at 11.30. Come on Tuesday about 12.30, will you? But perhaps you are busy? Still, we can meet, surely, some day. Your handwriting fascinates me, your praise charms me. Truly yours   OSCAR WILDE

To Philip Houghton

[?Late February 1894]   *16 Tite Street*

Dear Sir, I will send you a manuscript copy of my play, a little incomplete, but still enough to give you an idea of its ethical scheme. Your letter has deeply moved me. To the world I seem, by intention on my part, a dilettante and dandy merely – it is not wise to show one's heart to the world – and as seriousness of manner is the disguise of the fool, folly in its exquisite modes of triviality and indifference and lack of care is the robe of the wise man. In so vulgar an age as this we all need masks.

But write to me about yourself; tell me your life and loves, and all that keeps you wondering. Who are you? (what a difficult question for any one of us to answer!) I, at any rate, am your friend   OSCAR WILDE

In 1893 'Mrs Pat' had created the title role of Pinero's The Second Mrs Tanqueray *which had been running for nearly a year. Beardsley's drawing of her appeared shortly afterwards in the first number of the* Yellow Book, *a periodical started by John Lane with Beardsley as art director, in which, by common consent, Wilde was not involved.*

To Mrs Patrick Campbell

[March 1894]   *Box F [St James's Theatre]*
Dear Mrs Campbell, Mr Aubrey Beardsley, a very brilliant and wonderful young artist, and like all artists a great admirer of the wonder and charm of your Art, says that he must once have the honour of being presented to you, if you will allow it. So, with your gracious sanction, I will come round after Act III with him, and you would gratify and honour him much if you would let him bow his compliments to you. He has just illustrated my play of *Salomé* for me, and has a copy of the *édition de luxe* which he wishes to lay at your feet. His drawings are quite wonderful. Very sincerely yours   OSCAR WILDE

On Bosie's return from Egypt, he and Oscar were lunching at the Café Royal when his father, the Marquess, appeared. Bosie and his father had fallen out over Oscar the year before and the row was still simmering, but after all three had lunched together, a form of truce was called. It did not last long. By the beginning of April Queensberry's letters to his son were more abusive than ever, and at the end of June he called at Wilde's Tite Street house and all but accused him of sodomy. Wilde consulted his old friend the solicitor Sir George Lewis, but discovered to his dismay that Lewis had already been retained by Queensberry.

To Lord Alfred Douglas

[Circa 16 April 1894]   *16 Tite Street*
My dearest Boy, Your telegram has just arrived; it was a joy to get it, but I miss you so much. The gay, gilt and gracious lad has gone away – and I hate everyone else: they are tedious. Also I am in the purple valleys of despair, and no gold coins are dropping down from heaven to gladden me. London is very dangerous: writters come out at night and writ one, the

roaring of creditors towards dawn is frightful, and solicitors are getting rabies and biting people.

How I envy you under Giotto's Tower, or sitting in the loggia looking at that green and gold god of Cellini's. You must write poems like apple blossom.

The *Yellow Book* has appeared. It is dull and loathsome, a great failure. I am so glad.

Always, with much love, yours OSCAR

To Lord Alfred Douglas

[?20 April 1894] 16 *Tite Street*

My dearest Boy, Life here is much the same. I find a chastened pleasure in being shaved in Air Street: you are always enquired after, and sonnet-like allusions made to your gilt silk hair.

I saw an emissary from Mansfield, the actor, this morning. I think of writing *The Cardinal of Avignon* at once. If I had peace, I would do it. Mansfield would act it splendidly.

Max on Cosmetics in the *Yellow Book* is wonderful: enough style for a large school, and all very precious and thought-out: quite delightfully wrong and fascinating.

I had a frantic telegram from Edward Shelley, of all people! asking me to see him. When he came he was of course in trouble for money. As he betrayed me grossly I, of course, gave him money and was kind to him. I find that forgiving one's enemies is a most curious morbid pleasure; perhaps I should check it. With love, ever yours OSCAR

Edward Shelley was working for John Lane as an assistant when Wilde met him in 1892. Wilde was obviously attracted to him and invited him to dinner and to stay at an hotel on two occasions but, by Shelley's own admission, 'no improprieties occurred'. Wilde also had him to dine with Constance at Tite Street and offered him money to continue his education, in return for which Shelley helped Queensberry's lawyers and the Crown in all three of Wilde's trials.

To Mrs Bernard Beere

[?April 1894] 16 *Tite Street*

My dear Bernie, Of course: *we* must fly to Australia: I could not let you go alone. I have written to Cartwright – a bald genius who is dear Dot's agent – to ask him if it can be arranged. They have also *Mrs Tanqueray*, in which I long to see you.

I have also asked Cartwright if Dot is coming over – or I suppose I should say coming *up* from Australia. I believe that absurdly shaped country lies right underneath the floor of one's coal-cellar.

Why rusticate in this reckless way? You are wanted in town. *Once Upon a Time* was dreadful. Since the appearance of Tree in pyjamas there has been the greatest sympathy for Mrs Tree. It throws a lurid light on the difficulties of their married life.

Who is the fortunate mortal who has the honour of entertaining you? I dislike him more than I can tell you. Ever yours   OSCAR

To Lord Alfred Douglas

[?July 1894]   *New Travellers Club*
My own dear Boy, I hope the cigarettes arrived all right. I lunched with Gladys de Grey, Reggie and Aleck Yorke there. They want me to go to Paris with them on Thursday: they say one wears flannels and straw hats and dines in the Bois, but, of course, I have no money, as usual, and can't go. Besides I want to see you. It is really absurd. *I can't live without you.* You are so dear, so wonderful. I think of you all day long, and miss your grace, your boyish beauty, the bright sword-play of your wit, the delicate fancy of your genius, so surprising always in its sudden swallow-flights towards north or south, towards sun or moon – and, above all, you yourself. The only thing that consoles me is what the Sibyl of Mortimer Street (whom mortals term Mrs Robinson) said to me. If I could disbelieve her I would, but I can't, and I know that early in January you and I will go away together for a long voyage, and that your lovely life goes always hand in hand with mine. My dear wonderful boy, I hope you are brilliant and happy.

I went to Bertie, today I wrote at home, then went and sat with my mother. Death and Love seem to walk on either hand as I go through life: they are the only things I think of, their wings shadow me.

London is a desert without your dainty feet, and all the buttonholes have turned to weeds: nettles and hemlock are 'the only wear'. Write me a line, and take all my love – now and for ever.

Always, and with devotion – but I have no words for how I love you.

OSCAR

Mrs Robinson's prophecy was fulfilled the following January when Oscar and Bosie travelled to Algiers together. She is also said to have told Wilde, 'I see a very brilliant life for you up to a certain point. Then I see a wall. Beyond the wall I see

nothing.' Deeply in debt by this time owing to his hugely extravagant life with Douglas, Wilde prepared the scenarios of two plays for Alexander. The first one later became The Importance of Being Earnest.

To George Alexander

[?July 1894]   16 *Tite Street*

My dear Aleck, Thanks for your letter. There really is nothing more to tell you about the comedy beyond what I said already. I mean that the real charm of the play, if it is to have charm, must be in the dialogue. The plot is slight, but, I think, adequate.

Act 1. Evening party. 10 p.m.

Lord Alfred Rufford's rooms in Mayfair. Arrives from country Bertram Ashton his friend: a man of 25 or 30 years of age: his great friend. Rufford asks him about his life. He tells him that he has a ward, etc. very young and pretty. That in the country he has to be serious, etc. that he comes to town to enjoy himself, and has invented a fictitious younger brother of the name of George – to whom all his misdeeds are put down. Rufford is deeply interested about the ward.

Guests arrive: the Duchess of Selby and her daughter, Lady Maud Rufford, with whom the guardian is in love – Fin-de-Siècle talk, a lot of guests – the guardian proposes to Lady Maud on his knees – enter Duchess – Lady Maud: 'Mamma, this is no place for you.'

Scene: Duchess enquires for *her son Lord Alfred Rufford*: servant comes in with note to say that Lord Alfred has been suddenly called away to the country. Lady Maud vows eternal fidelity to the guardian whom she only knows under the name of *George* Ashton.

(PS The disclosure of the guardian of his double life is occasioned by Lord Alfred saying to him 'You left your handkerchief here the last time you were up' (or cigarette case). The guardian takes it – the Lord A. says 'but why, dear George, is it marked Bertram – who *is* Bertram Ashton?' Guardian discloses plot.)

Act II. The guardian's home – pretty cottage.

Mabel Harford, his ward, and her governess, Miss Prism, Governess of course dragon of propriety. Talk about the profligate George: maid comes in to say 'Mr George Ashton'. Governess protests against his admission. Mabel insists. Enter Lord Alfred. Falls in love with ward at once. He is reproached with his bad life, etc. Expresses great repentance. They go to garden.

Enter guardian: Mabel comes in: 'I have a great surprise for you – your brother is here.' Guardian of course denies having a brother. Mabel says 'You cannot disown your own brother, whatever he has done' – and brings in Lord Alfred. Scene: also scene between two men alone. Finally Lord Alfred arrested for debts contracted by guardian: guardian delighted: Mabel, however, makes him forgive his brother and pay up. Guardian looks over bills and scolds Lord Alfred for profligacy.

Miss Prism backs the guardian up. Guardian then orders his brother out of the house. Mabel intercedes, and brother remains. Miss Prism has designs on the guardian – matrimonial – she is 40 at least – she believes he is proposing to her and accepts him – his consternation.

Act III. Mabel and the false brother.

He proposes and is accepted. When Mabel is alone, Lady Maud, who only knows the guardian under the name of George, arrives alone. She tells Mabel she is engaged 'to George' – scene naturally. Mabel retires: enter George, he kisses his sister naturally. Enter Mabel and sees them. Explanations, of course. Mabel breaks off the match on the ground that there is nothing to reform in George: she only consented to marry him because she thought he was bad and wanted guidance. He promises to be a bad husband – so as to give her an opportunity of making him a better man; she is a little mollified.

Enter guardian: he is reproached also by Lady Maud for his respectable life in the country: a JP: a county-councillor: a churchwarden: a philanthropist: a good example. He appeals to his life in London: she is mollified, on condition that he never lives in the country: the country is demoralising: it makes you respectable. 'The simple fare at the Savoy: the quiet life in Piccadilly: the solitude of Mayfair is what you need etc.'

Enter Duchess in pursuit of her daughter – objects to both matches. Miss Prism, who had in early days been governess to the Duchess, sets it all right, without intending to do so – everything ends happily.

Result
Curtain
Author called
Cigarette called
Manager called

Royalties for a year for author.

Manager credited with writing the play. He consoles himself for the slander with bags of red gold.
Fireworks

Of course this scenario is open to alterations: the third act, after entrance of Duchess, will have to be elaborated: also, the local doctor, or clergyman, must be brought in, in the play for Prism.

Well, I think an amusing thing with lots of fun and wit might be made. If you think so, too, and care to have the refusal of it – do let me know – and send me £150. If when the play is finished, you think it too slight – not serious enough – of course you can have the £150 back – I want to go away and write it – and it could be ready in October – as I have nothing else to do – and Palmer is anxious to have a play from me for the States 'with no real serious interest' – just a comedy.

In the meanwhile, my dear Aleck, I am so pressed for money, that I don't know what to do. Of course I am extravagant, but a great deal of my worries come from the fact that I have had for three years to keep up two establishments – my dear Mother's as well as my own – like many Irish ladies she never gets her jointure paid – small though it is – and naturally it falls on me – this is of course *quite private* but for these years I have had two houses on my shoulders – and of course, am extravagant besides – you have always been a good wise friend to me – so think what you can do.

Kind regards to Mrs Aleck. Yours ever   OSCAR

For August and September the Wildes rented a house in Worthing for a family seaside holiday. It was there that he wrote most of Earnest *and sketched out his second scenario for Alexander. The play remained unwritten, but after his imprisonment, Wilde, by then living from hand to mouth, somewhat immorally sold the outline to several people, among them Frank Harris, who wrote it up as* Mr and Mrs Daventry *and produced it a month before Wilde's death.*

To George Alexander

[August 1894]   *The Haven, 5 Esplanade, Worthing*
Dear Aleck, What do you think of this for a play for you? A man of rank and fashion marries a simple sweet country girl – a lady – but simple and ignorant of fashionable life. They live at his country place and after a time he gets bored with her, and invites down a lot of fashionable *fin-de-siècle* women and men. The play opens by his lecturing his wife on how to behave – not to be prudish, etc. – and not to mind if anyone flirts with her. He says to her, 'I have asked Gerald Lancing who used to admire you so much. Flirt with him as much as you like.'

The guests arrive, they are horrid to the wife, they think her dowdy and dull. The husband flirts with Lady X. Gerald is nice and sweet and friendly to the wife.

Act II. The same evening, after dinner. Love scene between the husband and Lady X: they agree to meet in the drawing-room after everyone has retired. The guests bid good-night to the wife. The wife is tired and falls half asleep on a sofa. Enter husband: *he lowers the lamps*: then Lady X arrives; *he locks the door*. Love scene between them: wife hears it all. Suddenly violent beating on the door. Voice of Lady X's husband outside, desiring admittance. Terror of Lady X! Wife rises, turns up the lamp and goes to the door and unlocks it. Lady X's husband enters! Wife says 'I am afraid I have kept Lady X up too late; we were trying an absurd experiment in thought reading' (anything will do). Lady X retires with her husband. Wife then left alone with her own husband. He comes towards her. She says 'Don't touch me'. He retires.

Then enter Gerald, says he has been alarmed by noises, thought there were robbers. Wife tells him everything; he is full of indignation; it is evident he loves the wife. She goes to her room.

Act III. Gerald's rooms. Wife comes to see him: it is clear that they love each other. They settle to go away together. Enter servant with card. The husband has called. The wife is frightened, but Gerald consents to see him. Wife retires into another room.

Husband is rather repentant. He implores Gerald to use his influence with the wife to make her forgive him. (Husband is a gross sentimental materialist.) Gerald promises that he will do so. It is evident that it is a great act of self-sacrifice for him. Exit husband with maudlin expressions of gratitude.

Enter wife: Gerald asks her to go back to her husband. She refuses with scorn. He says 'You know what it costs me to ask you to do that. Do you not see that I am really sacrificing myself?' Etc. She considers: 'Why should you sacrifice me? I love you. You have made me love you. You have no right to hand my life over to anyone else. All this self-sacrifice is wrong, we are meant to live. That is the meaning of life.' Etc. She forces him by her appeals and her beauty and her love to take her away with him.

Three months afterwards: Act IV. Gerald and wife together. She is reading Act IV of *Frou-Frou*. They talk about it. A duel between Gerald and the husband is fixed for the day on which the scene takes place. She is confident he will not be killed. He goes out. Husband enters. Wife proclaims her love for her lover. Nothing would induce her to go back to her husband. Of the two she wishes him to die. 'Why?' says husband. 'Because the father of my child must live.' Husband goes out. Pistols are heard. He has killed himself.

Enter Gerald, the husband not having appeared at the duel. 'What a coward,' says Gerald. 'No,' she answers, 'not at the end. He is dead. We must love one another devotedly now.' Curtain falls with Gerald and the wife clinging to each other as if with a mad desire to make love eternal. *Finis.*

What do you think of this idea?

I think it extremely strong. *I want the sheer passion of love to dominate everything.* No morbid self-sacrifice. No renunciation. A sheer flame of love between a man and a woman. That is what the play is to rise to – from the social chatter of Act I, through the theatrical effectiveness of Act II, up to the psychology with its great *dénouement* in Act III, till love dominates Act IV and accepts the death of the husband as in a way its proper right, leaving love its tragedy, and so making it a still greater passion.

Of course I have only scribbled this off. I only thought of the plot this morning, but I send it to you. I see great things in it, and, if you like it when done, you can have it for America. Ever yours   OSCAR

While the Wildes were at Worthing, Douglas came to visit three times. What Constance made of his presence is not known, but on the second occasion he wrote to Robert Ross that he had become 'a bone of contention between Oscar and Mrs Oscar', possibly over a trip which he and Oscar proposed to take together to Dieppe. Alphonso Conway, a sometime newspaper seller on Worthing pier, later gave evidence to Queensberry's solicitors for the libel trial which Wilde brought against the Marquess the following year.

To Lord Alfred Douglas

[13 August 1894]   *5 Esplanade, Worthing*

My own dearest Boy, How sweet of you to send me that charming poem. I can't tell you how it touches me, and it is full of that light lyrical grace that you always have – a quality that seems so easy, to those who don't understand how difficult it is to make the white feet of poetry dance lightly among flowers without crushing them, and to those 'who know' is so rare and so distinguished. I have been doing nothing here but bathing and playwriting. My play is really very funny: I am quite delighted with it. But it is not shaped yet. It lies in Sibylline leaves about the room, and Arthur has twice made a chaos of it by 'tidying up'. The result, however, was rather dramatic. I am inclined to think that Chaos is a stronger evidence for an Intelligent Creator than Kosmos is: the view might be expanded.

Percy left the day after you did. He spoke much of you. Alphonso is still in favour. He is my only companion, along with Stephen. Alphonso always alludes to you as 'the Lord', which however gives you, I think, a Biblical Hebraic dignity that gracious Greek boys should *not* have. He also says, from time to time, 'Percy was the Lord's favourite,' which makes me think of Percy as the infant Samuel – an inaccurate reminiscence, as Percy was Hellenic.

Yesterday (Sunday) Alphonso, Stephen, and I sailed to Littlehampton in the morning, bathing on the way. We took five hours in an awful gale to come back! did not reach the pier till eleven o'clock at night, pitch dark all the way, and a fearful sea. I was drenched, but was Viking-like and daring. It was, however, quite a dangerous adventure. All the fishermen were waiting for us. I flew to the hotel for hot brandy and water, on landing with my companions, and found a letter for you from dear Henry, which I send you: they had forgotten to forward it. As it was past *ten* o'clock on a Sunday night the proprietor could not *sell* us any brandy or spirits of any kind! So he had to *give* it to us. The result was not displeasing, but what laws! A hotel proprietor is not allowed to sell 'necessary harmless' alcohol to three shipwrecked mariners, wet to the skin, because it is Sunday! Both Alphonso and Stephen are now anarchists, I need hardly say.

Your new Sibyl is really wonderful. It is most extraordinary. I must meet her.

Dear, dear boy, you are more to me than any one of them has any idea; you are the atmosphere of beauty through which I see life; you are the incarnation of all lovely things. When we are out of tune, all colour goes from things for me, but we are never really out of tune. I think of you day and night.

Write to me soon, you honey-haired boy! I am always devotedly yours

OSCAR

To W. B. Yeats

[?August–September 1894]   *5 Esplanade, Worthing*

Dear Yeats, With pleasure. I don't know that I think 'Requiescat' very typical of my work. Still, I am glad you like it.

I have just finished a play, so my handwriting is abominable.

Personally, I would sooner you chose a sonnet: that one on the sale of Keats's love letters: or the one beginning 'Not that I love thy children' with which my book opens, but the garden – such as it is – is yours to pluck from. Truly yours   OSCAR WILDE

In September Mathews and Lane terminated their partnership. Wilde was asked to state which partner he wished to follow and compromised by proposing to leave the plays with Lane and Mr W. H. with Mathews. In the event he remained uneasily with Lane whom he never much liked and after whom he named the manservant in Earnest. *As in all his correspondence with publishers, Wilde shows how unexpectedly astute he could be in matters of money and contracts.*

To Elkin Mathews and John Lane

[Circa 8 September 1894]   *5 Esplanade, Worthing*

Gentlemen, I have received your letters.

I am informed by Mr Lane that Mr Mathews declines to publish my story on Shakespeare's sonnets 'at any price' and that he himself will not publish it (at any price, I presume) unless he 'approves' of it!

Eighteen months ago nearly – at any rate considerably more than a year ago – Mr Lane on behalf of the firm, and using the firm's name, entered into an agreement with me to publish *The Portrait of Mr W. H.*: the number of copies to be printed, the royalties to be paid to me, the selection of the artist to whom the style of presentation of the work was to be confided, were all agreed upon: the book was subsequently advertised in the list of the coming publications of the firm: and notices to that effect have appeared in the literary columns of many newspapers. The agreement was stamped in my presence by Mr Lane, and signed by him on behalf of the firm. I do not suggest for a moment that he had not the authority to do so. He acted, I am quite sure, with the full authority of the firm of which he is, or was, a partner. If he did not, it is his affair, not mine.

It is the duty of the firm to publish my book, which they have now advertised for about sixteen months, and which they agreed with me to publish. I have a right to insist upon their doing so: and that right I retain. For the firm to break their agreement with me would be dishonourable, dishonest, and illegal.

Upon the other hand I am quite ready to enter into a compromise. You made an agreement to publish my book on certain terms: you have advertised the book as being about to appear: you have had the rights over the book since last July year. The delay in its publication has been very annoying to me, but I have always behaved towards your firm with perfect courtesy and kindness. Even now, when I am calmly told that one member of the firm refuses, after his stamped agreement nearly eighteen months old, to publish the book 'at any price': and the other calmly tells me that his publication of the book depends on his approval of it: I am not really angry:

I am simply amused. However, I am quite ready to let you off your agreement, on condition that you send me a cheque for £25, by return. I think you will agree with me that under the circumstances I am acting with great consideration towards your firm. If you do not think so I shall feel that I have been wrong in the estimate I have formed of your desire to act in an honourable and straightforward manner in your business relations with men of letters. Yours faithfully   OSCAR WILDE

The Green Carnation was published anonymously in September 1894. In its portrayal of Esmé Amarinth and Lord Reginald Hastings it came dangerously close to the truth of Oscar's relationship with Bosie. The author was Robert Hichens, a young homosexual whom Douglas had met in Cairo. It added to the growing feeling of public unease about Wilde's behaviour.

Telegram: To Ada Leverson

22 September 1894   *Worthing*

Esmé and Reggie are delighted to find that their Sphinx is not a minx after all, but are somewhat disappointed to learn that. Esmé feels a little jealous but hopes the Sphinx will remember that Sunday should be no exception to the general rule. Reggie goes up to town tonight – Cadogan Place. He proposes to call on the dear and rarely treacherous Sphinx tomorrow. The doubting disciple who has written the false gospel is one who has merely talent unrelieved by any flashes of physical beauty.

To Ada Leverson

[?23 September 1894]   [?*Worthing*]

Dear Sphinx, Of course you have been deeply wronged. But there are many bits not unworthy of your brilliant pen: and treachery is inseparable from faith. I often betray myself with a kiss.

Hichens I did not think capable of anything so clever. It is such a bore about journalists, they are so very clever.

I suppose you heard about our telegrams.

How sweet of you to have *Intentions* bound for me for your birthday! I simply love that book.

I shall be in town soon, and must come and charm the Sphinx with honeycakes. The trouble is I left my flute in a railway carriage – and the fauns take so long to cut new reeds. Ever yours   OSCAR WILDE

To the Editor of the *Pall Mall Gazette*

1 October [1894]   *Worthing*
Sir, Kindly allow me to contradict, in the most emphatic manner, the suggestion, made in your issue of Thursday last, and since then copied into many other newspapers, that I am the author of *The Green Carnation*.

I invented that magnificent flower. But with the middle-class and mediocre book that usurps its strangely beautiful name I have, I need hardly say, nothing whatsoever to do. The flower is a work of art. The book is not.

I remain, sir, your obedient servant   OSCAR WILDE

On Bosie's last visit to Worthing, he and Oscar moved into the Hotel Metropole in Brighton where Bosie caught influenza and Oscar nursed him. After a few days they moved into lodgings where Oscar in turn fell ill and Bosie abandoned him and went to London. Terrible scenes followed and, as Oscar later recalled, it was probably the last chance he had to end their relationship. But on 18 October Bosie's eldest brother, Viscount Drumlanrig, was killed in a shooting accident, rumoured to be suicide. Ives was a poet, penologist and low-key homosexual.

To George Ives

[Postmark 22 October 1894]   *16 Tite Street*
Dear George, I have been so upset by the terrible tragedy of poor Drumlanrig's death that I have not been able to answer your letter. It is a great blow to Bosie: the first noble sorrow of his boyish life: the wings of the angel of Death have almost touched him: their purple shadow lies across his way, for the moment: I am perforce the sharer of his pain.

The attack on you I have not read: I can't find it in the *Review of Reviews*: but congratulate you on it. When the prurient and the impotent attack you, be sure you are right.

Let me see you soon. Ever yours   OSCAR

To George Alexander

[Circa 25 October 1894]   *16 Tite Street*
My dear Aleck, I have been ill in bed for a long time, with a sort of malarial fever, and have not been able to answer your kind letter of invitation. I am quite well now, and, as you wished to see my somewhat farcical comedy, I send you the first copy of it. It is called *Lady Lancing* on the cover: but the real title is *The Importance of Being Earnest*. When you read the play, you will

see the punning title's meaning. Of course, the play is not suitable to you at all: you are a romantic actor: the people it wants are actors like Wyndham and Hawtrey. Also, I would be sorry if you altered the definite artistic line of progress you have always followed at the St James's. But, of course, read it, and let me know what you think about it. I have very good offers from America for it.

I read charming accounts of your banquet at Birmingham, and your praise of the English dramatist. I know and admire Pinero's work, but *who is Jones?* Perhaps the name as reported in the London papers was a misprint for something else. I have never heard of Jones. Have you?

Give my kind regards to Mrs Aleck, and believe me, sincerely yours

OSCAR WILDE

Adela Schuster lived at Cannizaro Park in Wimbledon (still in existence as an hotel). She was not a close friend of Wilde's, but was extraordinarily generous to him at the time of his crash, giving him £1000 for his personal use and taking a benevolent interest in his re-establishing himself after prison. Wilde always referred to her later as 'the Lady of Wimbledon'.

To Adela Schuster

[?November 1894]   [?London]
Thank you so much for your letter and for the book: but for the letter beyond all. Yes; that is the story. I wish I could write them down, these little coloured parables or poems that live for a moment in some cell of my brain, and then leave it to go wandering elsewhere. I hate writing: the mere act of writing a thing down is troublesome to me. I want some fine medium, and look for it in vain.

I was so happy at Cannizaro. Give please my kindest regards to your dear mother. Sincerely   OSCAR WILDE

Constance had collaborated with Humphreys, manager of Hatchard's bookshop in Piccadilly, to produce Oscariana, *a little collection of Wildean aphorisms, which was published in January 1895. Humphreys became her confidant for a while and, from extant correspondence, maybe briefly her lover at this time. As a gesture of solidarity to Wilde, Humphreys published a limited edition of 'The Soul of Man under Socialism' immediately after Wilde's conviction.*

To Arthur L. Humphreys

[Late November 1894]   *16 Tite Street*

Dear Mr Humphreys, The book is, as it stands, so bad, so disappointing, that I am writing a set of new aphorisms, and will have to alter much of the printed matter. The plays are particularly badly done. Long passages are quoted, where a single aphorism should have been extracted.

The book, well done, should be a really brilliant thing: no English writer has for years ever published aphorisms. But to do it well requires time, and I am busy, with heaps of things, but I work a little at it every morning. I enclose Copeland & Day's letter.

I think the book should be dearer than 2s.6d – all my books are dear – and it would look like underselling the other publishers, who have given their consent for extracts. I think also it should be bound in cloth, and look dainty and nice. I don't want a 'railway bookstall' book. In England a paper-covered book gets so dirty and untidy: I should like a book as dainty as John Gray's poems by Ricketts. I think also there should be fifty large-paper at a guinea: the book could be five shillings.

After the *Green Carnation* publication, this book of 'real Oscar Wilde' should be refined and distinguished: else, it will look like a bit of journalism.

Besides, *your* first book should be a work of art – something to be proud of. Please think over all this.

The *Saturday* was of course mine. Truly yours   OSCAR WILDE

I should prefer Copeland & Day to bring it out themselves separately, following our lines.

Wilde's own contribution to the Chameleon, *'Phrases and Philosophies for the Use of the Young', had appeared in the first (and only) number. Much was made of their 'immorality' by Queensberry's counsel, Edward Carson, in the libel trial, as well as Wilde's association with the sort of magazine which produced the overtly homoerotic story 'The Priest and the Acolyte'.*

To Ada Leverson

[Early December 1894]   *Albemarle Club*

Dear Sphinx, Your aphorisms must appear in the second number of the *Chameleon*: they are exquisite. 'The Priest and the Acolyte' is not by Dorian: though you were right in discerning by internal evidence that the author has a profile. He is an undergraduate of strange beauty.

The story is, to my ears, too direct: there is no nuance: it profanes a little by revelation: God and other artists are always a little obscure. Still, it has interesting qualities, and is at moments poisonous: which is something. Ever yours   OSCAR

Wilde and Douglas arrived in Algiers on 17 January. Wilde stayed for two weeks, returning for the rehearsals for The Importance of Being Earnest, *which opened on 14 February. Douglas remained for a month, only arriving back a week after the first night of the play. The interview 'Mr Oscar Wilde on Mr Oscar Wilde' in the* St James's Gazette, *largely a vehicle for his views on critics, censorship and his own plays, seems to have been a collaboration between him and Ross. Among his reported remarks there is a definite twenty-first-century ring to 'The more the public is interested in artists, the less it is interested in art'.*

To Robert Ross

[Circa 25 January 1895]   *Hôtel de l'Europe, Algiers*
Dearest Bobbie, Thank you so much. The interview is most brilliant and delightful, and your forwarding my letters really most sweet of you.

There is a great deal of beauty here. The Kabyle boys are quite lovely. At first we had some difficulty in procuring a proper civilised guide. But now it is all right, and Bosie and I have taken to haschish: it is quite exquisite: three puffs of smoke and then peace and love. Bosie wakes up at night and cries like a child for the best haschish.

We have been on an excursion into the mountains of Kabylia – full of villages peopled by fauns. Several shepherds fluted on reeds for us. We were followed by lovely brown things from forest to forest. The beggars here have profiles, so the problem of poverty is easily solved.

You are a great dear over my letters. Bosie sends his love, so do I. Ever yours
                                                                                    OSCAR
The most beautiful boy in Algiers is said by the guide to be 'deceitful': isn't it sad? Bosie and I are awfully upset about it.

To Lord Alfred Douglas

[Circa 17 February 1895]   *Thos Cook & Son, 33 Piccadilly*
Dearest Boy, Yes: the Scarlet Marquis made a plot to address the audience on the first night of my play! Algy Bourke revealed it, and he was not allowed to enter.

He left a grotesque bouquet of vegetables for me! This of course makes his conduct idiotic, robs it of dignity.

He arrived with a prize-fighter!! I had all Scotland Yard – twenty police – to guard the theatre. He prowled about for three hours, then left chattering like a monstrous ape. Percy is on our side.

I feel now that, without your name being mentioned, all will go well.

I had not wished you to know. Percy wired without telling me. I am greatly touched by your rushing over Europe. For my own part I had determined you should know nothing.

I will wire to Calais and Dover, and you will of course stay with me till Saturday. I then return to Tite Street, I think.

Ever, with love, all love in the world, devotedly your   OSCAR

After Queensberry's visit to Wilde's house the summer before and now this incident at the theatre, Wilde was determined to put a stop to the Marquess's harassment. He consulted his solicitor who in turn asked Alexander and the theatre staff if they would testify and was told they would not. Ironically, Wilde was informed of this by letter on the very day, 28 February, that he discovered the Marquess's insulting card 'For Oscar Wilde posing as somdomite [sic]' at his club. Egged on by Douglas he at once instructed his solicitors to obtain a warrant for Queensberry's arrest for criminal libel and the Marquess was arrested on 2 March. Percy (Lord Douglas of Hawick) was Bosie's elder brother.

To George Alexander

[February 1895]   *St James's Theatre*
Dear Aleck, I am much obliged to you for your cheque for £300.

If it is possible could you let me have the balance as soon as possible. I am already served with writs for £400, rumours of prosperity having reached the commercial classes, and my hotel is loathsome to me. I want to leave it.

On Sunday I hope to send you, or read you, the vital parts of my Florentine play. I think you will like it. In any case, some day soon I would like to talk to you about it. I am sorry my life is so marred and maimed by extravagance. But I cannot live otherwise. I, at any rate, pay the penalty of suffering. Ever yours   OSCAR

To Robert Ross

[28 February 1895]   *Hotel Avondale, Piccadilly*
Dearest Bobbie, Since I saw you something has happened. Bosie's father has left a card at my club with hideous words on it. I don't see anything now but a criminal prosecution. My whole life seems ruined by this man. The

tower of ivory is assailed by the foul thing. On the sand is my life spilt. I don't know what to do. If you could come here at 11.30 please do so tonight. I mar your life by trespassing ever on your love and kindness. I have asked Bosie to come tomorrow. Ever yours OSCAR

To Ernest Leverson

[?20 March 1895] *Cadogan Hotel, Sloane Street*

Dear Leverson, Can you do me a very great favour? Can you advance me £500 for my legal expenses, in this tedious and dreadful trial? Lord Douglas of Hawick, the eldest son, has promised to pay half my costs, and Lady Queensberry has promised to pay 'any amount required', but Lord Douglas is in Devonshire and Lady Queensberry in Florence, and the money is required by my lawyer at once.

If you would do this for me you would be repaid, as far as the money is concerned, within a week or ten days at most: my own indebtedness to you could never be repaid in any way. Will you kindly let me have your answer tomorrow morning by messenger if you can do it. I feel *sure* you will. Sincerely yours OSCAR WILDE

To Ernest Leverson

[?21 March 1895] *16 Tite Street*

Dear Ernest, Bosie and I cannot sufficiently thank you for your great kindness to us: we shall never forget it, but shall always cherish in affection and gratitude the friend who at a moment's notice came forward to help us, so gracefully, so kindly, so readily.

In a few days we hope to be free of our monetary obligation; the other obligation of gratitude and *reconnaissance* we would like to always keep.

Our homage to the dear and wonderful Sphinx, and believe me, dear Ernest, your sincere and grateful friend OSCAR WILDE

Cheque received.

Telegram: To Ada Leverson

25 March 1895 *Charles Street, Haymarket*

Thanks for charming letter. We have been to the Sibyl Robinson. She prophesied complete triumph and was most wonderful. OSCAR

The case opened on 3 April at the Old Bailey with Sir Edward Clarke prosecuting for Wilde and Edward Carson, who had been a student with Wilde at Trinity, defending the Marquess. Cross-examining Wilde, Carson gave him a few hours to defend his conduct with Douglas and his moral stance in his writings. Wilde acquitted himself well enough, though with touches of wit and frivolity which were distinctly out of place in a court of law. Carson then moved on to the evidence of the rent boys and Wilde struggled. By the morning of the third day, on the advice of his counsel, Wilde withdrew the prosecution.

To Constance Wilde

[?5 April 1895]
Dear Constance, Allow no one to enter my bedroom or sittingroom – except servants – today. See no one but your friends. Ever yours   OSCAR

To the Editor of the *Evening News*

5 April 1895   *Holborn Viaduct Hotel*
It would have been impossible for me to have proved my case without putting Lord Alfred Douglas in the witness-box against his father.

Lord Alfred Douglas was extremely anxious to go into the box, but I would not let him do so.

Rather than put him in so painful a position I determined to retire from the case, and to bear on my own shoulders whatever ignominy and shame might result from my prosecuting Lord Queensberry.   OSCAR WILDE

To Lord Alfred Douglas

[5 April 1895]   *[Cadogan Hotel]*
My dear Bosie, I will be at Bow Street Police Station tonight – no bail possible I am told. Will you ask Percy, and George Alexander, and Waller, at the Haymarket, to attend to give bail.

Would you also wire Humphreys to appear at Bow Street for me. Wire to 41 Norfolk Square, W.

Also, come to see me. Ever yours   OSCAR

The Prisoner

'Suffering is one long moment. We cannot divide it by seasons. We can only record its moods, and chronicle their return. . . . For us there is only one season, the season of Sorrow. The very sun and moon seem taken from us.'

No sooner had Wilde's libel action against the Marquess of Queensberry collapsed about midday on 5 April than the defence solicitors, Charles Russell, sent all their working papers, witness statements and other incriminating evidence to the Director of Public Prosecutions. The DPP consulted the two senior law officers and the Home Secretary, and a warrant was issued for Wilde's arrest, which took place at the Cadogan Hotel at 6.20 p.m. the same evening. He was charged at Bow Street Police Court the next morning and bail was refused, which was unusual since he was guilty only of a misdemeanour. Bosie visited Oscar almost every day while he was on remand in Holloway waiting for his trial, which began on 26 April. Two days beforehand the entire contents of Wilde's Tite Street home were auctioned by the sheriffs for outstanding debts. Douglas was made to go to France on the morning after the trial started for fear that he might in some way compromise Wilde's case, which ended on 1 May with a hung jury. A second trial was ordered. In the meantime Wilde was released on bail and was invited to stay with the Leversons until the new trial. He was finally convicted and sentenced to two years' hard labour on 25 May.

Early in April Constance had sent their two sons abroad to Switzerland where her brother was living, while she herself stayed behind, bravely offering what support she could until after Oscar's conviction. Then she, too, went abroad.

For the first two months Wilde was at Pentonville, before moving to Wandsworth in July and to Reading in November where he spent the rest of his sentence.

To Ada and Ernest Leverson

9 April 1895   *HM Prison, Holloway*
Dear Sphinx and Ernest, I write to you from prison, where your kind words have reached me and given me comfort, though they have made me cry, in my loneliness. Not that I am really alone. A slim thing, gold-haired like an angel, stands always at my side. His presence overshadows me. He moves in the gloom like a white flower.

With what a crash this fell! Why did the Sibyl say fair things? I thought but to defend him from his father: I thought of nothing else, and now –

I can't write more. How good and kind and sweet you and Ernest are to me.   OSCAR

To R. H. Sherard

13 April 1895   *HM Prison, Holloway*
My dear Robert, I cannot tell you how your letters have cheered and comforted me in this awful, terrible position in which I am placed, and how glad I am that Sarah, and Goncourt, and other artists are sympathising with me. Pray assure Louÿs, Stuart Merrill, Moréas, and all others how touched – touched beyond words – I am. I am sending you a telegram to ask you if you think Sarah would buy *Salomé* from me. I am so pressed by my creditors that I don't know where to turn. I would repay her of course, when all comes well, but perhaps if you mentioned to her the need I was in of 10,000 francs (£400) she might do it. Ever, with deepest affection and gratitude

OSCAR

Sherard did approach Bernhardt about Salomé. *In 1892 she had written in Constance's autograph book: 'Je vous promets, Madame, d'avoir un immense succès dans* Salomé, *et je vous confirme que le public français sera très fier d'avoir la première de cette pièce,' but now she said it was impossible, thought about sending money, prevaricated and did nothing.*

To Ada Leverson

23 April 1895   *HM Prison, Holloway*
My dear Sphinx, I have just had a charming note from you, and a charming note from Ernest. How good you both are to me!

Willie has been writing me the most monstrous letters. I have had to beg him to stop.

Today Bosie comes early to see me. My counsel seem to wish the case to be tried at once. I don't, nor does Bosie. Bail, or no bail, I think we had better wait.

Later

I have seen counsel, and Bosie. I don't know what to do. My life seems to have gone from me. I feel caught in a terrible net. I don't know where to turn. I care less when I think that he is thinking of me. I think of nothing else. Ever yours   OSCAR

To Lord Alfred Douglas

Monday Evening [29 April 1895]   *HM Prison, Holloway*

My dearest boy, This is to assure you of my immortal, my eternal love for you. Tomorrow all will be over. If prison and dishonour be my destiny, think that my love for you and this idea, this still more divine belief, that you love me in return will sustain me in my unhappiness and will make me capable, I hope, of bearing my grief most patiently. Since the hope, nay rather the certainty, of meeting you again in some world is the goal and the encouragement of my present life, ah! I must continue to live in this world because of that.

Dear —— came to see me today. I gave him several messages for you. He told me one thing that reassured me: that my mother should never want for anything. I have always provided for her subsistence, and the thought that she might have to suffer privations was making me unhappy. As for you (graceful boy with a Christ-like heart), as for you, I beg you, as soon as you have done all that you can, leave for Italy and regain your calm, and write those lovely poems which you do with such a strange grace. Do not expose yourself to England for any reason whatsoever. If one day, at Corfu or in some enchanted isle, there were a little house where we could live together, oh! life would be sweeter than it has ever been. Your love has broad wings and is strong, your love comes to me through my prison bars and comforts me, your love is the light of all my hours. Those who know not what love is will write, I know, if fate is against us, that I have had a bad influence upon your life. If they do that, you shall write, you shall say in your turn, that it is not so. Our love was always beautiful and noble, and if I have been the butt of a terrible tragedy, it is because the nature of that love has not been understood. In your letter this morning you say something which gives me courage. I must remember it. You write that it is my duty to you and to myself to live in spite of everything. I think that is true. I shall try and I shall do it. I want you to keep Mr Humphreys informed of your movements so that when he comes he can tell me what you are doing. I believe solicitors are allowed to see the prisoners fairly often. Thus I could communicate with you.

I am so happy that you have gone away! I know what that must have cost you. It would have been agony for me to think that you were in England when your name was mentioned in court. I hope you have copies of all my books. All mine have been sold. I stretch out my hands towards you. Oh! may I live to touch your hair and your hands. I think that your love will watch over my life. If I should die, I want you to live a gentle peaceful existence somewhere, with flowers, pictures, books, and lots of work. Try to let me hear from you soon. I am writing you this letter in the midst of great suffering; this long day in court has exhausted me. Dearest boy, sweetest of all young men, most loved and most loveable. Oh! wait for me! wait for me! I am now, as ever since the day we met, yours devoutly and with an immortal love   OSCAR

Once bail had been granted, Wilde sought refuge at his mother's house in Chelsea. The bail sureties were Percy Douglas and the Rev. Stewart Headlam who, though no friend of Wilde's, felt that his case was being prejudged. After a few days the Leversons offered him rooms in their Kensington house at Courtfield Gardens. They told the servants that they could have a month's wages if any wished to leave; none did and were 'proud to wait on poor Mr Wilde'.

To Ada Leverson

[?Early May 1895]   [?146 Oakley Street, Chelsea]
My dear Sweet Kind Friend, I have no words to thank you for all you do for me, but for you and Ernest Bosie and I have deepest love.

I hope to be in better spirits tonight. Your sweetness last night was wonderful. Your flowers are like him – your sending them like yourself. Dear, dear Friend, tonight I see you at 7.45. Ah! you are good and gentle and wonderful. Always devotedly yours   OSCAR

To Lord Alfred Douglas

[20 May 1895]   [?2 Courtfield Gardens, Kensington]
My child, Today it was asked to have the verdicts rendered separately. Taylor is probably being judged at this moment, so that I have been able to come back here. My sweet rose, my delicate flower, my lily of lilies, it is perhaps in prison that I am going to test the power of love. I am going to see if I cannot make the bitter waters sweet by the intensity of the love I bear you. I have had moments when I thought it would be wiser to separate. Ah! moments of weakness and madness! Now I see that that would have mutilated my life, ruined my art, broken the musical chords which make a perfect soul. Even covered with mud I shall praise you, from the deepest abysses I shall cry to you. In my solitude you will be with me. I am determined not to revolt but to accept every outrage through devotion to love, to let my body be dishonoured so long as my soul may always keep the image of you. From your silken hair to your delicate feet you are

perfection to me. Pleasure hides love from us but pain reveals it in its essence. O dearest of created things, if someone wounded by silence and solitude comes to you, dishonoured, a laughing-stock to men, oh! you can close his wounds by touching them and restore his soul which unhappiness had for a moment smothered. Nothing will be difficult for you then, and remember, it is that hope which makes me live, and that hope alone. What wisdom is to the philosopher, what God is to his saint, you are to me. To keep you in my soul, such is the goal of this pain which men call life. O my love, you whom I cherish above all things, white narcissus in an unmown field, think of the burden which falls to you, a burden which love alone can make light. But be not saddened by that, rather be happy to have filled with an immortal love the soul of a man who now weeps in hell, and yet carries heaven in his heart. I love you, I love you, my heart is a rose which your love has brought to bloom, my life is a desert fanned by the delicious breeze of your breath, and whose cool springs are your eyes; the imprint of your little feet makes valleys of shade for me, the odour of your hair is like myrrh, and wherever you go you exhale the perfumes of the cassia tree.

Love me always, love me always. You have been the supreme, the perfect love of my life; there can be no other.

I decided that it was nobler and more beautiful to stay. We could not have been together. I did not want to be called a coward or a deserter. A false name, a disguise, a hunted life, all that is not for me, to whom you have been revealed on that high hill where beautiful things are transfigured.

O sweetest of all boys, most loved of all loves, my soul clings to your soul, my life is your life, and in all the worlds of pain and pleasure you are my ideal of admiration and joy.   OSCAR

Under strict prison regulations Wilde was allowed to write and receive only four personal letters a year. He was permitted to see one outside visitor for twenty minutes every three months. One of his first letters, full of regret and begging her forgiveness, was to Constance. Like most of his letters to his wife it has not survived (see p. 85). By special dispensation of the Prison Commissioners, she was granted a visit in September 1895 at which she and Oscar sorted out their financial affairs. Oscar had a life-interest in Constance's marriage settlement in the event of her death and, in return for renouncing two-thirds of this she agreed to give him an annual allowance of £200 on his release. She also put aside any thoughts of divorce which she may have had. On 3 February 1896 Lady Wilde died and Constance travelled specially from Italy to break the news to him. It was but small compensation that Lugné-Poe, the French actor-manager, had staged Salomé a week after her death. More Adey, later an art-dealer and editor of the Burlington Magazine, *was a close friend of both Wilde and Ross. Although not a wealthy man, he had contributed to the costs of the libel trial. He took on the thankless task of trying to sort out Wilde's financial affairs while he was in prison.*

To Robert Ross

10 March 1896   *[HM Prison, Reading]*

My dear Robbie, I want you to have a letter written at once to Mr Hargrove, the solicitor, stating that as my wife has promised to settle one third on me in the case of her predeceasing me I do not wish any opposition to be made to her purchasing my life-interest. I feel that I have brought such unhappiness on her and such ruin on my children that I have no right to go against her wishes in anything. She was gentle and good to me here, when she came to see me. I have full trust in her. Please have this done *at once*, and thank my friends for their kindness. I feel I am acting rightly in leaving this to my wife.

Please write to Stuart Merrill in Paris, or Robert Sherard, to say how gratified I was at the performance of my play: and have my thanks conveyed to Lugné-Poe; it is something that at a time of disgrace and shame I should be still regarded as an artist. I wish I could feel more pleasure: but I seem dead to all emotions except those of anguish and despair. However, please let Lugné-Poe know that I am sensible of the honour he has done me. He is a poet himself. I fear you will find it difficult to read this, but as I am not allowed writing materials I seem to have forgotten how to write: you must excuse me.

Thank More for exerting himself for books: unluckily I suffer from headaches when I read my Greek and Roman poets, so they have not been of much use, but his kindness was great in getting them sent. Ask him to express also my gratitude to the lady who lives at Wimbledon. Write to me please in answer to this, and tell me about literature – what new books etc.: also about Jones's play and Forbes-Robertson's management: about any new tendency in the stage of Paris or London. Also, try and see what Lemaître, Bauër, and Sarcey said of *Salomé* and give me a little résumé: please write to Henri Bauër and say I am touched at his writing nicely. Robert knows him. It was sweet of you to come and see me: you must come again next time. Here I have the horror of death with the still greater horror of living: and in silence and misery [*some lines cut out by prison officials*] but I won't talk more of this. I always remember you with deep affection. Ever your friend

                                                   o. w.

I wish Ernest would get from Oakley Street my portmanteau, fur coat, clothes, and the books of *my own writing* I gave my dear mother. Ask Ernest in whose name the burial-ground of my mother was taken. Goodbye.

To Robert Ross

Saturday, 30 May 1896   *HM Prison, Reading*

Dear Robbie, I could not collect my thoughts yesterday, as I did not expect you till today. When you are good enough to come and see me will you always fix the day? Anything sudden upsets me.

You said that Douglas was going to dedicate a volume of poems to me. Will you write at once to him and say he must not do anything of the kind. I could not accept or allow such a dedication. The proposal is revolting and grotesque. Also, he has unfortunately in his possession a number of letters of mine. I wish him to at once hand all these without exception over to you; I will ask you to seal them up. In case I die here you will destroy them. In case I survive I will destroy them myself. They must not be in existence. The thought that they are in his hands is horrible to me, and though my unfortunate children will never of course bear my name, still they know whose sons they are and I must try and shield them from the possibility of any further revolting disclosure or scandal.

Also, Douglas has some things I gave him: books and jewellery. I wish these to be also handed over to you – for me. Some of the jewellery I know has passed out of his possession under circumstances unnecessary to detail, but he has still some, such as the gold cigarette-case, pearl chain and enamelled locket I gave him last Christmas. I wish to be certain that he has in his possession nothing that I ever gave him. All these are to be sealed up and left with you. The idea that he is wearing or in possession of anything I gave him is peculiarly repugnant to me. I cannot of course get rid of the revolting memories of the two years I was unlucky enough to have him with me, or of the mode by which he thrust me into the abyss of ruin and disgrace to gratify his hatred of his father and other ignoble passions. But I will not have him in possession of my letters or gifts. Even if I get out of this loathsome place I know that there is nothing before me but a life of a pariah – of disgrace and penury and contempt – but at least I will have nothing to do with him nor allow him to come near me.

So will you write at once to him and get these things: until I know they are in your possession I will be more miserable than usual. It is I know an ungracious thing to ask you to do, and he will perhaps write to you in terms of coarse abuse, as he did to Sherard when he was prevented publishing more of my letters, but I earnestly beg of you not to mind. *As soon* as you have received them please write to me, and make part of your letter just like your other, with all its interesting news of literature and the stage. Let me know why Irving leaves Lyceum etc., what he is playing: what at each theatre: who did Stevenson criticise severely in his letters: anything that will for an hour take my thoughts away from the one revolting subject of my imprisonment.

In writing to Douglas you had better quote my letter fully and frankly, so that he should have no loophole of escape. Indeed he cannot possibly refuse. He has ruined my life – that should content him.

I am deeply touched by the Lady of Wimbledon's kindness. You are very good to come and see me. Kind regards to More, whom I would so like to see. o. w.

To the Home Secretary

2 July 1896 *HM Prison, Reading*
To the Right Honourable Her Majesty's Principal Secretary of State for the Home Department.

The Petition of the above-named prisoner humbly sheweth that he does not desire to attempt to palliate in any way the terrible offences of which he was rightly found guilty, but to point out that such offences are forms of sexual madness and are recognised as such not merely by modern pathological science but by much modern legislation, notably in France, Austria, and Italy, where the laws affecting these misdemeanours have been repealed, on the ground that they are diseases to be cured by a physician, rather than crimes to be punished by a judge. In the works of eminent men of science such as Lombroso and Nordau, to take merely two instances out of many, this is specially insisted on with reference to the intimate connection between madness and the literary and artistic temperament, Professor Nordau in his book on 'Degenerescence' published in 1894 having devoted an entire chapter to the petitioner as a specially typical example of this fatal law.

The petitioner is now keenly conscious of the fact that while the three years preceding his arrest were from the intellectual point of view the most brilliant years of his life (four plays from his pen having been produced on the stage with immense success, and played not merely in England, America, and Australia, but in almost every European capital, and many books that excited much interest at home and abroad having been published), still that during the entire time he was suffering from the most horrible form of erotomania, which made him forget his wife and children, his high social position in London and Paris, his European distinction as an artist, the honour of his name and family, his very humanity itself, and left him the helpless prey of the most revolting passions, and of a gang of people who for their own profit ministered to them, and then drove him to his hideous ruin.

It is under the ceaseless apprehension lest this insanity, that displayed itself in monstrous sexual perversion before, may now extend to the entire nature and intellect, that the petitioner writes this appeal which he earnestly entreats may be at once considered. Horrible as all actual madness is, the terror of madness is no less appalling, and no less ruinous to the soul.

For more than thirteen dreadful months now, the petitioner has been subject to the fearful system of solitary cellular confinement: without human intercourse of any kind; without writing materials whose use might help to distract the mind: without suitable or sufficient books, so essential to any literary man, so vital for the preservation of mental balance: condemned to absolute silence: cut off from all knowledge of the external world and the movements of life: leading an existence composed of bitter degradations and terrible hardships, hideous in its recurring monotony of dreary task and sickening privation: the despair and misery of this lonely and wretched life having been intensified beyond words by the death of his mother, Lady Wilde, to whom he was deeply attached, as well as by the contemplation of the ruin he has brought on his young wife and his two children.

By special permission the petitioner is allowed two books a week to read: but the prison library is extremely small and poor: it hardly contains a score of books suitable for an educated man: the books kindly added at the prisoner's request he has read and re-read till they have become almost meaningless to him: he is practically left without anything to read: the world of ideas, as the actual world, is closed to him: he is deprived of everything that could soothe, distract, or heal a wounded and shaken mind: and horrible as all the physical privations of modern prison life are, they are as nothing compared to the entire privation of literature to one to whom Literature was once the first thing of life, the mode by which perfection could be realised, by which, and by which alone, the intellect could feel itself alive.

It is but natural that living in this silence, this solitude, this isolation from all human and humane influences, this tomb for those who are not yet dead, the petitioner should, day and night in every waking hour, be tortured by the fear of absolute and entire insanity. He is conscious that his mind, shut out artificially from all rational and intellectual interests, does nothing, and can do nothing, but brood on those forms of sexual perversity, those loathsome modes of erotomania, that have brought him from high place and noble distinction to the convict's cell and the common gaol. It is inevitable that it should do so. The mind is forced to think, and when it is deprived of the conditions necessary for healthy intellectual activity, such as books, writing materials, companionship, contact with the living world, and the like, it becomes, in the case of those who are suffering from sensual monomanias, the sure prey of morbid passions, and obscene fancies, and thoughts that defile, desecrate and destroy. Crimes may be forgotten or forgiven, but vices live on: they make their dwelling house in him who by horrible mischance or fate has become their victim: they are embedded in his flesh: they spread over him like a leprosy: they feed on him like a strange disease: at the end they become an essential part of the man: no remorse however poignant can drive them out: no tears however bitter can wash them away: and prison life, by its horrible isolation from all that could save a wretched soul, hands the victim over, like one bound hand and foot, to be possessed and polluted by the thoughts he most loathes and so cannot escape from.

For more than a year the petitioner's mind has borne this. It can bear it no longer. He is quite conscious of the approach of an insanity that will not be confined to one portion of the nature merely, but will extend over all alike, and his desire, his prayer is that his sentence may be remitted now, so that he may be taken abroad by his friends and may put himself under medical care so that the sexual insanity from which he suffers may be cured. He knows only too well that his career as a dramatist and writer is ended, and his name blotted from the scroll of English Literature never to be replaced: that his children cannot bear that name again, and that an obscure life in some remote country is in store for him: he knows that, bankruptcy having come upon him, poverty of a most bitter kind awaits him, and that all the joy and beauty of existence is taken from him for ever: but at least in all his hopelessness he still clings to the hope that he will not have to pass directly from the common gaol to the common lunatic asylum.

Dreadful as are the results of the prison system – a system so terrible that it hardens their hearts whose hearts it does not break, and brutalises those who have to carry it out no less than those who have to submit to it – yet at least amongst its aims is not the desire to wreck the human reason. Though it may not seek to make men better, yet it does not desire to drive them mad, and so, earnestly does the petitioner beg that he may be allowed to go forth while he has still some sanity left: while words have still a meaning, and books a message: while there is still some possibility that, by medical science and humane treatment, balance may be restored to a shaken mind and health given back to a nature that once knew purity: while there is still time to rid the temperament of a revolting madness and to make the soul, even for a brief space, clean.

Most earnestly indeed does the petitioner beg the Home Secretary to take, if he so desires it, the opinion of any recognised medical authorities on what would be the inevitable result of solitary confinement in silence and isolation on one already suffering from sexual monomania of a terrible character.

The petitioner would also point out that while his bodily health is better in many respects here than it was at Wandsworth, where he was for two months in the hospital for absolute physical and mental collapse caused by hunger and insomnia, he has, since he has been in prison, almost entirely lost the hearing of his right ear through an abscess that has caused a perforation of the drum. The medical officer here has stated that he is unable to offer any assistance, and that the hearing must go entirely. The petitioner, however, feels sure that under the care of a specialist abroad his hearing might be preserved to him. He was assured by Sir William Dalby, the great aurist, that with proper care there was no reason at all why he should lose his hearing. But though the abscess has been running now for the entire time of his imprisonment, and the hearing getting worse every week, nothing has been done in the way even of an attempted cure. The ear has been syringed on three occasions with plain water for the purpose of examination, that is all. The petitioner is naturally apprehensive lest, as often happens, the other ear may be attacked in a similar way, and to the misery of a shattered and debilitated mind be added the horrors of complete deafness.

His eyesight, of which like most men of letters he had always been obliged to take great care, has also suffered very much from the enforced living in a whitewashed cell with a flaring gas-jet at night: he is conscious of great weakness and pain in the nerves of the eyes, and objects even at a short distance become blurred. The bright daylight, when taking exercise in the prison-yard, often causes pain and distress to the optic nerve, and during the past four months the consciousness of failing eyesight has been a source of terrible anxiety, and should his imprisonment be continued, blindness and deafness may in all human probability be added to the certainty of increasing insanity and the wreck of the reason.

There are other apprehensions of danger that the limitation of space does not allow the petitioner to enter on: his chief danger is that of madness, his chief terror that of madness, and his prayer that his long imprisonment may be considered with its attendant ruin a sufficient punishment, that the imprisonment may be ended now, and not uselessly or vindictively prolonged till insanity has claimed soul as well as body as its prey, and brought it to the same degradation and the same shame. OSCAR WILDE

The Governor of Reading Gaol, Lt-Col. Isaacson, exercised his authority like a tyrant and did everything by the rule book, but shortly after this petition Isaacson was replaced by Major Nelson, whom Wilde later described as 'a man of gentle and humane character, greatly liked and respected by all the prisoners'. The petition resulted in Wilde being allowed writing materials in his cell and a more liberal supply of books, privileges which Nelson applied as generously as he was able.

To R. H. Sherard

Wednesday [26 August 1896]   *[HM Prison, Reading]*
My dear Robert, The Governor has told me that you have written to ask to see me. It is most kind and affectionate of you, but an order has already been sent to More Adey and Arthur Clifton (whom I have not seen yet) and, as you know, I am only allowed two visitors. I did not think there would have been any chance of your being in town. I hope you are well and writing a great deal. I often think of you and of our uninterrupted friendship, of twelve years' standing, and while I bitterly regret the sorrow that I have brought on you and others of my friends, I remember with pride and gratitude your chivalry and courage on my behalf. Should the end of my terrible punishment ever come, you are one of the few people I would like to see, and be with from time to time.

Please remember me very kindly to George Ives. I was greatly touched at hearing of his desire to come and see me. In the terrible solitude and silence in which one lives a message or a memory means a great deal. I hope he is hard at work writing books. I am very glad you know him. He is such a good fellow and so clever.

Should you have anything special to communicate to me – something separate from the sympathy and affection you have, I know, for me – More Adey, who is to write to me in the course of the next fortnight, will communicate it in his letter. He has to write to me on business.

I was so disappointed at not seeing you that I have been allowed as a favour to write this letter to you. Pray remember me to any of my friends who may ask after me, and believe me, dear Robert, sincerely yours OSCAR

To More Adey

Friday [25 September 1896]   *[HM Prison, Reading]*
My dear More, I was greatly delighted to get your letter. I was afraid that Bobbie might have been ill, and that that was the cause of the delay. It was a real pleasure to hear from him at such length, and to see his old wit and

pleasant satire running through his budget: I do hope he will be quite well soon: Please thank his mother for her kind messages. I am very glad she has been spared to watch over Bobbie in his illness.

I thank you very much for writing to the Home Secretary. I do hope it will have some effect. But pity seems to beat in vain at the doors of officialism; and power, no less than punishment, kills what else were good and gentle in a man: the man without knowing it loses his natural kindliness, or grows afraid of its exercise. Still, I hope something may be done. I admit that I look forward with horror to the prospect of another winter in prison: there is something terrible in it: one has to get up long before daybreak and in the dark-cold cell begin one's work by the flaring gas-jet; through the small barred window only gloom seems to find an entrance: and days often go over without one's being once even in the open air: days on which one stifles: days that are endless in their dull monotony of apathy or despair. If I could be released before the winter comes, it would be everything. On November 19th I will have had eighteen months of this black loathsome life: perhaps then something may be done. I know you will do your best: I have no words for my sense of your great wonderful kindness to me.

With regard to my children, I feel that for their own sake as well as for mine they should not be bred up to look on me with either hatred or contempt: a guardian amongst my wife's relations would be for this reason impossible. Of course I would like Arthur Clifton if he would undertake the charge. And so, would you ask Arthur to be my solicitor now: Humphreys is of course of no use: though paid an enormous fee through Leverson he never once came to see me about my Bankruptcy: so I was allowed to become insolvent when there was no reason. If Arthur will be my solicitor he can on application to the Home Secretary come and see me in the Solicitors' Room here for one hour without the presence of a warder, and with him I could discuss the whole affair, and then write to my wife on the whole subject. I would feel quite safe if Arthur was my children's guardian. And as a solicitor his advice would be of great service. If he could come within the next fortnight it would be a great thing.

I was greatly touched by the extract from the letter of the Lady of Wimbledon. That she should keep a gracious memory of me, and have trust or hope for me in the future, lightens for me many dreadful hours of degradation or despair. I have tried to remember and write down the *Florentine Tragedy*: but only bits of it remain with me, and I find that I cannot invent: the silence, the utter solitude, the isolation from all humane and humanising influences, kill one's brain-power: the brain loses its life: becomes fettered to monotony of suffering. But I take notes of books I read, and copy lines and phrases in poets: the mere handling of pen and ink helps me: the horror of prison is the horror of complete brutalisation: that is the abyss always in front of one, branding itself on one's face daily, and the faces of those one sees. I cling to my notebook: it helps me: before I had it my brain was going in very evil circles.

I am so glad you are friends with Robert Sherard: I have no doubt he is very indiscreet, but he is very true, and saved my letters from being published. I know there was nothing in them but expressions of foolish, misplaced, ill-requited, affection for one of crude and callous nature, of coarse greed, and common appetites, but that is why their publication would have been so shameful. The gibbet on which I swing in history now is high enough. There is no need that he of all men should for his own vanity make it more hideous.

I am so glad Pierre Louÿs has made a great name for himself. He was most cultivated, refined, and gentle. Three years ago he told me I would have to choose between his friendship and my fatal connection with A. D. I need hardly say I chose at once the meaner nature and the baser mind. In what a mire of madness I walked! . . . From your silence I see he still refuses to return my presents and letters . . . It is horrible he should still have the power to wound me and find some curious joy in doing so . . . I won't write about him any more today. He is too evil, and there is a storm outside . . .

Poor Aubrey: I hope he will get all right. He brought a strangely new personality to English art, and was a master in his way of fantastic grace, and the charm of the unreal. His muse had moods of terrible laughter. Behind his grotesques there seemed to lurk some curious philosophy . . .

As for my clothes, my fur coat is all I need really; the rest I can get abroad. Don't bother yourself. I hope Arthur will come and bring me good news of you and Robbie. Ever yours   OSCAR

To Robert Ross

[November 1896]   [HM Prison, Reading]
[*The first part of this letter is missing*]
For myself, dear Robbie, I have little to say that can please you. The refusal to commute my sentence has been like a blow from a leaden sword. I am dazed with a dull sense of pain. *I* had fed on hope, and now Anguish, grown hungry, feeds her fill on *me* as though she had been starved of her proper appetite. There are, however, kinder elements in this evil prison air than there were before: sympathies have been shown to me, and I no longer feel entirely isolated from humane influences, which was before a source of

terror and trouble to me. And I read Dante, and make excerpts and notes for the pleasure of using a pen and ink. And it seems as if I were better in many ways. And I am going to take up the study of German: indeed this seems to be the proper place for such a study. There is a thorn, however – as bitter as that of St Paul, though different – that I must pluck out of my flesh in this letter. It is caused by a message you wrote on a piece of paper for me to see. I feel that if I kept it secret it might grow in my mind (as poisonous things grow in the dark) and take its place with other terrible thoughts that gnaw me ... Thought, to those that sit alone and silent and in bonds, being no 'winged living thing', as Plato feigned it, but a thing dead, breeding what is horrible, like a slime that shows monsters to the moon.

I mean, of course, what you said about the sympathies of others being estranged from me, or in danger of being so, by the deep bitterness of the feelings I expressed about Alfred Douglas: and I believe that my letter was lent and shown to others with the part about him cut out by a pair of scissors. Now I don't like my letters shown about as curiosities: it is most distasteful to me: I write to you freely as to one of the dearest friends I have, or have ever had: and, with a few exceptions, the sympathy of others touches me, as far as its loss goes, very little. No man of my position can fall into the mire of life without getting a great deal of pity from his inferiors; and I know that when plays last too long, spectators tire. My tragedy has lasted far too long: its climax is over: its end is mean; and I am quite conscious of the fact that when the end *does* come I shall return an unwelcome visitant to a world that does not want me; a *revenant*, as the French say, as one whose face is grey with long imprisonment and crooked with pain. Horrible as are the dead when they rise from their tombs, the living who come out from tombs are more horrible still.

Of all this I am only too conscious. When one has been for eighteen terrible months in a prison cell, one sees things and people as they really are. The sight turns one to stone. Do not think that I would blame *him* for my vices. He had as little to do with them as I had with his. Nature was in this matter a stepmother to each of us. I blame him for not appreciating the man he ruined. An illiterate millionaire would really have suited him better. As long as my table was red with wine and roses, what did he care? My genius, my life as an artist, my work, and the quiet I needed for it, were nothing to him when matched with his unrestrained and coarse appetites for common profligate life: his greed for money: his incessant and violent scenes: his unimaginative selfishness. Time after time I tried, during those two wasted weary years, to escape, but he always brought me back, by threats of harm to himself chiefly. Then when his father saw in me a method of annoying his son, and the son saw in me the chance of ruining his father, and I was placed between two people greedy for unsavoury notoriety, reckless of everything but their own horrible hatred of each other, each urging me on, the one by public cards and threats, the other by private, or indeed half-public scenes, threats in letters, taunts, sneers . . . I admit I lost my head. I let him do what he wanted. I was bewildered, incapable of judgment. I made the one fatal step. And now . . . I sit here on a bench in a prison cell. In all tragedies there is a grotesque element. He is the grotesque element in mine. Do not think I do not blame myself. I curse myself night and day for my folly in allowing him to dominate my life. If there was an echo in these walls it would cry 'Fool' for ever. I am utterly ashamed of my friendship with him. For by their friendships men can be judged. It is a test of every man. And I feel more poignant abasement of shame for my friendship with Alfred Douglas . . . fifty thousand times more . . . than I do, say, for my connection with Charley Parker of which you may read a full account in my trial. The former is to me a daily source of mental humiliation. Of the latter I never think. It troubles me not. It is of no importance . . . Indeed my entire tragedy sometimes seems to me grotesque and nothing else. For as a result of my having suffered myself to be thrust into the trap Queensberry had laid for me – the trap he openly betted in the Orleans Club he would lure me into – as a result of that, the father ranks in history with the good parents of moral tales: the son with the Infant Samuel: and I, in the lowest mire of Malebolge, sit between Gilles de Retz and the Marquis de Sade. In certain places no one, except those actually insane, is allowed to laugh: and, indeed, even in their case it is against the regulations for conduct: otherwise I think I would laugh at that . . . For the rest, do not let Alfred Douglas suppose that I am crediting him with unworthy motives. He really had no motives in his life at all. Motives are intellectual things. He had passions merely. And such passions are False Gods that *will* have victims at all costs, and in the present case have had one wreathed with bay. He himself cannot but choose to feel *some* remorse. That he should really realise what he has done would be a burden too heavy for him to bear. But he must sometimes think of it. So in your letter tell me how he lives, what his occupations are, his mode of life.

And so now I have in my letter plucked the thorn out. That little scrawled line of yours rankled terribly. I *now* think merely of you getting quite well again, and writing at last the wonderful story of the little restaurant with the strange dish of meat served to the silent clients. Pray remember me, with my thanks, to your dear mother, and also to Aleck. The gilded Sphinx is I suppose wonderful as ever. And send from me all that in my thoughts and feelings is good, and whatever of remembrance and reverence she will accept, to the Lady of Wimbledon, whose soul is a sanctuary for those who are wounded, and a house of refuge for those in pain. Do not show this letter to others, nor discuss what I have written, in your answer. Tell me about that world of shadows I loved so much. And about his life and soul tell me also. I am curious of the thing that stung me: and in my pain there is pity.

OSCAR

In November 1895 Wilde had been declared bankrupt for Queensberry's costs in the libel action. Percy and Lady Queensberry had said they would contribute but only did so when it was too late three years later. Oscar's life-interest in Constance's marriage settlement was regarded as a small potential asset by the receiver and Oscar had been anxious that Constance should purchase it unopposed for a nominal sum. Ross and Adey thought that Wilde was being too conciliatory and, without Wilde's approval, bid against her. Constance assumed that Oscar had gone back on his word and threatened divorce. An ugly and unnecessary wrangle ensued, by the end of which Constance had reduced her offer of an annual allowance to £150 and had lost the last vestiges of trust in Oscar, which partly contributed to the fact that they never met again.

To More Adey

8 March 1897   *HM Prison, Reading*

My dear More, I am very much obliged to you for your letter, which the Governor has kindly allowed me to have and to answer. My business is I know unpleasant, but then it was not for pleasure that you took its burden on you, so I will write quite frankly to you.

Your news has distressed me a good deal. The claims of my own trustees and my brother-in-law would of course be easily withdrawn, and I thought I could, if the Queensberry debt was paid, as it should have been, by the Queensberry family, have made an effort at any rate to pay off my own personal creditors, who are really very few in number. I see, however, that this cannot be. I will now have to think of how to retain or buy my interest in my books and plays. I do not think they will be valued high. As £150 has been already paid to Humphreys who did nothing to help me (beyond of course forcing me to put in two appearances at the Bankruptcy Court where one would have been sufficient and engaging their own relative Mr Grain to appear as counsel where no counsel was required) I am reluctant to even write to them. I am very anxious however to know how I can be kept informed of the state of things, so that if my copyrights are to be sold I may have a chance of bidding for them. I am also anxious about my claim to the place in Ireland: it is now in utter rack and ruin, but I am reluctant to see it pass to a stranger: could Mr Holman, already in touch with the Receiver, let you know if anything happens? In the case of my brother's death, without male issue, the Irish property should fetch something: £4000 or £5000 at least.

As regards the Queensberry family, I of course feel very strongly about their allowing me to be made bankrupt by their father for the costs of the trial, and for such an absolutely contemptible sum; less than half, as I told you, of what in three wasted summer months I spent on Bosie at Goring – less than one half! Their idea that it would be a sort of 'score' off their father not to pay him his paltry claim showed how utterly blind they were to my feelings. As for Queensberry, I suppose nobody ever had such intense pleasure of a low order at such a low cost as he had. It was in the cheapest of markets that he bought his triumph. Indeed it was the only occasion in his life that he found his pleasures economical. To send a man like myself to prison for £900, and then to take him out and make him an insolvent for £700 more, was a piece of good fortune he never looked for. As regards my own debts, they were hardly anything. Their letting their father triumph a second time over me, rather than pay so petty, so abject a sum as £700, cut me very deeply. And people who live in the world of action don't understand that there is another world in which they who are not free live: a world in which nothing happens but emotions, and in which consequently emotions have a power, a proportion, a permanence that is beyond the possibility of description.

I was told, on Percy's behalf, that he had laid aside the sum of £600 for me, as the equivalent of his father's costs, to be used I suppose in buying back for me the property the Bankruptcy Receiver had seized, and possibly in other ways. I conveyed to him my thanks. I consider Percy a very good-hearted fellow, kind and considerate. I would very much like to see him again some time. He should of course have paid the costs, and left me then if necessary to settle my other debts. But he, I have no doubt, acted under advice. If he had realised matters a little more he would have seen that he merely doubled his father's delight and exultation by not interfering to prevent my insolvency. It was the only thing Queensberry was afraid of. He need not have been ... With regard to the whole question the Queensberry family must remember that through them I am in prison, through them a bankrupt, and that they can hardly allow people whom they ruined so completely to go to the workhouse.

I was touched and helped immeasurably by your telling me that some friends of mine have arranged that for eighteen months I am to have enough to live on: that gives me breathing space. But of course I cannot trespass for a lifetime on those on whom I have no more claim than any other of the poor and wretched and homeless people of whom God's world is so full. I couldn't do it. And I may live longer than eighteen months. A heart may be broken and yet fulfil its natural functions. The soul may sit in the shadow of death, and yet the body walk in the ways of life, and breathe and eat and know the sun and rain. I have no organic disease of any kind. I am troubled with insomnia, but I get my four or five hours of sleep every night. Supposing I live on? I should not be at all surprised if I did. I come of a long-lived race. The Queensberry family had better consider the point, the Douglases we will call them, as the other name is loathsome. There are debts of dishonour in a family as well as debts of honour. If the Douglas estates have to be burdened with a prospective claim of some paltry life-interest, let them be so burdened. A family cannot ruin a man like me, and look on the whole thing merely as a subject for sentiment or reminiscence over the walnuts and the wine. People, as somebody in one of Ibsen's plays says, don't do these things. It is dreadful that it should fall on me to remind them. They should consult their family solicitor, and let him communicate the result to my solicitor. That is all that is necessary.

You say in your letter that Bosie is so anxious to make 'some little return' to me for all I 'spent on him'. Unfortunately, I spent on him my life, my genius, my position, my name in history; for these no little, or big return is possible. But as regards the mere wretched pounds, shillings, and pence side of my ruin – the workhouse aspect – he must seriously consider the whole point. It is his duty to do so. His duty to himself as much, far more indeed, than to me. When people play a tragedy they should play it in the 'grand style'. All smallness, pettiness, meagreness of mood or gesture is out of place. If the Douglases don't recognise this, let me be informed. But I don't doubt that they will. It is a perfectly obvious matter. And as for me, my life will of course necessarily be one of great retirement, simplicity and economy of living, and many modes of self-denial, imposed and accepted. But a certain small permanence is requisite even for the practice of the virtues of thrift and economy. Bosie must consider the matter. I will be much obliged if you will copy out all that I have written, from the bottom of page one, and send it off to him. It will relieve my own letter to him of a very unpleasing duty, one that a little thought on his part would have spared me.

As regards my children, I sincerely hope I may be recognised by the Court as having some little, I won't say right, but claim to be allowed to see Cyril from time to time: it would be to me a sorrow beyond words if I were not. I do hope the Court will see in me something more than a man with a tragic vice in his life. There is so much more in me, and I always was a good father to both my children. I love them dearly and was dearly loved by them, and Cyril was my friend. And it would be better for them not to be forced to think of me as an outcast, but to know me as a man who has suffered. Pray let everything be done on my behalf that is possible. A little recognition by the Court would help me so much. And it is a terrible responsibility for the Law to say to a father that he is unfit to see his own children: the conscious-ness of it often makes me unhappy all day long.

As regards my life-interest, should Mr Hargrove make any proposal about it, it of course will be communicated to me by you *at once*. It will require grave consideration. The advances cannot come from me, can they? Should my own solicitor come to see me, pray let it be the last week in this month. I am quite distressed at the idea of his only charging £1.1 and expenses. I think he should have at least £3.3. Let the money be got from Leverson, and whatever Mr Stoker is owed be paid to him from the same fund in Leverson's hands.

I fear you see traces of bitterness in my business letters. Yes, that is so. It is very terrible. In the prison in which my body is I am shown much kindness, but in the prison in which my soul is I can show myself none. I hope that neither in your heart nor in Robbie's, nor in the heart of any that have been good to me, will bitterness of any kind ever find a place. It makes one suffer very deeply. Your affectionate friend   OSCAR WILDE
I quite see that I must accept, gratefully indeed, my discharge as a bankrupt, when I get it, and then set to work to try and pay off some of the debts. I suppose it won't be done till I go out of prison? I would like things held over, on account of the sale of copyrights etc. At present I receive no communication at all from the Receiver. That is, I suppose, right.

For the list of books, so many thanks. I am going to ask for a Bible in French: *la Sainte Bible*.

Around the beginning of 1897, with pen and paper now freely available to him, Wilde started a long letter to Douglas. When it was finished it ran to 50,000 words. Major Nelson consulted the Prison Commissioners who refused to allow its despatch and said that it could be given to the prisoner on his release, which it was. Despite Wilde's instructions to Ross, Douglas was neither sent a copy nor the original. What seems most likely is that Ross, taking Wilde's literary executorship seriously, persuaded him that keeping the manuscript was vital if, as seems to have been Wilde's ultimate intention, the letter was to be published. De Profundis, as it became known, was indeed published by Ross but in a much expurgated form five years after Wilde's death in 1905. Ross then gave the manuscript to the British Museum to be closed for fifty years and it first appeared unedited in 1962.

To Robert Ross

1 April 1897   *HM Prison, Reading*

My dear Robbie, I send you, in a roll separate from this, my letter to Alfred Douglas, which I hope will arrive safe. As soon as you, and of course More Adey whom I always include with you, have read it, I want you to have it carefully copied for me. There are many reasons why I wish this to be done. One will suffice. I want you to be my literary executor in case of my death, and to have complete control over my plays, books and papers. As soon as I find I have a legal right to make a will I will do so. My wife does not understand my art, nor could be expected to have any interest in it, and Cyril is only a child. So I turn naturally to you, as indeed I do for everything, and would like you to have all my works. The deficit that their sale will produce may be lodged to the credit of Cyril and Vyvyan.

Well, if you are my literary executor, you must be in possession of the only document that really gives any explanation of my extraordinary behaviour with regard to Queensberry and Alfred Douglas. When you have read the letter you will see the psychological explanation of a course of conduct that from the outside seems a combination of absolute idiocy with vulgar bravado. Some day the truth will have to be known: not necessarily in my lifetime or in Douglas's: but I am not prepared to sit in the grotesque pillory they put me into, for all time: for the simple reason that I inherited from my father and my mother a name of high distinction in literature and art, and I cannot, for eternity, allow that name to be the shield and catspaw of the Queensberrys. I don't defend my conduct. I explain it.

Also there are in the letter certain passages which deal with my mental development in prison, and the inevitable evolution of character and intellectual attitude towards life that has taken place: and I want you, and others who still stand by me and have affection for me, to know exactly in what mood and manner I hope to face the world. Of course from one point of view I know that on the day of my release I shall be merely passing from one prison into another, and there are times when the whole world seems to me no larger than my cell, and as full of terror for me. Still I believe that at the beginning God made a world for each separate man, and in that world which is within us one should seek to live. At any rate, you will read those parts of my letter with less pain than the others. Of course I need not remind you how fluid a thing thought is with me – with us all – and of what an evanescent substance are our emotions made. Still, I do see a sort of possible goal towards which, through art, I may progress. It is not unlikely that you may help me.

As regards the mode of copying: of course it is too long for any amanuensis to attempt: and your own handwriting, dear Robbie, in your last letter seems specially designed to remind me that the task is not to be yours. I may wrong you, and hope I do, but it really looks as if you were engaged in writing a three-volume novel on the dangerous prevalence of communistic opinions among the rich, or some dreadful subject of vital interest, or in some other way wasting a youth that I cannot help saying has always been, and will always remain, quite full of promise. I think that the only thing to do is to be thoroughly modern, and to have it type-written. Of course the manuscript should not pass out of your control, but could you not get Mrs Marshall to send down one of her type-writing girls – women are the most reliable, as they have no memory for the important – to Hornton Street or Phillimore Gardens to do it under your supervision? I assure you that the type-writing machine, when played with expression, is not more annoying than the piano when played by a sister or near relation. Indeed many, among those most devoted to domesticity, prefer it.

I wish the copy to be done not on tissue paper but on good paper such as is used for plays, and a wide rubricated margin should be left for corrections. The copy done and verified from the manuscript, the original should be dispatched to A. D. by More, and another copy done by the type-writer so that *you* should have a copy as well as myself. Also I would wish two type-written copies to be made from the fourth page of sheet 9 to the last page of sheet 14: from 'and the end of it . . . I must forgive you' down to 'Between art and myself there is none' (I quote from memory). Also on page 3 of sheet 18 from 'I am to be released if all goes well' to 'bitter herbs . . . whole' on page 4. These welded together with anything else you may extract that is good and nice in intention, such as first page of sheet 15, I wish sent, one copy to the Lady of Wimbledon – whom I have spoken of, without mentioning her name – the other to Frankie Forbes-Robertson. I know both these sweet women will be interested to know something of what is happening to my soul – not in the theological sense, but merely in the sense of the spiritual consciousness that is separate from the actual occupations of the body. It is a sort of message or letter I send them – the only one, of course, I dare send. If Frankie wishes she can show it to her brother Eric, of whom I was always fond, but of course it is a strict secret from the general world. The Lady of Wimbledon will know that too.

If the copying is done at Hornton Street the lady type-writer might be fed through a lattice in the door like the Cardinals when they elect a Pope, till she comes out on the balcony and can say to the world 'Habet Mundus Epistolam'; for indeed it is an Encyclical Letter, and as the Bulls of the Holy Father are named from their opening words, it may be spoken of as the *Epistola: In Carcere et Vinculis*.

There is no need to tell A. D. that a copy has been taken, unless he should write and complain of injustice in the letter or misrepresentation: then he should be told that a copy has been taken. I earnestly hope the letter will do him good. It is the first time anyone has ever told him the truth about himself. If he is allowed to think that the letter is merely the result of the influence of a plank-bed on style, and that my views are distorted by the privations of prison-life, no good will follow. I hope someone will let him know that the letter is one he thoroughly deserves, and that if it is unjust, he thoroughly deserves injustice. Who indeed deserves it more than he who was always so unjust to others?

In point of fact, Robbie, prison-life makes one see people and things as they really are. That is why it turns one to stone. It is the people outside who are deceived by the illusion of a life in constant motion. They revolve with life and contribute to its unreality. We who are immobile both see and know. Whether or not the letter does good to his narrow nature and hectic brain, to me it has done great good. I have 'cleansed my bosom of much perilous stuff', to borrow a phrase from the poet whom you and I once thought of rescuing from the Philistine. I need not remind you that mere expression is to an artist the supreme and only mode of life. It is by utterance that we live. Of the many, many things for which I have to thank the Governor there is none for which I am more grateful than for his permission to write fully to A. D. and at as great length as I desired. For nearly two years I had within me a growing burden of bitterness, much of which I have now got rid of. On the other side of the prison-wall there are some poor black soot-smirched trees that are just breaking out into buds of an almost shrill green. I know quite well what they are going through. They are finding expression.

There is another very serious thing about which I have to write to you, and I address myself to you because I have got to blame you, and I am far too fond of you to blame you to anyone else. On the 20th [*acually* 10th] March 1896, more than a year ago now, I wrote to you in the very strongest terms telling you that I could not bear the idea of any discord being made between myself and my wife on such a subject as money, after her sweetness in coming here from Italy to break to me the news of my mother's death, and that I desired my friends to withdraw their proposal to purchase my life-interest against her wishes. You should have seen that my wishes were carried out. You were very wrong not to do so. I was quite helpless in prison and I relied on you. You thought that the thing to do was the clever thing, the smart thing, the ingenious thing. You were under a mistake. Life is not complex. We are complex. Life is simple, and the simple thing is the right thing. Look at the result! Are you pleased with it?

Again, a complete error was made in the estimate formed of Mr Hargrove. He was regarded as a solicitor of the Humphreys class, one who would threaten to gain an end, bluster, extort, and the like. Quite the contrary. He is a man of very high character, and extremely good social position. Whatever he said he meant. The idea of putting me – a wretched prisoner and pauper – up to fight Mr Hargrove and Sir George Lewis was grotesque. The idea of bidding against them absurd. Mr Hargrove – the family solicitor of the Lloyds for thirty years – would advance my wife £10,000 if she wanted it, and not feel it. I asked Mr Holman whether in case of a divorce a settlement was not *ipso facto* broken. I received no answer. I find that it is as I suspected.

Again, how silly the long serious letters advising me 'not to surrender my rights over my children', a phrase that occurs seven times in the correspondence. My rights! I had none. A claim that a formal appeal to a Judge in Chambers can quash in ten minutes is not a right. I am quite astounded at the position I have been placed in. How much better if you had done as I asked you, as at that time my wife was kind and ready to let me see my two children and be with them occasionally. A. D. put me into a false position with regard to his father, forced me into it, and held me there. More Adey, with the best intentions, forced me into a false position with regard to my wife. Even had I any legal rights – and I have none – how much more charming to have privileges given to me by affection than to extort them by threats. My wife was very sweet to me, and now she, very naturally, goes right against me. Of her character also a wrong estimate was made. She warned me that if I let my friends bid against her she would proceed to a certain course, and she will do so.

Again, Swinburne says to Marie Stuart in one of his poems,

> But surely you were something better
> Than innocent!

and really my friends must face the fact that (setting aside such details in my indictment as belonged to my bosom-friend, three in number) I am not in prison as an innocent man. On the contrary, my record of perversities of passion and distorted romances would fill many scarlet volumes. I think it right to mention this – however surprising, and no doubt shocking, it will sound to many – because More Adey in his letter tells me that the opposite side will be obliged to furnish strict details of the dates and places and exact circumstances of the terrible charges to be brought against me. Does he seriously imagine that if I submitted to more cross-examination I would be believed? Does he propose I should do so, and repeat the Queensberry fiasco? It is the case that the charges are not true. But that is a mere detail. If a man gets drunk, whether he does so on white wine or red is of no importance. If a man has perverse passions, their particular mode of manifestation is of no importance either.

I said from the first that I relied entirely on my wife's condonation. I now learn that no condonation is of any value where more than one offence may be charged. My wife has simply to say that she condoned X, but knew nothing of Y, and would not hear of condoning Z. There is a little shilling book – ninepence for cash – called *Every Man his own Lawyer*. If my friends had only sent it to me, or even read it themselves, all this trouble, expense, and worry would have been saved. However, while I blame you *ab initio*, I am now in a mood of mind that makes me think that everything that happens is for the best, and that the world is not a mere chaos in which chance and cleverness clash. What I have to do is simply this. I have got to submit to my divorce. I don't think that the Government could possibly prosecute me again. Even for a British Government it would be too brutal a procedure. I have also, before that, to restore to my wife my interest in the settlement-money before it is taken from me. I have thirdly to state that I will accept nothing from her at all in the way of income or allowance. This seems to be the simple, straightforward, and gentlemanly thing to do. It is a great blow to me. I feel the legal deprivation of my children poignantly.

My friendship with A. D. brought me first to the dock of the Criminal Court, then to the dock of the Bankruptcy Court, and now to the dock of the Divorce Court. As far as I can make out (not having the shilling primer on the subject) there are no more docks into which he can bring me. If so, I can draw a breath of relief. But I want you to seriously consider my proposal, to ask More to do so, and his lawyer, and to write to me, and to get More to write to me, as soon as possible about it. I think my wife will have no objection to refunding the £75 paid for the *damnosa haereditas* of my life-interest. She is quite just on money matters. But personally I hope there will be no bargaining. A grave mistake has been made. Submission has to follow. I propose that my life-interest should be restored to my wife, its rightful owner, as a parting gift from me. It will render my exit from marriage less ignominious than to wait for its being done by legal coercion. Whether I am married or not is a matter that does not concern me. For years I disregarded the tie. But I really think that it is hard on my wife to be tied to me. I always thought so. And, though it may surprise some of my friends, I am really very fond of my wife and very sorry for her. I sincerely hope she may have a happy marriage, if she marries again. She could not understand me, and I was bored to death with the married life. But she had some sweet points in her character, and was wonderfully loyal to me. On this point of my surrendering everything, pray let More and yourself write at once, after you have considered the point.

Also, I would take it as a great favour if More would write to the people [*his brother Willie and his sister-in-law*] who pawned or sold my fur coat since my imprisonment, and ask them from me whether they would be kind enough to state where it was sold or pawned as I am anxious to trace it, and if possible get it back. I have had it for twelve years, it was all over America with me, it was at all my first nights, it knows me perfectly, and I really want it. The letter should be quite courteous, addressed first to the man: if he doesn't answer, to the woman. As it was the wife who pressed me to leave it in her charge, it might be mentioned that I am surprised and distressed, particularly as I paid out of my own pocket *since my imprisonment* all the expenses of her confinement, to the extent of £50 conveyed through Leverson. This might be stated as a reason for my being distressed. Their letters must be kept. I have a most particular reason for wishing it to be done – in fact, one vitally important. And the letter being one of civil request, with the reasons set forth, cannot involve argument or denial. I just require documentary evidence for my protection.

I hope to see Frank Harris on Saturday week, or soon. The news of the copying of my letter will be welcome, when I hear from you about my divorce. If Arthur Clifton would like to see the copy show it to him, or your brother Aleck. Ever yours   OSCAR WILDE

To More Adey

7 April 1897   [*HM Prison*] *Reading*
My dear More,
[*The first paragraphs of this letter, repeating much of what Wilde said to Ross in the previous letter, have been omitted*]

With regard to your letter about Alfred Douglas, I see of course that I must clearly ascertain what he and his family are going to do. On the occasion of my bankruptcy, which it was disgraceful of them to allow, I received through you and others a promise from Percy that £500 was to be at my disposal on my release, it being considered by him and his brother that it would be better to give the money to me instead of to their father. This promise will, I suppose, I don't doubt, be carried out, and as my release takes place in a few weeks and I am anxious to arrange my life for the next couple of years, will you kindly write to Percy and ask him to let you have the money for me. It must not go into Leverson's hands, as he would probably use it for his own purposes or in his business. I wish you to have it.

I also think it right that Percy should know a little of the mere outlines of my unfortunate acquaintance with his brother. The friendship began in May 1892 by his brother appealing to me in a very pathetic letter to help him in terrible trouble with people who were blackmailing him. I hardly knew him at the time. I had known him eighteen months, but had only seen him four times in that space. I was, however, I admit, touched by his letter, and his appeal, and did at once get him out of his trouble at considerable difficulty and annoyance to myself. Alfred Douglas was very grateful, and practically never left me for three years – not till he had got me into prison. I wish Percy to know of my incessant efforts to break off a friendship so ruinous to me artistically, financially, and socially.

In December 1893 I went so far as to fly abroad and leave a false address to try and escape from him. During the whole time he was in Egypt I refused to write to him or take any notice of his incessant letters and telegrams. It was only on his rushing back to Paris and sending me a telegram that seemed to threaten suicide that I consented even to see him. To get him out of my life was one of the objects of my life. I completely failed to accomplish it. Nothing that I could do could keep him out of my house.

As regards money, let Percy know that I spent on A. D. and with him more than £5000 in two years and a half, exclusive of bills. This I did not do as a pleasure to myself. I was forced to. I never remember on any one occasion from May 1892 to April 1895, the date of my arrest, A. D. having any money at all from either his father or his mother. He came to me for everything, nor is it any exaggeration to say that from his morning shave to his midnight hansom I was obliged to pay for every single item in his day's expenditure. He refused to have his meals at home and insisted on having them with me at the most expensive restaurants. He arrived at twelve o'clock every morning, and practically he never left me till after midnight. It was ruinous to me in every way, but I could not get rid of him. Explain to Percy that I never gave his brother large sums of money. His name hardly appears in my cheque-book. Where it does it was simply because when he was away or abroad he used to draw cheques on his own bank where his account was always overdrawn and telegraph to me to implore me to cover it by lodging to his account the amount so that his cheque might be honoured. The real expense was his support, left entirely to me.

Also, pray explain to Percy that the night A. D. arrived from Algiers I implored him to let us tell him (Percy) the truth. He absolutely refused, and insisted on the comedy of his father's delusions. Also, let Percy know the exact circumstances of my entering the absurd action. A. D. had brought to my hotel a companion of his own, one whose age, appearance, public and private profession, rendered him the most unsuitable companion possible for me in the terribly serious position in which I was placed. On my remonstrating with him, and asking him to let his companion return to his home, he made a violent scene, and preferring the society of his companion to mine retired at once to another hotel, where I subsequently had to pay the bill for them both, I need hardly say.

From his new quarters he began to bombard me with revolting letters. On the Thursday I went to my club and found Queensberry's hideous card. I returned at once to the hotel where I found a no less loathsome letter from Alfred Douglas. I felt I stood between Caliban and Sporus, and that I was in hideous danger from both of them, and, just as I had bolted from the son in December '93 to Paris, so I determined to bolt at once, to Paris again, from father as well as son. Unfortunately the bill for the ten days Alfred Douglas had planted himself on me, with his companion at the close of the period, was £148, and the hotel people would not allow my luggage to be removed till I had paid the bill in full, which I could not do. At that moment A. D. arrived, saw his father's card, and by taunts of cowardice and terror drove me to the fatal step. I stumbled like an ox into the shambles. My last straw for clutching to was the expense. I told Humphreys I had no money. A. D. at once interfered, said that his family would pay the whole expense, and be too delighted to do so. Humphreys, keen for a scandalous case, and scenting money, closed at once. I was brought in a four-wheeler by both of them to apply for a warrant, and here I am in prison. I think Percy should know these facts, as from Robbie's letter to me the Queensberry family seem to be talking foolishly about the case. So please write to Percy, and ask him from me to fulfil his promise.

Also, I want you to write to Leverson from me. During the time I was out on bail a sum of money was given to me by a friend to be of use to me in any way possible. I, not liking to have a large sum of money on me, asked Leverson and Reggie Turner to be trustees of this. They consented. Leverson personally took charge of the money. I gave Leverson a piece of paper on which my friend had written 'I desire this money to be employed for your own personal use and that of your children as you may direct'. These were the conditions of the trust. Leverson accepted it, but told me it would be better, more convenient, only to have one trustee, and that he had arranged with Reggie to retire. I was surprised, but made no objection.

On my way to Court to receive my sentence he began asking me in the carriage to repay him £250, the balance of £500 he had advanced to Alfred Douglas and myself for the first trial. I was astonished and wounded at his selecting such a moment to worry me over a debt, and told him that I could not discuss business then, and that the money held in trust was to be applied for my mother's wants primarily, and then, if it was necessary, for my children. He did disburse on my behalf to my mother some £280 or so: my children, my wife told me, required nothing. He now comes and proposes to deduct his debt of £250 before he hands over the balance. I cannot allow this for a single moment. He has to hand over the trust-money intact to me. He has no right to touch it for any claim of his own. He must know quite well that his proposing to pay himself in full, when my other creditors are receiving nothing, is an entire breach of the Bankruptcy Laws. This money was not given to me to pay my debts. It was given to me because I was at the time bankrupt and ruined, to be held in trust for me by a friend. Leverson first through you proposed to pay himself and to lend me an equivalent sum. I declined this entirely. When he came here, he calmly told me that 'money was tight in the City' and that he could not let me have the money that belonged to me! As if I cared whether money was tight in the City, or knew what it meant. I suppose it means that he was speculating with trust-money. That is a dangerous amusement. As a business man he should know better.

Kindly write to him and copy out what I have said and ask him to let me have the proper balance of the money entrusted to his care for my use. Of his original loan he has already had fifty per cent: the only one of my creditors who has had anything. For him to swoop down illegally and propose to collar the balance is not to be thought of. Nor will he do so. Of course, if he tried to do so I would never speak to him again or consent to see him, and would let everyone publicly and privately know of his dishonourable conduct. I would also take other measures.

There is also another matter: he bought for me at my sale my own portrait, the picture of A. D. I commissioned Will Rothenstein to do, and Shannon's pastel of the Moon. He may want to be paid for these, as he said they were a present to me from himself and his wife. If so, let him deduct from what is due to me his claim. The three things themselves I wish very much could be lodged somewhere for me – in a little garret in Hornton Street, or anywhere – so that I can get them when I want. Can you do this at once?

The Sphinx has (1) *The Duchess of Padua*. (2) The manuscript of *La Sainte Courtisane*. (3) A bundle of A. D.'s letters. Would you give her from me my kind regards and most affectionate wishes and ask her to let Robbie have them, as I want them all three as soon as I am released. This is a horrid letter, but how am I to write on horrid things but horridly? Ever yours

OSCAR

To More Adey

6 May 1897   *HM Prison, Reading*

My dear More, Many thanks for your letter. Hansell has written at last and forwarded a draft of the agreement to be drawn up between my wife and myself. It is couched in legal language, and of course quite unintelligible to me. The only thing I can make out is the close, where it is laid down that I am to be deprived of my £150 if I know any 'disreputable' people. As good people, as they are grotesquely termed, *will* not know me, and I am not to be *allowed* to know wicked people, my future life, as far as I can see at present, will be passed in comparative solitude. I have written to Hansell that artists and the criminal classes are the only people who will know me, and that the conditions would place him, if seriously insisted on, in an absurd position: but what I want now is a legal condonation from my wife of the past, so as not to have it raked up again and again. For the rest, to have been divorced would have been horrible of course, but now that the children are publicly taken from me by a Judge's order, and it is decided that I am unfit to be with Cyril, I am very disheartened: all I want is peace: all I ever wanted was peace: I loathe legal worries.

I don't know when you are coming: it had better be soon: I hope you have written to the *Commissioners* for permission to have the private room and a visit of an hour in duration: in the case of a special visit the Governor has no authority to grant these privileges himself, otherwise he would have gladly done so.

As to Ricketts, I see his presence troubles you: well, I thought, as he had applied so often, it was not for me to refuse a kindly offer from an artist of whom I am very fond, but I think that after half-an-hour I will ask Ricketts to leave us together to talk business: he will quite understand that I have lots of tedious and uninteresting things to settle. So then you and I and Robbie will have half-an-hour for everything.

As regards clothes etc.: Robbie kindly said he would get me a blue-serge suit from Doré and an ulster: this I suppose he has done. Frank Harris also offered me some kindnesses of the same kind, so I have already written to him to say what I want in the way of other clothes, *and boots*, and to ask for the things to be sent to you, not later than Thursday 13th. Hats I ought to have a lot of, but I suppose they have disappeared: Heath, Albert Gate, was my hatter, and understands my needs: I would like a brown hat, and a grey hat, soft felt, seaside things. Would you, if there is time, get me *eighteen* collars made after the pattern you have, or say two dozen. Also, order me two dozen white handkerchiefs, and a dozen with coloured borders. Also some neckties: some dark blue with white spots and diapers, and some of whatever is being worn for summer wear. I also want eight pair of socks, coloured summer things; my size in gloves is 8¼, as my hand is so broad, but my socks need only be for an 8 glove in proportion. Also, I want two or three sets of plain mother-of-pearl (by the way I want to make 'nacred' an English word) studs – nacred studs: you know how difficult they are to get abroad. Also, some nice French soap, Houbigant's if you can get it: Pritchard of King Street, St James's, used to have it for me: either 'Peau d'Espagne' or 'Sac de Laitue' would do: a case of three. Also, some scent; Canterbury Wood Violet I would like, and some 'Eau de Lubin' for the toilet, a large bottle. Also some of Pritchard's tooth-powder, and a medium toothbrush. My hair has become very grey: I am under the impression that it is quite white, but I believe that is an exaggeration: there is a wonderful thing called Koko Marikopas, to be got at 233 Regent Street, which is a wonderful hair-tonic: the name alone seems worth the money, so please get a large bottle. I want, for psychological reasons, to feel entirely physically cleansed of the stain and soil of prison life, so these things are all – trivial as they may sound – really of great importance. I don't know if there are any night-shirts? If not, please order me half a dozen; the size of my collar will show how wide the neck should be, also, the sleeve of my shirt for length of arm: the actual length – well, I am six feet, and I like long shirts. I like them made with a turn-down collar, and a breast-pocket for a handkerchief: coloured border to collar and cuffs. If 'the dreadful people' don't give up my two rugs, will you buy me one – a travelling Scotch rug, with a good fringe: *not* a tartan, of course: nor a shepherd's-plaid pattern: but the sort of fleecy striped thing. I feel I here convey no idea. All these, if possible, out of the wonderful £25: pray keep envelope of the latter, that I may try to guess from whose generous hand it has come.

As for Reggie Turner, please tell him from me how charmed and touched I am by his delightful present [*a dressing case*]: it is most sweet and generous of him, and I accept his gift with gratitude and delight: in fact I must thank him in person, if he will let me: I hope he will come to see me between the date of my leaving here, and my starting with Frank Harris. My plans are as follows. I have had no reply from the Home Secretary, I need hardly say; and as Hansell proposes to come on Saturday the 15th with the deeds for my signature, it makes it very troublesome. I must alter Hansell's date, I suppose. In any case my idea is this. If I am kept, as I suppose I shall be, till the 19th, I wish a carriage to be here at six o'clock: by 6.15 I will be ready. The carriage, by the Governor's permission, is to drive into the prison: it is to be a closed one. In this I go to *Twyford*, six miles off: there breakfast and change, and make my way to Folkestone, Twyford being on main line. Cross over by night-boat to Boulogne, and sleep there. Stay either at Boulogne, or in the immediate vicinity by the sea, for four or five days to recruit. Then join Frank Harris and go to the Pyrenees. So you see Reggie Turner could come to Boulogne, on the Thursday. Ask him to. Of course he is to keep all this a dead secret. Also, on no account is Alfred Douglas to be told. I will see him after my voyage with Frank Harris and receive from him my letters and what is left of my presents. But not before. For him to appear at Boulogne would be horrible. I could not stand it.

Bobbie wrote to me that Leverson would hand over the money all right: it should be about £450. If you or Bobbie would keep it for me I would be much obliged. Out of his original loan of £500 Leverson has already had £250: he must wait a little for the balance. I hope you will have received the money from him by the time I see you.

As regards Humphreys, I am under the impression that I left there my dressing bag containing my silver brushes and a suit of clothes and things: would you find out? and if so, the brushes and razors I would like. Razors and shaving things, by the way, are a necessity to be procured in England. If the bag with the silver brushes is not at Humphreys, it must be with the people who sold my furs, and they should be asked for it. They also have a dark ulster of mine.

I wish you would see if you could get me a travelling basket with strap for books: one that could go under the seat of a railway carriage: Lady Brownlow gave me one, of green wicker that was charming, but I don't know where it is now. In Bond Street, or at the Stores, I fancy you could get one. They are most useful. I will let Robbie know when he comes what English books I would like.

On the strength of Percy's promise to pay £500, Humphreys claims from me £150 for the expenses of Bankruptcy. I don't know if Leverson has paid this. Percy said he would pay half. It has to be paid, so if Percy does not pay half, I must pay it all through Leverson. Leverson will of course keep back what is necessary for Humphreys's bill.

I am still anxious to know if my bags with letters have been removed from Humphreys. I would like them to be at Hornton Street.

I am very sorry to hear Robbie has not been well. When I wrote to him about people giving me books, I meant that many literary people had sent messages through him, and I would have been touched by their giving me one of their books on my release: Stuart Merrill, Lugné-Poe, and the like. It was a whim I had. I don't know if Reggie ever hears from Charlie Hickey? If he does I wish he would ask Charlie to write to me (under cover to Reggie) and tell me how he is, and where. I have pleasant memories of him.

If the Twyford scheme is all right, perhaps this would be a good programme. Breakfast at Twyford: luncheon at Richmond with Frank Harris: dinner at Folkestone: supper at Boulogne. I would like to see Frank before my going to the Pyrenees. I wonder am I to see you on Saturday? I still suspect you of wishing to incarcerate me in a Trappist monastery, and will tax you with it in Robbie's presence. With thousand thanks, Ever yours

OSCAR WILDE

To More Adey

12 May 1897 *Reading Prison*

My dear More, I have received from the Governor your document and read it, with great pain, I need hardly say. To begin with, with regard to money-matters.

You and Robbie both assured me by letter and personally that enough money had been subscribed for me to enable me to live in comfort for 'eighteen months or two years'. I believed this. When one is in prison face to face with the realities of life one believes what is said to one. I now understand that there is no such sum at all, that all there is is £50, from which Hansell's and Holman's charges have to be deducted, so that nothing of any import will be left.

Let me say frankly that it was extremely wrong of you and Robbie to have made such a statement to me. It was wrong, unkind, and injudicious. Mr Holman also made a formal statement to Mr Hargrove that a considerable sum of money was to be placed at my disposal on my release. Mr Hargrove communicated this to my wife, and it conditioned her action with regard to refusing to increase her offer of £150 a year to £200. She wrote to me at Christmas telling me that she had received this information from Mr Holman through Mr Hargrove, and she very strongly urged me 'to purchase an annuity' with the sum of money in question. Mr Holman had represented it as a large sum. Subsequently, after I had mentioned to you that I was indebted to Mrs Napier for £150 (used to pay off the first instalment of Leverson's loan) Mr Holman declared through you (your letter lies before me) that this sum should be repaid 'at once' to Mrs Napier. I demurred, on the ground that I would sooner repay such a debt on my release personally, but suppose I had said 'yes'? Where was the money to come from? I naturally supposed that it was from the money you and Robbie had for me, to enable me to live without pecuniary anxiety for 'eighteen months or two years' at least. Did you, who strongly backed up Holman's suggestion, propose that it should come from the little money set apart for my use of which Leverson had got hold? That would have left me penniless. Where was it to come from?

At the same interview, when you urged me to authorise the payment of my debt to Mrs Napier, I asked Robbie to go to Brussels and engage a flat for me. I said I would like a studio, sleeping-room, kitchen etc. I naturally believed there was money forthcoming for me in your hands, and proposed to spend some of it in renting a good flat with studio in Brussels, which would have cost about £100 or £120 a year. Robbie listened quite seriously, and promised to do what I wished, as soon as I had definitely decided. Why was I not told that there was no money at all? That the statement made by you and Robbie to me, and by Mr Holman to my wife's solicitor, was utterly untrue in every detail? What advantage was gained by deceiving me and my wife? Why did you do it? What one wants in prison is the truth. You no doubt meant it to please me. So did Robbie. Mr Holman's object I don't know. Had the thing been done by others I would say it was a heartless, stupid and offensive hoax.

It has been done by others. On April 7th Frank Harris came to see me. He had come of his own accord, and in the two applications he had made for leave to see me had stated that it was on 'financial business'. When I saw him he was most cordial and friendly, told me that he had made a very large sum of money – some £23,000 in South Africa – and that he had come to put his cheque-book at my disposal. I was greatly touched, I admit, at his spontaneous and unsolicited kindness, and told him that if I were set free from money anxieties I thought I could produce some good art. He said he had come for the purpose of doing so, and would send me a cheque for £500 before my release. I admit that, in my unnerved state, I was very deeply moved at his generous present, and made no attempt to conceal my feelings, which were indeed beyond my control. I now learn that he has sent a verbal message through you to say he is very sorry but cannot do it. Of course nothing would induce me to go on this driving-tour with him after that. I hardly suppose he expects it. Would you kindly write to him that you gave me his message and that I was a good deal distressed, as I had unfortunately received similar messages from everyone else who had been kind enough to promise me money, and that I found myself in such a painful and parlous state as regards my finances that I could not think of any pleasant pleasure excursion such as he had proposed till I had in some way settled my affairs and seen a possible future. This will end the driving-tour, and there is nothing in the message that could hurt his feelings, so pray give it in my own words. In fact Frank Harris has no feelings. It is the secret of his success. Just as the fact that he thinks that other people have none either is the secret of the failure that lies in wait for him somewhere on the way of Life.

As regards Percy Douglas, who comes next in *his* refusal to carry out his promise, I remember you asked me to allow him spontaneously to break with the evil 'traditions of the Queensberry family'. I am afraid he has spontaneously shown that he is *bien le fils de son père*. One of the notes of the Queensberry character is that they are quite unscrupulous about money affairs, and extremely mean about them. On the occasion of my bankruptcy Percy stated that instead of paying off his father's costs he would reserve the money for me, as he thought it would be much better for me to have it for myself than for his father to enjoy it. I protested strongly against this view. Outside of Queensberry I had no debts of any size. I owed the Savory £86 and Lewis the jeweller £42! These came next. However, I was not consulted. I was told that Percy had insisted on his arrangement, and that the money, or £600 of it, was to be kept for me. I believed it. I never doubted it. Humphreys, on the strength of it, sends me in a bill for £150! I supposed my friends would naturally have got the money from Percy Douglas and kept it for me: perhaps put it into something that bears a little interest – Consols or something mysterious. Of course that is not done, and when Percy is asked to fulfil his promise, he gets out of it like Frank Harris does, but to show the generosity of his nature offers to pay *half* the solicitor's bill! I suppose the unfortunate man has spent the money on drink really. People like that give me a sense of nausea. I loathe the promise-makers. I could be humble and grateful to a beggar who gave me half of the crust out of his wallet, but the rich, the ostentatious, the false who ask one to a rich banquet and then when one is hungry and in want shut the door of house and heart against one and tell one to go elsewhere – I have nothing but contempt for them. The Frank Harrises of life are a dreadful type. I hope to see no more of them.

If anyone comes to you with promises and offers of help for me, tell them to give what they can give – if it be a piece of bread I could thank them – but don't let them promise anything. I won't have any more *promises*. People think that because one is in prison they can treat one as they choose. They should try to realise that where there is sorrow there is holy ground. They should know that sorrow is the most sensitive of all created things.

You see the state I am in. You saw it yesterday. I quiver in every nerve with pain. I am wrecked with the recurring tides of hysteria. I can't sleep. I can't eat. Why? Because on every side there comes in nothing but the tidings of evil, of indifference, of pretence. You and Robbie meant to please me, to comfort me, by inventing the story of the fund adequate for 'eighteen months or two years' of existence free from all monetary worries. I lived on the hopes of it. Then there was £600 from Percy – £500 from Frank Harris – and what do I find at the end of it all, *absolutely nothing*! My wife has most kindly given orders that I am to get my first quarter of my little £150 a year on the day I leave prison. I thank God for having put the thought in her beautiful heart. At the end of it all I shall owe to her my first cup of tea or dish of food. It will taste all the sweeter to me for it.

As regards Leverson – well, of course I understand now why you did not allow me to read the paper of statement yesterday. Robbie in his letter of Monday stated that Leverson had at last consented to hand over my money intact, minus what was paid for my mother out of it. From your statement I see this is not the case. He insists on claiming a right to repay himself, alone of all my creditors, in full, and to keep back £250. This is, of course, outrageous. The money was given to me, *after I had been served with a bankruptcy notice*, to be of use to me personally and to my children. On the occasion of my foolishly entrusting it to Leverson I gave him the title-deed of the trust, a piece of paper on which was written 'This is for your use and your children's'. I told Leverson I wished Reggie Turner to be co-trustee with him. For Leverson to come now and claim alone of all my creditors to be paid 100 per cent and have his pound of flesh is simple fraud and dishonesty. If he desired to rank as a creditor he should have put in his claim when I was bankrupt. I do not allow him to take this money. His account is to be as follows. He received £880: he disbursed for my mother's use at my request £280. I believe when Holman was so anxious for me to pay off all my debts in full from a fund that did not exist Arthur Clifton got £50: Humphreys claimed £150, of which Douglas of Hawick consents to pay half, viz. £75: so Leverson owes me about £475: will you please let me know *by return* why Robbie said Leverson would pay in full. I mean, was this an invention of Robbie's to please me, like the other, more serious one? Or had Leverson said so? Pray let me know this, and Leverson's private address.

I will write to him myself. On hearing from him, if it be unsatisfactory, I will consult my solicitor. I detest fraud, when united to gross sentimentality, and wordy, vulgar expressions of devotion. Please answer by return.

The other reason I regret your not having let me see the statement is about Robbie's meeting me. On February 27th, when you and Robbie were here, he told me he was going to meet me outside the prison. I begged him not to, but he insisted. I think that for many reasons, social, emotional, and others, it is much better he should not meet me. Yesterday I told him not to come to the prison, but to be at Twyford waiting for me. I consider it much better he should meet me abroad. My inability to go to Boulogne has rather upset me. It looks an evil omen, as though Alfred Douglas stood between me and the sun. Dieppe is relaxing, fashionable, and I am too well known there. I now see Havre is the best. There is a place close to Havre which is said to be *bracing*. I forget its name. Carlos Blacker used to be there a great deal.

Under these circumstances, it would be best to drive from here to *Mortimer*, which is on the Basingstoke line. At Mortimer I will breakfast and change. Something was said about Reggie. Would Reggie mind being at Mortimer, and bringing my things? All I want is that when I arrive a room should be ready for me to change in, and that breakfast should be served quickly. I would like all my luggage at Mortimer, as the chances of my suits *fitting* are questionable, so I would like a possibility of selection. As I no doubt shall be very much upset and hysterical, would you ask your doctor for any *nerve-sedative*. Nerves are not treated in prison. From Mortimer to Southampton there are many trains no doubt. I await with anxiety your answer about Leverson, about his address, and about Reggie. Robbie I hope to find at Havre, or rather he can follow. I don't know how often the boat runs now, but of course he can reach Havre in many ways. I write in great distress, because I am in great distress. Ever yours   OSCAR
Kindly let me have Reggie Turner's address by return.

To Robert Ross

13 May 1897   *HM Prison, Reading*

My dear Robbie, I am sorry that the last visit was such a painful and unsatisfactory one. To begin with I was wrong to have Ricketts present: he meant to be cheering, but I thought him trivial: everything he said, including his remark that he supposed time went very fast in prison (a singularly unimaginative opinion, and one showing an entirely inartistic lack of sympathetic instinct), annoyed me extremely. Then your letter of Sunday had of course greatly distressed me. You and More had both assured me that there was enough money waiting for me to enable me to live comfortably and at ease for 'eighteen months or two years'. I now find that there is exactly £50 for that purpose, and that out of this have to come the costs of two solicitors who have already had long interviews with Mr Hargrove and incurred much expense! The balance is for me!

My dear Robbie, if the £50 covers the law-costs I shall be only too pleased. If there is any balance remaining I don't want to know anything about it. Pray don't offer it to me. Even in acts of charity there should be some sense of humour. You have caused me the greatest pain and disappointment by foolishly telling me a complete untruth. How much better for me had you said to me, 'Yes, you will be poor, and there are worse things than poverty. You have got to learn how to face poverty'; simply, directly, and straightforwardly. But when a wretched man is in prison, the people who are outside either treat him as if he was dead, and dispose of his effects, or treat him as if he was a lunatic, and pretend to carry out his wishes and don't, or regard him as an idiot, to be humoured, and tell him silly and unnecessary lies, or look on him as a thing so low, so degraded, as to have no feelings at all, a thing whose entire life, in its most intimate relations with wife and child, and with all that wife and child represent to a ruined man, is to be bandied about like a common shuttlecock in a vulgar game, in which victory or failure are of really little interest, as it is not the life of the players that is at stake, but only someone else's life.

I am afraid that you don't realise what my wife's character and conduct have been towards me. You don't seem to understand her. From the very first she forgave me, and was sweet beyond words to me. After my seeing her here when we had arranged everything between us, and I was to have £200 a year during her life, and *one third* if I survived her, and our arrangements about the children and their transference to her guardianship had been made, so far as her expressing her desire to have nothing done in a public court but to have everything done privately between us was concerned, I wrote to you to say that all opposition to my wife's purchase of my life-interest was to be withdrawn, as she had been very sweet to me and I was quite satisfied with her offer, and I expressly stated that I begged that my friends would do nothing of any kind that would imperil the reconciliation and affection between myself and my wife.

You wrote at once to say that my wishes would be carried out, and that my friends would never dream of doing anything that would endanger my friendly relation with my wife. I believed you, and trusted you. You did not tell me the truth, you and my friends did not carry out my directions, and what is the result? Instead of £200 a year I have £150. Instead of one third of the interest, which on the death of my wife's mother will amount to about £1500 a year, I have no more than a bare £150 to the end of my days. My children will have £600 or £700 a year *apiece*. Their father will remain a pauper.

But that is not all. That is merely the common money side. My children are taken from me by an order of the court. I am legally no longer their father. I have no right to speak to them. If I try to communicate with them I can be put into prison for contempt of court. My wife also is of course wounded with me for what she considers a breach of faith on my part. On Monday I sign here a deed of separation of the most painfully stringent kind and of the most humiliating conditions. If I try to communicate with my wife against her will, or without her leave, I lose my wretched £150 a year at once. My life is to be ruled after a pattern of respectability. My friends are to be such as a respectable solicitor would approve of. *I owe this, Robbie, to your not telling me the truth, and not carrying out my instructions. I merely wanted my friends not to interfere.* I did not ask them to do anything. I begged them to do nothing.

More tells me that every single thing he did, he did with the sanction and advice of your brother Aleck, whom he describes as a 'sober business-like' person. Was Aleck aware that I distinctly forbade my friends to bid against my wife for my life-interest? That it was against my directions? Was it by his advice that you wrote me the letter containing the fatal untruth that has caused all this annoyance, loss, and misery? *'I have acted throughout under the advice of Aleck'* are More's words.

And the grotesque thing about it all is that I now discover, when it is too late to do anything, that the entire proceedings have been done at *my* expense, that I have had to pay for Holman, whose advice and opinions have been worthless and pernicious, and that the whole cost has fallen upon *me*: so that out of £150 given to More Adey *'for my use'* and aid nothing now remains at all but I suppose about £1.10s.6d.

Don't you see what a wonderful thing it would have been for me had you been able to hand me the £150 on my going out on Wednesday? How welcome such a sum would have been! Of what incalculable value! Now the whole thing, without my permission being asked, is spent in a stupid and ill-advised attempt to arrange my relations with my wife against my wife's wishes, in making discord, in promoting estrangement. My soul and the soul of my wife met in the valley of the shadow of death: she kissed me: she comforted me: she behaved as no woman in history, except my own mother perhaps, could have behaved. You and my other friends have so little imagination, so little sympathy, so little power of appreciating what was beautiful, noble, lovely and of good report that you can think of nothing better – you, More Adey and, I am told, your brother Aleck – than to rush in between us with an entirely ignorant solicitor and part us first and then make mischief between us.

[*Much of the middle of this letter repeats what Wilde had previously said to More Adey and has been omitted*]

The most shameful conduct on More Adey's part and the part of my friends was when my wife proceeded to the divorce. You were utterly regardless of me and my safety and position. You simply were gambling with my life. My father used to have a story about an English landlord who wrote from the Carlton to his Irish agent and said 'Don't let the tenants imagine that by shooting you they will at all intimidate me'. More Adey and you took up exactly the same position with regard to me. You did not care what happened.

Do you think I am writing mere rhetoric? Let me quote to you your friend More Adey's letter conveying to me the news that George Lewis was going to divorce me on appalling charges of a new and more infamous character. 'We,' he says, 'your friends' that is – 'we will have nothing whatever to do with your relations to your wife and we will not be *influenced by threats of a divorce, a matter in which we have no concern!*' . . .

There are your friend's words: that is the attitude of you, More Adey, and your brother Aleck, apparently. You were all keen to repeat the Queensberry scandal and affair. First a civil trial, with me cross-examined by Carson. Then a report by the judge to the Treasury. I am divorced, and re-tried and sent to prison! That is what you were working for. Oh! but, says More Adey, when we advised you to resist and meet the 'tainted' evidence we didn't mean it. We meant that you might 'have time to get abroad'. So the great scheme was that I should be divorced on hideous grounds, and should live in exile. As my divorce would annul my settlement I would of course have had no income at all. And when I was skulking abroad More Adey would have written to me and said, 'We have succeeded in all we aimed at: you have now no longer (1) any wife (2) any children (3) any income (4) any possibility of ever coming to London to produce a play. Mr Holman says he is very well satisfied on the whole.'

My dear Robbie, if that had happened, how would you have compared yourself, as a friend of mine, with wretched Alfred Douglas? I can only tell you that he would have shown up very well beside you. And really now that I reflect on your conduct and More Adey's to me in this matter I feel I have been unjust to that unfortunate young man.

In point of fact, Robbie, you had better realise that of all the incompetent people on the face of God's earth in any matter requiring wisdom, common sense, straightforwardness, ordinary intelligence, More Adey is undoubtedly the chief. I have written to him a letter about himself which I beg you will at once go and study. He is cultivated. He is sympathetic. He is kind. He is patient. He is gentle. He is affectionate. He is full of charming emotional qualities. He is modest – too much so – about his intellectual attainments. I value his opinion of a work of art far more than he does himself. I think he should have made, and still can make, a mark in literature. But in matters of business he is the most solemn donkey that ever stepped. He has neither memory, nor understanding, nor capacity to realise a situation, or appreciate a point. His gravity of manner makes his entire folly mask as wisdom. Every one is taken in. He is so serious in manner that one believes he can form an intellectual opinion. He can't. He is *extremely dense* in all matters requiring lucidity or imagination or instinct. In business matters he is *stupid*. The harm he has done me is irreparable, and he is as pleased as possible with himself. Now I have realised this, I feel it right, Robbie, that you should know it. If you have ever thought him sensible, give up the idea. He is incapable, as I have written to him, of managing the domestic affairs of a tom-tit in a hedge for a single afternoon. He is a *stupid man*, in practical concerns.

You are a dear affectionate, nice, loving fellow: but of course in all matters requiring business faculty utterly foolish. I didn't expect advice from you. I would have as soon expected it from Cyril. I merely expected the truth. I was quite disappointed. You have behaved very wrongly.

More gets my letter when you get this. He is to go to Leverson's *at once*. His accepting a *post-dated* cheque is really too idiotic. My plans he will tell you. Come when you like to this place near Havre. You shall be as welcome as a flower, and attacked till you know yourself. You have a heavy *atonement* before you. Kindly show Aleck this letter. Ever yours   o. w.

Of course it is understood that Alfred Douglas is not to be at Havre. You must write to him and say that I will receive any letter from him through you, but that he is not to attempt to see me, till I allow him. I believe he desires to return my letters and presents personally. He can do so, later on, in a month.

To More Adey

17 May 1897   *HM Prison, Reading*

Dear More, It is right to tell you that the Home Secretary against my earnest entreaties is to send me to London, the one place I wished to avoid. I am to be transferred to Pentonville tomorrow, the day announced in the papers for my transference to Wormwood Scrubs. The transference is to be conducted with humanity. I am to wear my own clothes, and not to be handcuffed. My clothes are so dreadful that I wish I had thought of having clothes here, but it will have to stand as it is.

I have written to Reggie to ask him to meet me and go abroad with me. I am so hurt with you and Robbie – not so much for what you have done, but for your failing to realise what you have done, your lack of imagination, which shows lack of sympathy, your blindness to your astounding conduct in spending money without my consent that would have been of priceless service to me – that if you came abroad with me it would only distress us both: I could talk to you of nothing but of the mode in which you very nearly repeated down to the smallest detail the whole of the Queensberry episode: forcing me into a civil trial, into a loathsome divorce, to be followed either by my arrest, in case I followed your advice and resisted the 'tainted evidence', or by my eternal exile, in case I followed your other advice and got 'safe abroad': in both cases being condemned to sheer pauperism, as the marriage settlement being broken *ipso facto* on my divorce, my prospective interest in it after my wife's death should I survive her would be absolutely *nil*. An order of the Court would have been obtained at once.

This, my dear More, is what you were preparing for me. If after a week you care to come to Havre and give me some explanation, I shall be delighted to see you. I hope Robbie will come with you.

5 o'clock

I have seen Hansell and signed the deed of separation. I do not really like going to Stewart Headlam's, as I don't care much about it. I know him but slightly, and a hotel would be better.

I have written to Reggie Turner to ask him to go and stay at a hotel so that I could go to his rooms and change: I mean a quiet hotel somewhere near Euston Road. Of course if it is impossible, it is impossible. But if Reggie engages rooms I can go there and change and breakfast. Only Reggie will have to sleep at the hotel.

Of course I really will be glad to see you the morning of my release, and I know you have taken a great deal of trouble about it. So come either to the prison with Reggie or to his rooms if that is more convenient. But we must not talk about business.

Receiving no telegram about Leverson is terrible. I am utterly upset.

I think you will agree with me that I have fully carried out your advice about Leverson and been most patient with him. It seems the wrong way to treat him. I feel sure that a man of that kind should be strongly dealt with. Your method at any rate has been a terrible failure.

I hear now that Dieppe has been fixed on. I am so well known there that I dislike it, and the air is relaxing, but I suppose one can move on. I am told Robbie is to be there. Very well, but you yourself would find little pleasure in my society. I feel so bitterly about so many things, that I forget many other acts of simple kindness that did me good not harm. I admit you have had endless trouble, but then you must remember I asked you through Robbie to leave my wife and myself alone: we were on terms of affection, and I was grateful to her. The rushing in to try to get more money for me was wrong. It has resulted in less money, and in a separation and the deprivation of my children, the last quite appalling.

Your intentions were always good and kind: your heart was always ready to vibrate in true sympathy: but your judgment was wrong: and the worse the results the worse your advice got. It was a miracle I escaped the divorce, the exile, the entire abandonment.

However, for your real heart-actions, your unwearying good nature, and desire to help me, I thank you very deeply. In a week I hope to be in a sweeter mood and to have lost some of my present bitterness. Then let us meet and talk about literature, in which your instinct is always right, your judgment castigated and serene, your sympathies intellectual. I hope you will hand all money to Reggie. As soon as Leverson has paid let me know. I of course cannot leave England without the money, and I don't want to have to go to his house for it. Ever yours   OSCAR

A Sort of Freedom

*'My desire to live is as intense as
ever, and though my heart is
broken, hearts are made to
be broken: that is why
God sends sorrow
into the world.'*

Wilde left Reading on the evening of 18 May 1897. Before he left, the Governor handed him the manuscript of his long letter to Douglas. Only two reporters were at the gates to see him go. Wearing his own clothes and now addressed as 'Mr Wilde' rather than his cell number 'C.3.3' by the two accompanying prison officers, he was driven in a cab to Twyford station, where they took the London train. They left it at Westbourne Park and travelled on by cab to Pentonville Prison, where Wilde spent the night.

At 6.15 next morning he was fetched in a cab by More Adey and Stewart Headlam. They managed to avoid the press and drove straight to Headlam's house, 31 Upper Bedford Place, Bloomsbury, where Wilde changed and breakfasted. Ada Leverson and her husband were among the first to greet him.

> We all felt intensely nervous and embarrassed. We had the English fear of showing our feelings, and at the same time the human fear of not showing our feelings. He came in, and at once put us at our ease. He came in with the dignity of a king returning from exile. He came in talking and laughing, smoking a cigarette, with waved hair and a flower in his button-hole, and he looked markedly better, slighter, and even younger than he had done two years previously. His first words were, 'Sphinx, how marvellous of you to know exactly the right hat to wear at seven o'clock in the morning to meet a friend who has been away! You can't have got up, you must have sat up.'

Other visitors came and went throughout the morning. For Wilde the opportunity to converse once more was as delightful as his new freedom. Predictably he and Adey missed the 10 a.m. 'Day Express' to Newhaven and the day boat to Dieppe. With time to spare, Wilde indulged himself with a visit to Hatchard's bookshop in Piccadilly where there was an act of kindness which he needed to acknowledge. The manager, Arthur Humphreys, had sent him a lavish parcel of books for his second Christmas in prison. Unfortunately while they were in the shop Wilde was recognised and they had to leave in a hurry.

They took the afternoon train to Newhaven, preferring to board it at East Croydon where there was less likelihood of Wilde being noticed than on the station concourse at Victoria. On their arrival Oscar sent a remorseful telegram to Robbie signed with his new exile pseudonym, a composite of his favourite saint and the hero of his great-uncle Charles Maturin's Gothic novel, Melmoth the Wanderer.

Telegram: To Robert Ross

19 May 1897, 6.25 p.m.   *Newhaven*

Arriving by night boat. Am so delighted at prospect of seeing you and Reggie. You must not mind the foolish unkind letters. More has been such a good friend to me and I am so grateful to you all I cannot find words to express my feelings. You must not dream of waiting up for us. In the morning we will meet. Please engage rooms for us at your hotel. When I see you I shall be quite happy, indeed I am happy now to think I have such wonderful friendship shown to me.   SEBASTIAN MELMOTH

To Ada Leverson

[20 May 1897]   *Hôtel Sandwich, Dieppe*

Dear Sphinx, I was so charmed with seeing you yesterday morning that I must write a line to tell you how sweet and good it was of you to be of the very first to greet me. When I think that Sphinxes are minions of the moon, and that you got up early before dawn, I am filled with wonder and joy.

I often thought of you in the long black days and nights of my prison life, and to find you just as wonderful and dear as ever was no surprise. The beautiful are always beautiful.

This is my first day of real liberty, so I try to send you a line, and with kind regards to dear Ernest whom I was pleased to see again, ever affectionately yours   OSCAR WILDE

I am staying here as Sebastian Melmoth – not Esquire but Monsieur Sebastien Melmoth. I have thought it better that Robbie should stay here under the name of Reginald Turner, and Reggie under the name of R. B. Ross. It is better that they should not have their own names.

Wilde and Adey arrived in Dieppe at 4.30 the next morning by the night boat. They were met by Turner and Ross on the quay. Wilde, Ross noted, had lost the coarse features of his pre-prison years but none of the conversational stamina:

Wilde talked until nine o'clock when I insisted on going to lie down. We all met at twelve for déjeuner, all of us exhausted except Wilde. In the afternoon we

drove to Arques and sat down on the ramparts of the castle. He enjoyed the trees and the grass and country scents and sounds in a way I had never known him do before, just as a street-bred child might enjoy them on his first day in the country: but of course there was an adjective for everything – 'monstrous', 'purple', 'grotesque', 'gorgeous', 'curious', 'wonderful'.

To Frank Harris

[Circa 20 May 1897]   *Hôtel Sandwich, Dieppe*
My dear Frank, Just a line to thank you for your great kindness to me, for the lovely clothes, and for the generous cheque.

You have been a real good friend to me, and I shall never forget your kindness: to remember such a debt as mine to you – a debt of kind fellowship – is a pleasure.

About our tour, later on let us think about it. My friends have been so kind to me here that I am feeling happy already. Ever yours OSCAR WILDE
If you write to me please do so under cover to R. B. Ross, who is here with me.

To Mrs Bernard Beere

[Circa 22 May 1897]   *Hôtel Sandwich, Dieppe*
My dear good beautiful Friend, Your letter has given me so much pleasure. I knew you would always be sweet and good to me – far more now, if that were possible, than ever, for now I need sympathy, and know its value: a kind word to me now is as lovely to me as a flower is, and love can heal all wounds.

I cannot write much for I am nervous – dazed with the wonder of the wonderful world: I feel as if I had been raised from the dead. The sun and the sea seem strange to me.

But, dear Bernie, although my life looks ruined to the outer world, to me it is not so. I know you will like to hear that somehow I feel that out of it all – out of the silence, the solitary life, the hunger, the darkness, the pain, the abandonment, the disgrace – out of these things I may get some good. I was living a life unworthy of an artist. It was wrong of me. Worse things might have happened to your old friend, dear, than two years' hard labour – terrible though they were. At least I hope to grow to feel so. Suffering is a terrible fire; it either purifies or destroys: perhaps I may be a better fellow after it all. Do write to me here – Monsieur Sebastian Melmoth is my name now to the world. With love and gratitude, ever yours   OSCAR

Delighted as he was to be a free man again, Wilde was nonetheless made brutally aware of his status as a social outcast. The English community avoided him as far as possible; one or two former acquaintances, notably the artists Beardsley and Blanche, showed themselves uncomfortable; and the proprietor of a Dieppe restaurant made it obliquely clear that he was not welcome, as his presence might adversely affect business. It was decided that he should live in Berneval, a few miles up the coast, initially in the small hotel by the beach run by the local estate agent, Monsieur Bonnet.

To Reginald Turner

[Postmark 27 May 1897]   *Hôtel de la Plage, Berneval-sur-Mer, Dieppe*
My dear Reggie, Thank you so much for the charming books: the poems are wonderfully fresh and buoyant: the guide-book to Berkshire is very lax in style, and it is difficult to realise that it is constructed on any metrical system. The matter, however, is interesting, and the whole book no doubt symbolic.

This is my first day here, Robbie and I arrived last night. The dinner was excellent, and we tried to eat enough for eight as we occupy so many rooms. However we soon got tired. Only the imagination of man is limitless. The appetite seems curiously bounded. This is one of the many lessons I have learnt.

I have just read Max's *Happy Hypocrite*, beginning at the end, as one should always do. It is quite wonderful, and to one who was once the author of *Dorian Gray*, full of no vulgar surprises of style or incident.

The population came at dawn to look at my dressing-case. I showed it to them, piece of silver by piece of silver. Some of the old men wept for joy. Robbie detected me at Dieppe in the market place of the sellers of perfumes, spending all my money on orris-root and the tears of the narcissus and the dust of red roses. He was very stern and led me away. I have already spent my entire income for two years. I see now that this lovely dressing-case with its silver vials thirsty for distilled odours will gradually lead me to the perfection of poverty. But it seemed to me to be cruel not to fill with rose-petals the little caskets shaped so cunningly in the form of a rose.

Dear Reggie, it was a great delight seeing you, and I shall never forget your kindness or the beauty of your friendship. I hope before the summer ends to see you again. Do write to me from time to time, and remember me to the Sphinx, and all those who do not know her secret. I know it of course. The open secret of the Sphinx is Ernest. Ever yours   OSCAR WILDE

To Max Beerbohm

[Circa 28 May 1897]   *Hôtel de la Plage, Berneval-sur-Mer*
My dear Max, I cannot tell you what a real pleasure it was to me to find
your delightful present waiting for me on my release from prison, and to
receive the charming and sweet messages you sent me. I used to think
gratitude a heavy burden for one to carry. Now I know that it is something
that makes the heart lighter. The ungrateful man seems to me to be one
who walks with feet and heart of lead. But when one has learnt, however
inadequately, what a lovely thing gratitude is, one's feet go lightly over sand
or sea, and one finds a strange joy revealed to one, the joy of counting up,
not what one possesses, but what one owes. I hoard my debts now in the
treasury of my heart, and, piece of gold by piece of gold, I range them in
order at dawn and at evening. So you must not mind my saying that I am
grateful to you. It is simply one of certain new pleasures that I have
discovered.

The Happy Hypocrite is a wonderful and beautiful story, though I do not
like the cynical directness of the name. The name one gives to one's work,
poem or picture – and all works of art are either poems or pictures, and the
best both at once – is the last survival of the Greek Chorus. It is the only
part of one's work in which the artist speaks directly in his own person, and
I don't like you wilfully taking the name given by the common spectators,
though I know what a joy there is in picking up a brickbat and wearing it as
a buttonhole. It is the origin of the name of all schools of art. Not to like
anything you have done is such a new experience to me that, not even for
a silver dressing-case full of objects of exquisite inutility such as dear Reggie
in his practical thoughtfulness provided for me on my release, shall I
surrender my views. But in years to come, when you are a very young man,
you will remember what I have said, and recognise its truth, and, in the
final edition of the work, leave the title unchanged. Of that I feel certain.
The gift of prophecy is given to all who do not know what is going to
happen to themselves.

The implied and accepted recognition of *Dorian Gray* in the story cheers
me. I had always been disappointed that my story had suggested no other
work of art in others. For whenever a beautiful flower grows in a meadow
or lawn, some other flower, so like it that it is differently beautiful, is sure
to grow up beside it, all flowers and all works of art having a curious
sympathy for each other. I feel also on reading your surprising and to me
quite novel story how useless it is for gaolers to deprive an artist of pen and
ink. One's work goes on just the same, with entrancing variations.

In case you should feel anxious about me, let me assure you frankly that the difference in colour between the two sheets of paper that compose this letter is the result not of poverty, but of extravagance. Do send me a line, to my new name. Sincerely yours   OSCAR WILDE

Despite the social snubs, there were some who went out of their way to show kindness to Wilde. The Norwegian painter, Frits Thaulow, and his wife had Wilde to dine on several occasions. Mrs Stannard, a prolific and popular novelist under her pseudonym John Strange Winter, and her husband invited him frequently to breakfast and lunch; once she even went out of her way to counter the ostentatious snubbing of Wilde by some English visitors to Dieppe, by crossing the street and suggesting in front of them that Wilde take her to tea.

To Mrs Stannard

[28 May 1897]   *Hôtel de la Plage, Berneval-sur-Mer*
Dear Mrs Stannard, Your kind husband gave me a very sympathetic and touching message from you yesterday, for which pray accept my most sincere thanks: he also asked me from you to call, a privilege of which I hope to avail myself tomorrow afternoon.

Of course I have passed through a very terrible punishment and have suffered to the very pitch of anguish and despair. Still I am conscious that I was leading a life quite unworthy of a son of my dear mother whose nobility of soul and intellect you always appreciated, and who was herself always one of your warmest and most enthusiastic admirers.

I am living quietly in a little *auberge* by the sea, and for the moment am quite alone. France has been charming to me and about me during all my imprisonment and has now – mother of all artists as she is – given me *asile*. To escape the foolish tongue and the prying eye I have for the moment taken the name of Sebastian Melmoth, a curious name which I will explain to you tomorrow.

Pray let my name and place of sojourn be quite a secret to all. I hope to live in solitude and peace. Accept these few flowers as a slight token of my gratitude and believe me truly yours   OSCAR WILDE

One of the first things that Wilde did when he reached France was to write a long and contrite letter to his wife asking to see her and the boys. The letter, since lost or probably destroyed, was described by Constance as one of the most beautiful he had ever written her. He also wrote for publication to the editor of the Daily Chronicle, *Henry Massingham, about the ill-treatment of children in prison which he had witnessed, about the dismissal of his own warder, Thomas Martin, for*

taking pity on the children and giving them biscuits, and about the case of a
mentally disturbed prisoner by the name of Prince in cell A.2.11. who was being
flogged regularly. His letter was published on 28 May under the heading 'The case
of warder Martin, some cruelties of prison life'.

To Robert Ross

[28 May 1897]   *Hôtel de la Plage, Berneval-sur-Mer*
My dear Robbie, This is my first day alone, and of course a very unhappy
one. I begin to realise my terrible position of isolation, and I have been
rebellious and bitter of heart all day. Is it not sad? I thought I was accepting
everything so well and so simply, and I have had moods of rage passing
over my nature, like gusts of bitter wind or storm spoiling the sweet corn,
or blasting the young shoots. I found a little chapel, full of the most fantastic
saints, so ugly and Gothic, and painted quite gaudily – some of them with
smiles carved to a *rictus* almost, like primitive things – but they all seemed
to me to be idols. I laughed with amusement when I saw them. Fortunately
there was a lovely crucifix in a side-chapel – not a Jansenist one, but with
wide-stretched arms of gold. I was pleased at that, and wandered then by
the cliffs where I fell asleep on the warm coarse brown sea-grass. I had
hardly any sleep last night. Bosie's revolting letter was in the room, and
foolishly I had read it again and left it by my bedside. My dream was that
my mother was speaking to me with some sternness, and that she was in
trouble. I quite see that whenever I am in danger she will in some way warn
me. I have a real terror now of that unfortunate ungrateful young man with
his unimaginative selfishness and his entire lack of all sensitiveness to what
in others is good or kind or trying to be so. I feel him as an evil influence,
poor fellow. To be with him would be to return to the hell from which I
do think I have been released. I hope never to see him again.

For yourself, dear sweet Robbie, I am haunted by the idea that many of
those who love you will and do think it selfish of me to allow you and wish
you to be with me from time to time. But still they might see the difference
between your going about with me in my days of gilded infamy – my
Neronian hours, rich, profligate, cynical, materialistic – and your coming to
comfort me, a lonely dishonoured man, in disgrace and obscurity and
poverty. How lacking in imagination they are! If I were rich again and
sought to repeat my former life I don't think you would care very much to
be with me. I think you would regret what I was doing, but now, dear boy,
you come with the heart of Christ, and you help me intellectually as no one
else can or ever could do. You are helping me to save my soul alive, not in

the theological sense, but in the plain meaning of the words, for my soul was really dead in the slough of coarse pleasures, my life was unworthy of an artist: you can heal me and help me. No other friend have I now in this beautiful world. I want no other. Yet I am distressed to think that I will be looked on as careless of your own welfare, and indifferent of your good. You are made to help me. I weep with sorrow when I think how much I need help, but I weep with joy when I think I have you to give it to me.

I do hope to do some work in these six weeks, that when you come I shall be able to read you something. I know you love me, but I want to have your respect, your sincere admiration, or rather, for that is a word of ill-omen, your sincere appreciation of my effort to recreate my artistic life. But if I have to think that I am harming you, all pleasure in your society will be tainted for me. With you at any rate I want to be free of any sense of guilt, the sense of spoiling another's life. Dear boy, I couldn't spoil your life by accepting the sweet companionship you offer me from time to time. It is not for nothing that I named you in prison St Robert of Phillimore. Love can canonise people. The saints are those who have been most loved.

I only made one mistake in prison in things that I wrote of you or to you in my book. My poem should have run, 'When I came out of prison you met me with garments, with spices, with wise counsel. You met me with love.' Not others did it, but you. I really laugh when I think how true in detail the lines are.

8.30. I have just received your telegram. A man bearded, no doubt for purposes of disguise, dashed up on a bicycle, brandishing a blue telegram. I knew it was from you. Well, I am really pleased, and look forward to the paper. I do think it will help. I now think I shall write my prison article for the *Chronicle.* It is interested in prison-reform, and the thing would not look an advertisement.

Let me know your opinion. I intend to write to Massingham. Reading between the lines of your telegram I seem to discern that you are pleased. The telegram was much needed. They had offered me serpent for dinner! A serpent cut up, in an umber-green sauce! I explained that I was not a *mangeur de serpents* and have converted the *patron.* No serpent is now to be served to any guest. He grew quite hot over it. What a good thing it is that I am an experienced ichthyologist!

I enclose a lot of letters. Please put money orders in them and send them off. Put those addressed to the prison in a larger envelope, each of them, addressed by yourself, if possible legibly. They are my debts of honour, and I must pay them. Of course you must read the letters. Explain to Miss

Meredith that letters addressed C.3.3, 24 Hornton Street are for you. The money is as follows. Of course it is a great deal but I thought I would have lots:

Jackson	£1.	
Fleet	£1.10s.	
Ford	£2.10s.	
Stone	£3.	
× Eaton	£2.	The letters must go *at once.*
× Cruttenden	£2.	At least those marked ×
Bushell	£2.10s.	
× Millward	£2.10s.	
Groves	£3.10s.	
	————	
	£20.10s.	
W. Smith	£2.	

How it mounts up! But now I have merely Jim Cuthbert December 2, Jim Huggins October 9, and Harry Elvin November 6. They can keep. On second thoughts I have sent only one to the prison. Please be careful not to mix the letters. They are all *nuanced.*

I want some pens, and some red ties. The latter for literary purposes of course.

I wrote to Courtenay Thorpe this morning: also to Mrs Stannard and sent her flowers.

More forwards me a poem from Bosie – a love-lyric! It is absurd.

Tardieu has written mysteriously warning me of dangerous friends in Paris. I hate mystery: it is so obvious.

Keep Romeike on the war-trail.

The *Figaro* announced me bicycling at Dieppe! They always confuse you and me. It really is delightful. I will make no protest. You are the best half of me.

I am very tired, and the rain is coming down. You will be glad to hear that I have not been planting *cacao* in plantain swamps, and that 'Lloyd' is not now sitting on the verandah, nor is 'Fanny' looking after the 'labour-boys', and that of 'Belle' I know nothing. So now, dear Colvin (what an awful pen!) I mean dear Robbie, good night.

With all love and affection, yours   OSCAR

The penultimate paragraph is a parody of R. L. Stevenson's Vailima Letters *to Sidney Colvin. The references are to Stevenson's stepson, wife and stepdaughter.*

To Major J. O. Nelson

[28 May 1897]   *Hôtel de la Plage, Berneval-sur-Mer*

Dear Major Nelson, I had of course intended to write to you as soon as I had safely reached French soil, to express, however inadequately, my real feelings of what you must let me term, not merely sincere, but *affectionate* gratitude to you for your kindness and gentleness to me in prison, and for the real care that you took of me at the end, when I was mentally upset and in a state of very terrible nervous excitement. You must not mind my using the word 'gratitude'. I used to think gratitude a burden to carry. Now I know that it is something that makes the heart lighter. The ungrateful man is one who walks slowly with feet and heart of lead. But when one knows the strange joy of gratitude to God and man the earth becomes lovelier to one, and it is a pleasure to count up, not one's wealth but one's debts, not the little that one possesses, but the much that one owes.

I abstained from writing, however, because I was haunted by the memory of the little children, and the wretched half-witted lad who was flogged by the doctor's orders. I could not have kept them out of my letter, and to have mentioned them to you might have put *you* in a difficult position. In your reply you *might* have expressed sympathy with my views – I think you would have – and then on the appearance of my public letter you might have felt as if I had, in some almost ungenerous or thoughtless way, procured your private opinion on official things, for use as corroboration.

I longed to speak to you about these things on the evening of my departure, but I felt that in my position as a prisoner it would have been wrong of me to do so, and that it would or might have put you in a difficult position afterwards, as well as at the time. I only hear of my letter being published by a telegram from Mr Ross, but I hope they have printed it in full, as I tried to express in it my appreciation and admiration of your own humane spirit and affectionate interest in *all* the prisoners under your charge. I did not wish people to think that any exception had been specially made for me. Such exceptional treatment as I received was by order of the Commissioners. You gave me the same kindness as you gave to everyone. Of course I made more demands, but then I think I had really more needs than others, and I lacked often their cheerful acquiescence.

Of course I side with the prisoners: I was one, and I belong to their class now. I am not a scrap ashamed of having been in prison. I am horribly ashamed of the materialism of the life that brought me there. It was quite unworthy of an artist.

Of Martin, and the subjects of my letter, I of course say nothing at all, except that the man who could change the system – if any one man can do so – is yourself. At present I write to ask you to allow me to sign myself, once at any rate in life, your sincere and grateful friend OSCAR WILDE

To Robert Ross

[29–30 May 1897] *Hôtel de la Plage, Berneval-sur-Mer*
My dear Robbie, Your letter is quite admirable, but, dear boy, don't you see how right *I* was to write to the *Chronicle*? All good impulses are right. Had I listened to some of my friends I would never have written.

I am sending a postscript to Massingham – of some importance: if he publishes it, send it to me.

I have also asked him if he wishes my prison experiences, and if he would share in a syndicate. I think now, as the length of my letter is so great, that I could do *three* articles on Prison Life. Of course much will be psychological and introspective: and one will be on Christ as the Precursor of the Romantic Movement in Life, that lovely subject which was revealed to me when I found myself in the company of the same sort of people Christ liked, outcasts and beggars.

I am terrified about Bosie. More writes to me that he has been practically interviewed about me! It is awful. More, desiring to spare me pain, I suppose, did not send me the paper, so I have had a wretched night.

Bosie can almost ruin me. I earnestly beg that some entreaty be made to him not to do so a second time. His letters to me are infamous.

I have heard from my wife. She sends me photographs of the boys – such lovely little fellows in Eton collars – but makes no promise to allow me to see them: she says *she* will see me, twice a year, but I want my boys. It is a terrible punishment, dear Robbie, and oh! how well I deserve it. But it makes me feel disgraced and evil, and I don't want to feel that. Let me have the *Chronicle* regularly. Also write often. It is very good for me to be alone. I am working. Dear Robbie, ever yours OSCAR

To Robert Ross

Monday Night, 31 May [1897] *[Hôtel de la Plage, Berneval-sur-Mer]*
My dearest Robbie, I have decided that the only way in which to get boots properly is to go to France to receive them. The *douane* charged three francs! How could you frighten me as you did? The next time you order boots please come to Dieppe to get them sent to you. It is the only way, and it will be an excuse for seeing me.

I am going tomorrow on a pilgrimage. I always wanted to be a pilgrim, and I have decided to start early tomorrow to the shrine of Notre Dame de Liesse. Do you know what Liesse is? It is an old word for joy. I suppose the same as Letizia, *laetitia*. I just heard of the shrine, or chapel, tonight, *by chance*, as you would say, from the sweet woman of the *auberge*, a perfect dear, who wants me to live always at Berneval! She says Notre Dame de Liesse is wonderful, and helps everyone to the secret of joy. I do not know how long it will take me to get to the shrine, as I must walk. But, from what she tells me, it will take at least six or seven minutes to get there, and as many to come back. In fact the chapel of Notre Dame de Liesse is just fifty yards from the hotel! Isn't it extraordinary? I intend to start after I have had my coffee, and then to bathe. Need I say that this is a miracle? I wanted to go on a pilgrimage, and I find the little grey stone chapel of Our Lady of Joy is brought to me. It has probably been waiting for me all these purple years of pleasure, and now it comes to meet me with Liesse as its message. I simply don't know what to say. I wish you were not so hard to poor heretics, and would admit that even for the sheep who has no shepherd there is a Stella Maris to guide it home. But you and More, especially More, treat me as a Dissenter. It is very painful, and quite unjust.

Yesterday I attended Mass at ten o'clock and afterwards bathed. So I went into the water without being a Pagan. The consequence was that I was not tempted by either Sirens, or Mermaidens, or any of the green-haired following of Glaucus. I really think that this is a remarkable thing. In my pagan days the sea was always full of tritons blowing conches, and other unpleasant things. Now it is quite different. And yet you treat me as the President of Mansfield College: and after I had canonised you, too!

Dear boy, I wish you would tell me if your religion makes you happy. You conceal your religion from me in a monstrous way. You treat it like writing in the *Saturday Review* for Pollock, or dining in Wardour Street off the fascinating dish that is served with tomatoes and makes men mad. I know it is useless asking you. So don't tell me.

I felt an outcast in chapel yesterday – not really, but a little in exile. I met a dear farmer in a cornfield, and he gave me a seat in his *banc* in church: so I was quite comfortable. He now visits me twice a day, and as he has no children, and is rich, I have made him promise to adopt three – two boys and a girl. I told him that if he wanted them, he would find them. He said he was afraid that they would turn out badly. I told him everyone did that. He really has promised to adopt three orphans! He is now filled with enthusiasm at the idea. He is to go to the *curé* and talk to him. He told me that his own father had fallen down in a fit one day as they were talking together, and that he had caught him in his arms, and put him to bed, where he died, and that he himself had often thought how dreadful it was that if he had a fit there was no one to catch him in his arms. It is quite clear that he must adopt orphans, is it not?

I feel that Berneval is to be my home. I really do. Notre Dame de Liesse will be sweet to me, if I go on my knees to her, and she will advise me. It is extraordinary being brought here by a white horse that was a native of the place, and knew the road, and wanted to see its parents, now of advanced years. It is also extraordinary that I knew Berneval existed, and was arranged for me.

M. Bonnet wants to build me a chalet! 1000 metres of ground (I don't know how much that is, but I suppose about 100 miles) and a chalet with a studio, a balcony, a *salle-à-manger*, a huge kitchen, and three bedrooms, a view of the sea, and trees – all for 12,000 francs, £480. If I can write a play I am going to have it begun. Fancy one's own lovely house and grounds in France for £480! No rent of any kind. Pray consider this, and approve, if you think right. Of course not till I have done my play.

An old gentleman lives here in the hotel. He dines alone in his rooms, and then sits in the sun. He came here for two days, and has stayed two years. His sole sorrow is that there is no theatre. Monsieur Bonnet is a little heartless about this, and says that as the old gentleman goes to bed at eight o'clock, a theatre would be of no use to him. The old gentleman says he only goes to bed at eight o'clock because there is no theatre. They argued the point yesterday for an hour. I side with the old gentleman, but Logic sides with Monsieur Bonnet, I believe.

I had a sweet letter from the Sphinx. She gives me a delightful account of Ernest subscribing to Romeike while his divorce suit was running, and not being pleased with some of the notices. Considering the growing appreci-ation of Ibsen I must say that I am surprised the notices were not better, but nowadays everybody is jealous of everyone else, except, of course, husband and wife. I think I shall keep this last remark of mine for my play.

Have you got back my silver spoon from Reggie? You got my silver brushes out of Humphreys, who is bald, so you might easily get my spoon out of Reggie, who has so many, or used to have. You know my crest is on it. It is a bit of Irish silver, and I don't want to lose it. There is an excellent substitute called Britannia metal, very much liked at the Adelphi and elsewhere. Wilson Barrett writes, 'I prefer it to silver.' It would suit dear Reggie admirably. Walter Besant writes, 'I use none other.' Mr Beerbohm Tree also writes, 'Since I have tried it I am a different actor. My friends hardly recognise me.' So there is obviously a demand for it.

I am going to write a Political Economy in my heavier moments. The first law I lay down is 'Wherever there exists a demand, there is *no* supply'. This is the only law that explains the extraordinary contrast between the soul of man, and man's surroundings. Civilisations continue because people hate them. A modern city is the exact opposite of what everyone wants. Nineteenth-century dress is the result of our horror of the style. The tall hat will last as long as people dislike it.

Dear Robbie, I wish you would be a little more considerate, and not keep me up so late talking to you. It is very flattering to me and all that, but you should remember that I need rest. Goodnight. You will find some cigarettes and some flowers by your bedside. Coffee is served *below* at eight o'clock. Do you mind? If it is too early for you, I don't at all mind lying in bed an extra hour. I hope you will sleep well. You should, as Lloyd is *not* on the verandah.

Tuesday morning [1 June 1897], 9.30.

The sea and sky one opal, no horrid drawing-master's line between them, just one fishing boat, going slowly, and drawing the wind after it. I am going to bathe.

Six o'clock

Bathed and have seen a chalet here, which I wish to take for the season – quite charming: a splendid view: a large writing-room; a dining-room, and three lovely bedrooms, besides servant's room, also a huge balcony.

I don't know the *scale* of my drawing. But the rooms are *larger* than the plan is.

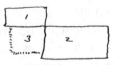

1. *Salle-à-manger.*   All on ground floor, with steps
2. *Salon*   from balcony to ground.
3. Balcony

The rent for the season or year is what do you think – £32. Of course I must have it: I will take my meals here, separate and reserved table: it is within two minutes' walk. Do tell me to take it: when you come again your room will be waiting for you. All I need is a *domestique*. The people here are most kind.

I made my pilgrimage. The interior of the chapel is of course a modern horror, but there is a black image of Notre Dame de Liesse. The chapel is as tiny as an undergraduate's room at Oxford. I hope to get the *curé* to celebrate Mass in it soon. As a rule the service is only held there in July–August: but I want to see a Mass quite close.

There is also another thing I must write to you about.

I adore this place. The whole country is lovely, and full of forest and deep meadow. It is simple and healthy. If I live in Paris I may be doomed to things I don't desire. I am afraid of big towns. Here I get up at 7.30. I am happy all day. I go to bed at ten o'clock. I am frightened of Paris. I want to live here.

I have seen the terrain. It is the best here, and the only one left. I must build a house. If I could build a chalet for 12,000 francs – £500 – and live in a home of my own, how happy I would be. I must raise the money somehow. It would give me a home, quiet, retired, healthy, and near England. If I lived in Egypt I know what my life would be. If I lived in the South of Italy I know I should be idle, and worse. I want to live here. Do think over this, and send me over the architect. Monsieur Bonnet is excellent, and is ready to carry out my ideas. I want a little chalet of wood and plastered walls, the wooden beams showing, and the white squares of plaster diapering the framework, like, I regret to say, Shakespeare's house: like old English sixteenth-century farmers' houses. So your architect has me waiting for him, as he is waiting for me.

Do you think this idea absurd?

I got the *Chronicle*: many thanks. I see the writer on Prince – A.2.11 – does not mention my name; foolish of her; it is a woman.

I, as you, the poem of my days, are away, am forced to write poetry. I have begun something that I think will be very good.

I breakfast tomorrow with the Stannards: what a great passionate splendid writer John Strange Winter is! How little people understand her work! *Bootle's Baby* is *une oeuvre symboliste*: it is really only the style and the subject that are wrong. Pray never speak lightly of *Bootle's Baby* – indeed, pray never speak of it at all; I never do. Ever yours   OSCAR

Please send a *Chronicle* to my wife, Mrs C. M. Holland, Maison Benguerel, Bevaix, près de Neuchâtel, just marking it, and if my second letter appears, mark that. Also one to Mrs Arthur Stannard, 28 Rue de la Halle-au-Blé, Dieppe. Also, cut out the letter and enclose it in an envelope to Mr Arthur Cruttenden, Poste Restante, GPO Reading, with just these lines:

Dear Friend, The enclosed will interest you. There is also another letter waiting in the Post Office for you from me, with a little money. Ask for it, if you have not got it. Yours sincerely   C.3.3

I have no one but you, dear Robbie, to do anything. Of course the letter to Reading must go *at once,* as my friends come out on *Wednesday* morning early.

Michael Davitt, Irish writer and socialist MP, had suffered frequent bouts in prison for Fenian and similar activities. He had already asked questions in the House of Commons about the dismissal of warder Martin.

To Michael Davitt

[Late May or early June 1897]   *Hôtel de la Plage, Berneval-sur-Mer*
Private and Confidential

Dear Mr Davitt, I have been sent a cutting from a Liverpool paper which states that you intend to ask a question about the treatment of A.2.11 in Reading prison. I do not of course know if this is true, but I sincerely hope that you are *in some way* stirring in the matter. No one knows better than yourself how terrible life in an English prison is and what cruelties result from the stupidity of officialism, and the immobile ignorance of centralisation. *You* suffered for what was done by someone else. I, in that respect more unfortunate, for a life of senseless pleasure and hard materialism and a mode of existence unworthy of an artist, and still more unworthy of my mother's son. But you know what prison-life is, and that there is no exaggeration in what I say. Everything that I state about the treatment of A.2.11 is absolutely true. With my own punishment I have nothing to do, except so far as it is the type of what is inflicted on much better, nicer fellows than myself. I have no bitterness at all, but I have learnt pity: and that is worth learning, if one has to tramp a yard for two years to learn it.

In any case I don't think they will flog A.2.11 again, and that is something. But of course I am quite powerless to do any more. I merely wrote as any other of the prisoners might have written, who had a pen he could use, and found a paper sufficiently large-minded to publish his letter. But with the letter I am forced to stop. It is part of my punishment – the new part that I have to face, and am facing very cheerfully and without any despair or making any complaint. I prefix to this letter *my name* for the present, and my address: but my letter requires no answer. It is simply the expression of a hope. I remain, yours faithfully   OSCAR WILDE

PS Enclosed letter has just been forwarded to me, through my solicitor. A.2.11 has apparently been flogged again – see postscript. I think it is simply revolting. After you have read the chap's letter, of course tear it up. I have his address.

Douglas, who had been abroad on the Continent since Wilde's first trial, was now living in Paris. He gave an interview to Le Jour, *which appeared on 28 May, in which he described Wilde's sufferings in prison and blamed English hypocrisy. The editorial comment was hostile, declaring that in Paris the name of Oscar Wilde was synonymous with 'pathologie passionnelle'.*

To Lord Alfred Douglas

[?2 June 1897]   *Hôtel de la Plage, Berneval-sur-Mer*
My dear Boy, If you *will* send me back beautiful letters, with bitter ones of your own, of course you will never remember my address. It is as above.

Of Lugné-Poe, of course, I know nothing except that he is singularly handsome, and seems to me to have the personality of a good actor, for personality does not require intellect to help it: it is a dynamic force of its own, and is often as superbly unintelligent as the great forces of nature, like the lightning that shook at sudden moments last night over the sea that slept before my window.

The production of *Salomé* was the thing that turned the scale in my favour, as far as my treatment in prison by the Government was concerned, and I am deeply grateful to all concerned in it. Upon the other hand I could not give my next play for nothing, as I simply do not know how I shall live after the summer is over unless I at once make money. I am in a terrible and dangerous position, for money that I had been assured was set aside for me was not forthcoming when I wanted it. It was a horrible disappointment: for I have of course begun to live as a man of letters should live – that is with a private sitting-room and books and the like. I can see no other way of living, if I am to write, though I can see many others, if I am not.

If then Lugné-Poe can give me no money, of course I shall not consider myself bound to him. But the play in question – being religious in surroundings and treatment of subject – is not a play for a *run*, at all. Three performances are the most I think I could expect. All I want is to have my artistic reappearance, and my own rehabilitation through art, in *Paris*, not in London. It is a homage and a debt I owe to that great city of art.

If anyone else with money would take the play, and let Lugné-Poe play the part, I would be more than content. In any case I am not bound, and, what is of more import, the play is not written! I am still trying to finish my necessary correspondence, and to express suitably my deep gratitude to all who have been kind to me.

As regards *Le Journal*, I would be charmed to write for it, and will try and get it regularly. I do not like to *abonner* myself at the office as I am anxious that my address should not be known. I think I had better do it at Dieppe, from where I get the *Echo de Paris*.

I hear the *Jour* has had a sort of interview – a false one – with you. This is very distressing: as much, I don't doubt, to you as to me. I hope however that it is not the cause of the duel you hint at. Once you get to fight duels in France, you have to be *always* doing it, and it is a nuisance. I do hope that you will always shelter yourself under the accepted right of any English gentleman to decline a duel, unless of course some personal fracas or public insult takes place. Of course you will never dream of fighting a duel for *me*: that would be awful, and create the worst and most odious impression.

Always write to me about your art and the art of others. It is better to meet on the double peak of Parnassus than elsewhere. I have read your poems with great pleasure and interest: but on the whole your best work is to me still the work you did two years and a half ago – the ballads, and bits of the play. Of course your own personality has had for many reasons to express itself *directly* since then, but I hope you will go on to forms more remote from actual events and passions. One can really, as I say in *Intentions*, be far more subjective in an *objective* form than in any other way. If I were asked of myself as a dramatist, I would say that my unique position was that I had taken the Drama, the most objective form known to art, and made it as personal a mode of expression as the Lyric or the Sonnet, while enriching the characterisation of the stage, and enlarging – at any rate in the case of *Salomé* – its artistic horizon. You have real sympathy with the Ballad. Pray again return to it. The Ballad is the true origin of the romantic Drama, and the true predecessors of Shakespeare are not the tragic writers of the Greek or Latin stage, from Aeschylus to Seneca, but the ballad-writers of the Border. In such a ballad as *Gilderoy* one has the prefiguring note of the romance of *Romeo and Juliet*, different though the plots are. The recurring phrases of *Salomé*, that bind it together like a piece of music with recurring *motifs*, are, and were to me, the artistic equivalent of the refrains of old ballads. All this is to beg you to write ballads.

I do not know whether I have to thank you or More for the books from Paris, probably both. As I have divided the books, so you must divide the thanks.

I am greatly fascinated by the *Napoléon* of La Jeunesse. He must be most interesting. André Gide's book fails to fascinate me. The egoistic note is, of course, and always has been to me, the primal and ultimate note of modern art, but *to be an Egoist one must have an Ego*. It is not everyone who says 'I, I' who can enter into the Kingdom of Art. But I love André personally very deeply, and often thought of him in prison, as I often did of dear Reggie

Cholmondeley, with his large faun's eyes and honey-sweet smile. Give him my fondest love. Ever yours   OSCAR

Kindly forward enclosed card to Reggie, with my address. Tell him to keep *both* a secret.

To Lord Alfred Douglas

Thursday [3 June 1897], 2.30   [*Hôtel de la Plage, Berneval-sur-Mer*]

My dear Boy, I have just received three copies of *Le Jour*, that I ordered from Dieppe; not knowing what day the supposed interview with you had taken place, I had ordered the numbers for Friday, Saturday, and Sunday.

The interview is quite harmless, and I am really sorry you took any notice of it. I *do* hope it is not with the low-class journalist that you are to fight, if that absurd experience is in store for you. If you ever fight in France let it be with someone who *exists*. To fight with the dead is either a vulgar farce or a revolting tragedy.

Let me know by telegram if anything has happened. The telegraph office is at Dieppe, but they send out on swift bicycles men in fantastic dresses of the middle-*class* age, who blow horns all the time so that the moon shall hear them. The costume of the *moyen-âge* is lovely but the dress of the middle-*class* age is dreadful.

Let me beg one thing of you. Please *always* let me see *anything* that appears about myself in the Paris papers – good or bad, but especially the *bad*. It is a matter of vital import to me to know the attitude of the community. All mystery enrages me, and when dear More wrote to say that a false interview with you of no importance had been published, I hired a *voiture* at once and galloped to Dieppe to try and find it, and ordered, as I have told you, three separate numbers. It wrecks my nerves to think of things appearing on me that are kept from me. If More had enclosed it in his letter, I would have been happy and satisfied. As it was, I was really unnerved. The smallest word about me tells.

If *Le Journal* would publish my letter to the *Daily Chronicle* it would be a great thing for me. I hope you have seen it.

Ernest Dowson, Conder, and Dal Young – what a name – are coming out to dine and sleep: at least I know they dine, but I believe they don't sleep. Ever yours   OSCAR

Ernest Dowson, a poet whom Wilde had met with Sherard in 1890, Charles Conder, the painter, and Dalhousie Young, the pianist and composer, all of them about thirty and living in Dieppe, were to give Wilde their unstinted friendship for the

next months. Dal Young, although unacquainted with Wilde at the time of his conviction, bravely published his Apologia pro Oscar Wilde *in May 1895 and later, when Wilde was in Naples, paid him to write a libretto, probably aware that the commission would never be completed, but afterwards complaining that Wilde had obtained the advance under false pretences.*

To Robert Ross

Thursday 3 June
2.45 p.m. (Berneval time)
AD 1897   *Latitude and Longitude not marked on the sea*
Dear Robbie, The entirely business-like tone of your letter just received makes me nervous that you are a prey of terrible emotions, and that it is merely a form of the calm that hides a storm. Your remark also that my letter is 'undated', while as a reproach it wounds me, also seems to denote a change in your friendship towards me. I have now put the date and other facts at the head of my letter.

I get no cuttings from Paris, which makes me irritable when I hear of things appearing. Not knowing the day of the false interview with Bosie I ordered, fortunately, copies of the paper for *three successive days*: they have just arrived, and I see an impertinent *démenti* of Bosie's denial.

Bosie has also written to me to say he is on the eve of a duel! I suppose about this. They said his costume was *ridicule*. I have written to him to beg him *never* to fight duels, as once one does it one has to go on. And though it is not dangerous, like our English cricket or football is, still it is a tedious game to be always playing.

Besides, to fight with the common interviewer is to fight with the dead, a thing either farcical or tragic.

Ernest Dowson, Conder, and Dal Young come out here this afternoon to dine and sleep – at least I know they dine, but I believe they never sleep.

I think the *Chronicle* are nervous. They have not answered yet or anything. Of course with them I am all right, if they take my work. Who is my Receiver? I want his name and address. Ever yours   OSCAR

To Robert Ross

Saturday, 5 June [1897]   *[Hôtel de la Plage, Berneval-sur-Mer]*
My dear Robbie, I propose to *live* at Berneval. I will *not* live in Paris, nor in Algiers, nor in southern Italy. Surely a house for a year, if I choose to continue there, at £32 is absurdly cheap! I could not live cheaper at a hotel.

You are penny foolish and pound foolish – a dreadful state for any financier to be in. I told M. Bonnet that my banker was *M. Ross et Cie, Banquiers célèbres de Londres*: and now you suddenly show me that you have really no place among the great financial people, and are afraid of any investment over £31.10. It is merely the extra 10/- that baffles you. As regards people living on me in the extra bedrooms: dear boy, there is no one who would stay with me but you, and you will pay your own bill at the hotel for meals, and as for your room the charge will be nominally 2 fr. 50 a night, but there will be *lots* of extras, such as *bougie, bain*, and hot water: all cigarettes smoked in the bedrooms are charged extra: washing is extra: and if any one does not take the extras, of course he is charged more. *Bain 25 c. Pas de bain 50 c. Cigarette dans la chambre-à-coucher, 10 c. pour chaque cigarette. Pas de cigarettes dans la chambre-à-coucher, 20 c. chaque cigarette.* This is the *système* in all good hotels. If Reggie comes, of course he will pay a little more. I cannot forget that he gave me a dressing-case. Sphinxes pay a hundred per cent more than anyone else. They always did in ancient Egypt. Architects, on the other hand, are taken at a reduction. I have special terms for architects.

But seriously, Robbie, if anyone stayed with me, of course they would pay their *pension* at the hotel. They would have to: except architects. A modern architect, like modern architecture, doesn't pay. But then I only know one architect, and you are hiding him somewhere from me. I am beginning to believe that he is as extinct as the Dado, of which now only fossil remains are found, chiefly in the vicinity of Brompton, where they are sometimes discovered by workmen excavating. They are usually embedded in the old Lincrusta-Walton strata, and are rare consequently.

I visited *M. le Curé* today: he has a charming house in a *jardin potager*: he showed me over the church: tomorrow I sit in the choir by his special invitation. He showed me all his vestments: tomorrow he really will be charming in his red. He knows I am a heretic, and believes that Pusey is still alive. He says that God will convert England on account of England's kindness to the *prêtres exilés* at the time of the Revolution. It is to be the reward of that sea-lashed island. Stained-glass windows are wanted in the church: he only has six: fourteen more are needed. He gets them at 300 francs (£12) a window in Paris! I was nearly offering half a dozen, but remembered you, and so only gave him something *pour ses pauvres*. You had a narrow escape, Robbie. You should be thankful.

I hope the £40 is on its way, and that the £60 will follow. I am going to hire a boat. It will save walking, and so be an economy in the end. Dear Robbie, I must start well. If the life of St Francis awaits me I shall not be angry. Worse things might happen. Ever yours   OSCAR

To Lord Alfred Douglas

Sunday night, 6 June [1897]   [*Hôtel de la Plage, Berneval-sur-Mer*]

My dearest Boy, I must give up this *absurd* habit of writing to you every day. It comes of course from the strange new joy of talking to you daily. But next week I must make a resolution to write to you only every *seven* days, and then on the question of the relations of the sonnet to modern life, and the importance of your writing romantic ballads, and the strange beauty of that lovely line of Rossetti's, suppressed till lately by his brother, where he says that 'the sea ends in a sad blueness beyond rhyme'. Don't you think it lovely? 'In a sad *blueness* beyond rhyme.' *Voilà 'l'influence du bleu dans les arts'*, with a vengeance!

I am so glad you went to bed at seven o'clock. Modern life is terrible to vibrating delicate frames like yours: a rose-leaf in a storm of hard hail is not so fragile. With us who are modern it is the *scabbard* that wears out the sword.

Will you do this for me? Get *Le Courier de la Presse* to procure a copy of *Le Soir*, the *Brussels* paper, somewhere between the 26th and the 31st of May last, which has an article on my letter to the *Chronicle*, a translation of it, I believe, and notices. It is of vital importance for me to have it as soon as possible. My *Chronicle* letter is to be published as a pamphlet with a postscript, and I need the *Soir*. I don't want to write myself for it, for obvious reasons. Dear boy, I hope you are still sweetly asleep: you are so absurdly sweet when you are asleep. I have been to Mass at ten o'clock and to Vespers at three o'clock. I was a little bored by a sermon in the morning, but Benediction was delightful. I am seated in the Choir! I suppose sinners should have the high places near Christ's altar? I know at any rate that Christ would not turn me out.

Remember, after a few days, only *one letter a week*. I *must* school myself to it.

En attendant, yours with all love   OSCAR
                                                    Poète-forçat

To Frank Harris

13 June 1897   *Hôtel de la Plage, Berneval-sur-Mer*

My dear Frank, I know you do not like writing letters, but still I think you might have written me a line in answer, or acknowledgement of my letter to you from Dieppe. I have been thinking of a story to be called 'The Silence of Frank Harris'.

I have, however, heard during the last few days that you do not speak of me in the friendly manner I would like. This distresses me very much.

I am told that you are hurt with me because my letter of thanks to you was not sufficiently elaborated in expression. This I can hardly credit. It seems so unworthy of a big strong nature like yours, that knows the realities of life. I told you I was grateful to you for your kindness to me. Words, *now*, to me signify *things*, actualities, real emotions, realised thoughts. I learnt in prison to be grateful. I used to think gratitude a burden. Now I know that it is something that makes life lighter as well as lovelier for one. I am grateful for a thousand things, from my good friends down to the sun and the sea. But I cannot say more than that I am grateful. I cannot make phrases about it. For *me* to use such a word shows an enormous development in my nature. Two years ago I did not know the feeling the word denotes. Now I know it, and I am thankful that I have learnt that much, at any rate, by having been in prison. But I must say again that I no longer make *roulades* of phrases about the deep things I feel. When I write directly to you I speak directly. Violin-variations don't interest me. I am grateful to you. If that does not content you, then you do not understand, what you of all men should understand, how sincerity of feeling expresses itself. But I dare say the story told of you is untrue. It comes from so many quarters that it probably is.

I am told also that you are hurt because I did not go on the driving-tour with you. You should understand that in telling you that it was impossible for me to do so, I was thinking as much of *you* as of myself. To think of the feelings and happiness of others is not an entirely new emotion in my nature. I would be unjust to myself and my friends, if I said it was. But I think of those things far more than I used to do. If I had gone with you, you would not have been happy, nor enjoyed yourself. Nor would I. You must try to realise what two years' cellular confinement is, and what two years of absolute silence mean to a man of my intellectual power. To have survived at all – to have come out sane in mind and sound of body – is a thing so marvellous to me, that it seems to me sometimes, not that the age of miracles is over, but that it is only just beginning; and that there are powers in God, and powers in man, of which the world has up to the present known little.

But while I am cheerful, happy, and have sustained to the full that passionate interest in life and art that was the dominant chord of my nature, and made all modes of existence and all forms of expression utterly fascinating to me always – still, I need rest, quiet, and often complete solitude. Friends have come to see me here for a day, and have been delighted to find me like my old self, in all intellectual energy and sensitiveness to the play of life, but it has always proved afterwards to have been a strain upon a nervous force, much of which has been destroyed. I have now no *storage* of nervous force. When I expend what I have, in an afternoon, nothing remains. I look to quiet, to a simple mode of existence, to nature in all the infinite meanings of an infinite word, to charge the cells for me. Every day, if I meet a friend, or write a letter longer than a few lines, or even read a book that makes, as all fine books do, a direct claim on me, a direct appeal, an intellectual challenge of any kind, I am utterly exhausted in the evening, and often sleep badly. And yet it is *three* whole weeks since I was released.

Had I gone with you on the driving-tour, where we would have of necessity been in immediate contact with each other from dawn to sunset, I would have certainly broken off the tour the third day, probably broken down the second. You would have then found yourself in a painful position: your tour would have been arrested at its outset; your companion would have been ill without doubt; perhaps might have needed care and attendance, in some little remote French village. You would have given it to me, I know. But I felt it would have been wrong, stupid, and thoughtless of me to have started an expedition doomed to swift failure, and perhaps fraught with disaster and distress. You are a man of dominant personality; your intellect is exigent, more so than that of any man I ever knew; your demands on life are enormous; you require response, or you annihilate. The pleasure of being with you is in the clash of personality, the intellectual battle, the war of ideas. To survive you one must have a strong brain, an assertive ego, a dynamic character. In your luncheon-parties, in old days, the remains of the guests were taken away with the *débris* of the feast. I have often lunched with you in Park Lane and found myself the only survivor. I might have driven on the white roads, or through the leafy lanes, of France with a fool, or with the wisest of all things, a child; with you it would have been impossible. You should thank me sincerely for having saved you from an experience that each of us would have always regretted.

Will you ask me why then, when I was in prison, I accepted with grateful thanks your offer? My dear Frank, I don't think you will ask so thoughtless a question. The prisoner looks to liberty as an immediate return to all his ancient energy, quickened into more vital forces by long disuse. When he goes out, he finds he has still to suffer. His punishment, as far as its effects go, lasts intellectually and physically, just as it lasts socially. He has still to pay. One gets no receipt for the past when one walks out into the beautiful air.

There is also a third thing. The Leversons kindly bought for me and presented to me my own life-size portrait of myself by Harper Pennington, and some other things, including a large pastel by my dear friend Shannon. These things they promised to store, or keep for me during my imprisonment. I knew, and realised with some natural amusement, that Leverson considered that Shannon's beautiful pastel might be demoralising to the female servants of his household. He told me so with tears in his eyes; his wife with laughter in hers. I was quite conscious of the very painful position of a man who had in his house a life-sized portrait, which he could not have in his drawing-room as it was obviously, on account of its *subject*, demoralising to young men, and possibly to young women of advanced views, and a pastel of the Moon, no less demoralising to housemaids on account of the *treatment* of the subject. I often felt the strongest sympathy with Leverson: a sentimentalist confronted with a fact either in Life or Art is a tragic spectacle to gods and men. Accordingly, the week before my release, as a slight token of my sympathy with him, I wrote to my friends to ask them to engage a small room in Hornton Street, Kensington, at my expense, where for a few shillings a week I could store the art of Pennington and of Shannon, in a seclusion where they would be as harmless as Art can be. I considered it, I may say, a plain act of manners and morals to do so. I asked them to relieve Leverson from his terrible charge: a portrait that was a social incubus, and a pastel dangerous to chambermaids.

I have now spent the whole of my Sunday afternoon – the first real day of summer we have had – in writing to you this long letter of explanation.

I have written directly and simply, and I need not tell the author of *Elder Conklin* that sweetness and simplicity of expression take more out of one than fiddling harmonics on one string. I felt it my duty to write, but it has been a distressing one. It would have been *better* for me to have lain in the brown grass on the cliff, or to have walked slowly by the sea. It would have been *kinder* of you to have written to me directly about whatever harsh or bitter or hurt feelings you may have about me. It would have saved me an afternoon of strain, and tension.

But I have something more to say. It is pleasanter to me, now, to write about others, than about myself.

The enclosed is from a brother prisoner of mine: released June 4th. Pray read it; you will see his age, offence, and aim in life.

If you can give him a trial, do so. If you see your way to this kind action, and write to him to come and see you, kindly state in your letter that it is about a situation. He may think otherwise that it is about the flogging of A.2.11, a thing that does not interest *you*, and about which *he* is a little afraid to talk.

If the result of this long letter will be that you will help this fellow-prisoner of mine to a place in your service, I shall consider my afternoon better spent than any afternoon for the last two years, and three weeks.

In any case I have now written to you fully on all things as reported to me.

I again assure you of my gratitude for your kindness to me during my imprisonment, and on my release, and am always your sincere friend and admirer   OSCAR WILDE

With regard to Lawley. All soldiers are neat, and smart, and make capital servants. He would be a good *groom*; he is, I believe, a Third Hussars man. He was a quiet well-conducted chap in Reading always.

To Lord Alfred Douglas

Wednesday, 16 June [1897]   *Berneval-sur-Mer*

My dear Boy, I am upset with the idea that you don't get my letters, or that the post goes wrong, or something. I daresay it is all absurd, but your last three letters dated the 10th, 11th, and 12th (whereas we are now at the 16th) contain no references to things I asked you, especially as regards our meeting.

I have asked you to come here on Saturday. I have a bathing costume for you, but you had better get one in Paris. Also bring me a lot of books, and cigarettes. I cannot get good cigarettes here or at Dieppe.

The weather is very hot, so you will want a straw hat and flannels. I hope you will get quietly out of Paris. On arriving at Dieppe, take a good *voiture* and tell him to drive to the Hôtel *Bonnet*, Berneval-sur-Mer, and go by the road by *Puys*, not by the *grande route* which is a straight line of white dust.

If you want a café at Dieppe on arriving, go to the Café Suisse.

It takes an hour and a half to get here, so arrive if you can at Dieppe about three o'clock and be here at five o'clock.

I hope to be in my chalet by Saturday: so you will stay with me there. I have a little walled-in place in the garden of the hotel where I have *déjeuner* and *dîner* – a *bosquet* of trees.

On Sunday I go to Mass, in a dark blue suit.

You must not have your letters sent on under your own name. It might do me serious harm. I still suggest – for the third time – Jonquil du Vallon, but any name you like will do.

Pray do not fail to write at once on receipt of this, and be careful of the date. Your *last* letter is dated the 12th: which was last *Saturday*.

It is lovely here today, and I am going to bathe at 10.30. Yesterday I drove Ernest Dowson back to Arques. I like him immensely.

Thanks for the *Soir*. You ask me other questions in your letter that I have answered in letters of my own to you: but I don't know if they reach you. I will wait for today's post, and write again tomorrow.

Bring also some perfumes and nice things from the sellers of the dust of roses.

Also bring yourself. Ever yours   OSCAR

Arthur Hansell, Wilde's solicitor, had got wind of the proposed meeting with Bosie, possibly from Ross who was trying to protect his friend's interests and who realised that if it became known, Wilde would immediately lose the allowance his wife was making him.

To Lord Alfred Douglas

Thursday, 17 June [1897] 2 o'clock p.m.   *Café Suisse, Dieppe*

My dearest Boy, I have been obliged to ask my friends to leave me, as I am so upset and distressed in nerve by my solicitor's letter, and the apprehension of serious danger, that simply I must be alone. I find that any worry utterly destroys my health, and makes me horrid and irritable and unkind, though I hate to be so.

Of course at present it is impossible for us to meet. I have to find out what grounds my solicitor has for his sudden action, and of course if your father – or rather Q as I only know him and think of him – if Q came over and made a scene and scandal it would utterly destroy my possible future and alienate all my friends from me. I owe to my friends everything, including the clothes I wear, and I would be wretched if I did anything that would separate them from me.

So simply we must write to each other: about the things we love, about poetry and the coloured arts of our age, and that passage of ideas into images that is the intellectual history of art. I think of you always, and love you always, but chasms of moonless night divide us. We cannot cross it without hideous and nameless peril.

Later on, when the alarm in England is over, when secrecy is possible, and silence forms part of the world's attitude, we may meet, but at present you see it is impossible. I would be harassed, agitated, nervous. It would be no joy for me to let you see me as I am now.

You must go to some place where you can play golf and get back your lily and rose. Don't, like a good boy, telegraph to me unless on a matter of vital import: the telegraph office is seven miles off, and I have to pay the *facteur*, and also reply, and yesterday with three separate *facteurs*, and three separate replies, I was *sans le sou*, and also mentally upset in nerve. Say please to Percy that I will accept a bicycle with many thanks for his kindness: I want to get it here, where there is a great champion who teaches everyone, and has English machines: it will cost £15. If Percy will send me £15 to enclosed name and address in a cheque, it will make me very happy. Send him my card.

Ever yours (rather maimed and mutilated)   OSCAR

To Lord Alfred Douglas

Wednesday, 23 June [1897]   *Café Suisse, Dieppe*

My darling Boy, Thanks for your letter received this morning. My *fête* was a huge success: fifteen *gamins* were entertained on strawberries and cream, apricots, chocolates, cakes, and *sirop de grenadine*. I had a huge iced cake with *Jubilé de la Reine Victoria* in pink sugar just rosetted with green, and a great wreath of red roses round it all. Every child was asked beforehand to choose his present: they all chose instruments of music!!!

> *6 accordions*
> *5 trompettes*
> *4 clairons*

They sang the Marseillaise and other songs, and danced a *ronde*, and also played 'God save the Queen': they said it was 'God save the Queen', and I did not like to differ from them. They also all had flags which I gave them. They were most gay and sweet. I gave the health of *La Reine d'Angleterre*, and they cried *'Vive la Reine d'Angleterre'*!!!! Then I gave *'La France, mère de tous les artistes'*, and finally I gave *Le Président de la République*: I thought I had better do so. They cried out with one accord *'Vivent le Président de la République et Monsieur Melmoth'*!!! So I found my name coupled with that of the President. It was an amusing experience as I am hardly more than a month out of gaol.

They stayed from 4.30 to seven o'clock and played games: on leaving I gave them each a basket with a jubilee cake frosted pink and inscribed, and *bonbons*.

They seem to have made a great demonstration in Berneval-le-Grand, and to have gone to the house of the Mayor and cried, *'Vive Monsieur le Maire! Vive la Reine d'Angleterre. Vive Monsieur Melmoth!'* I tremble at my position.

Today I have come in with Ernest Dowson to dine with the painter Thaulow, a giant with the temperament of Corot. I sleep here and go back tomorrow.

I will write tomorrow on things. Ever, dearest boy, yours   OSCAR

To Robert Ross

6 July [1897]   *[Chalet Bourgeat] Berneval-sur-Mer*
Dearest Robbie, I have had no time to write lately, but I have written a long
letter – of twelve foolscap pages – to Bosie, to point out to him that I owe
everything to you and your friends, and that whatever life I have as an artist
in the future will be due to you. He has now written to me a temperate letter,
saying that Percy will fulfil his promises when he is able. Of course he will. But
the occasion of his ability is certainly distant, and my wants were pressing.

I also wrote to him about his calling himself a *grand seigneur* in comparison
to a dear sweet wonderful friend like you, his superior in all fine things. I
told him how grotesque, ridiculous, and vulgar such an attempt was.

I long to see you. When are you coming over? I have a lovely bedroom
for More, and a small garret for you, with my heart waiting in it for you.

The photograph of Constance has arrived. It was most sweet of you to
send it. She writes to me every week.

Ernest Dowson is here for a few days: he leaves tomorrow. He stays at
Arques-la-Bataille.

Could you send me my pictures? Would it cost much? I long for them.

Today is stormy and wet. But my chalet is delightful, and when I pass
through Berneval-le-Grand they still cry '*Vivent Monsieur Melmoth et la Reine
d'Angleterre!*' It is an astonishing position.

With best love. Ever yours   OSCAR
I hope *you* will be firm with Bosie.

*Carlos Blacker had been an old friend of Wilde's since the 1880s when Wilde
dedicated* The Happy Prince *to him. In 1890, having been accused (unjustly as it
turned out) of cheating at cards, he went abroad and lived mostly in Paris for the
rest of his life. His American wife strongly disapproved of Wilde and was ultimately
the cause of their friendship ceasing. Messalina was the faithless and depraved wife
of the Emperor Claudius, and Sporus the effeminate favourite of the Emperor Nero,
with whom, according to Suetonius, he went through a form of marriage.*

To Carlos Blacker

12 July 1897   *[Chalet Bourgeat] Berneval-sur-Mer*
My dear old Friend, I need not tell you with what feelings of affection and
gratitude I read your letter. You were always my staunch friend and stood
by my side for many years.

Often in prison I used to think of you: of your chivalry of nature, of your limitless generosity, of your quick intellectual sympathies, of your culture so receptive, so refined. What marvellous evenings, dear Carlos, we used to have! What brilliant dinners! What days of laughter and delight! To you, as to me, conversation – that υεϱπνον κακον [delightful wickedness] as Euripides calls it – that sweet sin of phrases – was always among the supreme aims of life, and we tired many a moon with talk, and drank many a sun to rest with wine and words. You were always the truest of friends and the most sympathetic of companions. You will, I know, wish to hear about me, and what I am doing and thinking.

Well, I am in a little chalet, with a garden, over the sea. It is a nice chalet with two great balconies, where I pass much of my day and many of my nights: Berneval is a tiny place consisting of a hotel and about twenty chalets: the people who come here are *des bons bourgeois* as far as I can see. The sea has a lovely beach, to which one descends through a small ravine, and the land is full of trees and flowers, quite like a bit of Surrey: so green and shady. Dieppe is ten miles off. Many friends, such as Will Rothenstein, the artist, Conder, who is a sort of Corot of the sunlight, Ernest Dowson, the poet, and others have come to see me for a few days: and next month I hope to see Ricketts and Shannon, who decorated all my books for me, dear Robbie Ross, and perhaps some others. I learnt many things in prison that were terrible to learn, but I learnt some good lessons that I needed. I learnt gratitude: and though, in the eyes of the world, I am of course a disgraced and ruined man, still every day I am filled with wonder at all the beautiful things that are left to me: loyal and loving friends: good health: books, one of the greatest of the many worlds God has given to each man: the pageant of the seasons: the loveliness of leaf and flower: the nights hung with silver and the dawns dim with gold. I often find myself strangely happy. You must not think of me as being morbidly sad, or wilfully living in sadness, that sin which Dante punishes so terribly. My desire to live is as intense as ever, and though my heart is broken, hearts are made to be broken: that is why God sends sorrow into the world. The hard heart is the evil thing of life and of art. I have also learnt sympathy with suffering. To me, suffering seems now a sacramental thing, that makes those whom it touches holy. I think I am in many respects a much better fellow than I was, and I now make no more exorbitant claims on life: I accept everything. I am sure it is all right. I was living a life unworthy of an artist, and though I do not hold with the British view of morals that sets Messalina above Sporus, I see that any materialism in life coarsens the soul, and that the hunger of the body and the appetites of the flesh desecrate always, and often destroy.

Of course I am troubled about money, because the life of a man of letters

– and I hope to be one again – requires solitude, peace, books and the opportunity of retirement. I have, as I dare say you know, only £3 a week: but dear Robbie Ross and some other friends got up privately a little subscription for me to give me a start. But of course they are all quite poor themselves, and though they gave largely from their store, their store was small, and I have had to buy everything, so as to be able to live at all.

I hope to write a play soon, and then if I can get it produced I shall have money – far too much I dare say: but as yet I have not been able to work. The two long years of silence kept my soul in bonds. It will all come back, I feel sure, and then all will be well.

I long to see you, dear friend. Could you come here with your wife? Or to Dieppe? The hotel here is a charming little *auberge* with a capital cook: everything very wholesome and clean, and daintily served besides. I must talk over my future, for I believe that God still holds a future for me, only I must be wise, and must see my way.

Will you do this? It would help me very much to see you – more than I can say.

And now, dear friend, I must end my letter. I have only said a little in it, but writing is strangely difficult for me from long disuse.

Write to me as Monsieur Sebastian Melmoth. It is my new name. I enclose a card. Pray offer my homage to your wife, and believe me, ever gratefully and affectionately yours   OSCAR WILDE

On Wilde's release, an ex-convict, William Dixon, wrote offering his secretarial services. Wilde must have discussed earlier with Ross the possibility of having Dixon proof-read the typescript of De Profundis. *Strangely, given the importance which his prison letter seems to have assumed for him, this is the last time that Wilde refers to the letter in his correspondence. He began work on* The Ballad of Reading Gaol *in the second week of July.*

To Robert Ross

20 July [1897]   *Chalet Bourgeat, Berneval-sur-Mer*
My dearest Robbie, Your excuse of 'domesticity' is of course most treacherous: I have missed your letters very much. Pray write at least twice a day, and write at length. You now only write about Dixon. As regards him, tell him that the expense of bringing him to London is too heavy. I don't think I would like the type-written manuscript sent to him. It might be dangerous. Better to have it done in London, scratching out Bosie's name, mine at the close, and the address. Mrs Marshall can be relied on.

The pictures, as I said, insure for £50.

As regards Bosie, I feel you have been, as usual, forbearing and sweet, and too good-tempered. What he must be made to feel is that his vulgar and ridiculous assumption of social superiority must be retracted and apologised for. I have written to him to tell him that *quand on est gentilhomme on est gentilhomme*, and that for him to try and pose as your social superior because he is the third son of a Scotch marquis and you the third son of a commoner is offensively stupid. There is no difference between gentlemen. Questions of titles are matters of heraldry – no more. I wish you would be strong on this point; the thing should be thrashed out of him. As for his coarse ingratitude in abusing you, to whom, as I have told him, I owe any possibility I have of a new and artistic career, and indeed of life at all, I have no words in which to express my contempt for his lack of imaginative insight, and his dullness of sensitive nature. It makes me quite furious. So pray write, when next you do so, quite calmly, and say that you will not allow any nonsense of social superiority and that if he cannot understand that gentlemen are gentlemen and no more, you have no desire to hear again from him.

I expect you on August the First: also, the architect.

The poem is nearly finished. Some of the verses are awfully good.

Wyndham comes here tomorrow to see me: for the adaptation of Scribe's *Le Verre d'Eau*: which of course you have to do. Bring *Esmond* with you, and any Queen Anne chairs you have: just for the style.

I am so glad More is better.

The sketch of Frank Harris in *John Johns* is superb. Who wrote the book? It is a wonderful indictment. Ever yours   OSCAR

Constance was suffering increasingly from spinal problems and, with much restricted movement, was finding it hard to lead a normal life. Although both she and Oscar seem to have been keen to meet, it appears to have been the meddlesome but well-meaning family and friends who kept them apart, as much as anything to avoid the social dilemma they would have faced, had Oscar and Constance remade their life together. Cyril and Vyvyan spent much of July and August with Carlos and his wife in the Black Forest before returning to Italy and taking a house at Nervi on the Italian Riviera, just outside Genoa. Neither she nor the two children ever saw Oscar again.

To Carlos Blacker

Thursday, 29 July 1897   *Café Suisse, Dieppe*

Dear Friend, I am terribly distressed about what you tell me about Constance. I had no idea it was so serious.

Of course she could not come here. I see that. She would require the attendance of a maid, and I have only my man-servant, and the journey would be too much.

Do you think I should go and see her in about three weeks? I really think it would be better for her to see me, and have it over. I would only stay a couple of days. I think that she is afraid I am fearfully altered. I don't think I am in appearance. My friends say I am not. Just try and advise me.

I am so glad she is with you and your charming, brilliant wife.

For myself, I really am quite heart-broken. Nemesis seems endless.

With many thanks, dear old friend, ever yours   OSCAR

To Reginald Turner

Saturday [Postmark 31 July 1897]   *Berneval-sur-Mer*

My dear Reggie, The most lovely clock has arrived, and I hear it is from you. It is most sweet of you to give it to me, and you will be pleased, and perhaps astonished, to hear that though it is quite beautiful, and has a lovely face and wonderful slim restless hands, yet it is strangely punctual in all its habits, business-like in its methods, of ceaseless industry, and knows all that the sun is doing. I hope you will come here and see it. It has been greatly admired by all the inhabitants. Come any time you like. I am not responsible for the architecture of the chalet: all that I am responsible for at Berneval are the sunsets and the sea.

I don't know if you are with Bosie, but send this to his care. Affectionately yours   OSCAR

To Reginald Turner

Tuesday [3 August 1897]   *Berneval-sur-Mer*

Dearest Reggie, I am so sorry you are ill: I was in hopes of seeing you here soon. Do get well, and come over. I long for your delightful companionship and sympathetic friendship. The horizon of the English stage seems dark with Hichens. Do finish your play and stop him.

Robbie was to have come here yesterday, but has not arrived. I suspect a conspiracy with ramifications. I suppose ramifications are a sort of dagger?

I wrote to you care of Bosie to thank you for the lovely clock: I hope he forwarded my letter. The clock *still goes*: and is quite astounding in its beauty and industry. It even works at night, when no one is watching it.

Aubrey, and Conder, and Dal Young are at Dieppe, and the place is very full. I have made Aubrey buy a hat more silver than silver: he is quite wonderful in it.

Do get well soon. Ever yours affectionately   OSCAR

To Carlos Blacker

[Postmark 4 August 1897]   *Café Suisse, Dieppe*
My dear Friend, I am simply heart-broken at what you tell me. I don't mind *my life* being wrecked – that is as it should be – but when I think of poor Constance I simply want to kill myself. But I suppose I must live through it all. I don't care. Nemesis has caught me in her net: to struggle is foolish. Why is it that one runs to one's ruin? Why has destruction such a fascination? Why, when one stands on a pinnacle, *must* one throw oneself down? No one knows, but things are so.

Of course I think it would be much better for Constance to see me, but you think not. Well, you are wiser. My life is spilt on the sand – red wine on the sand – and the sand drinks it because it is thirsty, for no other reason.

I wish I could see you. Where I shall be in September I don't know. I don't care. I fear we shall never see each other again. But all is right: the gods hold the world on their knees. I was made for destruction. My cradle was rocked by the Fates. Only in the mire can I know peace. Ever yours

OSCAR

Laurence Housman had just sent Wilde All-Fellows, *his book of imaginary legends. A. E. Housman, his brother, had published* A Shropshire Lad *in 1896, which he sent to Wilde on his release and parts of which may have influenced Wilde's choice of metre for his own* Ballad.

To Laurence Housman

9 August [1897]   *Chalet Bourgeat, Berneval-sur-Mer*
Dear Mr Housman, I cannot tell you how gratified and touched I was to receive your charming letter, and the beautiful book that it so gracefully heralded.

Your prose is full of cadence and colour, and has a rhythmic music of words that makes that constant appeal to the ear, which, to me, is the very condition of literature. The 'King's Evil', the 'Tree of Guile', and the 'Heart of the Sea' are quite beautiful: and their mysticism, as well as their meaning, touches me very deeply: and while they are of course dramatic, still one is conscious – as one should be in all objective art – of one personality dominating their perfection all through.

The whole book, with its studied and imaginative decorations and its links of song, is a very lovely and almost unique work of art. Your title pleases me little, but every one has some secret reason for christening a child: some day you must tell me yours. Ricketts and Shannon, those good kind friends of mine, are coming to see me this month. It would be charming if you came with them.

I have lately been reading your brother's lovely lyrical poems, so you see you have both of you given me that rare thing happiness. With renewal of my thanks, believe me truly yours OSCAR WILDE

To Reginald Turner

Tuesday, 10 August [1897] *[Dieppe]*
My dear Reggie, Will you come over here on Saturday next, by the afternoon boat? Robbie is here, and we want you so much. It is quite quiet and the weather is charming. Also last night acrobats arrived. Smithers, the publisher and owner of Aubrey, comes over on Sunday and we all dine with him: then we go to Berneval.

I do not know if you know Smithers: he is usually in a large straw hat, has a blue tie delicately fastened with a diamond brooch of the impurest water – or perhaps wine, as he never touches water: it goes to his head at once. His face, clean-shaven as befits a priest who serves at the altar whose God is Literature, is wasted and pale – not with poetry, but with poets, who, he says, have wrecked his life by insisting on publishing with him. He loves first editions, especially of women: little girls are his passion. He is the most learned erotomaniac in Europe. He is also a delightful companion, and a dear fellow, very kind to me.

You will on arrival proceed without delay to the *Café Suisse*, where Robbie and I will be waiting for you.

If you don't come I shall be quite wretched. I long to see you again. Ever yours OSCAR

Rothenstein's book, published the following year and entitled English Portraits, *was to consist of twenty-four lithographed drawings, with a brief note on each sitter. These were to be anonymous and by different hands; Wilde had been asked*

to describe W. E. Henley. Wilde's humorous restraint, given Henley's earlier attacks on his work, is remarkable.

To William Rothenstein

14 August 1897   *Berneval-sur-Mer*

My dear Will, I don't know if the enclosed will suit. If so, pray use it. Also don't forget to come and see me as soon as possible. I simply long for your delightful companionship. Robbie Ross and Sherard are here at present: the latter goes away today. We all go to Dieppe to dine with Smithers. Ever yours   O. W.

He founded a school, and has survived all his disciples. He has always thought too much about himself, which is wise; and written too much about others, which is foolish. His prose is the beautiful prose of a poet, and his poetry the beautiful poetry of a prose-writer. His personality is insistent. To converse with him is a physical no less than an intellectual recreation. He is never forgotten by his enemies, and often forgiven by his friends. He has added several new words to the language and his style is an open secret. He has fought a good fight, and has had to face every difficulty except popularity.

!!! !!!

Despite Wilde's previous correspondence with Smithers, it seems they did not meet until introduced by Ernest Dowson at Dieppe in July. Smithers published Dowson's poems and a number of his translations from the French, but Louÿs's Aphrodite *was never done. Vincent O'Sullivan, an Irish-American poet and novelist, was a good friend of both Dowson and Smithers, and lived most of his life in France. His anecdotal memoir* Aspects of Wilde *is one of the most perceptive and reliable books on the subject.*

To Ernest Dowson

18 August [1897]   *Berneval-sur-Mer*

My dear Ernest, I think your translating *Aphrodite* a capital idea: I do hope you will get someone to make good terms for you. Why not Smithers? The Bacchic, the Dionysiac!

You should make a lot of money by royalties. The book, if well puffed, might be a great *succès*.

Robbie Ross is here with me, and Sherard left on Saturday. Smithers is devoted, and breakfasts here every Monday. I like him immensely. He is a most interesting and, in some respects, a charming personality.

I have not yet finished my poem, but I hope to do so soon. I wrote four splendid stanzas yesterday. I am going to try and get a lot of money for it from the *New York World*. Robert Sherard will, he says, arrange it for me.

Vincent O'Sullivan has been twice here to dine. I *now* like him. At first I loathed him.

As for the cheque: I know, dear Ernest, you will send it as soon as you can. I scramble on somehow, and hope to survive the season. After that, Tunis, rags, and hashish! Ever yours OSCAR

To Leonard Smithers

Sunday, 22 August 1897 *Chalet Bourgeat, Berneval-sur-Mer*
My dear Smithers, I look forward to seeing you on Saturday, and thank you for your kind letters.

Your wife, whose sweetness and kindness to me I shall never forget, came out to tea on Wednesday: the Stannards and Dal and others were here. I don't think you will do much with Dal's art, but Anquetin is a different thing: however *Les Trois Mousquetaires* is too *obvious*, and Stanley Weyman has rewritten Dumas for the British public – I must say, very well indeed. From what Thaulow tells me (I dined on Friday with him) Anquetin's art is at his best with nymph and satyr; he is a sort of erotic Michelangelo. Would an edition of Beckford be any use? Perhaps you have already done one.

Will Rothenstein, as I expected, is too nervous to publish my little appreciation of Henley. He says he is the editor of 'a *paying* magazine'. That seems a degrading position for any man to occupy. I have recommended Symons: he will do just what is unnecessary: it is his *métier*.

I enclose you a letter for Daly, which you can read. I don't feel really at liberty to take his money, though I would like it. I have never done that sort of thing, and I can't begin. It is merely the weakness of the criminal classes that makes me refuse.

Conder is now a *vineyard*: the Youngs are very serious about him, and there is a moral atmosphere about Dieppe that you should come over and dissipate. Sincerely yours OSCAR WILDE

To Laurence Housman

22 August 1897 *Chalet Bourgeat, Berneval-sur-Mer*
Dear Mr Housman, Thank you for your kind letter. I hope some day to see you here, or elsewhere.

It is absurd of Ricketts and Shannon not to see the light lyrical beauty of your brother's work, and its grace and delicate felicity of mood and music. I can understand Ricketts not liking them, for he is dominated by the sense of definite design and intellectual architecture, nor can he see the wonderful strangeness of simple things in art and life: but Shannon is inexcusable: you must get him alone, and read them to him: you can tell him I think your brother's poems exceedingly like his own lithographs!

With regard to what you ask me about myself – well, I am occupied in finishing a poem, terribly realistic for me, and drawn from actual experience, a sort of denial of my own philosophy of art in many ways. I hope it is good, but every night I hear cocks crowing in Berneval, so I am afraid I may have denied myself, and would weep bitterly, if I had not wept away all my tears. I will send it to you, if you allow me, when it appears. Believe me truly yours   OSCAR WILDE

To Leonard Smithers

Wednesday, 25 August 1897   *Dieppe*
My dear Smithers, Will you do me a great favour and have the poem I send you type-written for me, and bring it over with you on Saturday, or, if you cannot come, send it by post to Sebastian Melmoth, c/o Hôtel Sandwich, Dieppe, where I shall be? I want it done on good paper, *not* tissue paper, and bound in a brown paper cover. If you will let me know what it will cost – or rather has cost – I will let you have the money on Saturday. It is not yet finished, but I want to see it type-written. I am sick of my manuscript.

I hope you are doing wonderful things in Art and Life. Always sincerely yours   OSCAR WILDE

Throughout the summer Oscar and Bosie had been corresponding, Bosie anxious to meet but Oscar fearful of the consequences. By the end of August Oscar's resolve weakened; his wife still vacillated about seeing him and giving him access to the children; his friends had come and gone; the summer season in Dieppe was drawing to a close; Berneval seemed more remote and lonely than ever. The prospect of spending the winter in Naples with Bosie was mad and therefore irresistible.

To Lord Alfred Douglas

Tuesday, 7.30 [?31 August 1897]   *Café Suisse, Dieppe*
My own Darling Boy, I got your telegram half an hour ago, and just send you a line to say that I feel that my only hope of again doing beautiful work in art is being with you. It was not so in old days, but now it is different,

and you can really recreate in me that energy and sense of joyous power on which art depends. Everyone is furious with me for going back to you, but they don't understand us. I feel that it is only with you that I can do anything at all. Do remake my ruined life for me, and then our friendship and love will have a different meaning to the world.

I wish that when we met at Rouen we had not parted at all. There are such wide abysses now of space and land between us. But we love each other. Goodnight, dear. Ever yours   OSCAR

To Robert Ross

4 September 1897   *Café Suisse, Dieppe*
My dearest Robbie, The pictures arrived safe.

I am delighted you have come back, as you will now be able to join me in *Rouen* – Hôtel d'Angleterre, I go in half an hour. I simply cannot stand Berneval. I nearly committed suicide there last Thursday – I was so bored.

I have not yet finished my poem! I really want you. I have got in about the kiss of Caiaphas: it is very good.

I am going at Rouen to try to rewrite my *Love and Death* – *Florentine Tragedy*.

Yes: I saw Bosie, and of course I love him as I always did, with a sense of tragedy and ruin. He was on his best behaviour, and very sweet.

Do come to Rouen at once. Ever yours   OSCAR

To Carlos Blacker

Monday [Postmark 6 September 1897]   *Grand Hôtel de France, Rouen*
My dear Carlos, The weather has been so dreadful at Berneval that I have come here, where the weather is much worse. I cannot stay in the North of Europe; the climate kills me. I don't mind being alone when there is sunlight, and a *joie de vivre* all about me, but my last fortnight at Berneval has been black and dreadful, and quite suicidal. I have never been so unhappy. I am trying to get some money to go to Italy, and hope to be able to find my way to Sicily, but the expenses of travelling are frightening. I don't suppose I shall see you before I go, as I think you said you could not come to France before the end of September, and the journey from Basle is, I suppose, very long and tedious.

I am greatly disappointed that Constance has not asked me to come and see the children. I don't suppose now I shall ever see them. Ever yours

OSCAR

Write to me at Berneval-sur-Mer.

To Leonard Smithers

Tuesday [Postmark 14 September 1897]   *Café des Tribunaux, Dieppe*

My dear Smithers, It has been a great blow not seeing you again. I hope your leg is better.

I leave here for Paris tomorrow – address Sebastian Melmoth, Hôtel d'Espagne, Rue Taitbout, Paris – and from there I want to get on to Naples, in three days. At Naples I intend to finish my poem, and begin my play. I have now only three stanzas to add to the poem, and I intend, by the advice of Clyde Fitch, to ask the *New York Journal* for £200. In the meanwhile I am, of course, fearfully hard up. I suppose you are the same, but could you advance me £20 on my poem? I think I am sure to get at least £100 from the New York paper. They offered £1000 for an interview, so for poetry they could not give less than £100. If you can do this I would of course tell Pinker to hand you over whatever sum he gets for the poem, and you could send me the balance. But if you can do this, will you let me have the £20 *at once*, to Paris. I don't want to stay in Paris: I want to get away to Italy, but must have money. Sincerely yours   OSCAR WILDE

The Second Time Around

'My going back to Bosie was
psychologically inevitable . . .
the mere fact that he
wrecked my life
makes me love
him.'

On 15 September Wilde left Dieppe for Paris where he stayed for three days. There he met Vincent O'Sullivan who gave him the money to continue on to Italy. Bosie joined him at Aix. They spent a day in Genoa and arrived in Naples on 20 September. Within ten days they had taken a villa in a suburb of the city at Posillipo. Constance, having sent Cyril and Vyvyan back to their separate boarding schools, wrote to Oscar asking him to stay, but the letter sent to France arrived after his departure. No sooner did Constance learn what had happened than she stopped his allowance for 'associating with disreputable people' against the terms of their separation agreement.

To Robert Ross

Tuesday, 21 September 1897   *Hôtel Royal des Étrangers, Naples*
My dearest Robbie, Your letter has reached me here.

My going back to Bosie was psychologically inevitable: and, setting aside the interior life of the soul with its passion for self-realisation at all costs, the world forced it on me.

I cannot live without the atmosphere of Love: I must love and be loved, whatever price I pay for it. I could have lived all my life with you, but you have other claims on you – claims you are too sweet a fellow to disregard – and all you could give me was a week of companionship. Reggie gave me three days, and Rowland a sextette of suns, but for the last month at Berneval I was so lonely that I was on the brink of killing myself. The world shuts its gateway against me, and the door of Love lies open.

When people speak against me for going back to Bosie, tell them that he offered me love, and that in my loneliness and disgrace I, after three months' struggle against a hideous Philistine world, turned naturally to him. Of course I shall often be unhappy, but still I love him: the mere fact that he wrecked my life makes me love him. *'Je t'aime parce que tu m'as perdu'* is the phrase that ends one of the stories in *Le Puits de Sainte Claire* – Anatole France's book – and it is a terrible symbolic truth.

We hope to get a little villa or apartments somewhere, and I hope to do work with him. I think I shall be able to do so. I think he will be kind to me; I only ask that. So do let people know that my only hope of life or literary activity was in going back to the young man whom I loved before with such tragic issue to my name.

No more today. Ever yours   OSCAR

To Leonard Smithers

Wednesday, 22 September [1897]   *Hôtel Royal des Étrangers, Naples*
My dear Smithers, Thanks for your letters.

With regard to the poem, I hope really to complete it this week when I will send it to you but till the last three days I have been too unhappy and distressed to write anything. Now I feel all my old power coming back to me. I am quite happy now.

In Paris I met at Henri Davray's a wonderful young artist called Hermann who is very anxious to do a cover and a frontispiece design for the poem. He is a most interesting genius, and would do something very fine. He talked to me about a method of printing etchings in four colours, which he says has great possibilities. His genius is sombre, troubled and *macabre*. Can you go and see him in Paris? He is going to send me some drawings for cover etc. here. I will, of course, send them on to you.

I don't know his price, but will find out. I now feel that the poem should be published in a very artistic form, with a wonderful cover (paper of course), frontispiece, initial letters, *culs-de-lampe* etc. and should be 5/-. What do you say?

With regard to terms I think we should share profits – that when really carried out by the publisher, as I know will be the case with you, seems to me always fair to both, and in the present case there will be the expense of the artist: but there should I think be a limit on the *advertisements* – I should say a £10 margin. Would this be enough?

If my poem is *not* published in any English paper, I think you should give me something in advance – say £20: if it *is* published, I of course will wait till accounts are made up. Hermann's address is: Henri Hermann, 65 rue Lepic, Montmartre, Paris. Please get into communication with him as soon as possible.

Pray remember me to your kind, charming wife and believe me sincerely

OSCAR WILDE

PS The drawings by Hermann are so strong and full of such great masses of black, and strong curves and contrasts, that I feel the *type* of the poem should be large and strong too. Would you let me see the strongest, blackest, finest type you have?

Despite Wilde's enthusiasm for Hermann's work, the projected illustrations were never done, but the following year Davray, a young author and Anglophile, published his prose translation of The Ballad *with the* Mercure de France.

To Carlos Blacker

Thursday, 22 September [1897]   *Hôtel Royal des Étrangers, Naples*
My dear Carlos, Your letter was forwarded to me here from Paris. I will go and see Constance in October.

I know that all you have written to me about my coming here comes from the sympathy and loyalty of your great generous heart, and I am sorry that my being here gives you pain. It gives pain to most of my friends: but I cannot help it: I must remake my maimed life on my own lines. Had Constance allowed me to see my boys, my life would, I think, have been quite different. But this she would not do. I don't in any way venture to blame her for her action, but every action has its consequence.

I waited three months. At the expiration of that long, lonely time, I had to take my life into my own hands.

I intend to winter here. Perhaps live here. Much depends of course on my ability to write again.

You must not, dear Carlos, pass harsh judgments on me, whatever you may hear. It is not for pleasure that I come here, though pleasure, I am glad to say, walks all round. I come here to try to realise the perfection of my temperament and my soul. We have all to choose our own methods. I have chosen mine. My friends in England are greatly distressed. Still, they are good friends to me: and will remain so, most of them at any rate. You must remain so too. Ever yours   OSCAR

To Robert Ross

Friday [1 October 1897]   *Villa Giudice, Posillipo, Naples*
Dearest Robbie, I have not answered your letters, because they distressed me and angered me, and I did not wish to write to *you* of all people in the world in an angry mood. You have been such a good friend to me. Your love, your generosity, your care of me in prison and out of prison are the

most lovely things in my life. Without you what would I have done? As you remade my life for me you have a perfect right to say what you choose to me, but I have no right to say anything to you except to tell you how grateful I am to you, and what a pleasure it is to feel gratitude and love at the same time for the same person.

I dare say that what I have done is fatal, but it had to be done. It was necessary that Bosie and I should come together again; I saw no other life for myself. For himself he saw no other: all we want now is to be let alone, but the Neapolitan papers are tedious and wish to interview me, etc. They write nicely of me, but I don't want to be written about. I want peace – that is all. Perhaps I shall find it.

Now to literature. Of course I want you to help me.

I have sent Smithers my poem with directions for a type-written copy to be sent at once to *you*: please send me any suggestions and criticisms that occur to you.

Also, see Smithers, and *Pinker*: Pinker lives at Effingham House. I must have £300 at least – more, if possible. The poem is to be published simultaneously in the *New York Journal* and by *Smithers*. I think bits of the poem very good now, but I will never again out-Kipling Henley.

Bosie has written three lovely sonnets, which I have called 'The Triad of the Moon' – they are quite wonderful. He has sent them to Henley. I have also got him to send his sonnet on Mozart to the *Musician*.

Tomorrow I begin the *Florentine Tragedy*. After that I must tackle *Pharaoh*.

We have a lovely villa over the sea; and a nice piano. I take lessons in Italian conversation from Rocco three times a week.

My handwriting is now dreadful, as bad as yours. Ever yours   OSCAR

To Leonard Smithers

Friday [?1 October 1897]   *Villa Giudice, Posillipo*
Dear Smithers, Your letter has just arrived, and as the enclosure seems to have slipped out I wired at once to you to ask you to *telegraph* the £20 through Cook's office. I do hope you will do so. The crisis is of a grave and usual character – were it unique I would not feel so agitated.

I have decided long ago that I would not send my poem to the *Chronicle*, as it is far too long for a paper. It is now 600 lines almost, so Symons need not prophesy – he is unnecessary.

I am going to ask £300 for my poem from America! It is well worth it.

Do at once send me specimen type.

Also have you good initial letters? Let me see them. By spacing the intervals of the poem well I think it will be almost a book. Wherever a space occurs one should have a fresh page – begin a fresh page.

One can always fall back on vegetable parchment for a cover; it is rather nice really, and is very good for jam and poetry.

How *can* you keep on asking is Lord Alfred Douglas in Naples? You know quite well he is – we are together. He understands me and my art, and loves both. I hope never to be separated from him. He is a most delicate and exquisite poet, besides – far the finest of all the young poets in England. You have got to publish his next volume; it is full of lovely lyrics, flute-music and moon-music, and sonnets in ivory and gold. He is witty, graceful, lovely to look at, loveable to be with. He has also ruined my life, so I can't help loving him – it is the only thing to do.

My wife's letter came too late. I had waited four months in vain, and it was only when the children had gone back to school that she asked me to come to her – whereas what I want is the love of my children. It is now irretrievable, of course. But in questions of the emotions and their romantic qualities, unpunctuality is fatal.

I dare say I may have more misfortunes yet. Still, I can write as well, I think, as I used to write. Half as well would satisfy me.

With regard to the postal arrangements in France, I am still of opinion that one *can*. The bet holds good, for the third time now. Ever yours

OSCAR WILDE

To Leonard Smithers

Sunday [?3 October 1897]   *Villa Giudice, Posillipo*

My dear Smithers, I have heard nothing from Cook yet, but I have no doubt at all that you have done what I asked you. You see how wonderful my confidence in you is.

You must remember that I am not asking you for an ordinary loan of money at all. I am asking for a small advance on my poem which you are about to publish.

When you asked me my terms at Dieppe I said I would be ready to leave the entire question to you. You said you would give me the entire profits of the book. This offer, I may say, was made before, not after, dinner at the Café des Tribunaux. I said I could not agree to it, as I did not think it was fair to you or business-like in any way, but that I would take half the profits. This was agreed to.

At that time I proposed to publish first in some paper, but since then I decided not to, so you have now the perfect virginity of my poem for the satyrs of the British public to ravish. Previous publication would of course have damaged your sale. People will not pay half a crown for what they can buy for a penny. Why, I cannot understand, but it is so everywhere except perhaps at Naples.

So after having refused to take advantage of your generosity in offering me the entire profits, and also having let you have the virginity of the poem unsoiled by any liaison with the newspapers, I don't think I am really asking a great favour in saying that I wish you to advance me £20 on account. It is an ordinary thing to do, as I have already given you a certain *quid pro quo*, by reassigning half the profits of the book, and leaving you to be its first producer. I give you a clear market and offer you a virgin who has never even been engaged to Arthur Symons – harmless though such a thing would have been in the eyes of all sensible people.

The fact is, my dear Smithers, I really don't think you are business-like: it is a painful thing to have to say of anyone: but in your case it is sadly true. I hope you won't mind my having spoken frankly about it.

In case that you have not yet grasped the idea that an advance of £20 on my poem is really a thing that I have a perfect right to expect on business grounds, pray do so at once. Application to you for a personal or private loan may, and I have no doubt will, follow later on, but up to the present time our relations have been merely the usual ones of poet and publisher, with the usual complete victory for the latter. I also, such is the generosity of my nature, send you enclosed *four* more verses of great power and romantic-realistic suggestion. Twenty-four lines in all, each worth a guinea in any of the market-places for poetry. Will you kindly give them at once to the type-writer and ask her to insert them in Part II of the poem: after the sixth stanza, the one ending 'has such a sin to pay'. They come in there splendidly and improve Part II, as it was a little too short compared to the others.

Your telegraphic address is still too long, and costs a heap of money. Leonardo, London, would be enough.

I hope you have seen Pinker and that in his business capacity he carried out the extraordinary promise of his name. Also, I hope that you have already written to me on the question of having an illustrated *second* edition of the poem. The *Musician*, editor Robin Grey, wants to publish the whole poem before you do so in book form, but I have refused, though they offered large sums. So you see what sacrifices I make for you. I refuse money from others in order that you may have the first fruits of my poem, and yet you have not, up to the present, consented to advance me *less than half* of what the *Musician* offered me: and there is a tone of levity in your letters – at least in the business part of them – that pains me.

I do hope you will be serious now; it will help you in your business more than you know. Sincerely yours   OSCAR WILDE

To Robert Ross

Sunday [?3 October 1897]   *Villa Giudice, Posillipo*
My dear Robbie, I hope you have received a type-written copy of the poem by this. I have just sent Smithers four more stanzas, for insertion – one of them very good – in the romantic vein that you don't quite approve of, but that on the whole will I think make a balance in the poem. I can't be always 'banging the tins'. Here it is:

> It is sweet to dance to violins
>   When Life and Love are fair:
> To dance to flutes, to dance to lutes,
>   Is delicate and rare:
> But it is not sweet with nimble feet
>   To dance upon the air.

On the whole I like the poem now, except the second and third stanzas of Part III. I can't get that part right.

I am awaiting a thunderbolt from my wife's solicitor. She wrote me a terrible letter, but a foolish one, saying '*I forbid you*' to do so and so: 'I will not *allow* you' etc.: and 'I *require* a distinct promise that you will not' etc. How can she really imagine that she can influence or control my life? She might just as well try to influence and control my art. I could not live such an absurd life – it makes one laugh. So I suppose she will now try to deprive me of my wretched £3 a week. Women are so petty, and Constance has no imagination. Perhaps, for revenge, she will have another trial: then she certainly may claim to have for the first time in her life influenced me. I wish to goodness she would leave me alone. I don't meddle with her life. I accept the separation from the children: I acquiesce. Why does she want to go on bothering me, and trying to ruin me? Another trial would, of course, entirely destroy me. On the whole, dear Robbie, things are dark with storm.

The solitude of our life here is wonderful, and no one writes to either of us. It is lucky that we love each other, and would be quite happy if we had money, but of course Bosie is as penniless as usual – indeed he has nothing at all to speak of, and unless Pinker gets me £300 we will not be able to get food. Up to the present I have paid for almost everything.

Do stir Pinker to acts of daring. Tell him that £500 is the proper price.

Smithers is displaying levity in his business-relations with me: it is very annoying.

It is very curious that none of the English colony here have left cards on us. Fortunately we have a few simple friends amongst the poorer classes.

When do you go to America?

Give my love to Reggie.

I expect a long letter from you about my poem. Pray go through it carefully, and note what you don't like. Ever yours   OSCAR

To Robert Ross

Friday [8 October 1897]   *Villa Giudice, Posillipo*

My dear Robbie, Thanks so much for your letter. Smithers took my letter a little too seriously. It was unfair of him, as I certainly did not take his advice seriously, though he gave me a great deal of it, with reference to my wife, through the medium of his type-writer. He is a very good fellow, and most kind to me.

With much of your criticism I agree. The poem suffers under the difficulty of a divided aim in style. Some is realistic, some is romantic: some poetry, some propaganda. I feel it keenly, but as a whole I think the production interesting: that it is interesting from more points of view than one is artistically to be regretted.

With regard to the adjectives, I admit there are far too many 'dreadfuls' and 'fearfuls'. The difficulty is that the objects in prison have no shape or form. To take an example: the shed in which people are hanged is a little shed with a glass roof, like a photographer's studio on the sands at Margate. For eighteen months I thought it *was* the studio for photographing prisoners. There is no adjective to describe it. I call it 'hideous' because it became so to me after I knew its use. In itself it is a wooden, oblong, narrow shed with a glass roof.

A cell again may be described *psychologically*, with reference to its effect on the soul: in itself it can only be described as 'whitewashed' or 'dimly-lit'. It has no shape, no contents. It does not exist from the point of view of form or colour.

In point of fact, describing a prison is as difficult artistically as describing a water-closet would be. If one had to describe the latter in literature, prose or verse, one could merely say it was well, or badly, papered: or clean or the reverse: the horror of prison is that everything is so simple and commonplace in itself, and so degrading, and hideous, and revolting in its effect.

The *Musician* expressed a great desire to publish the poem: I refused then: now I think I would accept *any* English paper. If the *Musician* would offer £50, it would be a great thing. But, of course, I would prefer the *Sunday Sun*, or *Reynolds*. If the *Saturday* will take it, well and good. I can't offer it myself, but Smithers might.

It is very annoying that I cannot get a copy of the poem. I sent it exactly two weeks ago, and until I get it I cannot pull it together. I write daily on the subject to Smithers. He takes no notice. I am not reproaching him for this: I am merely stating a fact.

I am going to retain the opening of Part IV, but to cut out three stanzas at opening of Part III.

As regards the spirits, I think the *grotesqueness* of the scene to a certain degree makes their speech possible, but Bosie agrees with you: though we do not hold your views on the Ghost in *Hamlet*: there is so little parallel between lyrical and dramatic poetry or method.

I have had no money at all for three days, so cannot buy note-paper. This is *your* foolscap. Ever yours   OSCAR

To Reginald Turner

Friday [15 October 1897]   *Villa Giudice [Posillipo]*
Dear Reggie, Thank you so much for sending me the copy of *Salomé*, and please tell the Sphinx how kind it was of her to part with such a treasure.

If it is acted at Naples, it will really be, if successful, a great thing for me here. I simply now, from all the letters I get from England, seem utterly isolated, and people who have nothing to do with my life write long tedious letters to me informing me that I have wrecked my life for the second time.

Of the worldly-success point-of-view I really cannot say: it may be so: but I myself feel that I am happier with Bosie than I could be if all my laurels were given back to me. Somehow, he is my life: of course, he is unchanged: he is just what he was: kinder, and more considerate in a thousand ways: but still the same wilful, fascinating, irritating, destructive, delightful personality. If we had money, we would be all right, but he is in his usual state, and I have raised on prospective work all I can. Our sole hope of food is in Pinker and *The Ballad of Reading Gaol*, for which I ask £500! I hope to get £300, at least. I now think of beginning my play for George Alexander, but I cannot see myself writing comedy. I suppose it is all in me somewhere, but I don't seem to feel it. My sense of humour is now concentrated on the grotesqueness of tragedy.

I have extracted, after three weeks of telegrams, £10 from Smithers! It is absurd. However, with it we go to Capri for three days. I want to lay a few simple flowers on the tomb of Tiberius. As the tomb is of someone else really, I shall do so with the deeper emotion.

I don't at all approve of Max collaborating with anyone. He is too individual a genius. I am pleased to hear that his brother is still acting, and hope he will have a success, some day. I read Max on Clement Scott lately – his last appreciation. It was very dainty and witty. England has more subjects for art than any other country: I suppose that is the reason it has fewer artists.

Pray write whenever you have something better to do. Ever yours

OSCAR

Robert Sherard in London, on hearing that Wilde had returned to Bosie Douglas, was openly critical of what he saw as his friend's self-destructive behaviour.

To Vincent O'Sullivan

19 October 1897   *Villa Giudice, Posillipo*

Dear Vincent O'Sullivan, I am delighted to hear from Smithers that there is really some chance of your being at Naples this winter, and look forward with the greatest pleasure, I need hardly say, to seeing you again.

I have also heard incidentally of something that happened at the Authors' Club last week: and I cannot express to you adequately how deeply touched I was by the position you took up with regard to me, and by the dignity and, I cannot help saying, justice of your rebuke to Sherard. I feel it all the more as, in old days of high position and the like, I had not had the privilege of counting you amongst my intimate friends. I hope, however, you will not consider yourself bound to tilt at every blundering windmill that whistles on the high hill of Folly: you would have no time left in which to write jewelled verse or strange and subtly-coloured prose. Whatever future may be in store for me depends entirely on my art, and the possibility of my art coming again into touch with life. I have no inclination to propitiate Tartuffe, nor indeed is that monster ever to be propitiated.

Pray let me know when your next volume comes out. In your poetry you seem to be a Catholic, in your prose a Pagan. Is this a mood, or a principle of music? Both are equally important in art. Sincerely yours

OSCAR WILDE

To Leonard Smithers

Tuesday, 19 October 1897   *Hôtel Royal des Étrangers, Naples*

Dear Smithers, As an edition of 500 – of which 100 will go to press, author, etc. practically – will only just pay expenses, and leave me £20 in your debt, I now think that it would be better after all to publish the poem in a paper. It is too long for the *Chronicle*, and Frank Harris has been so offensive to me and about me that I don't think negotiations possible with him.

My idea is *Reynolds*. It has, for some odd reason, always been nice to me, and used to publish my poems when I was in prison, and write nicely about me. Also, it circulates widely amongst the criminal classes, to which I now belong, so I shall be read by my peers – a new experience for me. I have written to Robbie Ross about the matter.

There are, I think, still 400 people left amongst the lovers of poetry to buy our edition up.

I have had a letter from Ernest Dowson to say he gave you £10 of his debt to me to send to me. This seems improbable, as I have heard nothing of it from you, but I have no doubt he 'means well'.

I am eagerly waiting for the type-written copies. Truly yours

OSCAR WILDE

To Leonard Smithers

[22 October 1897]   *Villa Giudice, Posillipo*

My dear Smithers, In the desert of my life you raised up the lovely mirage of the great sum of £20: you said that its conversion into reality was a matter of days. On the score of this I took a lovely villa on the Bay of Naples which I cannot inhabit as I have to take all my meals at the hotel. This is the simple truth. Upon the other hand I am very sorry indeed that I should have in any way given you pain or, if that is too big a word, annoyance for the moment. You have always been most kind and sympathetic to me and about me and as for going to another publisher, that is of course nonsense. I rely entirely on you, and am very proud to have my work brought out by you – and hope that you will always accord me that privilege.

Now to minor matters:

(1) Of course Pinker is to have a copy of the poem. I said so in my letter to you of last Friday week. How else could Pinker sell the work? People are told not to buy a pig in a poke – that may or may not be true. I don't think people should buy pigs at all. But certainly no one can buy poets in a poke. Pinker is a literary agent who sells wares and must have the wares before

289

he sells. Pray at once let him have one. Also I hear of one Murphy the accredited representative of the *New York Journal,* invented by Reggie Turner; if he is ready to make an offer, let him see the poem. But Pinker is my agent at ten per cent.

(2) I have been waiting for the two type-written copies for myself. I cannot understand why they have not arrived. I must see that the poem is correct.

(3) You never acknowledged four extra verses I sent you. Did you get them? I hope so as I have no copy of them. They were sent, I think, on Monday week last.

(4) The type you sent me *is,* as you say yourself, too small. I await the one you promise.

(5) I have written to Pinker to suggest the *Sunday Sun* or *Reynolds* to be approached for publication. I see that our edition will only just pay expenses and leave me still £20 in your debt. So if I could get even £50 from an English paper it would enable me to repay you and leave me £30.

(6) Your letter received today is dated Monday last, and Dowson wrote to me that he had given you £10 for me on Saturday. What does he mean? Will you write to him and ask an explanation? It seems a disgraceful thing for him to have said. I will write to him myself about it.

(7) Will you carefully consider the question of printing only one side of the page so as to give the book thickness and solidity. I don't approve of it as a principle or practice but perhaps it may improve the format. I have now added three more verses so the poem is fairly long.

(8) By letting me have the typewritten copies at once, you will save much extra expense in correction. Also I cannot complete any bargain with America till I have the poem in a regular and revised form.

(9) The tragedy of my present position is so awful that I began today a modern social comedy, and would in consequence have had an excellent appetite for dinner had there been any dinner. Sincerely yours

OSCAR WILDE

Hansell, having resigned as Wilde's solicitor after hearing that Bosie was to visit Oscar in Berneval, had now become the 'arbitrator' in matters to do with the Wildes' separation agreement. Constance and her solicitor, Hargrove, had appealed to him as soon as it was confirmed that Oscar and Bosie were living together in Naples. In his correspondence Oscar still refers to Hansell as his solicitor, probably to exaggerate what he sees as 'the monstrous injustice' of having his allowance from Constance stopped.

To Robert Ross

Tuesday, 16 November 1897   *Villa Giudice, Posillipo*

My dear Robbie, I received this afternoon a letter from Hansell to say he was going to decide that I was to be deprived of my absurd income because I was with Bosie. I don't suppose that anything will prevent him from doing this, but I felt it due to myself and to Bosie to write to him a letter of protest, on the ground that I do not think it just or socially-speaking accurate to describe Bosie as a 'disreputable person'. After all, no charge was made against him at any of my trials, nor anything proved, or attempted to be proved.

Nor do I think that it is fair to say that I have created a 'public scandal' by being with him. If newspapers chronicle the fact, that is their business; I can't help that. If I were living here with you they would chronicle my being here with equal venom and vulgarity: or if I were living with someone of unblemished reputation and unassailable position. I think I should only be held accountable for any scandal caused by my getting into trouble with the law. My existence is a scandal. But I do not think I should be charged with creating a scandal by continuing to live: though I am conscious that I do so. I cannot live alone, and Bosie is the only one of my friends who is either able or willing to give me his companionship. If I were living with a Naples renter I would I suppose be all right. As I live with a young man who is well bred and well born, and who has been charged with no offence, I am deprived of all possibility of existence.

This is the point I have made to Hansell. I merely tell it to you, not that you should worry about a pre-judged matter, but because I tell you everything: you tried your best to create a possible life for me, but it was one my own temperament could not suffer. I could not live alone, and so inevitably I took the love and companionship that was offered to me. It seemed to me to be the only gate to any life, but I did it conscious of all the new ruin it might bring on me. I was not blind to what I was doing. You know what beautiful, wise, sensible schemes of life people bring to one: there is nothing to be said against them: except that they are not for oneself.

But don't think I am complaining: I wish merely to tell you what has occurred. I suppose you knew it already. I myself felt it was coming.

You have not written to me for ages except about the worrying business of my unsaleable poem. You had, I know, great worry about it. I had no idea that there were such barriers between me and publication in America. I thought I would romp in, and secure a good lump sum. It is curious how vanity helps the successful man, and wrecks the failure. In old days half of my strength was my vanity.

Please let me know what books are being published, and what is going on. I sometimes see English papers, but not often. They are so dear. I read all about Carton's play – an absurd production.

I wish you could come out here for a little. I suppose it is impossible but, of course, we are terribly isolated. I dare say Paris would have been better, but Bosie said he could not winter there.

I have written to Ernest Leverson for some of my money, but I don't know if anything will come of it. Of course do not say anything to him about it.

George Ives has sent me his poems – of course without an inscription. His caution is amusing. He means well, which is the worst of it.

Give my love to Reggie. Ever yours, dearest Robbie   OSCAR

Ernest Leverson had lent Wilde £500 at the time of the libel case and some weeks later proposed that he pay himself back out of Adela Schuster's £1000 which Wilde had entrusted to Leverson's safe-keeping (see pp. 218–19). On leaving prison Wilde accused Leverson of withholding money which he felt was rightly his – an accusation which was largely unfounded. Now, desperately short of money, Wilde raised the matter again. The production of Salomé *which he had hoped for in Naples, with the title role performed by Eleonora Duse, was never staged.*

To Ada Leverson

16 November 1897   *Villa Giudice, Posillipo*

My dear Ada, I have never answered your many sweet and brilliant letters because I have been so hurt and wounded at Ernest's conduct to me in retaining money entrusted to him for my use. It has nothing to do with you at all, and you yourself told me how deeply you regretted his proposed action towards me, but still, I could not write to you with the freedom and affection I would like while I felt so bitterly about Ernest. I have now, after waiting five months for the letter you said he was writing to me, written to him myself. I deferred doing so, as I know how strongly he dislikes parting with money – even the money of other people – till I was absolutely penniless, and in want. But now, as the absurd income I had – £3 a week – has been stopped by my trustees because I am here with Bosie, the only friend I have who either is able or willing to be with me, I am forced to do so, and I find that I cannot get my poem – a long poem of 700 lines – accepted even by the most revolting New York paper. So I am face to face with starvation, not in any rhetorical sense, but as an ugly fact. Of course Bosie, as you know, has only £25 a month, and naturally that is not enough for his own wants. He cannot, financially, help me with either the smallest sum or the most meagre assistance. He simply has not got the money.

These are the circumstances under which I have written very strongly to Ernest to say that of the money of mine that he has at any rate £100 must be telegraphed at once to me through Cook's agency: there is nothing else for him to do.

For yourself, dear Sphinx, I have always the deepest love and admiration, and Bosie and I often talk over your delightful sayings, and your brilliant and beautiful personality – unique, troubling, and imaginative.

I will send you your *Salomé* tomorrow. I must have it done up properly. It was most kind of you to lend it.

I have no good news to tell you. I am in such distress and misery, but it is pleasant to tell you that I am always your affectionate and devoted admirer.
OSCAR

To Leonard Smithers

Tuesday, 16 [November 1897]   *Villa Giudice, Posillipo*

My dear Smithers, Do remember that what is comedy to you may be the reverse of comic to others.

Since I received your letter in which you said 'I expect that before the arrival of this letter you will have received the £10', I have been down twice *a day* to Naples to Cook's office, and have just returned from a third visit now – 5.30. Of course there was nothing, and I am really so ashamed of my endless enquiries about a sum of £10 to be telegraphed from London. Perhaps you only wrote what you did to give me hope, but, my dear fellow, hope constantly disappointed makes one's bread bitter, especially as I have just heard from *my own* solicitor to say that as I am in Naples with Alfred Douglas he is going to give his decision that I am leading an infamous life, and so deprive me of my sole income – £38 a quarter! For one's own solicitor this seems a little strong. Unluckily he has it in his power to stop my wretched allowance, and is going to do so, and as I see my poem is a very unsaleable affair I simply have starvation or suicide before me – the latter, as I dislike pain, for choice. Alfred Douglas has no money, not enough for his own wants, and cannot do anything, even temporarily, for me.

I am anxious however to correct my proofs before retiring from a world of injustice and wrong and annoyance. So do let me have them. You said you would send them last Wednesday – as yet no sign of them.

I should not like to die without seeing my poem as good as I can make a poem, whose subject is all wrong, and whose treatment too personal. I hope to receive the proofs this week. As regards the cover, do what you like – the simpler the better.

I won't write any more about America. I have no hopes: but I do trust you will copyright it in the States: there is a *chance* – just a chance – of a big sale.

The weather is entrancing, but in my heart there is no sun. Ever yours

O. W.

Although Smithers promised Wilde that he would copyright The Ballad *in America, he appears not to have done so and several pirated editions of it appeared even before Wilde's death three years later.*

To Leonard Smithers

Friday, 19 [November 1897]   *Villa Giudice, Posillipo*

My dear Smithers, Your telegram has just arrived: and I am very much obliged to you for your kindness, as in the midst of my hideous worries the lack of any money at all was paralysing. Now, I can really think about my position, and form some judgment as to whether it is worth while fighting on against the hideous forces of the world. Personally I don't think it is, but Vanity, that great impulse, still drives me to think of a possible future of self-assertion. It seems absurd to be beaten by the want of money. And yet I feel that every problem in life must be solved on its own conditions. And Financial Problems can be solved only by Finance. Genius, Art, Romance, Passion, and the like are useless when the point at issue is one of figures. A solution for an algebraic problem is not to be found in the sense of Beauty, however developed.

The proofs also have arrived: in old days of power and personality I always insisted that my proofs should be sent to me on the paper to be ultimately used. Otherwise I would not have been able to judge of the look of a page. Of course the paper of these proofs is awful, and the whole thing looks to me mean in consequence. The type is good: though I think the ?s lacking in style, and the stops, especially the full-stops, characterless. But setting this aside, the whole thing looks too meagre for a 3/6 book. When one remembers what thick cloth-bound volumes the public buys nowadays for 3/6 or 2/6, it seems to me that they will think twice before they pay 3/6 for what looks like a thin sixpenny pamphlet, lacking in all suggestion of permanence of form. The public is largely influenced by the *look* of a book. So are we all. It is the only artistic thing about the public.

I had intended that wherever there was a break (marked by a leaf) in my poem, a *new* page should begin. This would give the book thickness and an air of responsibility. Whether it would really look well, I cannot say: you are, of course, the better judge. Failing this, it really would be better to print on alternate leaves, as you suggested. As it stands, it is not adequate to 3/6.

The drawback of beginning a new page at every break is that it makes the poem look piecemeal, and robs it of the impression of continuous unity of development. The advantage is the increase of the number of pages. I really think that printing on alternate pages is the best. You say this will necessitate a cloth binding. Well, let us have one. A plain olive-green, or cinnamon cloth, with a white back gold-lettered. The colours, nowadays, in cloths are lovely.

The title-page is not good. (I hope, by the way, you have a double proof?) The 'By C.3.3.' is far too small. Also, as a general rule in art, I think that the less the type is changed on a page the better. Too many types spoil the looking. Nor do I care for, or indeed stand, the placing of the 'By C.3.3.'.

Why not

The

Ballad of Reading Gaol

By

C.3.3.

Indeed place 'By C.3.3.' quite at the side, so as to draw down the type-design to the publisher's lines and fill the page. As a rule in English books the publisher's name looks a sudden intrusion into a page more candid without it, whereas it should be part of it all.

I would suggest the same type for the full title and the suggestion of the author. The publisher's name and address, of course, smaller.

The type for the Dedication is *revolting*. It is like a bad brass by Gilbert Scott. There need be no suggestion of a Pugin tombstone about it. Joy and Assertion are its notes.

At the close of each Canto a leaf is out of place. It marks transition, not finality.

The 'In Memoriam' page is an example of what I mean by the inartistic effect of changing type: it looks like a page of specimen-types for a printer's apprentice. It should be quite simple, and no tombstone Gothic about the words 'In Memoriam'. On the whole I think now that the combination of Latin and English is wrong. What do you say to this? (not in tombstone-type)

In Memory
of
R. J. M.
late of H. M. Dragoon Guards.
Died in H. M. Prison, Reading
July 13
1896.

Or, shall we put 'Her Majesty's' in full? Perhaps not, as it would go badly with Gaol or Prison: though the official address on prison notepaper (paper of a loathsome blue colour) is *H. M. Prison*. Perhaps 'Died in Reading Gaol, Berkshire' would suit the title better. It would not suggest that there was any sneer in the title.

Do you think 'Hanged in Reading Gaol' would either be too like G. R. Sims, or give away the plot of the poem?

Or do you think that the words 'In Memory of R. J. M'. would be enough? I now, sometimes, think so. It would excite interest, without giving away the plot. It is a difficult point. Please consult with Robbie. Alfred Douglas thinks that if I don't put that R. J. M. died in Reading Prison people might think that it was all imaginary. This is a sound objection.

As regards the doctor, I have written to you today. To sacrifice the stanza on the dung-heap of the Chiswick Press would be absurd. Would you kindly say that the description is generic, and that the Reading doctor is a thin sallow man with an aquiline nose, and that the description is imaginary, just like the yellow face of the Governor, or the Caiaphas-chaplain. It does not occur in any description of Reading Gaol. It is abstract. The only people I have libelled in the poem are the Reading warders. They were – most of them – as good as possible to me. But to poetry all must be sacrificed, even warders.

Robbie has written me a very acrimonious letter to assure me that he never showed you any letters of mine, except passages on business. But you wrote to me 'Is it *kind* or *just* of you to write to Ross that I dictated to my type-writer advice about your wife and your conduct to her?' So Robbie must have thought my remarks on the subject of a business-character. They really were not. But Robbie is on horseback at present. He can ride everything, except Pegasus.

I hope to send you the proofs tomorrow. Do you think that copyrighting *portions* of the poem will prevent the piracy of quotation in the papers? I don't. I think the only chance is to go for a big thing and to publish the poem in America at one dollar. This of course would rank as general expenses. So you would have half the profits in America, and they *may* be great. But the moment you publish in England, the American papers, under pretence of criticism, will publish the whole affair. That is certain.

I now think that we must wait till after Christmas. If we are to secure America we must. And the 1st of January would not be a bad date. Consider the point.

You suggest 'gray' instead of 'grey' in one passage. But I have 'grey' everywhere else. Is there any rule about it? I only know that Dorian *Gray* is a classic, and deservedly. Excuse this brief letter. I am in a hurry to buy cigarettes – the first for four days. Sincerely yours   OSCAR WILDE

To More Adey

Sunday [Postmark 21 November 1897]   *Villa Giudice, Posillipo*
My dear More, I cannot tell you the utter astonishment with which I read your letter.

You tell me that you, and Bobbie, on being asked whether Bosie was 'a disreputable person' felt bound at once to say yes: and that you declared that my wife was acting 'strictly within her legal rights according to the agreement' in depriving me of my allowance, because I have the pleasure of Bosie's companionship, the only companionship in the world open to me.

In what way, my dear More, is Bosie more disreputable than either you or Robbie?

When you came to see me at Reading in November 1895, my wife, on being informed of this by my sister-in-law, wrote to me a most violent letter, in which she said – I quote from her letter now before me – 'I hear with horror that Mr More Adey has been to see you. Is this your promise to lead a new life? What am I to think of you if you still have intercourse with your old infamous companions? I require you to assure me that you will never see him again, or any people of that kind' etc. etc.

That is my wife's view of you, based on the information supplied to her by George Lewis about you, and Robbie, and other friends of mine. My wife also knows what Robbie's life is and has been.

May I ask, if you had come to give me the pleasure of your companionship in my lonely life, whether Robbie would have at once agreed that you were a 'disreputable person' and that I had forfeited all claim to my allowance in consequence?

If Robbie had lived with me, would you have taken the same course?

I simply don't know how to describe my feelings of utter amazement and indignation.

As for Hansell, he calmly writes to me that he considers 'any member of the Queensberry family' is 'a disreputable person'. Conceive such ignorance, such impertinence. If Lord Douglas of Hawick offered me the shelter of his roof I was to be left a pauper!

Hansell is bound to decide according to the legal agreement: it is his duty to do so. I say nothing about his failing in his duty to me as a client. That would only give him pleasure. But simply as an arbitrator, in a question of life and death practically, he utterly ignores the wording of the agreement, and gives a decision entirely illegal, entirely unjust, in order, I suppose, to curry favour with Mr Hargrove, or to experience for the first time in his life the priggish pleasure of what he ignorantly thinks is a moral attitude.

When he tells me in black and white that if Percy came and stayed with me he would regard me as living with a disreputable person, he shows his entire disregard of the legal agreement of whose clauses he was stupidly made arbitrator.

As for you and Robbie calmly acquiescing in this monstrous injustice, I do not know what to think about either of you. I simply cannot comprehend it, nor can I write, today, any more about it. Ever yours   OSCAR

By this time Sybil Queensberry, Bosie's mother, had joined the chorus of disapproval and had threatened to stop her son's allowance. The two men were effectively starved into submission. Lady Queensberry did, however, accede to Bosie's conditions for their separation: the settlement of their outstanding bill at the Hôtel Royale des Étrangers; the payment of a quarter's rent at the Villa Giudice; and a lump sum of £200 to be paid to Oscar in two instalments through More Adey. This, too, became the subject of some acrimony, with Wilde claiming that Bosie's family had promised to pay £500 of the libel case costs and that after this payment £300 was still owing (see pp. 208, 225). Adrian Hope, a neighbour from Tite Street and related by marriage to Constance, had been made guardian to the Wildes' children and a trustee under their separation agreement. After Constance's death Wilde asked Hope if he could write letters to his sons to be delivered when they came of age, but was told that any such letters would be destroyed.

To Robert Ross

Thursday [25 November 1897]   *Villa Giudice, Posillipo*
My dear Robbie, Thanks for writing to me. The situation is appalling.

I will begin by a few literary notes. I have put back the stanzas I expunged, because I think they are dramatically necessary for the narrative. I think people will want to know what the man did after his conviction, so the narrative is improved, though the poetry is not good, but while it is possible to correct a good verse, it is almost impossible to correct a bad one.

I have put 'The Governor was *strict* upon The Regulations Act'. I now think that 'strong' is better. The verse is meant to be colloquial – G. R. Sims at best – and when one is going for a coarse effect, one had better be coarse. So please restore '*strong*'.

You did not like 'The man in red who reads the Law', because you said it reminded you of the 'man in blue' for a policeman. The reminiscence it brought to me was the '*Voilà! l'homme rouge qui passe*' of Hugo's *Marion De Lorme*, and I like the expression, but 'who reads *one's doom*' would I think be better. Will you alter this for me? Unless you think I have fiddled too often on the string of Doom.

Smithers has been very kind and has sent me £5. He promises another this week; but it has not yet arrived. I think after Christmas would be better for publication: I am hardly a Christmas present.

What astonishes and interests me about my present position is that the moment the world's forces begin to persecute anyone they *never leave off*. This seems to me a historical fact, as well as an interesting psychological problem. To leave off persecution is to admit that one has been wrong, and the world will never do that. Also, the world is angry because their punishment has had no effect. They wished to be able to say 'We have done a capital thing for Oscar Wilde: by putting him in prison we have put a stop to his friendship with Alfred Douglas and all that that implies'. But now they find that they have not had that effect, that they merely treated me barbarously, but did not influence me, they simply ruined me, so they are furious.

I have written to Adrian Hope, but have not yet heard anything. To Hansell I have written violently. Of dear More I have made a holocaust: it had to be. But he will survive any pyre: in the ashes his heart – *cor cordium* – will be found untouched.

I will write tomorrow, but for the future cannot afford stamps! Ever yours   OSCAR

To More Adey

Saturday [Postmark 27 November 1897]   *Villa Giudice, Posillipo*
My dear More, I have not yet heard anything from you in answer to my letter. But Hansell has written to me stating that his decision is irrevocable.

I now want to know if there cannot be a compromise made. I am quite ready to agree not to live in the same house with Bosie again. Of course to promise to cut him, or not to speak to him, or not to associate with him, would be absurd. He is the only friend with whom I can be in contact, and to live without some companion is impossible. I had silence and solitude for two years: to condemn me now to silence and solitude would be barbarous.

It is not a matter of much importance, but I never wrote to my wife that I was going 'to keep house with Alfred Douglas'. I thought 'keep house' was only a servant-girl's expression.

My wife wrote me a very violent letter on September 29 last saying: 'I *forbid* you to see Lord Alfred Douglas. I forbid you to return to your filthy, insane life. I forbid you to live at Naples. I will not allow you to come to Genoa.' I quote her words.

I wrote to her to say that I would never dream of coming to see her against her will, that the only reason that would induce me to come to see her was the prospect of a greeting of sympathy with me in my misfortunes, and affection, and pity. That for the rest, I only desired peace, and to live my own life as best I could. That I could not live in London, or, as yet, in Paris, and that I certainly hoped to winter at Naples. To this I received no answer.

I do think that, if we engage not to live together, I might be still left the wretched £3 a week – so little, but still something. How on earth am I to live?

Do, if possible, try to arrange something. I know you all think I am wilful, but it is the result of the nemesis of character, and the bitterness of life. I was a problem for which there was no solution. Ever yours   OSCAR

To Leonard Smithers

Sunday [?28 November 1897]   *Posillipo*
Dear Smithers, Do try and make the Chiswick Press less mad and less maddening. I now have 'While *some* coarse-mouthed doctor straddles by, with *a* flattened bulldog nose, fingering *the* watch' etc. If they ask you is there no offence in it, say it is simply miching mallecho, but to say it with style wear sables. However, if they kick, I cannot sacrifice the lines about the watch, so I enclose a feeble substitute, but I shall be outraged and perhaps outrageous if it is used.

I wish you would start a Society for the Defence of Oppressed Personalities: at present there is a gross European concert headed by brutes and solicitors against us. It is really ridiculous that after my entire life has been wrecked by Society, people should still propose to exercise social tyranny over me, and try to force me to live in solitude – the one thing I can't stand. I lived in silence and solitude for two years in prison. I did not think that on my release my wife, my trustees, the guardians of my children, my few friends, such as they are, and my myriad enemies would combine to force me by starvation to live in silence and solitude again. After all in prison we had food of some kind: it was revolting, and made as loathsome as possible on purpose, and quite inadequate to sustain life in health. Still, there *was* food of some kind. The scheme now is that I am to live in silence and solitude and have no food at all. Really, the want of imagination in people is appalling. This scheme is put forward on moral grounds! It is proposed to leave me to die of starvation, or to blow my brains out in a Naples urinal. I never came across anyone in whom the moral sense was dominant who was not heartless, cruel, vindictive, log-stupid, and entirely lacking in the smallest sense of humanity. Moral people, as they are termed, are simple beasts. I would sooner have fifty unnatural vices than one unnatural virtue. It is unnatural virtue that makes the world, for those who suffer, such a premature Hell.

All this has, of course, direct reference to my poem: and indeed is the usual way in which poets write to publishers.

I have decided to put back the opening of Canto *Three*, because it is dramatically necessary for the telling of the story. The reader wants to know where the condemned man was, and what he was doing. I wish it were better, but it *isn't* and can't be. I think it aids the narrative immensely. So stick it in. For the rest I think I have corrected enough. The popularity of the poem will be largely increased by the author's painful death by starvation. The public love poets to die in that way. It seems to them dramatically right. Perhaps it is. Ever yours   O. W.

To More Adey

Sunday [Postmark 29 November 1897]   *Villa Giudice, Posillipo*
My dear More, I am sorry my letter gave you pain: very sorry indeed: but then your action gave me still greater pain: not that I suggest or think that any protest from you would have prevented my wife from doing what she has done: but that I do think you would have been entitled to say that you did not regard Bosie as a 'disreputable person' in the legal meaning of the word in a legal document. I was hurt at your saying to me that you felt bound to admit that 'Mrs Wilde was acting strictly within her legal rights according to the agreement'. I do not think that that is the case. Though had there been no agreement, and my wife was merely making me an

allowance of her own free will, I quite admit that her action would have been natural, from the point of view of the passions and emotions of human nature, and popular, from the point of view of social approval by ordinary people. It seemed to me that you gave up unnecessarily and prematurely: a protest from you would not have stopped the confiscation, but it would have enabled me to make a stronger protest to Adrian Hope than I have done.

At present my own friends have given away my position. I am fighting without support. And, as you knew what Hansell's decision would probably, if not certainly be, you might have, and I think should have, said that the terms of the agreement did not *legally* apply to Bosie.

You can understand I feel sore about it, and the position in which I have placed myself makes me bitter.

At present I don't know what to do. Bosie will probably go back to Paris. I see nothing to do but to stay on here, and try to get to literary work. Of course I am depressed by the difficulty of reaching an audience; the adventures of my American poem have been a terrible blow to my ambition, my vanity, and my hopes.

Perhaps Adrian Hope may recommend my wife to continue the allowance on condition of my not ever again living in the same house as Bosie, and we are both ready to accept the inevitable, forced now on him as well as on me. We have no option. Whether Adrian Hope will help me, I don't know. Ever yours   OSCAR

To Leonard Smithers

30 November [1897]   *Villa Giudice, Posillipo*
My dear Smithers, Robbie Ross has sent me a copy of a letter he has written you, in which he states that he finds he has no longer my confidence in business matters, and so does not wish to be connected with my affairs.

I write at once to assure you that Robbie writes under a complete misapprehension due to a misinterpretation of a phrase or sentence used by someone else.

Robbie has done everything for me in business that anyone on earth could do, and his own generosity and unwearying kindness are beyond any expression of praise on my part, though, I am glad to say, not beyond my powers of gratitude.

Robbie may not wish to be worried any more by my business affairs. He has had endless worry for two years over them but it would be fairer of him to say that it is too much worry to go on, than that he finds he has not my confidence. Such a statement is childish and, if taken seriously by you, would lead you to think that I was at once dense of judgment and coarsely ungrateful in nature. Sincerely yours   OSCAR WILDE

Bosie left Naples at the beginning of December and went to Rome. From there he wrote to his mother to say that despite still loving and admiring Oscar he was glad to be free of the tie. 'If I hadn't rejoined him and lived with him for two months, I should have never got over my longing for him.' Although the two men later saw each other regularly in Paris, the intensity of their relationship was never the same again.

To Leonard Smithers

Tuesday [?30 November 1897]   *Villa Giudice, Posillipo*
My dear Smithers, Your letter just received.

I am very glad you are going to print on one side only: my suggestion of a new page after each closing stanza was merely in case you did not wish to print on one side only. But I was always conscious it would give a casual piecemeal air to the work.

As regards the cover, I am quite content with paper; we must see how it all makes up. Also as regards price, your judgment is of course better than mine. I am myself in favour of 2/6.

Do send a copy at once to Miss Marbury, and Reynolds: they *cannot* get an offer unless the poem is read: and I don't think that a New York paper of standing would pirate, any more than the editor of a magazine. All my plays went to Miss Marbury. She is a woman of the highest position, and would not allow any nonsense. So pray let her have a copy at once. Reynolds I don't know, but he can have access to hers. I think that £5 would copyright the poem in the States: I used to copyright my plays for £20 each, through Miss Marbury. She does all that sort of work.

With regards to the notes of interrogation, I really think that it would be best to discuss vital points like this *en tête-à-tête*, so I hope you will come out to Naples and see me.

As I have lost my entire income, of course I cannot live with Alfred Douglas any more. He has only just enough for himself. So he is going back to Paris, and I shall be alone here. I do not know if, now that we are going to separate, there is any likelihood of my income being restored to me. I unluckily have now no one to plead my cause aright. I have alienated all my friends, partly through my own fault, partly through theirs. The Paris *Journal* has a sympathetic paragraph to say I am starving at Naples, but

French people subscribe nothing but sonnets when one is alive, and statues when one is not.

With regard to Daly, it would be very kind of you if you would write to him and say that I will begin a comedy for him for £100 down, and £100 for each completed act, the royalties to be such as I received for my last American play. Miss Marbury will let him know the contract. This would of course see me through the winter.

As regards the ownership of the publishing rights of my plays, the Bankruptcy trustee made no claim on them at all: they are not amongst my assets. Robbie will tell you who the trustee is. He is, I believe, very friendly disposed, and will make no claim: it would be absurd.

I still think that, to secure American copyright, it would be best to publish after Christmas, though Miss Marbury could copyright the thing in a week for you.

I hope Robbie is not behaving so unkindly as his letter to me suggested. After all it is on me that the whole tragedy has fallen: and it is mere sentimentality for the spectators to claim the crown of thorns as theirs, on the ground that their feelings have been harrowed.

You give me no news about the verse about the doctor. I think that with my alteration ('some' etc.) it should stand, but other alternatives were given.

My handwriting – once Greek and gracious – is now illegible: I am very sorry: but I really am a wreck of nerves. I don't eat, or sleep: I live on cigarettes. Ever yours   O. W.

To Leonard Smithers

Saturday [11 December 1897]   *Villa Giudice [Posillipo]*
My dear Smithers, A holograph letter from you is indeed a curiosity of literature, and I treasure it for its manner no less than for its matter.

As for dear Robbie, if he will kindly send me out a pair of his oldest boots I will blacken them with pleasure, and send them back to him with a sonnet. I have loved Robbie all my life, and have not the smallest intention of giving up loving him. Of all my old friends he is the one who has the most beautiful nature; had my other friends been like him, I would not be the pariah-dog of the nineteenth century. But natures like his are not found twice in a life-time.

When dear Robbie heavily bombarded me (an unfair thing, as unfortified places are usually respected in civilised war) I bore it with patriarchal patience. I admit, however, that when he seemed to me slightly casual about someone else, I sent up a rocket of several colours. I am sorry I did so. But what is there in my life for which I am not sorry? And how useless it all is! My life cannot be patched up. There is a doom on it. Neither to myself, nor others, am I any longer a joy. I am now simply an ordinary pauper of a rather low order: the fact that I am also a pathological problem in the eyes of German scientists is only interesting to German scientists: and even in their works I am tabulated, and come under the law of *averages*! *Quantum mutatus*!

Now to the title-page, which I enclose. The *C.3.3.* is not good. It is too thin. It should be as black and thick as the title. There may be some difficulty about the numerals, but the *C* seems to me much thinner than the *G* in 'Gaol'.

Also, your name is too large. I am not discussing the relative values of publisher and poet, as the poet's name is not mentioned. But the title of the poem is the foremost thing. By printing your name in the same type, or near it, the printers have spoiled the page. There is no balance, and it looks as if the poem was by Leonard Smithers.

It was much better in the second proof. You have marked on that that your name is to be 'one size larger type'. They seem to have made it three sizes larger. Personally, I think that there should be simply *two* types – one for the title and pseudonym, the other for publisher and address and date. If you wish a third type, take the one of L. S. in the title-page of O'Sullivan's book. Also, surely the spacing of the full title should be equalised. There seems to me too much white between

Gaol

——>

By

——>

3.

I do think it would look better together, made more of a block of. In any case your name is evidently out of all proportion – I speak typographically.

I think that you had better send me no more proofs of the poem. I have the *maladie de perfection* and keep on correcting. I know I have got it now to a fairly high standard, but I don't want to polish for ever. So *after you get* the proofs, I think you yourself could see that all my corrections were carried out, and let me have merely the title-page and 'In Memoriam' page. This is out of regard for your time and pocket. I would also like to see the cover.

I think that if you try and get in your name and address on the back, where the lettering is to be, it will be too crowded. I propose simply 'The Ballad of Reading Gaol'. But you will see yourself. However, I see your name is all right on O'Sullivan's back.

Robbie has just sent me the *Weekly Sun*. I do not know if this is a sign of forgiveness or the reverse. Ever yours   OSCAR WILDE

Between 20 and 30 December, on the strength of the first £100 from Lady Queensberry, Wilde went to Taormina in Sicily. 'C. T. W.' was Charles Thomas Wooldridge, the dedicatee of The Ballad, *a soldier who murdered his wife in a crime passionel and was hanged while Wilde was in Reading. Earlier, Wilde had even proposed giving him false intials to disguise his identity entirely.*

To Leonard Smithers

9 January 1898   *31 Santa Lucia [Naples]*
My dear Smithers, The revise has never arrived, and I have waited from day to day for it. To wait longer would be foolish.

I am sure it is all right. As regards your suggestion, or request, that I should revert to 'in God's sweet world again', instead of 'for weal or woe again' (Canto Two somewhere), certainly. Pray mark the correction yourself. Second thoughts in art are always, or often, worst.

The C.3.3. I enclose seems excellent. The C. T. W. of the In Memoriam page was better larger, as before. *'trooper'* (same page) should have a *capital T*.

I *think* that *'in* the Royal Horse Guards' should be *'of* the R. H. G'. I don't know, however; you might ask. *'Of* seems nicer. The cover etc. I leave to you.

The post here is impossible, so pray bring it all out as soon as possible, without further consultation. I, as all poets, am safe in your hands.

As regards America, I think it would be better now to publish there *without* my name. I see it is my *name* that terrifies. I hope an edition of some kind will appear. I cannot advise about what should be done, but it seems to me that the withdrawal of my name is essential in America as elsewhere. And the public like an open secret. Half of the success of Marie Corelli is due to the no doubt unfounded rumour that she is a woman. In other respects pray do as you like about America, but do see that there is *some* edition.

I have had many misfortunes since I wrote to you – influenza, the robbery, during my absence in Sicily, of *all* my clothes etc. by a servant whom I left at the villa, ill-health, loneliness, and general *ennui* with a tragi-comedy of an existence, but I want to see my poem out before I take steps. Ever yours
O. W.

To Leonard Smithers

[Postmark 7 February 1898]   *31 Santa Lucia [Naples]*
I am really charmed with the book. It is quite right, except the final signature
of C.3.3 (page 31). That is awful; it should have been cut. In the remote case
of a second edition, please have one cut. The cover is very nice, and the
paper excellent. The title-page is a masterpiece – one of the best I have ever
seen. I am really so cheerfully grateful to you, my dear fellow, for the care
and trouble you have taken.

I have sent you the title-pages. Robbie Ross will give you the addresses,
except Alfred Douglas's, which is Hôtel Bellevue, Mentone.

The Final Years

*'Like dear St Francis of Assisi I am
wedded to Poverty: but in my
case the marriage is not a
success. . . . I live now on
echoes and have little
music of my own.'*

Just as at Berneval five months before, the loneliness of Posillipo without Bosie was
intolerable. Vincent O'Sullivan came to visit for a few days, but no other friends
had any inclination to make the long trip to southern Europe. Constance was still
furious at what she saw as his weakness in going back to Bosie and any hope of
reconciliation there had vanished. Oscar needed companionship and intellectual
stimulation, so he returned to the only city where he knew he could find it – Paris
– and arrived there on 13 February, the day on which The Ballad of Reading
Gaol *was published. In the end he did persuade Smithers to increase the first*
edition to 800 copies.

To Robert Ross

[?18 February 1898]   *Hôtel de Nice, rue des Beaux-Arts, Paris*
My dearest Robbie, Thanks so much for the cuttings.

Smithers is absurd, only printing 400 copies, to begin with, and not
advertising. I fear he has missed a popular 'rush'. He is so fond of 'suppressed'
books that he suppresses his own. Don't tell him this from me. I have
written to him.

It is very unfair of people being horrid to me about Bosie and Naples. A
patriot put in prison for loving his country loves his country, and a poet in
prison for loving boys loves boys. To have altered my life would have been
to have admitted that Uranian love is ignoble. I hold it to be noble – more
noble than other forms. Ever yours   OSCAR

To R. B. Cunninghame Graham

[Circa 20 February 1898]   *Hôtel de Nice*

My dear Cunninghame Graham, A thousand thanks for your charming letter, and its generous, and most welcome, praise of *The Ballad*.

I read with great interest your article in the *Saturday* last June, and wish we could meet to talk over the many prisons of life – prisons of stone, prisons of passion, prisons of intellect, prisons of morality, and the rest. All limitations, external or internal, are prison-walls, and life is a limitation.

I hope you will be in Paris this spring, and come and see me. I often hear scraps of news about you from that good little chap Will Rothenstein. Ever yours   OSCAR WILDE

Constance was sent a copy 'With the author's compliments' and wrote to her brother, 'It is frightfully tragic and makes one cry,' but, as she confided to a friend, there was the additional sadness in that it was the only one of his books not personally inscribed to her.

To Robert Ross

Sunday [?20 February 1898]   *Paris*

Dear Robbie, Certainly: it would be very kind of you to give Smithers the names of the people who should have copies. I have asked him to print slips for insertion 'with the compliments of the author'. Arthur Clifton, of course, and Dal Young, and anyone else you can think of. I have sent *O. B.* one at King's.

Miss Frances Forbes-Robertson should have one. Do you know her address? I suppose I would have no right to send *Miss Schuster* one? It is a great pity. I would like Sydney Grundy to have a copy.

I fear that the press will boycott the work. It is very bitter and unfair, but I have not much hope of recognition.

Who are the people who object to my having been with Bosie at Naples, and spent my days with Heliogabalus, and my nights with Antinous? I mean are they people who were ever my friends? Or are they simply those to whom Uranian love is horrible? If the latter, I cannot care. If the former, I do.

I am sending my wife a copy.

I have hardly seen anyone in Paris. I am waiting to distribute twelve copies to my friends here, Henri Bauër, Mirbeau, and others.

A poem gives one *droit de cité*, and shows that one is still an artist.

There was an MP who was nice about me, through Miss Schuster; I forget his name. Would you have a copy sent to him also, with a slip?

I have had a charming letter from Cunninghame Graham, but, except you and Reggie, none of the people to whom I sent copies have written to me. The lack of imagination in people is astonishing. I wish I could see you. I see no one here, but a young Irishman called Healy, a poet. Ever yours

OSCAR

What does Aleck think of *The Ballad*?

To More Adey

Monday [21 February 1898]   *Hôtel de Nice*

My dear More, I see your beautiful handwriting on the cover of the *Echo*, which reached me this morning. Many sincere thanks. It is a capital review, but, of course, I want the literary papers to criticise it. It is not *altogether* a pamphlet on prison-reform. I wonder what that good kind fellow Major Nelson thinks of it. I sent him a copy.

I wish you could come over here and see me, but I suppose that is difficult. The intellectual atmosphere of Paris has done me good, and I now have ideas, not merely passions. Naples was fatal.

Are you writing?

Are you in love?

Are you happy? Ever yours   O. W.

To William Rothenstein

[Late February 1898]   *Hôtel de Nice*

My dear Will, I cannot tell you how touched I am by your letter, and by all you say of my poem. Why on earth don't you write literary criticisms for papers? I wish *The Ballad* had fallen into your hands. No one has said things so *sympathiques*, so full of delicate insight, so large, from the point of view of art, as you. Your letter has given me more pleasure, more pride, than anything has done since the poem appeared.

Yes: it is something to have made a 'sonnet out of skilly' (Cunninghame Graham will explain to you what skilly is. You must never know by personal experience). And I *do* think the whole affair 'realised', and that is triumph.

I hope you will be in Paris some time this spring, and come and see me.

I see by the papers that you are still making mortals immortal, and I wish you were working for a Paris newspaper, that I could see your work making *kiosques* lovely. Ever yours   OSCAR

To Frank Harris

[End February 1898]   *Hôtel de Nice*

My dear Frank, I cannot express to you how deeply touched I am by your letter: it is *une vraie poignée de main*. I simply long to see you, and to come again in contact with your strong, sane, wonderful personality.

I cannot understand about the poem. My publisher tells me that, as I had begged him to do, he sent the two *first* copies to the *Saturday* and the *Chronicle*, and he also tells me that Arthur Symons told him he had written specially to you to ask you to allow him to do a *signed* article. I suppose publishers are untrustworthy. They certainly always look it. I hope *some* notice will appear, as your paper, or rather yourself, is a great force in London, and when you speak men listen. I, of course, feel that the poem is too autobiographical and that *real* experiences are alien things that should never influence one, but it was wrung out of me, a cry of pain, the cry of Marsyas, not the song of Apollo. Still, there are some good things in it. I feel as if I had made a sonnet out of skilly! And that is something.

When you return from Monte Carlo please let me know. I long to dine with you.

As regards a comedy, my dear Frank, I have lost the mainspring of life and art, *la joie de vivre*; it is dreadful. I have pleasures, and passions, but the joy of life is gone. I am going under: the morgue yawns for me. I go and look at my zinc-bed there. After all, I had a wonderful life, which is, I fear, over. But I must dine once with you first. Ever yours   o. w.

To Leonard Smithers

[Postmark 28 February 1898]   *Paris*

My dear Smithers, I am still looking for you in Paris. Are you here, or in London? Please be serious, and let me know. In the Author's Edition I would like the dedication inserted. It would give an interest to the edition, and an air of psychological mystery. Robbie has written to me about people to whom I should send copies – people who have been kind to me and about me. He will bring you the list. Please enter them to my account. Also, do send me some money – a fiver at any rate – I have just twenty-two francs left. I long to hear about America. There are great possibilities there for a coup. Do try and work some papers for more reviews: they help immensely.

o. w.

To Laurence Housman

[February–March 1898]   *Hôtel de Nice*

Dear Mr Housman, I am so glad you got the copy I ordered to be sent to you. I was in Naples, so had to deny myself the pleasure of writing your name on the fly-leaf.

I thank you very much for all you have said to me about *The Ballad*: it has greatly touched me. I quite hold with you on all you say about the relation of human suffering to art; as art is the most intense mode of expression, so suffering is the most real mode of life, the one for which we are all ultimately created.

I read some wonderful extracts from *Spikenard* in the *Chronicle*, but to have the book itself would be a great honour and a great pleasure. Yours most sincerely   o. w.

To Robert Ross

Wednesday [?2 March 1898]   [*Paris*]

My dear Robbie, A thousand thanks for all the trouble you are taking for me. You, although a dreadful *low-Church* Catholic, as a little Christian sit in the snow-white rose. Christ did not die to save people, but to teach people how to save each other. This is, I have no doubt, a grave heresy, but it is also a fact.

I have *not* read your letter to Constance. I would sooner leave it to you. You have the tact of affection and kindness, and I would sooner return it unread.

The facts of Naples are very bald and brief.

Bosie, for four months, by endless letters, offered me a '*home*'. He offered me love, affection, and care, and promised that I should never want for anything. After four months I accepted his offer, but when we met at *Aix* on our way to Naples I found that he had no money, no plans, and had forgotten all his promises. His one idea was that I should raise money for us both. I did so, to the extent of £120. On this Bosie lived, quite happy. When it came to his having, of course, to repay his own *share*, he became terrible, unkind, mean, and penurious, except where his own pleasures were concerned, and when my allowance ceased, he left.

With regard to the £500, which he said was 'a debt of honour' etc. he has written to me to say that he admits that it is a debt of honour, but that 'lots of gentlemen don't pay their debts of honour', that it is 'quite a common thing', and that no one thinks anything the worse of them.

I don't know what you said to Constance, but the bald fact is that I accepted the offer of a *'home'*, and found that I was expected to provide the money, and that when I could no longer do so, I was left to my own devices.

It is, of course, the most bitter experience of a bitter life; it is a blow quite awful and paralysing, but it had to come, and I know it is better that I should never see him again. I don't want to. He fills me with horror. Ever yours

O. W.

To Frank Harris

[Circa 3 March 1898]   *Hôtel de Nice*

My dear Frank, You have been so good and generous to me that I hate to have to ask you to be generous again. But I am entirely without money, and if you could let me have £5 you would be doing me a great kindness. I have had no money from my trustees for six months, and am trying to get back my little £3 a week, through Robbie Ross, always a good friend to me, but there are delays, and in the meanwhile I drift in ridiculous impecuniosity, without a sou. So, if you can, do something.

I long to see you here, and to have the dinner you asked me to at *Reading*. Ever yours   OSCAR WILDE

The first edition of The Ballad was sold out in days and a week later a second edition followed. The signed 'Author's Edition' came out in March and by May six editions had been printed totalling over 5000 copies. The critical reception was on the whole good, with the notable exception of W. E. Henley who clearly felt that he still had some old scores to settle and wrote, 'The trail of the Minor Poet is all over it.' Maurice Gilbert was one of Wilde's closest and most devoted friends during these last years. Except that his father was English and his mother French, and that he was a young soldier in the marine infantry, nothing is known of him.

To Leonard Smithers

[Postmark 3 March 1898]   *Hôtel de Nice*

My dear Smithers, Very well: no dedication for the Author's Edition. You are always wise and prudent (about other people's affairs). Please send the money you promise for tomorrow in a bank-note, as no banks are open on Sunday, and I may not get it till too late on Saturday. I enclose an absurd review from the *Herald* – of today.

I think the poem will appear in a French edition, with translation, either in a book or a review. This will be capital. I am not at all well and also am very unhappy, but dear Robbie Ross is bestirring himself in my interests, like the good chap he is.

There is going to be a recitation in a French translation of some of my poems in prose at the Odéon – at a literary matinée.

Maurice has won twenty-five games of bezique and I twenty-four: however, as he has youth, and I have only genius, it is only natural that he should beat me. Ever yours   OSCAR WILDE

To Henry D. Davray

Monday [7 March 1898]   *Hôtel de Nice*
My dear Davray, I am delighted that my poem is to appear with a translation by you, and will go and see Vallette tomorrow morning. I have told my publisher to send you a copy of the Second Edition which contains some corrections. You will receive it on Wednesday. I will also bring Vallette a copy, so that he can have it set up in type.

I need not say with what pleasure I would see your translation. Of course, there are many words, relating to prison life, for which the proper French *prison* equivalents must be found: words that, though not *argot*, are still *technical*. I am always free, so pray let me know when I can see you, on the completion of the poem.

I have written to my publisher to suggest his printing 250 copies with your translation on the opposite page, to appear simultaneously with the *Mercure*, and to bear, of course, the name of the *Mercure* on it – on the title-page – as well as that of the London publisher. Your sincere friend

OSCAR WILDE

To Frank Harris

[Circa 7 March 1898]   *Hôtel de Nice*
My dear good friend, Just a line to thank you for your generosity, and the sweet way in which you make your generosity dear to one. Many can do acts of kindness, but to be able to do them without wounding those who are helped in their trouble is given only to few: to a few big, sane, large natures like yours.

I long to see you, and catch health and power from your presence and personality.

The *Mercure de France* is going to publish my poem here, with a prose translation by a young poet who knows English, so I have something to think of besides things that are dreary or dreadful, and I am starting on a play, so perhaps there is something for me in the future.

With a thousand thanks, your sincere and grateful friend   OSCAR WILDE

To Carlos Blacker

[Postmark 9 March 1898]   *Hôtel de Nice*

My dear Carlos, I cannot express to you how thrilled and touched by emotion I was when I saw your handwriting last night. Please come and see me tomorrow (Thursday) at five o'clock if you possibly can: if not, pray make some other appointment: I want particularly to see you, and long to shake you by the hand again, and to thank you for all the sweet and wonderful kindness you and your wife have shown to Constance and the boys.

I am living here quite alone: in one room, I need hardly say, but there is an armchair for you. I have not seen Alfred Douglas for three months: he is I believe on the Riviera. I don't think it probable that we shall ever see each other again. The fact is that if he is ever with me again he loses £10 a month of his allowance, and as he has only £400 a year he has adopted the wise and prudent course of conduct.

I am so glad my poem has had a success in England. I have had for some weeks a copy for you – of the first edition – by me, which I long to present to you.

It appears with a French translation in the *Mercure de France* for April, and I hope to have it published in book form also, in a limited edition of course, but it is my *chant de cygne*, and I am sorry to leave with a cry of pain – a song of Marsyas, not a song of Apollo; but Life, that I have loved so much – too much – has torn me like a tiger, so when you come and see me, you will see the ruin and wreck of what once was wonderful and brilliant, and terribly improbable. But the French men of letters and artists are kind to me, so I spend my evenings reading the *Tentation* by Flaubert. I don't think I shall ever write again: *la joie de vivre* is gone, and that, with will-power, is the basis of art.

When you come ask for Monsieur Melmoth. Ever yours   OSCAR

To Frank Harris

[Circa 15 March 1898]   *Hôtel de Nice*

My dear Frank, It gave me great pleasure to find that the most sensitive and intellectual appreciation of my poem appeared in your paper. I am greatly touched by Symons's article; it is most admirably phrased, and its mode of approach is artistic and dignified. A thousand thanks to you, and to him.

When do you arrive?

I have a *faim de loup* for your presence, and for dinner. I am eating the *vache enragée* [having a rough time] with a vengeance, which perhaps accounts for my Greek handwriting having become a scrawl.

I wish you would let me have the *Saturday* from time to time: papers are so dear here. Ever yours   OSCAR

To Robert Ross

[Postmark 17 March 1898]   *Hôtel de Nice*

My dear Robbie, Thanks for your letter.

My wife wrote to Carlos Blacker that she had sent you £40 for me, but she has evidently changed her mind. I think it is absurd my not having the arrears of my allowance – nearly £80 – now due to me, and lopping me from £150 to £120 is of course absurd also. However, it is something, and I am glad to get it.

It is quite untrue that I received £200 from Lady Q. on condition of not living with Bosie.

Bosie owed me £500. He admitted this a debt of honour, and got his brother to formally guarantee it etc. He paid me £200 of this, but I have had no communication with that mischievous foolish woman; I simply received less than half of what Bosie owes me. I know that Bosie made terms with his mother, but that is not my concern. In paying debts of honour people cannot make terms. So pray tell my wife that it is quite untrue, or that you know nothing about it. The former statement would be the true one.

As soon as the £10 arrives I am going to see how to live on it. I must try and invent some scheme of poverty, and have found a restaurant where for 80 francs a month one can get nothing fit to eat – two chances a day – so shall *abonner* myself there. But you don't realise what a problem it is, to live on 250 francs a month. However, I must try.

Today is the *Mi-Carême*, a detestable day of clowns and confetti, so I am writing in a *café*, where I get this paper for nothing.

I am charmed with Symons's article in the *Saturday*.

My writing has gone to bits – like my character. I am simply a self-conscious nerve in pain. Ever yours   O. W.

To Leonard Smithers

[Postmark 17 March 1898]   *Hôtel de Nice*

My dear Smithers, Can you give me any idea of the prospective profits of my poem? I suppose we can depend on a sale of 4000 copies, some of which are dearer than the others. I don't care to be always worrying you for money, but of course I see no prospect for me except advances, not on problematic successes, but on an achieved sale.

Of course you have to wait for the booksellers' accounts, but still as the money is assured I should like to have some if I have not already overdrawn, which I cannot believe.

My handwriting has gone to bits, because I am nervous and unhappy. I never could understand mathematics, and life is now a mathematical problem. When it was a romantic one, I solved it – too well. Ever yours   O. W.

To Carlos Blacker

[Circa 17 March 1898]   *Hôtel de Nice*

My dear Friend, A thousand thanks for your good kindly letter. I do hope to see you soon. I have heard from Robbie Ross. It seems that my wife *will not* pay the arrears of my allowance – £80 – nor any portion of it. She says she will let me have £10 a month: that is all she promises, and she has as yet sent nothing.

In the meanwhile I am in dreadful straits, as I was forced to pay my hotel bill with the money you kindly lent me. I don't know what to do, and I have pawned everything I had. It was very kind of you writing to my wife, but I have a sort of idea she really wants me to be dead. It is a horrible and persistent thought, and I daresay she would be relieved to hear you had recognised me at the Morgue. Ever yours   OSCAR

Aubrey Beardsley died of tuberculosis at Menton on 16 March aged twenty-five.

To Leonard Smithers

[Circa 18 March 1898]   [*Paris*]

My dear Smithers, I was greatly shocked to read of poor Aubrey's death. Superbly premature as the flowering of his genius was, still he had immense development, and had not sounded his last stop. There were great possibilities always in the cavern of his soul, and there is something macabre and tragic in the fact that one who added another terror to life should have died at the age of a flower.

You never write now. I know nothing of *yesterday's* sales!! What were they? I suppose you have seen enclosed? All *Galignani's* said was 'wonderfully weird verses'.

The book has had quite a sale here at Brentano's and Galignani's, so if you print a leaflet let them each have one.

When do you come over? I hear Miss D'Or is looking pale and sad, but on such topics I only speak at second-hand.

Maurice is well and begs to be remembered. Ever yours   o. w.

To Robert Ross

Friday [?18 March 1898]   [*Paris*]

My dear Robbie, Many thanks for the cheque, which I received this morning. The absurd money-changer, blind to his own interests, declared that he did not know your name! So I have to wait till Monday to touch the gold, but I have borrowed twenty francs from the concierge, so am all right.

I wish you could come over – for three days at any rate.

Bosie is, I believe, going to Venice, but I have not heard from him for ages. What do you think of his going back to London? He tells me he returns there with his mother in May. I think it is premature. I mean of course from the point of view of 'social recognition' which he desires so much, and, I fear, so much in vain. It is not his past, but his future, that people so much object to, I am afraid.

I suppose you know that he made his mother leave the hotel at Mentone because the proprietor refused to publish his name among the fashionable arrivals. They have rooms now, I believe.

The reviews you sent me are excellent, and really the Press has behaved very well, and Henley's hysterical personalities have done no harm, but rather the contrary. I am quite obliged to him for playing the rôle of the *Advocatus Diaboli* so well. Without it my beatification as a saint would have been impossible, but I shall now live as the Infamous St Oscar of Oxford,

Poet and Martyr. My niche is just below that of the Blessed St Robert of Phillimore, Lover and Martyr – a saint known in *Hagiographia* for his extraordinary power, not in resisting, but in supplying temptations to others. This he did in the solitude of great cities, to which he retired at the comparatively early age of eight. Ever yours   o. w.

Constance Wilde to Carlos Blacker

20 March 1898   *Villa Elvira, Bogliasco [Genoa]*

My dear Mr Blacker, I did send £40 to Mr Ross, but he would not, and I expect rightly did not, send more than £10 at a time to him. I enclose you letters that I have had from Robbie which at any rate are truthful, which I know that Oscar is not.

The actual sum that I owe him, if you call it owing, is at the rate of £12.10. a month. £62.10. and not £80. This is counting it from the month of November when I stopped giving him his allowance to the end of this present month. I have said that I would give him £10 a month, so at the most I owe him little more than £20! By his own account to me he received £30 from Smithers, and he seems to have had money since. Also he had £10 of mine which he more than ignores in his letter to you, for he says that he has had nothing from me.

Oscar is so pathetic and such a born actor, and I am hardened when I am away from him. No words will describe my horror of that BEAST, for I will call him nothing else, A. D. Fancy Robbie receiving abusive letters from him, and you know perfectly well that they are sent with Oscar's knowledge and consent. I do not wish him dead, but considering how he used to go on about Willie's extravagance and about his cruelty in forcing his mother to give him money, I think that he might leave his wife and children alone. I beg that you will not let him know that you have seen these letters, only I wish you to realise that he knew perfectly well that he was forfeiting his income, small as it was, in going back to Lord A., and that it is absurd of him to say now that I acted without his knowledge.

He owes, I am certain, more than £60 in Paris, and if I pay money now he will think that he can write to me at any time for more. I have absolutely no one to fall back upon, and I will not get into debt for anyone. The boys' expenses will go on increasing until they are grown up and settled, and I will educate them and give them what they reasonably require. As Oscar will not bargain or be anything but exceedingly extravagant, why should I do with my money what is utterly foreign to my nature? If I were living on someone else's money, it would be a different thing and pride would make me do even what I hate. But Oscar has no pride. When he had this disastrous law-suit, he borrowed £50 from me, £50 from my cousin, and £100 from my aunt. The £50 I repaid my cousin, the £100 never has been, and I suppose never will be, repaid. I was left penniless, and borrowed £150 from Burne-Jones, and I have never borrowed a penny since. I still owe money in London which I am trying to pay, but all these things are nothing to Oscar as long as someone supports him! I paid all my tradespeople immediately and I had £60 advanced to me out of my settlement to pay for the boys' education.

You will say in the face of all this why did I ask you to go and see him in Paris? Well, I thought you would have nothing to do with his money affairs, and I strongly advise you to leave them alone. I knew that you were not in your own house, and therefore could not ask him to dinner, and I was silly enough to think that you would merely give him the intellectual stimulus he needed. I don't know what name he is living under in Paris. Is it his own or the name he took when he left England? If he was fixed anywhere, I could make an arrangement to pay 10 francs a day for his board to the hotel, not to him, for I know that he would never pay it. In the winter I paid at the hotel here 9 francs a day. Of course the good hotels are about 18 francs but I knew I could not afford that and did not go to them. He ought to go to a pension and live a great deal cheaper than this, for you see it only leaves him about 12 francs a month. At Heidelberg I paid about 4 marks a day, which is more his style, only I know he would think it horrible, and I did not particularly like it! [. . .] Love to all. Yours ever CONSTANCE HOLLAND

In spite of the exasperated tone of Constance's letter to Carlos Blacker, she was able to write around the same time to her old friend Arthur Humphreys, 'For the sake of the boys I am bound to keep apart, but it goes terribly against the grain, as unfortunately when I care for a person once, I care for them always, and angry as I am with him for his treatment of me, I think that if I saw him I should forgive everything.'

To Frank Harris

[Circa 20 March 1898]   *Hôtel de Nice*

My dear Frank, The *Saturday* arrived last night, and I read your article on Shakespeare with intense interest, and this morning I got your letter. I am much obliged for your kind promise to let me have the *Saturday* regularly, and I will duly acquaint the office with any change of name, address, or personal appearance. To read it keeps me in touch with you, and though you do not blow through all the horns and flutes, or beat on *all* the drums, still I feel you are there, just as in the old days there was always the aroma of poor old Lady Pollock's weak tea and literary twaddle – the 'five o'clock' of their reminiscences and butter. I envy you your phrase the 'rose-mist of passion'. You should save it for a sonnet.

I wish you would have a good article on Aubrey Beardsley – as a personality. Robbie Ross knew him intimately. Ever yours   OSCAR

To George Ives

[Postmark 21 March 1898]   *Hôtel de Nice*
My dear George, Thanks so much for your letter. Your charming friend came to see me one morning at the hotel, and was most delightful. I hope to see him again in a few days. He seems quite fascinated by Paris.

Thanks so much for ordering my book: it is now in its fifth edition. Smithers has put a flaming advertisement into the *Athenaeum*, headed

'3000 copies sold in three weeks'.

When I read it I feel like Lipton's tea!

Yes: I have no doubt we shall win, but the road is long, and red with monstrous martyrdoms. Nothing but the repeal of the Criminal Law Amendment Act would do any good. That is the essential. It is not so much public opinion as public officials that need educating. Ever yours   OSCAR

At the end of March Wilde moved into the Hôtel d'Alsace in the rue des Beaux-Arts, which was to become his main Paris address until his death. The proprietor, Jean Dupoirier, was unexpectedly kind to Wilde, allowing him extended credit and even, in August 1899, paying off his debts at another hotel which had impounded his clothes.

To Carlos Blacker

Monday [28 March 1898]   *Hôtel d'Alsace, rue des Beaux-Arts, Paris*
My dear Carlos, Thanks for your *petit bleu* [telegram]. I am so sorry you can't come to see me, as I have not been out since Friday, except one night when I was dragged out to meet *Esterhazy* at dinner! The Commandant was astonishing. I will tell you all he said some day. Of course he talked of nothing but Dreyfus *et Cie*.

What happened to me was simply that through the horse coming down I was thrown almost through the front window of a fiacre, and cut my lower lip almost in two. It was quite dreadful, and, of course, a hideous shock to my nerves. It is so horrible to have no one to look after one, or to see one, when one is cooped up in a wretched hotel. I hope to go out tomorrow.

I had a very nice letter from Constance yesterday. Ever yours   o. w.

Constance had gone into a private clinic just outside Genoa at the beginning of April for an operation to relieve her spinal problems. She survived the operation but died from post-operative complications on 7 April. Shortly beforehand she had reinstated Oscar's allowance of £3 per week and he continued to receive it after her death.

Telegram: To Robert Ross

12 April 1898   *Paris*
Constance is dead. Please come tomorrow and stay at my hotel. Am in great grief.   OSCAR

To Carlos Blacker

[12 or 13 April 1898]   *[Paris]*
My dear Carlos, It is really awful. I don't know what to do. If we had only met once, and kissed each other.

It is too late. How awful life is. How good you were to come at once.

I have gone out as I don't dare to be by myself. Ever yours   OSCAR

To Robert Ross

[Circa 1 May 1898]   *[Paris]*
My dear Robbie, More paper has arrived! How good you are. I really must begin 'The Sphere'.

I enclose you Hargrove's letter: it seems conclusive. Will you show it to Holman? My allowance should begin *now* – May the 1st – but did Holman not understand the circumstances? There was clearly no necessity to write to Adrian at all. He is bound to pay.

Bosie has not gone into his flat yet, but I chose some nice furniture for him at Maples. He will move in tomorrow, I hope. He apparently goes to races every day, and loses of course. As I wrote to Maurice today, he has a faculty of spotting the loser, which, considering that he knows nothing at all about horses, is perfectly astounding.

Ernest has been in Paris again. He invited Bosie to dinner at the Café Anglais – but did not even come to see me. He avoids me with the artificial modesty of the debtor.

Edmond is very smart, and directs his little band of brigands on the Boulevard with great success. His book, *Les Chevaliers du Boulevard*, is begun, but he says he finds poetry very difficult. That promises well for his future as an artist.

I dined with the Thaulows the other night, and on Saturday I went to the *vernissage* at the Salon. Rodin's statue of Balzac is superb – just what a *romancier* is, or should be. The leonine head of a fallen angel, with a dressing-gown. The head is gorgeous, the dressing-gown an entirely unshaped cone of white plaster. People howl with rage over it. A lady who had gazed in horror on it had her attention directed to Rodin himself who was passing by. She was greatly surprised at his appearance. '*Et pourtant il n'a pas l'air méchant*' was her remark.

Do you love Maurice? Ever yours   OSCAR

To Leonard Smithers

[2 May 1898]   *[Paris]*

My dear Smithers, Do you think that a shilling edition (on 'grey paper' but not in 'blunt type') would sell? – of *The Ballad*. I think so. I suppose the type still stands, so that expense is saved. The cover should be grey with red letters – vermilion – and at the end we might have a good selection of 'press notices'. If someone like Davitt would write a preface it would add to it very much. Could you get an estimate of 1000 copies at 1/-? The poem should still be on *one* side only of the paper, I think, unless the paper is too bad to bear the test of a blank surface. I sent Robbie the *Revue Blanche* for you to look at: a capital review.

Would you kindly let me have *eight* copies of *The Ballad*, and a copy of *Dorian Gray* also, as soon as possible. Ever yours   OSCAR
Did you send Stead a copy?

To Robert Ross

Sunday [8 May 1898]   *[Paris]*

My dear Robbie, Something must be done. Friday and Saturday I had not a penny, and had to stay in my room, and as they only give breakfast at the hotel, *not* dinner, I was dinnerless. My quarter is really due the 18th May: it began the 18th May and was always paid in advance. The November allowance was suppressed, but the February was paid by my wife, and the May is due on the 18th.

In any case, as I would like it always paid through you, could you get someone to advance the money, so as to be paid now, and when it is paid you simply hand over the cheque.

I enclose what seems a legal document. I judge solely from its want of style. Armed with this, surely, dear Robbie, you could get me £30 at least, if not £38.10. I am quite off my balance with want and worries, and have also had to have an operation on my throat, unpaid for yet, except in pain. Ever yours   OSCAR

After his success with Wilde's Ballad, Smithers agreed to publish the two plays which had been running at the time of Wilde's arrest, An Ideal Husband *and* The Importance of Being Earnest *(here referred to by the name of Jack Worthing's fictitious friend 'Bunbury'). They appeared in February and July 1899 respectively, but instead of Wilde's name on the title pages, there appeared only 'By the author of* Lady Windermere's Fan'. *Rowland Strong was the Paris correspondent of the* Observer *to which he sold later in the year Esterhazy's confession of guilt in the Dreyfus affair.*

To Robert Ross

Tuesday [10 May 1898]   [*Paris*]

My dear Robbie, Thanks for the letter of the wicked Holman. By reading between the lines I can discern passionate remorse underlying the apparent coldness.

Personally, as the allowance was from the first paid *in advance*, I cannot understand how the trustees can possibly take on themselves to alter an arrangement made by my wife. I have written, in my nicest style, to Hargrove on the subject.

I have had a very bad time lately, and for two days had not a penny in my pocket, so had to wander about, filled with a wild longing for *bock* and cigarettes: it was really like journeying through Hell. I was in the 'Circle of the Boulevards', one of the worst in the Inferno, and I could only get breakfast here, not dinner, so was dinnerless.

I hope to get a type-written copy of *Bunbury* soon, and to work on it. In type, size, paper, and the like, it should be identical with the other plays, and Shannon should do the cover.

The chance of a popular edition of *The Ballad* depends entirely on Smith's bookstalls.

Bosie is at Nogent, with Strong: very angry because I won't join him. Best love. Ever yours   OSCAR

To Leonard Smithers

Tuesday evening [10 May 1898]   [*Paris*]

My dear Smithers, I have been *seven* times to Cook's, and also went at seven o'clock, two hours after their bank closes, and woke them up. Of course nothing at all had arrived, so I have had no dinner. I hope you had a good one. Ever yours   O. W.

To Robert Ross

Tuesday, 24 May [1898]   [*Paris*]

Dear Robbie, Thanks for your letter. I hope the £10 will arrive tomorrow. It will be a sunlit moment when it does. If it doesn't I am afraid I shall be obliged to telegraph to you daily.

As regards the rooms, the difficulty about taking furnished apartments is this.

If one has *furnished* apartments one is entirely at the mercy of the *propriétaire*, who can ask one to leave whenever he chooses, and all houses in Paris where there are furnished rooms are a form of hotel. Other people live there, and might object to my living at the same address. The *propriétaire* would of course find out my real name and ask me to go.

This would not be a question of my conduct, but of my personality. Besides, he would see all my visitors, and might object to some of them. At the rue Tronchet Bosie had great trouble because Maurice used to stay with him. The proprietor demanded Maurice's name, and said he was bound to take the names of people who passed the night in the house. He also objected to others of Bosie's visitors arriving with him at midnight and leaving at 3.15 in the morning.

Furnished apartments would be impossible for me. I am undisturbed as yet at my hotel, because it is a very poor and unsanitary place. People won't stay there as there is no drainage.

Also, I am very anxious to be able always to breakfast in, and sometimes to dine in: otherwise work is impossible. In furnished apartments one is charged hotel prices, and a furnished flat with a kitchen would cost about £80 a year at least.

If I had an unfurnished flat with a kitchen, I could have, as Bosie has, a woman to come in every morning to clean and cook, and to return, if required, at six o'clock to cook some dinner. The saving is enormous. Such breakfast as I take, a couple of eggs and a cutlet, costs very little if you buy the things yourself.

But the chief point is that, if you take unfurnished rooms, you are your own master. Your visitors go up directly to call on you; the concierge is not seen nor consulted; no one can interfere. I have been several times to see Bosie, and I have not yet seen the concierge. If Bosie could not live in the rue Tronchet, is it likely that I could live anywhere under similar conditions?

At the present moment if the *patron* of the Hôtel d'Alsace asked me to leave, I would have to go at once. Ashton, as you know, was turned out of his hotel by a *commissaire de police* because he was intoxicated. He was in bed at the time, and asleep, and Maurice and I had to dress him and take him out of the hotel at 10.15 at night. The *Juge d'Instruction*, whom I saw personally at the Police Station, told me that the proprietor of furnished rooms could turn out any person he chose, at any time. That is the French law. In unfurnished rooms one can do as one chooses.

So you see that for *me* the only chance I have is to take unfurnished rooms. I don't take them for the purpose of riotous living – lack of money, to put it on the lowest grounds, entails chastity and sobriety – but I do not want to be disturbed, and if Edmond comes to see me at tea-time I don't want the proprietor to question me about his social status.

To suggest I should have visitors of high social position is obvious, and the reason why I cannot have them is obvious also. But, as I said, in unfurnished rooms I can live quietly and at peace. Please seriously consider this point.

Also, my dear Robbie, do not listen to stories about my being expelled from Paris; they are childish. I live a very ordinary life. I go to cafés like Pousset's where I meet artists and writers. I don't frequent places like the Café de la Paix. I dine in modest restaurants for two or three francs. My life is rather dull. I cannot flaunt or dash about: I have not got the money, nor the clothes. When I can I go to the Quartier Latin under the wing of a poet, and talk about art.

I suppose Carlos is the author of the *canard*? It is unkind of him. Ever yours   OSCAR

To Robert Ross

[Circa 28 May 1898]   *[Paris]*

My dear Robbie, A thousand thanks for the cheque. May I ask *when* the June £10 comes due? Of course the 1st of the month; otherwise I will never be able to keep my accounts straight.

Of course nothing can be done about rooms till you decide, and have the collection for the sweet sinner of England in hand, but I still suspect you of having a flat of some kind concealed about your person. My instinct in such points is unerring.

I wish you would write and tell me how much you love Maurice. He is a great dear, and loves us all, a born Catholic in romance; he is always talking of you and Reggie.

Yesterday he and I and Bosie went to the Salon. As modern art had a chastening effect on Maurice, and he seemed sad, we went afterwards to the *Foire aux Invalides*, where Maurice won a knife, by foolishly throwing a ring over something.

Robert Sherard is here. On Wednesday he created a horrible scene in Campbell's Bar by bawling out '*A bas les juifs*', and insulting and assaulting someone whom he said was a Jew. The fight continued in the street, and Robert tried to create an Anti-Semite, Anti-Dreyfusard demonstration. He succeeded, and was ultimately felled to the ground by the Jew!

Bosie and I met him at Campbell's by chance on the next day. Campbell told him that the only reason he would consent to serve him was that Bosie and I had shaken hands with him! This rather amused me, when I remember Robert's monstrous moralising about us, and how nobody should know us. Robert looked quite dreadful, all covered with cigar-ash, stains of spilt whiskey, and mud. He was unshaven, and his face in a dreadful state. He had no money, and borrowed a franc from Bosie.

Yesterday he turned up again, and had to receive a rather insolent lecture from Campbell, who told him he preferred Jews to drunkards in his bar. He was much depressed, so of course I gave him drinks and cigarettes and all he wanted. To show his gratitude he insisted on reciting *The Ballad of Reading Gaol*, at the top of his voice, and assuring me that I was '*le plus grand maître de la littérature moderne, et le plus grand homme du monde*'. At the end he got very tedious, and lest I might love my poem less than I wish to, I went away. Poor Robert, he really is quite insane, and unbearable, except to very old friends who bear much. He begged me to lunch with him and to bring Maurice, but I declined, feigning temporary good health as my excuse! His asking me to bring Maurice was astounding, as when he was last in Paris he refused to call on me because M. was staying with me, and generally was offensive about a lovely and loveable friendship. He has gone to the country today; I hope he will get better. Years ago he was a very good and dear fellow.

I dined last night with Robert d'Humières, a very charming young Frenchman, whom I first met, years ago, at Frank Schuster's. He had asked a poet to meet me, and I believe I was rather wonderful.

I liked the review you sent me immensely. Do you know the writer? It is a very good appreciation.

This letter seems not at all business-like, but Maurice's account of you has somewhat disturbed the severe Spartan Ideal I had formed of you lately. Ever yours   OSCAR

Georgina Weldon was a well-known, eccentric London figure in the 1880s when Wilde had corresponded briefly with her. She was largely responsible for securing the reform of the Lunacy Act under which unscrupulous husbands could have wives committed rather than go through expensive and troublesome divorce proceedings. She had written to Wilde a few days before to say, as she recorded in her diary, 'that, as he had given up his insane and unnatural penchants, I did not see any reason why an old lady like me should hold him at arm's distance and that, if he wished, I would see him when I came to Paris'.

To Georgina Weldon

31 May 1898   *Hôtel d'Alsace*

My dear Mrs Weldon, So Philip Treherne is your nephew! When he gave me his card I wondered if he was kith and kin with that lady whom friends of mine remember as the 'beautiful Miss Treherne' and whom the world will always remember as Mrs Weldon. But we talked of books and art and the idea passed from my mind. How cultivated he is! and so well bred in his nice quiet gravity and courteous ways. I enjoyed my meeting with him very much and hope he will do well in literature. At present he has perhaps just a little too much appreciation of other people's work to be able to realise his own creative energy, but admiration is the portal to all great things.

Yes: I think that, aided by some splendid personalities like Davitt and John Burns, I have been able to deal a heavy and fatal blow at the monstrous prison-system of English justice. There is to be no more starvation, nor sleeplessness, nor endless silence, nor eternal solitude, nor brutal floggings. The system is exposed, and, so, doomed. But it is difficult to teach the

English either pity or humanity. They learn slowly. Next, the power of Judges (an extremely ignorant set of men – ignorant, that is, of what they are doing, their power to inflict the most barbarous sentences on those who are brought before them) must be limited. A Judge, at present, will send a man to two years' hard labour or to five years' penal servitude with utter callousness, not knowing that all such sentences are sentences of death. It is the lack of imagination in the Anglo-Saxon race that makes the race so stupidly, harshly cruel. Those who are bringing about Prison Reform in Parliament are Celtic to a man. For every Celt has inborn imagination.

For myself, of course, the aim of life is to realise one's *own* personality – one's *own* nature, and now, as before, it is through Art that I realise what is in me. I hope soon to begin a new play, but poverty with its degrading preoccupation with money, the loss of many friends, the deprivation of my children, by a most unjust law, by a most unjust Judge, the terrible effects of two years of silence, solitude and ill-treatment – all these have, of course, to a large extent, killed if not entirely that great joy in living that I once had. However, I must try, and the details of Prison Reform will have to be worked out by others. I put the fly in motion but I cannot drive the wheels. It is enough for me that the thing is coming and that what I suffered will not be suffered by others. That makes me happy.

One word more. Your letter gave me great pleasure, but when you allude to my life being in some respects 'unnatural and insane' you are judging of the life of another by an alien standard. Those very expressions – *unnatural and insane* – were often used of you in reference to your conduct as a wife with duties of affection, and a woman, with duties of rational conduct. You know that they were unjustly so used. I know it too. But there were many who had a different estimate: there are many still who have a different estimate. They make the harsh error of judging another person's life without understanding it. Do not you – of all people – commit the same error. Charity is not a sentimental emotion: it is the only method by which the soul can attain to any knowledge – to any wisdom. Very sincerely yours

OSCAR WILDE

To Robert Ross

1 June 1898   *[Paris]*

My dear Robbie, People who repent in sackcloth are dreary, but those who repent in a suit by Doré, and intend this suit for another, are worthy of Paradise. It is most sweet of you, and the colour I would like is *blue*, like the suit I had last year.

A rather painful fact, apparent to all, must now be disclosed. Pray mention it to no one but Doré, and break it to him gently. I am distinctly stouter than I was when the last suit was made. I should say a good inch and a half. I *can* still button the old Doré suit, but it is tight, and the two lower buttons drag. I would like the same stuff, if possible; it is such good stuff, and has lasted so well.

Bosie is now inseparable from Maurice; they have gone again to Nogent. I made Maurice put a postscript into a rather silly letter, inspired by Bosie, which he sent off to you today. I think letters of that kind quite stupid and witless, but Bosie has no real enjoyment of a joke unless he thinks there is a good chance of the other person being pained or annoyed. It is an entirely English trait, the English type and symbol of a joke being the jug on the half-opened door, or the distribution of orange-peel on the pavement of a crowded thoroughfare.

I hope that the beautiful blue suit will be brought over by either you or Reggie. If not, let Smithers be told that the duty is his. I hear that the Custom House is exorbitant, and sends you papers on which they have thrown sand.

I find I have written the beginning of a letter to a French poet on the other side of this, so cannot write more. Fabulet is the author of *La Crise*, an attempt at an anarchical poem, a dull thing at best. Ever yours   OSCAR

To Robert Ross

[Early June 1898]   [Paris]

My dear Robbie, Thanks so much for cheque.

I hope you replaced Oxford in the right way. It is sad to think I may have of disciples 'but few or none' in that sweet grey city that nurtured me.

Georgette Leblanc, Maeterlinck's mistress, sent me seats last night for *Sapho* at the Opéra Comique. She is one of the most wonderful artists I ever saw. The music meandered aimlessly about, as Massenet's usually does, with endless false alarms of a real melody, and incessant posing of themes that are not resolved into any development, but her acting was really a marvel. Bosie was with me, and she looked at us with wonderful eyes, and on her 'calls' gave us her bows to the exclusion of the rest of a crowded house. Bosie was seated next a *German* who exhaled in strange gusts the most extraordinary odours, some of them racial (it is smell that differentiates races); others connected with all kinds of trades from leather-dressing and carpentry, to vitriol-works and the keeping of an Italian warehouse; others such as are found only among '*les mangeurs des choses immondes*'; others connected with gas, fuel, and candles. In the last act he became like a petroleum lamp. Bosie bore it very well indeed: but had practically to sit in my pocket.

Maurice, unfortunately under the influence of his mother, who seems to be devoted to betting, spends all his days at suburban race-courses. Of course he always wins: he is a child of the Sun, not a σεληνιζόμενος [moon-struck] as you and I are, but in spite of betting, and 'spotting the winner', the curves of his mouth are more wonderful than ever. His mouth, when he talks, and he is never silent, is the most beautiful mouth I know. It has the curves of Greek art and English flowers.

Bosie preys on his *femme-de-ménage*, who now pays for everything, including cigars. When he gives his orders she 'looks upon the wondering sky with unreproachful stare', she is so bewildered. She apparently thought that Bosie was going to pay for everything. Of course she finds that that is out of the question. Her psychological condition is extraordinary.

Edmond tells me he wrote you an absurd letter. I *can't* understand why he called with a young champion bicyclist. Ever yours   OSCAR

To Frank Harris

[Postmark 13 August 1898]   *Hôtel d'Alsace*
My dear Frank, How are you? I read your appreciation of Rodin's 'Balzac' with immense pleasure, and am looking forward to more Shakespeare. You will of course put all your Shakespearean essays into a book, and, equally of course, I must have a copy. It is a great era in Shakespearean criticism, the first time that one has looked in the plays, not for philosophy, for there is none, but for the wonder of a great personality – something far better, and far more mysterious, than any philosophy. It is a great thing that you have done. I remember writing once in *Intentions* that the more objective a work of art is in form, the more subjective it really is in matter, and that it is only when you give the poet a mask that he can tell you the truth. But you have shown it fully in the case of the one artist whose personality was supposed to be a mystery of deep seas, a secret as impenetrable as the secret of the moon.

Paris is terrible in its heat. I walk in streets of brass, and there is no one here. Even the criminal classes have gone to the seaside, and the *gendarmes* yawn and regret their enforced idleness. Giving wrong directions to English tourists is the only thing that consoles them.

You were most kind and generous last month in letting me have the £10: it gives me just the margin to live on and to live by. May I have it again this month? Or has gold flowed away from you? Ever yours   OSCAR

To Robert Ross

3 October 1898   *Paris*

My dear Robbie, Thanks so much for the £17.10, duly received.

I wish you and Reggie could have stopped in Paris a night, but I hope you will pass some days here on your return. It is ages since I saw Reggie.

Bosie is back from Aix: his mother on leaving gave him £30 to go to Venice with. He of course lost it all at once at the Casino, and arrived in Paris on the proceeds of his sleeve-links. For the moment he is penniless.

Frank Harris is at St Cloud. I have breakfasted and dined with him, of course, many times, and have brought Bosie, to whom Frank is very nice. Frank has bought a hotel at Monaco, and hopes to make lots of money. He wants me to go to a place called Napoule, near Cannes, where he is going to winter. In Paris I certainly do nothing.

Charlie Owen is here, and we all dined one night together. He is really very handsome and amusing. He thinks of going to Japan, and then to winter in India.

Great rows here over Strong selling Esterhazy's confession. He is violently attacked by his old *confrères*, and Robert Sherard writes terrific diatribes.

Do write, and give my love to dear Reg. Ever yours   OSCAR

To Robert Ross

[Circa 23 November 1898]   *Grand Café, 14 boulevard des Capucines, Paris*

My dear Robbie, The clothes are quite charming – suitable to my advanced age. The trousers are too tight round the waist. That is the result of my rarely having good dinners: nothing fattens so much as a dinner at 1 fr. 50, but the blue waistcoat is a dream. Smithers I received in the same parcel. He was quite wonderful, and depraved, went with monsters to the sound of music, but we had a good time, and he was very nice.

Would it bother you if I asked you to let me have my allowance for December now? A wretched inn-keeper at Nogent to whom I owe 100 francs, out of a bill of 300, threatens to sell Reggie's dressing-case, my overcoat, and two suits, if I don't pay him by Saturday. He has been detaining the things, and now threatens a sale. It is less than a week, so perhaps you might manage it without too much worry to yourself.

Sir John was astonishing, went through a romance with an absurd Boulevard boy, who, of course, cheated him, and treated him badly. The reason was that Sir John had given him a suit of clothes – an admirable reason. To undress is romance, to dress, philanthropy. You are quite philanthropic to me, but you are also romantic – the sole instance of the lack of philosophy in clothes. Do let me have a cheque: if you can, by return. Ever yours OSCAR

To Robert Ross

Friday [25 November 1898]   *Paris*
My dear Robbie, I am so sorry about my excuse. I had forgotten I had used Nogent before. It shows the utter collapse of my imagination, and rather distresses me.

Do let me know about Bosie. I suppose that London takes no notice at all: that is the supreme punishment.

I have corrected two-thirds of my proofs, and await the last act. I don't want to make threats, but remember that the dedication is not yet written, and I may write

To
R. B. Ross
in recognition of his good advice.

That would be terrible, so do not lecture till *after Dec. 7th.*

I see a great deal of La Jeunesse, who is more intolerable than ever, and I dined with Strong, who has reduced Maurice to a state of silent frightened idiocy. Dogma without Literature is bad for boys. Ever yours   OSCAR

Wilkinson, a seventeen-year-old Radley schoolboy, had invented the Ipswich Dramatic Society purely to enable him to write to Wilde about dramatising Dorian Gray. *Despite plans to do so, Wilde and Wilkinson never met.*

To Louis Wilkinson

[Postmark 14 December 1898]   *Hôtel d'Alsace*
Dear Mr Wilkinson, Certainly: you can dramatise my play, but please tell me if the version is yours, and how the play is constructed.

Who acts Dorian Gray? He should be beautiful.

My work is so far in your hands that I rely on your artistic instinct that the play shall have some quality of beauty and style.

You can have four performances, and if there should be any notices of the play in papers, pray let me see them.

Your letter of last summer gave me great pleasure. Pray let me know all about yourself. Who are you? What are you doing or going to do? Send me your photograph.

Write to me at the above address, and direct the envelope to *Sebastian Melmoth*, a fantastic name that I shall explain to you some day. Sincerely yours   OSCAR WILDE

Although Harris was in many ways a scoundrel, a liar and a cheat, one of the nicest things about him was his almost unfailing generosity and kindness to Wilde in his years of exile. In the winter of 1898, Harris had offered Wilde a three months' stay on the French Riviera in an attempt to rekindle some of his old desire to write.

To Robert Ross

Wednesday [14 December 1898]

Taverne F. Pousset, 14 boulevard des Italiens, Paris

My dear Robbie, Just a line to say that I leave with Frank Harris for Napoule, near Cannes, tomorrow night. Frank has been most kind, and nice, and, of course, we have dined and lunched together every day at Durand's. At least I lunch at one o'clock, and dine at eight o'clock. Frank arrives at 2.30 and 9.15. It is rather a bore, and no one should make unpunctuality a formal rule, and degrade it to a virtue, but I have admirable, though lonely, meals. Frank insists on my being always at high intellectual pressure; it is most exhausting; but when we arrive at Napoule I am going to break the news to him – now an open secret – that I have softening of the brain, and cannot always be a genius. I shall send you my address tomorrow.

Ashton is with me; he is more penniless than ever, poor dear fellow; and Walter, that snub-nosed little horror, has just gone back to England, so Sir John is sad and sentimental. Ever yours   OSCAR

To Louis Wilkinson

28 December [1898]   *Hôtel des Bains, Napoule*

Dear Mr Wilkinson, Thank you so much for your long and interesting letter. I envy you going to Oxford: it is the most flower-like time of one's life. One sees the shadow of things in silver mirrors. Later on, one sees the Gorgon's head, and one suffers, because it does not turn one to stone.

I am on the Riviera, in blue and gold weather, the sun warm as wine, and apricot-coloured. The little hotel where I am staying is right on the Golfe de Juan, and all round are pine-woods with their pungent breath: the wind growing aromatic as it moves through the branches: one's feet crushing sweetness out of the fallen needles: I wish you were here.

In your second letter you tell me that you enclose your photograph for

me, but no photograph was in the envelope. Your thoughts must have been in the crystal of the moon. Call them back, and let me have your portrait. Sincerely yours
OSCAR WILDE

Mellor, the neurotic son of a Bolton cotton spinner, was a wealthy young man living at Gland on Lake Geneva. Wilde went to stay with him in the spring, happy to accept his hospitality but quick to criticise him in correspondence with friends. From this time on Wilde's money worries dominated his life, compromising his integrity as well as his friendships. He even managed, rather unscrupulously, to sell the scenario of his play Mr and Mrs Daventry *(see p. 176) to at least four people including Frank Harris, who to his annoyance was forced to pay some of the others out when he wrote it up and produced it in October 1900.*

To Robert Ross

2 January 1899
Napoule

My dear Robbie, The cheque on Cook arrived this morning: many thanks. The proprietor was looking a little anxious – rather yellow in fact – but has now quite regained his spirits, as I have told him I shall pay him this afternoon.

No sign yet of Frank Harris: it is a great bore. There is a charming fellow called Harold Mellor (sent away from Harrow at the age of fourteen for being loved by the captain of the cricket eleven) who is staying with his mother near Cannes, and comes over on his bicycle to breakfast every morning. He is about twenty-six, but looks younger. Sometimes a very pretty, slim, fair-haired Italian boy bicycles over with him. His name is *Eolo*; his father, who sold him to Harold for 200 lire, having christened all his children – seventeen in number – out of the *Mythological Dictionary*. Harold is a nice fellow, but his boy bores him. It is dreadfully sad.

He took me to Nice on Friday and we saw Sarah in *La Tosca*. I went round to see Sarah and she embraced me and wept, and I wept, and the whole evening was wonderful. I wish to goodness you would come here. I need you immensely. As regards my marrying again, I am quite sure that you will want me to marry this time some sensible, practical, plain, middle-aged boy, and I don't like the idea at all. Besides I am practically engaged to a fisherman of extraordinary beauty, age eighteen. So you see there are difficulties.

Love to Reggie. Ever yours
OSCAR

To Reginald Turner

[Postmark 19 January 1899]   *Hôtel des Bains, Napoule*

My dear Reggie, I was charmed to hear from you, but it is absurd your being in bad spirits about Life. You used to be such a light-hearted lad. The influence of the *DT* is obviously of the worst kind.

I am still sitting on porphyry rocks, or roaming through pine-woods. Occasionally my friend Harold Mellor orders a bottle of Pommery for dinner. Then the exquisite taste of ancient life comes back to me. And twice a week I look at the shop-windows in Cannes.

The weather is lovely, and the mimosa in flower – such powdered gold-dust dancing in the sun, the dainty feather-like leaves always tremulous with joy.

I am very anxious to go to Corsica. Would you like a long Corsican knife marked '*Vendetta*'? They are deadly and inexpensive, and you have many friends. It might be useful.

If you hear any news of poor Sir John do let me know. Ever yours

OSCAR

To Robert Ross

2 February 1899   *Napoule*

My dear Robbie, Thank you for the cheque, duly received. Your account of Henry James has much amused Frank Harris: it is a delightful story for your memorabilia.

Today, for the first time, rain – quite an Irish day. Yesterday was lovely. I went to Cannes to see the *Bataille des Fleurs*. The loveliest carriage – all yellow roses, the horses with traces and harness of violets – was occupied by an evil-looking old man, English: on the box, beside the coachman, sat his valet, a very handsome boy, all wreathed with flowers. I murmured 'Imperial, Neronian Rome'.

I have signed the copies of the play for Smithers, a 'Japanese' for you. Smithers will show you my list: if I have forgotten anyone, let me know. Of course dear More Adey has a 'large-paper': and also Reggie.

Harold Mellor will be in London at the end of the month. He is going there to get me some neckties. I have asked him to write and let you know. He is a charming fellow, very cultivated, though he finds that Literature is an inadequate expression of Life. That is quite true: but a work of Art is an adequate expression of Art; that is its aim. Only that. Life is merely the *motif* of a pattern. I hope all things are well with you. Frank Harris is upstairs,

thinking about Shakespeare at the top of his voice. I am earnestly idling.
Ever yours   OSCAR

To Reginald Turner

[Postmark 3 February 1899]   *Hôtel des Bains, Napoule*
My dear Reggie, I hope you are in better spirits. Poor dear Sir John was
always in the best spirits (and water): the most good-hearted of the alcoholic.
Life goes on very pleasantly here. Frank Harris is of course exhausting. After
our literary talk in the evening I stagger to my room, bathed in perspiration.
I believe he talks the Rugby game.

Max's caricature in the *Chronicle* is a masterpiece – as far as George Moore
goes: it is a most brilliant and bitter rendering of that vague formless obscene
face. The Archer is *manqué* – not at all like. I showed the drawing to Frank,
who was in ecstasies over the Moore, and would like to have a replica of it
by Max.

I am sending you, of course, a copy of my book. It was extraordinary
reading the play over. How I used to toy with that tiger Life! I hope you
will find a place for me amongst your nicest books, not near anything by
Hichens or George Moore. I should like it to be within speaking distance of
Dorian Gray. You will also get a copy addressed to Charlie Hickey. How is
that dear boy? I wish you would import him.

There is a *Carnaval* at Nice on Sunday. I hope to run over: on Sundays
there are no confetti, which is a blessing. Ever yours   OSCAR

To Frank Harris

[Circa 22 February 1899]   *Hôtel Terminus & Cosmopolitain, Monte Carlo*
My dear Frank, I am in great trouble, and am obliged to come over to
Monte Carlo and see you.

As I was, of course, unable to leave the hotel at Nice, not having enough
money to pay the whole bill last Saturday, I have been forced to stay on,
and to have my meals at *table-d'hôte*, though naturally at a separate table.
The middle-class English who are at the hotel have objected to my presence,
and this morning I was presented with my bill and requested to leave by
twelve o'clock.

I declined to do this, and said I could not pay the bill today. They have
given me till tomorrow at noon, and have asked me not to have my meals
in the hotel, so I have come over to Monte Carlo, having raised ten francs
on my ring.

You have not forgotten that you invited me to spend three months on the Riviera as your guest. My bill at Napoule for eight weeks amounted to £35, of which you gave me £30, and I cannot think that it was very extravagant of me. The choice of Napoule was yours, and £4 a week is not very extravagant. Of course at Nice it is different. My bill is forty francs a day at the hotel. You asked me to go there, and to look out for a villa for you. My one anxiety has been to leave the place, but I have not been able. Now I am turned out, and everyone at the hotel knows it. My dear Frank, you must come down and see me here for a few moments. You cannot, and you will not, abandon me. I won't go to the Palace, because it would not be good for your hotel for me to be seen there. This little place is quiet. Please come. Ever yours   o. w.

To Robert Ross

[Circa 1 March 1899]   *Gland, Canton Vaud, Switzerland*
My dear Robbie, Thanks for your charming letter, which I found waiting for me here on my arrival from Genoa yesterday.

It was a great pleasure writing your name on the page of dedication. I only wish it was a more wonderful work of art – of higher seriousness of intent – but it has some amusing things in it, and I think the tone and temper of the whole thing bright and happy.

I went to Genoa to see Constance's grave. It is very pretty – a marble cross with dark ivy-leaves inlaid in a good pattern. The cemetery is a garden at the foot of the lovely hills that climb into the mountains that girdle Genoa. It was very tragic seeing her name carved on a tomb – her surname, my name, not mentioned of course – just 'Constance Mary, daughter of Horace Lloyd, QC' and a verse from *Revelations*. I brought some flowers. I was deeply affected – with a sense, also, of the uselessness of all regrets. Nothing could have been otherwise, and Life is a very terrible thing.

This is a pretty house on the Lake. We look over to the snows and hills of Savoy. Geneva is half an hour by rail. You are to come whenever you like. April is lovely here, I believe, and flaunts in flowers.

There is an Italian cook, also the lad Eolo, who waits at table. His father told Mellor at Spezia that he was christened Eolo because he was born on a night on which there was a dreadful wind! I think it is rather nice to have thought of such a name. An English peasant would probably have said 'We called him John, sir, because we were getting in the hay at the time'.

There is no truth at all in Sedger's advertisement, and I am very angry about it. It is quite monstrous. My only chance is a play produced anonymously.

Otherwise the First Night would be a horror, and people would find meanings in every phrase.

I am going to try a bicycle. I have never forgotten the lesson you so kindly gave me: even my leg remembers it.

Do write again soon. Have I forgotten anyone to whom I should send a copy? Ever yours   OSCAR

To More Adey

[March 1899]   *Gland, Switzerland*

My dear More, I am so glad you liked the play, and that it arrived safe. As a rule Smithers suppresses all my presentation copies. I am staying, as I dare say you know, in a villa on the Lake of Geneva. There is much beauty of an obvious, old-fashioned kind – snow-capped mountains, blue sky, pine-trees and the like. But the sunlight is golden: brazen rather. I don't like my host, and the Swiss are so ugly to look at that it conveys melancholy into all my days.

I am much interested to hear of your book on Dante. I have not read Dante for ages: it is a great pity. He is the supreme modern poet: Greek tragedy deals with the elemental difficulties of life – the terrible things external to us – but in Dante are all the complexities of the modern soul. Robbie, with ostentatious modesty, has told me nothing about his story at all.

I was very happy on the Riviera – lovely weather – and at Nice beautiful people and beautiful flowers. As one nears Italy physical beauty comes running to meet one. At Nice I knew three lads like bronzes, quite perfect in form. English lads are chryselephantine. Swiss people are carved out of wood with a rough knife, most of them; the others are carved out of turnips.

I have been reading much of Maupassant lately, and I now find much tenderness in him – a great pity for life. I don't agree with the attacks on him for *brutalité* or the praise of him for it. And *Une Vie* is a masterpiece: Balzac would have been filled with wonder at it. Maupassant always thought that Flaubert was his master, lived and died under that impression, but, of course, his master was Balzac.

There are lovely walks here by the Lake, through the grounds of others: but I am a born trespasser. Prince Napoleon's villa is quite close – the one he used to have. He had lovely bronze and marble statues set everywhere, and a splendid fountain with a bronze centaur strangling a bear from whose gullet rushes the water. Nyon, a little village, is three miles off. I go there on foot daily and have a *bock* and buy French papers.

I often think of your wonderful visits to me when I was in pain, and of your tenderness, and kindness to me. I fear that, in consequence, your stay in the Purgatorio – where the poets are – will be too brief. However, you will find Statius in heaven. I wish he was a better poet. Ever yours   OSCAR

Willie Wilde died on 13 March. He had inherited Moytura House by Loch Corrib on his father's death in 1876 and it now passed by entailment to Oscar since Willie had no male heirs. The bankruptcy receiver eventually got wind of the inheritance and sold it a year after Oscar's death to pay off some of his debts.

To Robert Ross

Wednesday [15 March 1899]   *Gland, Switzerland*

My dear Robbie, Thank you very much for your thoughtfulness in wiring to me about my brother's death. I suppose it had been expected for some time. I am very sorry for his wife, who, I suppose, has little left to live on. Between him and me there had been, as you know, wide chasms for many years. *Requiescat in Pace.*

I don't know what position I hold about this absurd Irish property. It comes to me by entail, but I suppose my creditors will claim it. I wish I had asked for my discharge. It was most foolish of me not to. Could you ask some solicitor what is likely to be done? If I could sell it for a fair sum, and have the money, I would give my sister-in-law something of course, but I don't know if I can sell.

I hope to write more tomorrow. I don't like Mellor very much, and would like to get away, but, at present, it is impossible. Ever yours   O. W.

To Reginald Turner

[Postmark 20 March 1899]   *Gland, Switzerland*

My dear Reggie, Thanks so much for your letter. I am delighted you are pleased with your copy of the play. I like the play's irresponsibility and its *obiter dicta*, but it is essentially an acting play: it should have been a classic for the English Theatre, but alas! the author was struck by madness from the moon.

Did you get the copy for Charlie Hickey? I wrote his name on a flyleaf, and sent it to Smithers to be forwarded to you.

Here the weather is bright and sunny. Across the Lake I see Mont Blanc, showing above the Savoy mountains: but it has lost the virginity of the snows: spinsters and curates climb it: its terrors are over.

The villa is pretty and comfortable: but I don't like Mellor: he is a silent, dull person, cautious, and economical: revolting Swiss wines appear at meals: he is complex without being interesting: has Greek loves, and is rather ashamed of them: has heaps of money, and lives in terror of poverty: so I regard it as a sort of Swiss *pension*, where there is no weekly bill.

I have been twice to Geneva, which is beautifully situated and full of swans and bridges, but the Swiss are really too ugly. I feel sure that the reason they have produced nobody – except sterile things like Amiel and *Obermann* – is their lack of physical beauty: they never gain an impulse from the vision of perfection of form: life is robbed of its first great element: the people are formless, colourless; one longs for Italy, or England, where beauty walks in the sun.

I read a great deal, and correct the proofs of *An Ideal Husband*, shortly to appear. It reads rather well, and some of its passages seem prophetic of tragedy to come.

On my way I stopped at Genoa, where I met a beautiful young actor, a Florentine, whom I wildly loved. He has the strange name of Didaco. He had the look of Romeo, without Romeo's sadness: a face chiselled for high romance. We spent three days together.

Write and tell me some of your adventures, and what new stars have crossed your way. Are you in love? If not, why not?

I don't know how long I shall stay here. I can't get away, having neither gold nor silver. I wait on Fortune, like a discarded lover. Ever yours   OSCAR

To Robert Ross

Tuesday [21 March 1899]   *Gland, Switzerland*
My dear Robbie, Thank you so much for your long letter. For the first time in my life I was glad that your handwriting was illegible, so I was able to miss a lot, or rather forced to.

The position is this. Moytura is entailed on me, but not beyond me. One can only entail I believe for two lives: in this case my brother's and mine. So the place is mine to sell, and should fetch £3000 or a little more. It is beautifully situated, and there are lovely trees etc.

As regards my bankruptcy, if my *trustees* heard of it, they would no doubt try to seize it. I fancy I had best remain passive, and receive the rents, such as they are. My brother was bankrupt, and received the rents. Why should not I? The only thing is to ascertain *how* the rents are paid, whether through an agent or not. This my sister-in-law would be able to tell you. I would be ready to give her £40 a year, if I received £140 (gross), as she has a child. The whole affair is a great bore. I wonder whether a private sale would be illegal. Of course, what one wants is a solicitor who will be able to show how one can escape the law. In gaining legal possession of an entailed estate I wonder has one to go to a Court of Probate? I wonder does the Court of Bankruptcy take cognisance of anything without a creditor applying? But I have not much hope of anything good. However, one can try.

I dislike Mellor, because he is unsocial, taciturn, wretched company, and taking no pains to please or gratify his guest. He is very well off, but absurdly mean in everything. He gives me at dinner the most horrid Swiss *vin ordinaire*, though he has a capital cellar, and is quite amused by the fact that I don't like it. There is insanity in his family. His mother is under restraint, and his brother went mad and killed himself. His own insanity is misanthropy, and meanness. I am philosophic about it now; indeed we only meet at meals. In the evening he reads *The Times*, or sleeps – both audibly. But I should love to get away.

I never dreamed of having Smithers to bring alcoholic experience to bear on my affairs. It was a joke.

I shall write to Arthur, and also to my sister-in-law. If you see her, you need not say anything about my proposal to give her £40 a year, if I get £140. There is no necessity to worry you too much. The weather here is bright and sunny, but cold; snow has fallen on the mountains. Ever yours

OSCAR

To Robert Ross

[29 March 1899]   *Gland, Switzerland*

My dear Robbie, Thanks so much for the cheque. I hope to be able to 'toucher' (excellent expression) on Saturday. If so, I shall leave for Genoa on Sunday morning.

I could not stay any longer at Mellor's: he really is too insane, and impossible. I never disliked anyone so thoroughly. My visit has taught me a curious and bitter lesson. I used to rely on my personality: now I know that my personality really rested on the fiction of *position*. Having lost position, I find my personality of no avail. Mellor has treated me as I would not have treated the most dull and unimportant of the lower middle-classes. I feel very humble, besides feeling very indignant: the former being my intellectual realisation of my position, the latter an emotion that is a 'survival' of old conditions.

I won't go to Paris, because I should spend all my money in no time. I can't live in Paris under £1 a day; it is impossible. Near Genoa I hope to find some little spot, and sunlight counts as half one's income.

Your news about Moytura *are* crushing. That octopus the Law! One cannot escape. I don't know what to do. Do you think that if I applied for my discharge I would get it? It depends on Hargrove. *Could he be sounded?*

Thanks so much for the *Outlook*: it is a good notice, well written.

Could you not come to Genoa? *Do*: for a month. We never see each other now. My address will be Albergo di Firenze, Genoa.

Please write, and please come. Ever yours   OSCAR

To Robert Ross

1 April [1899]   *Café du Nord, Geneva*
My dear Robbie, I have left Gland. Mellor wept at my departure, apologised, implored me to stay, and put his conduct under the aegis of the Hereditary Furies of insanity that beset his race. I really was very sorry for him, but I could not stay. However, we parted amicably on my side, and on his with protestations of admiration and remorse.

I leave tomorrow morning for Genoa – Albergo di Firenze – a small inn on the quay, rather *mal-famé* but cheap. Then I think of some little place in the environs. There is no good my going to Paris; I can't afford to live there.

The only thing I see to do now, is to see what Hargrove will do if I ask for my discharge. Of course if he insists I suppose everything will be seized.

The weather has become very hot – quite summer: I expect Italy will be delightful. Could you not come for three weeks to Genoa? I never see you. You would do me no end of good. And there is More, who is apparently sentenced to life-long imprisonment in Great Britain: cannot he get away? I should love to have you both near at hand for a little. It would be delightful. Please do this. I believe that at the holy season of Easter one is supposed to forgive all one's friends.

I hope to find at Genoa, waiting for me, a young lad, by name Edoardo Rolla, one of the sea-farers. He has fair hair, and is always in dark blue. I have written to him. After the chill virginity of Swiss Alps and snow, I long for the red flowers of life that stain the feet of summer in Italy. Ever yours

O. W.

To Frances Forbes-Robertson

[Mid-May 1899]   *Hôtel Marsollier, rue Marsollier, Paris*
My dear, sweet, beautiful Friend, Eric has just sent me your charming letter, and I am delighted to have a chance of sending you my congratulations on your marriage, and all the good wishes of one who has always loved and

admired you. I met Eric by chance, and he told me he had been over to the marriage. He was as picturesque and sweet as usual, but more than usually vague. I was quite furious with him. He could not quite remember who it was you had married, or whether he was fair or dark, young or old, tall or small. He could not remember where you were married, or what you wore, or whether you looked more than usually beautiful. He said there were a great many people at the wedding, but could not remember their names. He remembered, however, Johnston being present. He spoke of the whole thing as a sort of landscape in a morning mist. Your husband's name he could not for the moment recall: but said he thought he had it written down at home. He went dreamily away down the Boulevard followed by violent reproaches from me, but they were no more to him than the sound of flutes: he wore the sweet smile of those who are always looking for the moon at mid-day.

So, dear Frankie, you are married, and your husband is a 'king of men'! That is as it should be: those who wed the daughters of the gods are kings, or become so.

I have nothing to offer you but one of my books, that absurd comedy *The Importance of Being Earnest*, but I send it to you, in the hopes it may live on one of your bookshelves and be allowed to look at you from time to time. Its dress is pretty: it wears Japanese vellum, and belongs to a limited family of *nine*: it is not on speaking terms with the popular edition: it refuses to recognise the poor relations whose value is only seven and sixpence. Such is the pride of birth. It is a lesson.

Ah! how delightful it would be to be with you and your husband in your own home! But my dear child, how could I get to you? Miles of sea, miles of land, the purple of mountains and the silver of rivers divide us: you don't know how poor I am: I have no money at all: I live, or am supposed to live on a few francs a day: a bare remnant saved from shipwreck. Like dear St Francis of Assisi I am wedded to Poverty: but in my case the marriage is not a success: I hate the Bride that has been given to me: I see no beauty in her hunger and her rags: I have not the soul of St Francis: my thirst is for the beauty of life: my desire for its joy. But it was dear of you to ask me, and do tell the 'king of men' how touched and grateful I am by the invitation you and he have sent me.

And, also, sometimes send me a line to tell me of the beauty you have found in life. I live now on echoes as I have little music of my own. Your old friend   OSCAR

In May Wilde had sent Fullerton, the Paris correspondent of The Times, *a copy of* The Importance of Being Earnest, *smartly followed by a letter trying to borrow 100 francs.*

To W. Morton Fullerton

Dimanche, 25 Juin [1899]   *Trouville*

My dear Fullerton, Thanks for your letter, which has just been forwarded to me from Paris. I am glad to say the momentary difficulty I was in has quite passed away. It was not very serious, but it is always a bore to find oneself without pocket-money. Balzac's *héros métallique* still dominates our age, as do indeed all Balzac's heroes; and the French have not yet realised that the basis of all civilisation is unlimited credit. Empires only fall when they have to pay their bills: at that moment the Barbarians arrive.

But what a Johnsonian letter you have written me! 'I grope at the hope that you will not have occasion to put either me or anyone else again into such a position of positive literal chagrin': so might the great lexicographer have written (though perhaps he might have found tautology in 'positive . . . literal'). In so slight a matter, my dear Fullerton, sentiment need not borrow stilts.

I am glad you received my play safely, and were amused by it. It is a bit of nonsense, with style: a form of art the French are rich in, but the English sadly to seek.

So you have been in Stendhal's *patrie*. I fear I don't know where it is; I think of him as *Arrigo Beyle: Milanese* – so, I think, he wished his epitaph to run.

Trouville is boring, so I return to Paris tomorrow or next day, and hope to come across you, but you must not be Johnsonian: Theocritean were better. Sincerely yours   OSCAR WILDE

To Leonard Smithers

[August 1899]   *Hôtel d'Alsace, rue des Beaux-Arts, Paris*
                                                From Sebastian Melmoth

My dear Smithers, I am back at my old hotel: the country was too dear.

I don't know if you have received the proof-sheets yet: you have never acknowledged them. I also think you might have sent me a copy of the book when it appeared. I have only seen it at Galignani's. It looked very nice.

The address of '*Frankie*' in one of the copies is Mrs Harrod, Amlwch, Anglesey, Wales. The other addresses are I think all indicated.

Did you get my letter about Percy and the £300 which is owing to me? It is just a hope.

Also, can you let me have my September allowance in advance? £10. Robbie cannot himself advance it, and I have no money at all. I am in a dreadful state, as all my clothes are at the Hôtel Marsollier, where I owe a bill. I am really in the gutter.

Do send me *at once* a cheque on Betts. Since Sunday I have only had seven francs to live on. Ever yours   OSCAR

To Arthur L. Humphreys

Sunday [August 1899]   *Hôtel d'Alsace*
My dear Humphreys, I am so glad you received your copy of my play all right. I think it looks very nice in its pale purple and noble gold. I hope it will do well, but I don't think the reviewers have written anything yet. It is very horrid of them, and very stupid.

I was greatly delighted, I need hardly tell you, with what you wrote about my work in your monthly message, and the footnote was admirable. If the critics had your sense of literature and of life they would treat me in a different manner.

Paris is burning hot – streets of brass in which the passers – few in number – crawl like black flies. I wish I had the means to go away, but I am in dreadful want – no money at all. I wonder would you lend me £5? If you could I think you would. I have been passing through a terrible time. Sincerely yours   OSCAR WILDE

Lewis Waller had produced An Ideal Husband *in 1895 and acted in it with his wife Florence. They had also toured* A Woman of No Importance *for Beerbohm Tree in 1893, of which they now appear to have given a few more performances.*

To Florence Waller

[?December 1899]   *Grand Café, 14 boulevard des Capucines, Paris*
Dear Mrs Waller, Thanks so much for your letter. I heard from many of my friends how wonderfully the play went, and how really great you and your husband were in the last act. The general silence of the papers is ignoble, and unjust to you as to me.

Yes, I shall be here all the month. Last year I was on the Riviera with roses, but this year I fear I shall have to stay in the icy north. One can't get railway-tickets on credit: it is such a bore!

It will be a great pleasure to see you again. You shall retell me your triumphs. Sincerely yours OSCAR WILDE

To George Ives

12 February [1900] *Hôtel d'Alsace*
My dear George, Thank you for the article, which is very suggestive and interesting.

Do, when again, if ever, you come to Paris let me know, and also let me know your address. Don't have with *me* the silly mania for secrecy that makes you miss the value of things: to you it is of more importance to conceal your address from a friend, than to see your friend.

You called on me twice, but would not leave either your name or address with the concierge: please don't do that again: I dislike to be told that a young man – you are still young of aspect – called twice, and refused to give his name. It annoys me.

Also, when you send me a *petit bleu* to ask me to make an appointment with you, please put your address: otherwise I can't reply. I received your *dépêche* all right, but could not answer.

As regards seeing you in private in preference to seeing you in public, the matter is indifferent to me as far as the place is concerned. It is a pleasure to me to see you. I don't invite my friends to my hotel because my room is cold and uncomfortable and I dislike it. The ordinary meeting-places are clubs in London and cafés in Paris. You must not imagine that people in cafés listen to the conversation of others; nobody bothers to do anything of the kind. People in life listen primarily to their own conversation, then to the conversation of the person or persons with whom they are, if the latter are interesting.

Your proposal that I should breakfast with you in a cabaret the other side of the Arc de Triomphe, frequented, you said, only by *cochers de fiacre* was too appalling. There are seemly inexpensive restaurants in proper quarters where two gentlemen can breakfast quietly, without the noisy and vulgar surroundings of your cabmen.

Nor, finally, have you and I, when we meet, to discuss business, which often requires privacy of a severe kind. I like to talk to you about literature, life, the progress of thought, its power to touch the world, its practical energy – subjects of no interest to others than ourselves. It is not necessary to go to a remote cabman's shelter for such discussions.

On the whole, George, you are a great baby. One can't help being angry with you. Ever yours OSCAR

In January Robert Sherard had found Ernest Dowson penniless and ill in a garret on the Euston Road. He took him back to his own house in Catford where he and his wife nursed Dowson for a month. But self-neglect, drink and depression had taken their toll and Dowson died in Sherard's arms on 23 February. The artist Althea Gyles illustrated an edition of Wilde's poem 'The Harlot's House' which Smithers pirated in 1904.

To Leonard Smithers

[Circa 24 February 1900]   [Paris]

My dear Smithers, I am greatly distressed to hear of Ernest's death: how sudden it must have been! Poor wounded wonderful fellow that he was, a tragic reproduction of all tragic poetry, like a symbol, or a scene. I hope bay-leaves will be laid on his tomb, and rue, and myrtle too, for he knew what love is.

He was a sweet singer, with a note all the lovelier because it reminds us of how thrushes sang in Shakespeare's day. If he is not yet laid to rest or unrest, do put some flowers for me on his grave.

I have been very ill, in bed since Monday, some disease with a hybrid-Greek name: it attacks the throat and the soul.

How is Althea? Has she still the green wand? Ever yours   OSCAR WILDE

To Robert Ross

Wednesday [?28 February 1900]   *Hôtel d'Alsace*

My dear Robbie, How could I have written to you during the last three months considering that I have been in bed since last Monday. I am very ill and the doctor is making all kinds of experiments. My throat is a lime kiln, my brain a furnace and my nerves a coil of angry adders. I am apparently in much the same state as yourself.

Maurice – you remember Maurice? – has kindly come to see me and I've shared all my medicines with him, shown him what little hospitality I can. We are both horrified to hear that Bosie's suspicions of you are quite justified. That and your being a Protestant make you terribly *unique* (I have told Maurice how to spell the last word as I was afraid that he might have used a word which often occurs in the Protestant bible).

Aleck lunched with Bosie and me one day and I lunched alone with him another. He was most friendly and pleasant and gave me a depressing account of you. I see that you, like myself, have become a *neurasthenic*. I have been so for four months, quite unable to get out of bed till the afternoon, quite unable to write letters of any kind. My doctor has been trying to cure me with arsenic and strychnine but without much success, as I became poisoned through eating mussels, so you see what an exacting and tragic life I have been leading. Poisoning by mussels is very painful and when one has one's bath one looks like a leopard. Pray never eat mussels.

As soon as I get well I'll write you a long letter, though your letter asking me to stay with you in Rome never reached me.

Thanks so much for the cheque, but your letter was really too horrid. With love, ever yours   OSCAR

To Robert Ross

16 April [1900]   *c/o Cook & Son, Piazza di Spagna, Rome*
My dear Robbie, I simply cannot write. It is too horrid, not of me, but to me. It is a mode of paralysis – a *cacoethes tacendi* [craving for silence] – the one form that malady takes in me.

Well, all passed over very successfully. Palermo, where we stayed eight days, was lovely. The most beautifully situated town in the world, it dreams away its life in the Conca d'Oro, the exquisite valley that lies between two seas. The lemon-groves and the orange-gardens were so entirely perfect that I became again a Pre-Raphaelite, and loathed the ordinary Impressionists, whose muddy souls and blurred intelligences would have rendered but by mud and blur those 'golden lamps hung in a green night' that filled me with such joy. The elaborate and exquisite detail of the true Pre-Raphaelites is the compensation they offer us for the absence of motion; Literature and Music being the only arts that are not immobile.

Then nowhere, not even at Ravenna, have I seen such mosaics. In the Cappella Palatina, which from pavement to domed ceilings is all gold, one really feels as if one was sitting in the heart of a great honeycomb *looking* at angels singing; and looking at angels, or indeed at people singing, is much nicer than listening to them. For this reason the great artists always give to their angels lutes without strings, pipes without vent-holes, and reeds through which no wind can wander or make whistlings.

Monreale you have heard of, with its cloisters and cathedral. We often drove there, the *cocchieri* most dainty finely-carved boys. In them, not in the Sicilian horses, is race seen. The most favoured were Manuele, Francesco, and Salvatore. I loved them all, but only remember Manuele.

I also made great friends with a young Seminarist who lived *in* the Cathedral of Palermo, he and eleven others in little rooms beneath the roof, like birds.

Every day he showed me all over the Cathedral, and I really knelt before the huge porphyry sarcophagus in which Frederick the Second lies. It is a sublime bare monstrous thing, blood-coloured, and held up by lions, who have caught some of the rage of the great Emperor's restless soul. At first, my young friend, Giuseppe Loverde by name, gave *me* information: but on the third day I gave information to him, and re-wrote History as usual, and told him all about the Supreme King and his Court of Poets, and the terrible book that he never wrote. Giuseppe was fifteen, and most sweet. His reason for entering the Church was singularly mediaeval. I asked him why he thought of becoming a *clerico*: and how.

He answered 'My father is a cook, and most poor, and we are many at home, so it seemed to me a good thing that there should be in so small a house as ours one mouth less to feed, for, though I am slim, I eat much: too much, alas! I fear.'

I told him to be comforted, because God used poverty often as a means of bringing people to Him, and used riches never, or but rarely. So Giuseppe was comforted, and I gave him a little book of devotion, very pretty, and with far more pictures than prayers in it; so of great service to Giuseppe, whose eyes are beautiful. I also gave him many *lire*, and prophesied for him a Cardinal's hat, if he remained very good, and never forgot me. He said he never would: and indeed I don't think he will, for every day I kissed him behind the high altar.

At Naples we stopped three days. Most of my friends are, as you know, in prison, but I met some of nice memory, and fell in love with a Sea-God, who for some extraordinary reason is at the Regia Marina School, instead of being with Triton.

We came to Rome on Holy Thursday. H. M. left on Saturday for Gland, and yesterday, to the terror of Grissell and all the Papal Court, I appeared in the front rank of the pilgrims in the Vatican, and got the blessing of the Holy Father – a blessing they would have denied me.

He was wonderful as he was carried past me on his throne, not of flesh and blood, but a white soul robed in white, and an artist as well as a saint – the only instance in History, if the newspapers are to be believed.

I have seen nothing like the extraordinary grace of his gesture, as he rose, from moment to moment, to bless – possibly the pilgrims, but certainly me. Tree should see him. It is his only chance.

I was deeply impressed, and my walking-stick showed signs of budding; would have budded indeed, only at the door of the chapel it was taken from me by the Knave of Spades. This strange prohibition is, of course, in honour of Tannhäuser.

How did I get the ticket? By a miracle, of course. I thought it was hopeless, and made no effort of any kind. On Saturday afternoon at five o'clock Harold and I went to have tea at the Hôtel de l'Europe. Suddenly, as I was eating buttered toast, a man, or what seemed to be one, dressed like a hotel porter, entered and asked me would I like to see the Pope on Easter Day. I bowed my head humbly and said '*Non sum dignus*', or words to that effect. He at once produced a ticket!

When I tell you that his countenance was of supernatural ugliness, and that the price of the ticket was thirty pieces of silver, I need say no more.

An equally curious thing is that whenever I pass the hotel, which I do constantly, I see the same man. Scientists call that phenomenon an obsession of the visual nerve. You and I know better.

On the afternoon of Easter Day I heard vespers at the Lateran: music quite lovely: at the close a Bishop in red, and with red gloves – such as Pater talks of in *Gaston de Latour* – came out on the balcony and showed us the relics. He was swarthy, and wore a yellow mitre. A sinister mediaeval man, but superbly Gothic, just like the Bishops carved on stalls or on portals. And when one thinks that once people mocked at stained-glass attitudes! They are the only attitudes for the clothed. The sight of this Bishop, whom I watched with fascination, filled me with the sense of the great realism of Gothic art. Neither in Greek nor in Gothic art is there any pose. Posing was invented by bad portrait-painters, and the first person who ever posed was a stockbroker, and he has gone on ever since.

Homer talks much – a little too much – of you. He slightly suspects you of treachery, and your immediate return seems to him problematical. Your allusion to his conduct on a postcard was mysterious. How was the 'revision' painful?

I have added one Pietro Branca-d'Oro to the group. He is dark, and gloomy, and I love him very much.

I send you a photograph I took on Palm Sunday at Palermo. Do send me some of yours, and love me always, and try to read this letter. It is a labour of a week to read it.

Kindest regards to your dear mother. Always   OSCAR

To Robert Ross

Saturday [21 April 1900]   *Rome*

My dear Robbie, A thousand thanks for all your trouble. The cheque arrived safely this morning.

Of course I got your telegram, from Milan, and wrote to you at the Hôtel

Cavour – a long, interesting, and of course seriously compromising letter. Should it fall into the hands of the authorities you will be immortal.

I have not seen the Holy Father since Thursday, but am bearing up wonderfully well. I am sorry to say he has approved of a dreadful handkerchief, with a portrait of himself in the middle, and basilicas at the corners. It is very curious the connection between Faith and bad art: I feel it myself. Where I see the Pope I admire Bernini: but Bernini had a certain dash and life and assertion – theatrical life, but life for all that: the handkerchief is a dead thing.

By the way, did I tell you that on Easter Sunday I was completely cured of my mussel-poisoning? It is true, and I always knew I would be. Five months under a Jewish physician at Paris not merely did not heal me, but made me worse: the blessing of the Vicar of Christ made me whole. Armand Point, the French painter, a bad Botticelli-Jones artist, is here, and has promised to do me a *tabella votiva*. The only difficulty is the treatment of the mussels. They are not decorative, except the shells, and I didn't eat the shells.

I have been three times to see the great Velasquez of the Pamfili Pope: it is quite the grandest portrait in the world. The entire man is there. I also go to look at that beautiful voluptuous marble boy I went to worship with you at the Museo Nazionale. What a lovely thing it is!

I have given up Armando, a very smart elegant young Roman Sporus. He was beautiful, but his requests for raiment and neckties were incessant: he really bayed for boots, as a dog moonwards. I now like Arnaldo: he was Armando's greatest friend, but the friendship is over. Armando is *un invidioso* [jealous] apparently, and is suspected of having stolen a lovely covert-coat in which he patrols the Corso. The coat is so delightful, and he looks so handsome in it, that, although the coat wasn't mine, I have forgiven him the theft.

Omero has never received your letter. I need not say I have not given him your London address – at least not your real one: he now believes that your real name is Edmondo Gosse, and that your address is the Savile. I also added that some of your more intimate friends prefer to write to you as

Reginaldo Turner

Avvocato

The Reform Club:

but that I, from old associations, prefer to address you as

Sir Wemyss Reid,

so I fancy there will be many interesting letters arriving in London.

Yesterday a painful thing happened. You know the terrible, the awe-inspiring effect that Royalty has on me: well, I was outside the Caffè Nazionale taking iced coffee with *gelato* – a most delightful drink – when the King drove past. I at once stood up, and made him a low bow, with hat doffed – to the admiration of some Italian officers at the next table. It was only when the King had passed that I remembered I was *Papista* and *Nerissimo!* I was greatly upset: however I hope the Vatican won't hear about it.

I enclose you a little cutting that appeared in Palermo while I was there. My incognito vanished in three hours, and the students used to come to the café to talk – or rather to listen. To their great delight I always denied my identity. On being asked my name, I said every man has only one name. They asked me what name that was. 'Io' was my answer. This was regarded as a wonderful reply, containing in it all philosophy.

Rome is burning with heat: really terrible: but at 4.30 I am going to the Borghese, to look at daisies, and drink milk: the Borghese milk is as wonderful as the Borghese daisies. I also intend to photograph Arnaldo. By the way, can you photograph cows well? I did one of cows in the Borghese so marvellous that I destroyed it: I was afraid of being called the modern Paul Potter. Cows are very fond of being photographed, and, unlike architecture, don't move.

I propose to go to Orvieto tomorrow: I have never seen it, and I must revisit Tivoli. How long I shall stay here I don't know – a fortnight perhaps.

Write always to Cook's. Love to More and Reggie. Ever yours   OSCAR

To Robert Ross

14 May [1900]   *Rome*

Dearest Robbie, You never write to me now, so I don't know if it is worth while informing you of my movements. However, I leave Rome tomorrow for Naples, thence by boat to Genoa, thence to Chambéry, where Harold Mellor awaits me, or should do so, with his automobile – and so to Paris. I suppose one of us will arrive safe; I hope it will be me.

Rome has quite absorbed me. I must winter here; it is the only city of the soul. I have been to Albano, and Nemi, and Tivoli, and seen much of Armand Point, who is really a dear fellow, gay and romantic, simple and intellectually subtle, with an inordinate passion for beauty in its most complete expression, and an inordinate love of life.

My photographs are now so good that in my moments of mental depression (alas! not rare) I think that I was intended to be a photographer.

But I shake off the mood, and know that I was made for more terrible things of which colour is an element.

Today I bade goodbye, with tears and one kiss, to the beautiful Greek boy who was found in my garden – I mean in Nero's garden. He is the nicest boy you ever introduced to me.

In the mortal sphere I have fallen in and out of love, and fluttered hawks and doves alike. How evil it is to buy Love, and how evil to sell it! And yet what purple hours one can snatch from that grey slowly-moving thing we call Time! My mouth is twisted with kissing, and I feed on fevers. The Cloister or the Café – there is my future. I tried the Hearth, but it was a failure. Ever yours   OSCAR

Write to Paris

Bosie's father, 'the Screaming Scarlet Marquess' as Oscar called him, had died on 31 January and Bosie had come into about £15,000. He and Percy had been in Paris in February where Oscar described them as being 'in deep mourning and the highest spirits. The English are like that.' Later in the year, at Robbie's suggestion, Oscar proposed that Bosie should help him out of his continuing financial difficulties with some sort of small annuity; the result was an ugly scene.

To Robert Ross

[May–June 1900]   *Hôtel d'Alsace, Paris*

Dearest Robbie, I have at last arrived. I stayed ten days with Harold Mellor at Gland: the automobile was delightful, but, of course, it broke down: they, like all machines, are more wilful than animals – nervous, irritable, strange things: I am going to write an article on 'nerves in the inorganic world'.

Frank Harris is here, also Bosie. I asked Bosie what you suggested – without naming any sum at all – after dinner. He had just won £400 at the races, and £800 a few days before, so he was in high spirits. When I spoke to him he went into paroxysms of rage, followed by satirical laughter, and said it was the most monstrous suggestion he had ever heard, that he would do nothing of the kind, that he was astounded at my suggesting such a thing, that he did not recognise I had any claim of any kind on him. He was really revolting: I was quite disgusted. I told Frank Harris about it, and he was greatly surprised: but made the wise observation 'One should never ask for anything: it is always a mistake'. He said I should have got someone to sound Bosie, and ask him for me. I had also the same idea, but you did not seem to like the prospect of a correspondence with Bosie where money was concerned, and I am not surprised.

It is a most horrible and really heart-breaking affair. When I remember his letters at Dieppe, his assurances of eternal devotion, his entreaties that I should always live with him, his incessant offers of all his life and belongings, his desire to atone in some way for the ruin he and his family brought on me – well, it sickens me, it gives me nausea.

The affair occurred in the Café de la Paix, so, of course, I made no scene. I said that if he did not recognise my claim there was nothing more to be said.

We dined last night with Frank Harris at Maire's. I was quite as usual, but he really is, now that he has money, become mean, and narrow, and greedy. He always accused you of having the bourgeois commercial view of money, instead of the generous, chivalrous, aristocratic view, but he really has out-Heroded Herod this time. 'I can't afford to spend anything except on myself' was one of his observations. I thought of you, and dear More, and all your generosity and chivalry and sacrifice for me. It is an ugly thing; it taints life.

Send me my cheque, like a good boy. Ever yours   OSCAR

I am horrified about Smithers [*who had gone bankrupt*]. It really is too bad.

To Robert Ross

[Circa 29 June 1900]   [*Paris*]

My dear Robbie, Thanks for the cheque. I enclose receipt.

I am horrified at what you tell me about Grissell: its impertinence, its coarseness, its lack of imagination: I should really write to him if I were you. He who seven times sought and seven times received the blessing of the Holy Father is not to be excommunicated on postcards by the withered eunuch of the Vatican Latrines. (By 'He' I mean myself.)

It is a curious, and therefore natural thing, but I cannot stand Christians because they are never Catholics, and I cannot stand Catholics because they are never Christians. Otherwise I am at one with the Indivisible Church.

By the way, I suppose the great revival of architecture, Gothic and Renaissance, was due simply to the fact that God found he could only live in temples made by hands: in the heart of man he could not live, he was not the first.

I have seen Maurice lately; we spent two evenings at the Exhibition. He was pale, and sweet, and gentle. He now forms part of a *ménage à trois*: none of the members sleep: the girl – a rose-like thing I hope – lies in the middle, and knows the pleasure and insecurity of the *Via Media*. Maurice won't tell me the name of the other partner, but admits he has a slight moustache. He does odd jobs for Strong, and quarrels with him incessantly. I find I am very fond of Maurice still. He is a dear fellow.

From your silence about Reggie my worst suspicions are confirmed: is it a sprightly lady-journalist who led him astray? Or was it one of those typical English women with their 'fatal gift of duty'?

Bosie I have not seen for a week. I feel sure he will do nothing. Boys, brandy, and betting monopolise his soul. He is really a miser: but his method of hoarding is spending: a new type.

Love to R. Ever yours   OSCAR

At the time of Wilde's bankruptcy, George Alexander purchased the acting rights in Lady Windermere's Fan *and* The Importance of Being Earnest. *There was little that he could do with the plays until after Wilde's death, but he generously made some voluntary payments to Wilde in the last few months of his life and bequeathed the rights back to Wilde's son, Vyvyan, on his death in 1918.*

To George Alexander

[?21 July 1900]   *Hôtel d'Alsace*

My dear Aleck, It was really a great pleasure to see you again, and to receive your friendly grasp of the hand after so many years. Nor shall I forget your dear wife's charming and affectionate greeting of me. I know now how to value things like that.

With regard to your proposal to spread the payment for the plays over a certain time, I know it was dictated by sheer kindness and the thoughtfulness of an old friend.

If you would send Robert Ross £20 on the first of every month for me it would be a great boon. He would send it on to me, as he looks after all my affairs. His address is R. B. Ross, 24 Hornton Street, Kensington W. I would then have before me a year free from worry, and perhaps may do something you would like. Could you do this for me?

I was delighted to see you so well, and so unchanged.

Kindest wishes to your wife. Sincerely yours   OSCAR WILDE

To Robert Ross

Saturday, 1 September [1900]   *[Paris]*

My dear Robbie, Thanks for the cheque. Your letter is very maddening: nothing about yourself: no details, and yet you know I love middle-class tragedies, and the little squabbles that build up family life in England. I have had delightful letters from you quite in the style of Jane Austen. You, I know, are the Cinderella of your family, and lead them all a dreadful life, like your *Märchen*-prototype. You turned your dear mother's carriage into a pumpkin, and won't let your sisters wear your slippers, and always have the comfortable ingle-nook by the fire, except in summer, when you make poor Aleck sit there.

The 'Mellor cure' was dull, but I got better. He is now in Paris with his slave Eolo, who like all slaves is most tyrannical. He and I, however, are great friends. I think Harold is on the verge of acute melancholia. At present he has almost arrived at total abstinence – drinks and talks mineral waters. I like people who talk wine.

So Bosie is in London: where is he staying? Do you think he has really spent all his money? It is a great pity if he has. How is dear More? And Reggie? Paris is full of second-rate tourists. German and American are the only languages one hears. It is dreadful. Ever yours   OSCAR

Epilogue

On 10 October Wilde had an operation performed on his ear which had been troubling him for some time. The operation itself was successful, but soon complications set in and finally, on 27 November, cerebral meningitis was diagnosed by the two doctors attending him. Any further surgical intervention was pointless, they declared, and early in the afternoon of 30 November 1900 Oscar Wilde died in his room in the Hôtel d'Alsace. Robbie Ross's letter to 'the Lady of Wimbledon', who had taken a discreet interest in Wilde's progress after his release, sums up Robbie's feelings and the last weeks of Oscar's life.

Robert Ross to Adela Schuster

23 December 1900   *Hôtel Belle Vue, Mentone*

Dear Madam, Oscar Wilde began to be in failing health about a year ago. Like his brother he was inclined to take too much alcohol at times, but never regularly, and he never bore outward signs of it. In fact owing to his extraordinary constitution he was able (unfortunately perhaps) to take a great deal too much without being affected. He never became incapable. When I was with him in Genoa in the spring of 1899, just after his brother's death, I managed to frighten him so much on the subject that he quite reformed for six months. Had circumstances permitted me to be with him more than I was, I might have done something with him as he liked being ordered about by people whom he knew were fond of him.

In March and April of this year he came to Rome where I was wintering with my mother and I noticed that a great change had come over his health, but he was in very good spirits. He wanted me then to introduce him to a priest with a view to being received into the Church, and I reproach myself deeply for not having done so, but I really did not think he was quite serious. Being a Catholic myself, I really rather dreaded a relapse, and having known so many people under the influence of sudden impulse, aesthetic or other emotion become converts, then cause grave scandal by lapsing, that I told him I should never *attempt his conversion* until I thought he was serious. You, who once knew him so well, will appreciate the great difficulty. He was never quite sure himself where and when he was serious. Furthermore I did not know any priest in Rome sufficiently well to prepare for a rather grave intellectual conflict. It would have been no use getting an amiable and foolish man who would have treated him like an ordinary person and entirely ignored the strange paradoxical genius which he would have to overcome or convince. Mr Wilde was equipped moreover for controversy, being deeply read in Catholic philosophy especially of recent years. I need hardly say he made a good story out of his stay with me in Rome, and told people that whenever he wanted to be a Catholic I stood at the door with a flaming sword which only turned in *one* direction and prevented him from entering.

Shortly after his release when Mr Adey and I left him at Berneval, he made friends with a French priest and was very nearly received then, he told me, and of course you know that as a young man he was only prevented from doing so by his father and Professor Mahaffy. When I went for the priest to come to his deathbed he was quite conscious and raised his hand in response to questions and *satisfied* the priest, Father Cuthbert Dunne of the Passionists. It was the morning before he died, and for about three hours he understood what was going on (and knew I had come from the South in response to a telegram), that he was given the last sacraments. The doctors said that if he recovered consciousness in a few days, it would be a signal that the end was near.

He was in Paris from last June but had been away to Switzerland for a few weeks, and underwent a slight operation on October 10. He did not even wire for me, but on the 11th I got a telegram saying 'Operated on yesterday try and come over soon'. He knew that I was to pass through Paris at the end of the month. I was then in England. I came over on October 15. He was looking extremely well and seeing various friends at intervals during the day, and sometimes was in the highest spirits. He was, as he always was at least twice a year, financially embarrassed, and this worried him a good deal. He was quarrelling with Frank Harris, who had really been most generous to him over the play *Mr and Mrs Daventry*. He owed about £170, most of which was due to the proprietor of the hotel, and the doctor told me that his recovery was being retarded by this circumstance. Had it been an outside debt he would not have troubled very much. I may here say that the proprietor of the Alsace was a most charitable and humane man, that he never spoke to Mr Wilde on the subject from the time of the operation, paid *himself* for luxuries and necessities ordered by the physicians, and never even spoke to me about it until after the funeral, while all the other creditors of course flocked round directly they heard the case was hopeless. I trust that Mr Harris will be able to settle the proprietor's bill at all events, as he has promised to do. I merely mention this point because there is an *unfounded* report which has been reproduced in the newspapers that Mr Wilde died in a sort of neglected and sordid way. Of course the hotel is rather a shabby little place compared to what he would have liked to stay in, but it is perfectly comfortable as I know by staying there often, and Mr Wilde wanted for *nothing* in the last weeks of his life. He had a special nurse, food sent in from a restaurant, the Embassy doctor Tucker; Hobean a well-known specialist operated, and Mr Turner and myself had in a brain specialist, Dr Kleiss, when meningitis declared itself. As long as he was allowed champagne, he had it *throughout* his illness.

To continue. I saw him every day and sometimes twice a day from October 15 till November 13th. He drove out in the Bois with me on several occasions. On November 1st the doctor took me aside and told me that although he was getting well, his general condition was serious, and that unless he pulled himself up he could not live for more than five years. I had no idea before then that such was the state of the case. I talked the next day very straightly as I always did to Mr Wilde. He of course laughed and said he could never outlive the century as the English people would not stand it, that he was already responsible for the failure of the Exhibition, as English people on seeing him there had gone away. However he made plans for coming to the South of France in order to be near me when he was better and Harris had sent him over the money due for his play. I asked a Mr Turner, an old friend of mine who had been very kind to Mr Wilde since his release, to look him up every day while I was absent and send me bulletins, and Mr Turner more than fulfilled my request.

The night before I went away, when I paid a farewell visit, I found Mr Wilde in a very excited state. He asked Mr Turner and the nurse to leave the room, and then burst into hysterical tears, saying he would never see me again. Here again I rather reproach myself, for I did not think him nearly so ill as he must have been, and I knew he had been taking morphia a good deal, and I became rather stern, as you are told always to be with people in hysteria. I simply attributed the whole scene to general weakness after his illness. As I mentioned before, he was nervous about his finances and the issue of his dispute with Harris. In this respect again, melancholy and dreadful though his death was in many ways, his poverty has been exaggerated. To *my* knowledge since January last he had £400 over and above the annuity of £150 paid from his wife's trustees through me – £300 came from the Queensberry family and £100 from a theatrical manager, while his expenses in Italy were all paid by a Mr Mellor who was travelling with him and has always been most kind to him. There are so many sad and grievous circumstances in his later career, that there is no necessity for those who were interested in him to be harrowed by imaginary pictures of his poverty. The debts you will observe were very small comparatively, for him especially, out of the £170, £50 being due to the general practitioner Dr Tucker, and £96 to the proprietor of the hotel.

About five days before I left for Nice he caught a slight cold in the ear and this developed into an abscess rapidly, *causing him great pain*. No importance was attached to it by the English doctor, but the French doctor regarded it as a grave symptom. It was much better on November 13th. It was, however, the abscess which eventually produced inflammation of the brain. Mr Turner sent me several letters to Nice reporting progress and several drives in the Bois. On Sunday the 25th he did not get up, complained of giddiness and during the evening became light-headed. I think I told you the last details in my former letter. He was never able to *articulate* after my arrival. It was most fortunate that Mr Turner, whom he knew very well, was with him the whole of the last week of his life. Till Sunday 25th he was able to laugh and talk, though he got easily tired and slept a great deal and spoke constantly of coming south, so I hardly think he believed he was dying. I am thankful I arrived in time, as there was no other person there who could assume any authority or knew of his affairs. Owing to his being *registered* at his hotel under an assumed name (contrary to French law it seems) his body was nearly taken to the Morgue. The French authorities could not understand the absence of relatives or legal representatives. By great efforts and kind assistance of others I was able to prevent such a ghastly contingency. Mr Hope, the guardian of his children, for some reason or other did not communicate with me, although I wired to him directly I arrived in Paris asking for instructions in case of his death.

Please do not mention these personal matters. I blame Mr Hope very much, but I dare say he acted according to his view and of course could not be expected to take much interest in the matter. He communicated with me after everything was over and all difficulties overcome, through *my solicitor*. I think on the children's account he might have taken a little more interest, at all events when he knew Mr Wilde was dead. But on the other hand he had every reason to distrust me as a friend of the father, and suspected my motives at all times since the difficulty about the annuity. He highly disapproved of *Mrs Wilde* corresponding with me as she did, after her husband's release. I believe I told you that the grave is at Bagneux in a *temporary* concession. I shall either purchase the ground outright later on and erect a suitable monument, or move the remains to a permanent resting place. Though everyone who knew him well enough to *appreciate* his wonderful power and the sumptuous endowment of his intellect will regret his death, apart from personal affection the terrible commonplace 'it was for the best' is really true in his case.

Two things were absolutely necessary for him, contact with comely things, as Pater says, and social position. Comely things meant for him a certain standard of living, and this, since his release, he *was able to have* except for a few weeks at a time, or perhaps months. Social position he realised after five months he could not have. Many people were kind to him, but he was too proud, or too vain, to be forgiven by those whom he regarded as social and intellectual inferiors. It galled him to have to appear grateful to those whom he did not, or would not have regarded, before the downfall. You who knew him so well in former years will understand what others will never understand I suppose. He chose therefore a Bohemian existence, entirely out of note with his genius and temperament. There was no use arguing or exhorting him. The temporary deprivation of his annuity produced no result. You cannot ask a man who started on the top rung of the ladder to suddenly start again from the lowest rung of all. Among his many fine qualities he showed in his later years was that he never blamed anyone but himself for his own disasters. He never bore any ill-will to anybody, and in a characteristic way was really surprised that anyone should bear any resentment against him. For example he really did not understand how cruel he was to his wife, but I never expect anyone to believe that.

I was not surprised by the silence of the press. Journalists could hardly say very much, and it was better to be silent than point a moral. Later on I think everyone will recognise his achievements; his plays and essays will endure. Of course you may think with others that his personality and conversation were far more wonderful than anything he wrote, so that his written works give only a pale reflection of his power. Perhaps that is so, and of course it will be impossible to reproduce what is gone for ever. I am not alas a Boswell, as some friends have kindly suggested I should become. But I only met him in '86 and only became intimate with him when he was writing *Lady Windermere*, but there were long intervals when I never saw him, and he never corresponded with me regularly until after the downfall. I stayed with him in '87 for two months and used then to write down what he said, but to tell you a *great secret* which I ought not to do, I gave him my notes and he used a great deal of them for one of his later plays which was written in a great hurry and against time as he wanted money. This of course is *private*. I think it would be a great pity myself to dwell too much on the sad and later part of his life with which I am of course more familiar, and the difficulties of collecting material for the 'great period', as one may call it, would be immense. A great many people would dislike admitting their former intimacy with him, and if they have kept his letters would not care to lend them. I could only give a personal impression of him, and that really would not be of much value to the world or to his friends. You want the whole man from every side. In this letter to you I fear you will already be tired of my own views and remarks, but I wanted to try and tell you what you wanted, and it is difficult to edit out one's own personality from a hastily written letter.

Some time I should be very grateful if you allowed me to have your views as to the advisability of a memoir, and its scope or plan, and if done with discretion whether it would please and interest his friends. I would not care for it to appeal to morbid curiosity, and I remember Mr Wilde's remark 'that it is always Judas who writes the biography'. You are in a better position to judge of this question, and to gauge the value of the interest taken in his work and career prior to the downfall. Sincerely yours

ROBERT ROSS

Wilde's funeral took place on 3 December at the Church of St Germain des Prés. After a mass was said by Father Cuthbert Dunne, the funeral procession set off for Bagneux, an hour and a half away in a suburb to the south of the city. The stark fact was that no one had the money to pay for a proper grave in one of the main Parisian cemeteries. A plain tombstone was later set above the grave at Bagneux, bearing these words from the twenty-ninth chapter of the Book of Job: Verbis meis addere nihil audebant et super illos stillabat eloquium meum *[to my words they dared to add nothing and my eloquence dropped upon them].*

In 1909, with Wilde's debts paid off and his works beginning to earn some royalties, Robert Ross was able to purchase a concession à perpétuité *in the cemetery of Père Lachaise, where Wilde's remains now rest under Jacob Epstein's monument and his own words from* The Ballad of Reading Gaol:

> *And alien tears will fill for him*
> *Pity's long-broken urn*
> *For his mourners will be outcast men,*
> *And outcasts always mourn.*

The grave was classified as a French Historic Monument in 1995.

A commemorative plaque was unveiled on Wilde's house (now 34 Tite Street) on the centenary of his birth in 1954; a memorial window to him was installed in Poets' Corner, Westminster Abbey on 14 February 1995; and a publicly funded sculpture, A Conversation with Oscar Wilde *was erected in Adelaide Street, London, in 1998.*

Index of Recipients

General Index

Abbots Hill 120

Adam, Madame 101, 103

Adey, More 195–6, 215–16; his contribution to W's legal costs 196; handles W's financial affairs while in prison 196; his petition to Home Secretary 203; and W's marriage settlement 207, 214, 229–30; and MS of *De Profundis* 211; blamed for misleading W 223–4, 226, 228 232; incompetence in business affairs 231; W distressed by conduct of 232–3; fetches W from prison 237; accompanies W to Dieppe 238; blamed for agreeing with lawyers 297–8, 299, 301–2; sent copies of W's plays 339, 342

Aeschylus 15, 16, 27, 254

Ainslie, Douglas 84, 97

Alexander, George: and *Lady Windermere* 134, 146–51; W in debt to 138; plot of *Importance* outlined to 174–6; plot of *Mr & Mrs Daventry* outlined to 176– 8; and staging of *Importance* 182–3; thanked for money 186; *Florentine Tragedy* promised to 186; stands bail for W 188; W thinks of writing play for 287; purchases acting rights of *Lady Windermere* and *Importance* 359; voluntary payments to W 359

Algiers 173, 185

Allen, Grant 135

Allen, Revd W. D. 25, 31

Allhusen, Beatrice 123

Alma-Tadema, Lawrence 27

Amiel, H. F. 344

Anderson, Mary 68–9, 73, 74–5

Anderson, Mr 144

Anquetin, Louis 273

Anstey, F. 105

Archer, William 155–6, 340

Aristotle: *Poetics* 16

Armando (boy) 355

Arnaldo (boy) 355, 356

Arnold, Matthew 44, 45, 64, 135

Ashton, I. D. W. ('Sir John') 329, 335, 337, 339, 340

Atalanta 105

Athenaeum, The 324

Athens 23, 37

Atkins, Fred 158

Augustus, Emperor 105

Austen, Jane 360

Auteri-Manzocchi, Salvatore: *Dolores* 13–14

Authors' Club 288

Babbacombe Cliff 156, 157, 158, 160, 162–3

Bagneux 367, 368

Balcombe, Florence 25, 32–3, 43, 108, 161

Ballad of Reading Gaol, The 113, 267, 270, 280, 282; Davray's prose translation 281; illustrated second edition proposed 284; quoted 285; Ross's criticism of 286; publishing discussed 287, 289–90, 296–7; piracy issue 294, 296, 303; proofs arrive 294; dedication 295, 306, 314, 316; title-page 295, 305, 307; 'In Memoriam' page 295–6, 305, 306; W's corrections 299, 301; W charmed with appearance of 307; publication 311; Constance on 312; recipients list 312, 314; reviews 312–14, 316, 319, 326; press expected to boycott 312; Author's (signed) Edition 314, 316; second and later editions 316, 324; French translation 316–17; W's *chant de cygne* 318; shilling edition suggested 326, 327; quoted on W's tomb 368

Balzac, Honoré de 66, 326, 342, 348

Barlas, John 145

Barnett, Henrietta 119

Barrett, Lawrence 68–9, 118, 134, 135, 143–4

Barrett, Wilson 42, 249

Barrow, John Burton 30

Baudelaire, Charles 93, 96

Bauër, Henri 196, 312

374